Christmas Memories Cookbook

Gilded Peacock · Sandtarts · Gingerbread · The Wassail Bowl · Sugar Plums · Confections · Plum Pudding · The Boar's Head · Sweetmeats · Mince Pie · Twelfth Cake · Salsify · Oyster Soup · Marzipan · Comfits

Lynn Anderson
History, Art & Calligraphy

Lois Klee & Connie Colom
Recipe Testing & Editing

Published by Mystic Seaport Museum Stores · Mys...

Net income earned from the **Christmas Memories Cookbook** will go toward supporting the programs at Mystic Seaport Museum, a non-profit educational institution.

For additional copies of the **Christmas Memories Cookbook**, use the Order Blank in the back of the book or write directly to:

Mystic Seaport Museum Stores
Bookstore
Mystic, CT 06355

or for credit card orders:

Call toll free (800) 331-BOOK
or (203) 572-8551

Suggested retail price: $14.95 + $4.00 for packing and shipping charges (Connecticut residents add State Sales Tax.)

The **Christmas Memories Cookbook** may be obtained by organizations for fund-raising projects or by retail outlets at special rates. Write to the above address for all of the details or call the above number.

Designed and typeset by Mim-G Studios, Inc.

ISBN 0-939510-03-0

First Printing 1985
Second Printing 1986
Third Printing 1988
Fourth and Fifth Printings 1989
Sixth Printing 1990
Seventh Printing 1991

Contents

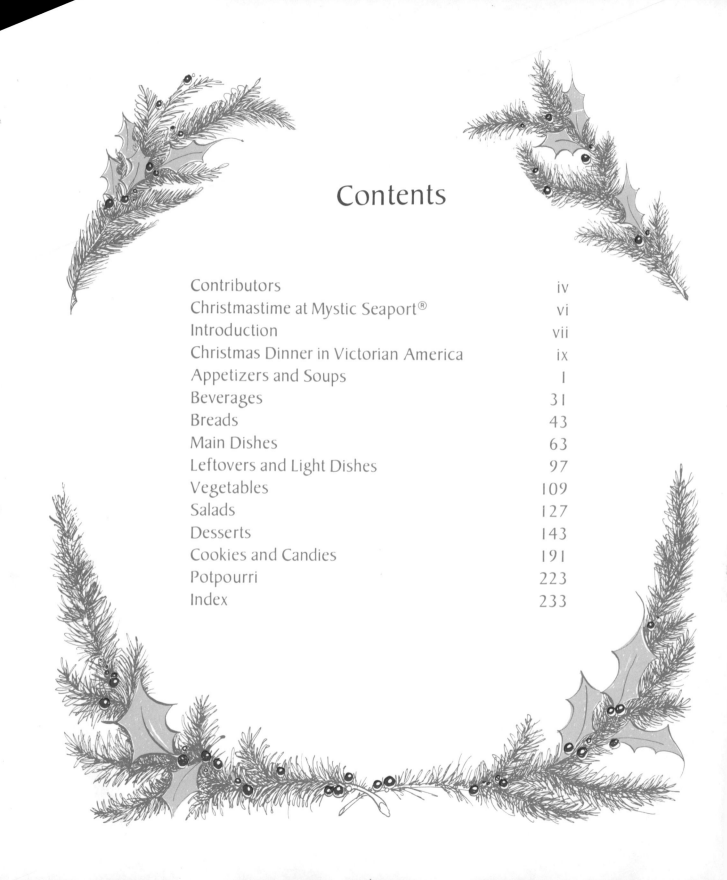

Recipe Contributors

**A special thank you to all the Members of Mystic Seaport
who made this cookbook possible.**

Mrs. Carol Aageson
Mr. Tom Aageson
Donna Reeves Abbott
Binti Ackley
Mrs. C. Adie
M/M Peter Agnew
Mrs. Carol A. Alvarez
Lynn Anderson
Mrs. Axel L. Anderson
M/M David Anderson
Nora Andrews
Mrs. Toni Armitage
Barbara Backus
Phyllis K. Baker
Mrs. Frederick Ball
Eleanor Barber
Mrs. H.B. Barlow, Jr.
Thora Knapp Barnes
Mrs. Eleanor J. Barron
Serena Bates
Mrs. Charles Beaumont
Mrs. Milton Beckwith
Sandra Rose Bellisle
Mrs. James L. Bement, Sr.
Jean Bergamo
Carol Brandon Bergeron
Camilla Bertsche
Grace Bishop
Mrs. Arline Blau
Laurie Blefeld
Mrs. George F. Bliven, Jr.
Constance Boehm
Mrs. Elisabeth Bohlen
Jeannie Booth
M/M Raymond Booth
Mrs. William Bornstein
Shirley M. Bower
Mrs. Barbara Boyden
Clare R. Bray
Nancy Broberg
Mrs. Richard L. Brooks
Mrs. Corinna N. Brown
Mr. James McE. Brown
Mrs. Florence Brown
Mrs. Margaret Brown
Sheila Jackson Brown
Lisa Brownell
Dr. Marion Gilmour Buck
Mrs. Fisher Ames Buell
Fran Bulot

Southie Burgin
Mr. F.W. Butterworth III
Mrs. Paula L. Callahan
Elizabeth Carlson
Mrs. Milton V. Carlson
Pat Carlson
Mrs. Lillian B. Carney
Mrs. Betsy Carr
Mr. Peter C. Cawthorn
Mr. Paul Cerullo
Mrs. Betty Chapman
Mrs. James F. Chase
Kay Chester
Cynthia A. Clapp
Pamela G. Clarke
Charlotte R. Coe
Mrs. Frank K. Cole
Mrs. Fran Colie
Mrs. Elizabeth D. Colson
Margaret Connolly
Mrs. Paul Connor
Nancy Cook
Mrs. Victoria C. Cooke
Mrs. Stanley M. Cooper
Jo Ann Cooper-Relyea
Mrs. Lee Cote
Mrs. A.S. Crandon
Ann Crowley
Mrs. Judy A. Crump
Marilyn D. Curtis
Mrs. John T. Curtiss
Yoland J. D'Elia
Mrs. Karl M. Davies
Mrs. Diane Curran Davis
Patricia Dean
Mrs. Mary Derosier
Mrs. Marie Despres
Patricia Deveau
Mrs. Jane Donnell
Carolyn Dranginis
Kay R. Dreher
Mrs. Sheila Drometer
Jackwyn Durrschmidt
Pamela Ehrlich
Mrs. William Emswiler
Mrs. Carolyn T. Fackler
Flora H. Fairchild
Judith Fales
Joy Fast
Meredith Feldman

Susan L. Fennell
Mrs. Alex Fenwick
Alvonia H. Fitzhugh
Mrs. Ruth Florentino
Judi Samuels Fonsh
Mrs. Richard L. Foote
Jane Foster
Mrs. Clarke Freeman, Jr.
Mrs. Jan Fuller
Mr. Donald E. Furber
Mrs. June D. Gates
Mrs. David L.R. Gearing
Mrs. Richard L. Geismar
Barbara Gilderdale
Kathy Gill
Roberta E. Goldman
Mrs. Patricia Ann Goodrich
Mrs. Robert Groat
Mrs. Christine Guille
Mrs. Kathleen Hanning
Mary Claire Hanson
Grace Harger
Mrs. Carol Harker
Noralyn Harlow
Mrs. Ron Harnish
Jan Hart
Theresa Heacock
Mrs. Marguerite Heipt
Barbara M. Henderson
Miss Olive Hillman
Mrs. Mildred G. Hodgson
Mrs. F. M. Holby
Mrs. Herbert A. Holmstedt
Mrs. William Holub
Betsy Honey
Darlene Hopkins
Mrs. H.M. Horner
June M. Hotchkiss
Marilee Kenney Hunt
Beverly Hutton
Bonnie James
Doris Jannke
Mrs. Henry Jarisch, Jr.
Veronica Jeffers
Mrs. Harrison L. Jewett
Carmen Johnson
Kathleen Johnson
Mrs. Irving Johnson
Virginia Jones
Mrs. Winifred T. Josephson

Sandra A. Jump
Elizabeth Kennedy
Caroline Kinney
Honey Odom Kirila
Mrs. Kathleen Kjerulff
Mrs. Elwood H. Koontz
Mrs. Pamela Kozora
Mr. A.T. Kraemer
Rebecca A. Kraimer
Carol Kraus
Mrs. Edwin R. Krodel
Mrs. Robert V. Krusewski
Barbara Lamond
Mrs. Robert E. Land
Mrs. Marie Lanzillo
Mrs. Breck S. Lardner
Pat Latham
Mr. James W. Lathrop
Janette R. Law
Mrs. William Leroy
Mrs. Winthrop T. Lewis
Mrs. Trudy Loy
Mrs. Philip Lublin
Mrs. Robert M. Lynch
Merrily Werz Lyon
Mrs. W.A. Macaulay
Mrs. Ronald W. MacDonald
Mrs. Lydia L. Main
Mrs. Julie Maisch
Leela M. Mallon
Grace Malloy
Barbara K. Marr
Dorothy Marson
Mary Martin
Mrs. Crystal Matejek
Lil Maxwell
Carol Mazour
Sally McBee
Evelyn McCall
Ellen H. McGuire
Mrs. Francis F. McGuire
Christa McGuire
Mrs. Marilyn B. McKernan
Nancy McLoughlin
Martha McMahon
Mrs. Thelma D. Meek
Pat Meston
Mr. Bert Mielke
Peggy Miller
Ceseli Milstein
Mrs. William C. Missimer, Jr.
Mrs. Margaret Montzingo
Mrs William F. Moran
Sue Holly Morrell

Mrs. Sally Mallory Morris
Gail E. Munn
Catherine C. Murphy
Susan Musselwhite
Mrs. Louise S. Mutschler
Jean Lee Myers
Mr. Bruce D. Nelson
Mrs. Colleen C. North
Noreen O. O'Toole
Mrs. Dorothy Oberg
Helen Otfinoski
Mrs. Robert Palmer
Mrs. Rosemary Palmer
Deborah S. Palmer
Mr. Fred Parker
Mrs. Douglass Hale Parsons
Mrs. William Patterson
Mrs. Joy Lee Peterle
Shirley Phelps
Sarah Phelps
Mrs. Donald Pillsbury, Jr.
Mrs. Arthur Pintauro
Jo Plant
Mrs. T.C. Powden-Wardlaw
Sheri M. Polen
Dorothy A. Poole
Mary Katherine Porter
Mrs. John E. Porter, Jr.
Mrs. Charles W. Poston
Mrs. Ellin Pothier
Mrs. Samuel F. Powel, III
Mrs. John C. Prizer, Jr.
M/M Santo Puglisi
Mrs. Madeline Quincy
Mrs. L.V. Ragsdale
Mrs. Christine M. Reaske
Vicki Holman Reid
Marjorie R. Reid
Terry Reilly
Jane Ressler
Mrs. Thomas F. Richardson
Mrs. Nancy Richartz
Elaine Rigazio
Mrs. Angie Robinson
Mrs. Bernard Rolsma
Mary Ann Root
Terry Roper
Mrs. Thomas B. Rowe
Marjorie Russell-Hains
Mrs. Doris Rutherford
Pam Ryley
Mrs. Marjorie D. Sabin
Janice W. Sargent
Ellen S. Schattan

Mrs. Jane Schmidt
Charlotte Schoonover
Dorothy B. Schrader
Mrs. Jan Scottron
Mrs. Fran Scully-Power
Diane Secchiaroli
Jeannette A. Semon
Carol Sharpe
Mary E. Shea
Martha Sherman
Mrs. Lucille M. Showalter
Sue Simonsen
Mrs. J. Donald Simpson
Eleanor Smith
Mrs. Hugh R. Smith
Mrs. Y.E. Soderberg
Mrs. Georgia A.P. Spratt
Mrs. Alden Stanton
Dr. Gwendolyn Stevens
Mrs. Trudy D. Stevens
Jackie Stoltz
Dr/M Donald M. Swanson
Mrs. Constance Swinglehurst
Mrs. Dodie Taylor
Estelle Thibeault
Mrs. Emilie Thomas
Shirley J. Tirrell
Mrs. James T. Todd
Dorcas F. Toney
Mrs. Dottie Tower
Janet Travers
Mrs. Marie F. Underwood
Patricia A. Varholy
Mr. Joseph M. Vrooman
Mrs. Eleanor Walker
Mrs Johnnie Mae Wasserman
Mrs. Barbara Weakley
Mrs. Andrew Webster
Mrs. Margaret A. Wheeler
Louise White
M/M James Y. Whittier
Mrs. Jan Wickersham
Beatrice A. Widger
Mrs. Kathleen Wielosznski
Alice Wilkins
Susan Williams
Mrs. Benjamin Witkin
Mrs. Jayne R. Woods
Mrs. Colleen R. Woods
Sue Yacovino
Mrs. Arden Yinkey, Jr.
Mrs. Nancy Young
Cindy Young
Mrs. John Zimmerman

Christmastime at Mystic Seaport®

For many people, Christmas just wouldn't be Christmas without a visit to Mystic Seaport. Setting the stage with all the warmth of yesterday's tradition, the Seaport always delivers the Christmas spirit early.

Seasonal activities at this maritime museum include daytime "Yuletide Tours", a Star of Bethlehem Show at the Planetarium, Children's Victorian Tours and a community carol sing. The popular Lantern Light Tours take people through the Seaport's 19th Century village and aboard a vessel to hear the story of Christmas past from period "personalities" of the 1800's.

Throughout December, decorations in the Seaport's 19th Century village, from wreaths on doorways to evergreen trees atop ships' masts, make any excursion to the Seaport a merry one.

Daytime "Yuletide Tours" explore the theme, "Christmas at Sea and Ashore". Escorted by costumed guides, groups are given an intimate look at the Seaport's village and exhibits.

No matter what the day or occasion, December is a favorite month for families to visit the Seaport. The onset of chilly weather does not limit the offerings of the nation's largest maritime museum and all the 40 exhibits and three major ships remain open to sightseers.

For the 1980's shopper, the lavishly decorated Mystic Seaport Stores at the Museum's South Gate offer the buyer the contents of 12 stores under one roof — Christmas ornaments, reproduction toys, nautical gifts, scrimshaw, fresh country baked goods, nautical books and maritime art.

In December, Lantern Light Tours bring small groups of visitors on a sensory visit to another era. Leaving the 20th Century behind, they will spend the next hour smelling gingerbread, dancing to a fiddler's tune in the tavern, singing Christmas carols and meeting a cast of characters from the past.

Housewives, sailors, fishermen and sea captains all appear in the lanternlit journey that unfolds like scenes in a play, one in which everyone has a role. There's even a surprise appearance by St. Nicholas, the 19th Century forerunner of Santa Claus.

Led by a guide in the costume of the last century, visitors are welcomed as guests in several historic homes, learning as they go how Christmas customs evolved in the past generations. In the course of the evening, participants also go aboard the whaleship CHARLES W. MORGAN and walk through the cramped quarters below decks where sailors spent many a holiday at sea, thousands of miles from their New England homes.

Though the Seaport streets may be dusted with snow, tour-goers are warmed by open hearth fireplaces and pot-bellied stoves along their way. When the tour is over, many choose to enjoy a traditional roast goose dinner, complete with all the trimmings, at Seamen's Inne. Wassail and plum pudding are other treats to sample from the menu.

Christmas at Mystic Seaport is a time truly to live New England traditions which reach back in history over 100 years. Many of the members' recipes in this cookbook reflect that history.

Introduction

The Victorian scene depicted on the cover evokes charming images, but the contemporary cook, grateful for food processors and microwaves, is equally grateful that that era has passed! Our recollections of our own mothers laboring for days over Christmas specialties are awe-inspiring, if not overwhelming. Yet we are faced with the realization that it is our turn to be the memory makers and we desire to make our Christmas meals quite special.

For some of us, "special" means an elaborate crown roast or a traditional flaming steamed pudding; for others it means a return to "old-fashioned" cooking, a reflection of our sentimentality for simpler lives, with such dishes as corn pudding or peanut brittle. Still others recall their families' heritages by preparing traditional ethnic dishes such as Swedish Glögg or Spanish Flan. As editors, we have tried to reflect these special differences by our choices for this book.

Christmas Memories Cookbook is a collection of family favorites. We think you will find these recipes uncomplicated and, most often, simple to prepare. Many dishes can be prepared beforehand and stored, thus reducing the number of those requiring lengthy, last-minute preparation. Should you have an occasional question regarding techniques or ingredients, please consult a "big, fat all-purpose" cookbook.

A warm thank you to our many contributors and our own families and friends who allowed us to share these recipes so that they might become a part of your Christmas memories and those of future generations.

Merry Christmas!
The Editors

P.S. Please consider this more than a seasonal cookbook. Many of these recipes will undoubtedly become a part of your special menus throughout the year.

Christmas Dinner in Victorian America

As the family arrived home from church on Christmas Day 1880, rich aromas of spices, turkey, pies and evergreens greeted them in the entryway. Pine boughs were generously draped across the mantles, over the doors and above the windows. Mistletoe "kissing balls" hung in the doorways. Mother, Father, children and servants busied themselves with the cooking, putting the final touches on the elaborately set diningroom table, or adjusting the decorations on the floor-to-ceiling Christmas tree in the parlor.

Not long before this time in America the family might not have been observing Christmas with decorations, gifts and feasting — early restrictions of many American churches forbade celebrating Christmas and it wasn't a legal holiday in all of the United States until 1890. During the 19th century, however, churches gradually began to celebrate on December 25th with special sermons, hymns and even community Christmas trees for the children and it was at this time in Victorian America when Christmas began to assume its present characteristics.

In the Victorian home family and friends began to

arrive. The menu had been decided months ago and many of the comfits, cookies, breads and pies had been prepared far ahead. Handmade decorations, candies and presents had busied hands for weeks in anticipation of this day and most important feast. As aunts, uncles, grandparents and cousins arrived, bowler hats, fur muffs, scarves, capes, overcoats and gloves were shed and bits of news of family, town and country were exchanged. Mother and Father led the way as gentlemen escorted ladies into the elaborately decorated diningroom.

     Exclamations of delight warmed the hostess' heart as the visitors viewed for the first time her patiently crafted decorations . With instructions from. the "Ladies Home Journal" the hostess had fashioned a huge bright red bell which hung from the chandelier. From the red satin bow beneath it long red ribbons were draped down to each carefully lettered place card. Rising from table were three "epergnes", many-tiered stands made, according to "Godey's Lady's Book", by placing glass bowls, goblets and plates on top of one another with wet sand to hold everthing in place and with fruit, holly, ivy and flowers overflowing the epergne and ceramic figurines "artistically arranged" at the base. The entire dinner, minus the desserts, was arranged on the table, filling every space between the decorations and the china and wine glasses at each place.

     Gentlemen seated ladies, who removed their gloves as the

hostess served the oyster soup.   No one asked for seconds on soup—there was too much turkey, roast beef, stuffed ham, turnips, potatoes, beets, cole slaw, fried celery, oysters, salsify, candied sweet potatoes, and oyster gravy to be enjoyed for the next two hours.   After the table was cleared for the pies, cakes, dried fruits and nuts, came the zenith of the feast—the blazing plum pudding.   As it was ushered into the room, the children squealed with delight, the host beamed with pride and the hostess smiled with satisfaction that the glorious Christmas feast had been happily successful once more.

Appetizers and Soups

Appetizers and Soups

APPETIZERS
Dips and Spreads
Blitzen's Hot Crab Dip 4
Bourbon Spread 4
Crab Filled Cocktail Puffs 5
Caviar Mousse 6
- Chili Cheese Ball with Herbs 5
- Christmas Wreath Cheese Spread 7
Curried Chutney Spread 6
Date Nut Ball 7
Dill 'n Onion Dip 8
Hot Beef Dip 8
Hot Crab Dip 9
Layered Vegetable Paté 10
Molded Seafood 9
Mushroom Paté 8
Mustard Sauce for Cream Cheese 11
Pita Crisps 11
Pesto Layered Torte 12
- Poor Man's Boursin 12
Salmon Paté 13
Shrimp Spread 14
Souffle Crackers 13
Spinach Spread 11

Hot Appetizers
Asparagus Fingers 14
Baked Brie 15
Cheese Puffs 15
Goat Cheese and Roasted Pepper Tart 16
Italian Stuffed Mushrooms 17
Marie's Roll-Ups 16
Merry, Merry, Merry Meatballs 19
Minted Cocktail Meatballs
   with Cucumber Dip 18
Sausage Biscuit Bites 17

Cold Appetizers
Gingerbread Muffins with
   Smoked Turkey 18
Marinated Mushrooms 20
Norwegian Herring 21
Smoked Salmon Cheesecake 20
Stuffed Canapes 21

• Indicates items suitable for gift giving

SOUPS
Carrot Soup 24
Cheddar Cheese Soup 25
Chesapeake Oyster Stew 28
Creamed Turkey Rice Soup 26
Cream of Crab-Broccoli Soup 25
Cream of Mushroom Soup 27
Ham and Corn Chowder 28
Hearty Beef-Vegetable Soup 26
Lynn's Seafood Bisque 24
Mushroom Soup 29
Pumpkin Soup in Pumpkin Shell 29
Super Soup 28
Oysters Rockefeller Soup 27

Appetizers

The Victorian hostess would have applauded the modern custom of predinner "finger foods" and beverages had she known about this ideal social icebreaker. Instead, according to a very popular household handbook, Mrs. Beeton's All About Cookery, published in 1861, the hostess greeted her guests and braved the half hour before dinner without either cocktails or hors d'oeuvres, two customs to arrive in America from Europe during WWI. The "gentleman's punchbowl" or rum grog tradition of the 18th century had vanished, leaving an often vacuous interval and a panicky start to the evening for the hostess, who was forced to invent some diversion to keep the guests from falling into awkward silence, which would not bode well for the rest of the evening. Mrs. Beeton offered several suggestions to help ease the ordeal, including a curiosity of art, an article of vertu, a new book, a rare plant, a photograph, crest album, bit of music or a grotesque sculpture.

Blitzen's Hot Crab Dip

Yield: about 2 cups

As fast as Santa's reindeer!

8 ounces crabmeat
8 ounces cream cheese
½ cup mayonnaise
1 tablespoon chives
¼ teaspoon Tabasco sauce
   (or more to taste)
½ teaspoon Worcestershire sauce

Dip may be made in a conventional manner by combining all ingredients in an ovenproof bowl, mixing by hand or with electric mixer until smooth and creamy. Heat in 300° oven for 25 to 30 minutes, or until hot and bubbly.

1. Place all ingredients in bowl of food processor. Process 30 to 60 seconds, until smooth and creamy.
2. Spoon dip into a 1-quart ceramic or glass dish. Microwave on high power for 90 seconds, or more, until hot and bubbly. (Or refrigerate after mixing until ready to use.)
3. Serve with crackers or vegetable crudities. Or as an accompaniment to entrée, place dip on tomato halves and broil them until crab is hot and bubbly.

Bourbon Spread

Yield: about 2 cups

1 package unflavored gelatin
¼ cup bourbon
1 can beef consommé
1 can Sell's liver paté, room temperature
3 ounces cream cheese, softened
Jalapeño pepper, optional

Must be made ahead.

1. Soak gelatin in bourbon in small saucepan. Add consommé and heat until gelatin is dissolved.
2. Pour half (about ¾ cup) into a 1-pint mold. Refrigerate until set. Set remaining comsommé mixture aside.
3. When refrigerated mixture is set, combine remaining consommé mixture with cream cheese and paté. Pour carefully onto the molded portion and chill until firm.
4. Unmold to serve. Place on bed of dark green lettuce.
5. Finely chopped Jalapeño pepper may be added to second half of mold.

Crab Filled Cocktail Puffs

Yield: 4 cups

Crab Filling:

1 pound crabmeat, flaked
4 hard-cooked eggs, finely chopped
⅔ cup celery, chopped
½ cup onion, finely chopped
1 tablespoon fresh parsley, minced
2 tablespoons chili sauce
1½ to 2 cups mayonnaise
salt and pepper to taste

**Puffs and Filling may be made ahead;
fill just before serving.**

1. Mix all ingredients together, adding enough mayonnaise to bind.
2. Refrigerate until shortly before serving. Fill cocktail puffs. (Do not fill puffs too far ahead or they may become soggy.)

Cocktail Puffs

Yield: 60 puffs

1 cup water
½ cup (1 stick) butter
1 cup sifted flour
4 eggs

**Cut puffs and discard excess inner dough
BEFORE freezing.**

1. Bring water to boiling; add butter. Stir until melted. Add flour, stirring briskly until dough forms a ball.
2. Beat eggs until very thick and lemony-colored. Stir into cooled dough; blend thoroughly.
3. Drop by teaspoonfuls onto baking sheet. Bake in preheated 400º oven for 15 minutes. Cool on rack. (May be frozen). To serve: slice and fill at last minute.

Chili Cheese Ball with Herbs

Yield: one 1-pound cheese ball

An unusual blend of flavors.

8 ounces cream cheese, softened
8 ounces sharp Cheddar cheese, grated
2 teaspoons chili powder
1 teaspoon sesame seeds
1 teaspoon poppy seeds
½ teaspoon thyme
¼ teaspoon rosemary
1 clove garlic, minced
2 teaspoons grated onion
1 teaspoon sherry (optional)

Must be made ahead.

1. Mix together cheeses; add remaining ingredients and beat thoroughly. (Or put all ingredients in the bowl of food processor and process until smooth).
2. Refrigerate cheese mixture for about 30 minutes, or until easier to handle. Shape into a ball or log and roll in chili powder to coat. Wrap tightly in wax paper; place inside a plastic bag. Refrigerate at least 24 hours before serving. (Flavors blend with age). Serve with crackers.

Caviar Mousse

Yield: about 3 cups

Combines chopped egg with caviar for ease in serving.

6 hard-cooked eggs
1 cup mayonnaise
1/8 teaspoon salt
½ teaspoon white pepper
1½ teaspoons unflavored gelatin
2 tablespoons lemon juice
2 tablespoons water
1 teaspoon Worcestershire sauce
2 teaspoons minced onion
dash Tabasco sauce
1 3½-ounce jar red lumpfish caviar, rinsed
Garnish: sour cream, one 3½-ounce jar red lumpfish caviar, fresh dill weed (optional)

Must be made ahead.

1. In food processor chop eggs finely. Add mayonnaise, salt and pepper; process just until mixed with egg.
2. In a small saucepan, combine gelatin, lemon juice, water, Worcestershire, onion and Tabasco. Cook over low heat until gelatin is dissolved; cool slightly.
3. Combine gelatin mixture with egg mixture, stir in 3½-ounce jar of caviar. Pour into a greased 3- or 4-cup mold. Cover, chill overnight.
4. To serve: unmold on plate. Garnish with sour cream in center, topped by additional caviar, if desired, and surrounded with fresh dill weed. Serve with party-size sliced pumpernickel bread or rye crackers.

Curried Chutney Spread

Yield: approximately 2 cups

Keep copies of this recipe on hand or you'll develop writers' cramp responding to requests.

8 ounces cream cheese, softened
½ 10-ounce jar chutney, Raffeto Chut Nut or Major Grey's, finely chopped (about ½ cup)
1 to 2 teaspoons curry powder
¼ teaspoon dry mustard
⅓ cup chopped onion
⅓ cup chopped toasted pecans.

Must be made ahead.

1. Combine all ingredients, mixing well with fork. Pack into serving dish or form into ball or log and roll in more pecans.
2. Refrigerate several hours or overnight. Serve at room temperature. Wonderful on most crackers but try garlic bagel crisps.

Christmas Wreath Cheese Spread   Yield: about 3 cups

Impress your guests with your creativity!

2 8-ounce packages cream cheese, softened
½ cup mayonnaise
½ cup grated Parmesan cheese
10 slices bacon, cooked crisp and crumbled
½ cup smoked almonds, chopped
¼ cup sliced green onion
pimento strips
one bunch fresh parsley, chopped
   (preferably flat-leafed)

Must be made ahead.

1. In food processor, or with mixer, cream together cream cheese, mayonnaise, and Parmesan until smooth.

2. Mix in crumbled bacon, nuts and green onions. Refrigerate 30 minutes.

3. Form cheese into a long roll; shape into a "wreath", approximately 8 to 10 inches in diameter. (Use hands; cheese will be soft even though chilled.)

4. Liberally cover wreath with chopped parsley. Select long strips of pimento and shape into a bow on wreath. Dot wreath with bits of pimento to resemble berries. Chill.

Variations:

1. Substitute ½ cup chopped ham, ¼ cup green pepper and ¼ cup chopped onion for bacon and green onion.

2. Substitute ½ cup chopped cooked chicken or turkey for bacon; add 1 tablespoon curry powder.

Date Nut Ball   Yield: One 3-inch ball

Has incredible appeal. Everyone wonders about the "secret" ingredient.

1 8-ounce package cream cheese, softened
2 tablespoons maple syrup
¾ cup dates, chopped
1¼ cups walnuts, chopped and toasted

1. Combine cheese and syrup until thoroughly mixed.

2. Add ½ cup nuts and dates.

3. Form into ball and roll in remaining nuts. Refrigerate until needed. Serve with McVities' Wheatalo or Peak Freen's Sweet Meal crackers.

Dill 'n Onion Dip

Yield: 1⅓ cups

⅔ cup mayonnaise
⅔ cup sour cream
1 tablespoon onions, finely chopped
1 tablespoon fresh parsley, finely chopped
1 teaspoon dill weed
1 teaspoon Beau Monde seasoning
1 large sweet red pepper, hollowed

Vegetables for dipping: broccoli, pea pods, green pepper strips, scallions, etc.

Must be made ahead.

1. Blend mayonnaise and sour cream. Mix in remaining ingredients.
2. Cover and chill several hours or overnight to blend flavors.
3. To Serve: place dip in hollowed-out sweet red pepper as bowl. Surround with bright green veggies for dipping.

Hot Beef Dip

Yield: 4 cups

2 8-ounce packages cream cheese
1 cup sour cream
¼ cup milk
4 tablespoons minced onion
¼ teaspoon pepper
2 teaspoons Worcestershire sauce
1 large jar dried beef, chopped
½ cup chopped nuts

Dip is also delicious spread on melba toast or French bread slices and put under broiler until hot and bubbly.

Must be made ahead.

1. In food processor, or with electric mixer, combine first six ingredients; mix until smooth.
2. Stir in dried beef; mix. Pour dip into a 1½ quart baking dish. Sprinkle nuts on top. Refrigerate until ready to use. (Flavor improves with age).
3. Heat dip in 350° oven for 20 minutes, until hot and bubbly. Serve with crackers.

Mushroom Paté

Yield: approximately 2 cups

1 clove garlic, crushed
1 medium onion, chopped (about ½ cup)
12 ounces fresh mushrooms
2 tablespoons butter
1½ teaspoons dried dill weed
1½ teaspoons lemon juice
½ teaspoon Dijon mustard
4 ounces cream cheese, softened
½ teaspoon salt
freshly ground black pepper

1. In medium frying pan, sauté garlic, onion & mushrooms in butter, until juice is evaporated. Add lemon and dill.
2. In food processor or blender, combine cream cheese, and mustard. Add mushrooms, salt and pepper and process until smooth. Chill well. Serve with dark pumpernickel or crackers.

Hot Crab Dip

Yield: 4 cups

Leftovers make a great sauce over vegetables.

3 8-ounce packages cream cheese, softened
1 cup mayonnaise
8 ounces (2 cups) shredded Cheddar cheese
3 to 4 teaspoons lemon juice
1 tablespoon Worcestershire sauce
4 hard-cooked eggs, chopped finely
12 to 16 ounces shredded crabmeat
  or seafood sticks

An attractive way to serve dip is in a round loaf of bread which has been hollowed out to form a bowl. Use the inside bread, cut into cubes, to dip crabmeat.

1. In food processor, or with electric mixer, cream together cream cheese and mayonnaise; add Cheddar, lemon juice and Worcestershire and process until smooth.
2. Fold in crabmeat and chopped egg. Pour into a 2½ quart oven-proof casserole. Refrigerate until ready to serve.
3. To serve: heat in a 350° oven until hot and bubbly. (Also may be heated in microwave). Serve with crackers.

Molded Seafood

Yield: approximately 4 cups

2 envelopes (2 tablespoons)
  unflavored gelatin
½ cup cold water
1 tablespoon fresh lemon juice
1 cup mayonnaise
1 3-ounce package cream cheese, softened
½ cup chopped celery
1 teaspoon onion
1 teaspoon dill weed
dash Tabasco sauce
salt and pepper to taste
1 4½-ounce can tiny shrimp, rinsed
12 ounces sea sticks or imitation crabmeat
  or 1 7½-ounce can crabmeat and 1 cup
  cooked, flaked fish

Garnish: black olives, pimento, salad greens, lemon slices, sea shells

Attractive prepared in a fish-shaped mold if possible. May be made in individual molds for use as a first course.

Must be made ahead.

1. In a heatproof measuring cup, combine gelatin and cold water. Place cup in a pan of hot water, over low heat and stir to dissolve gelatin (or heat in microwave 10 seconds.) Add lemon juice.
2. "Paint" inside of chilled fish mold with about a teaspoon of gelatin mixture; place a black olive slice in mold for eye of fish and pimento slice for fin. Chill.
3. Beat together softened cream cheese and mayonnaise; add remaining gelatin mixture, celery, onion and seasonings. Fold in seafood.
4. Spoon into chilled mold, cover with plastic wrap and chill until firm.
5. To serve: unmold on platter of greens or parsley and decorate with lemon slices and seashells, if desired. Accompany with assorted crackers.

Layered Vegetable Paté

A food processor makes this easier than it may appear.

Spinach layer:

2 10-ounce packages chopped spinach, cooked and well drained
2 shallots, finely chopped
2 tablespoons butter
½ cup light cream
½ teaspoon nutmeg
3 eggs, lightly beaten
¼ cup dry bread crumbs
¼ cup grated Parmesan cheese
½ teaspoon salt

Mushroom layer:

1 pound fresh mushrooms
1 tablespoon lemon juice
¼ cup (½ stick) butter
1 cup chopped onion
2 tablespoons dry sherry
1 teaspoon salt
¼ teaspoon pepper
2 eggs, lightly beaten
4 tablespoons dry bread crumbs

Carrot layer:

3 8-ounce cans sliced carrots, drained
2 tablespoons butter
2 tablespoons flour
¼ cup light cream
½ teaspoon salt
1½ teaspoons curry
2 eggs, lightly beaten

Garnish: whole mushrooms and fresh dill weed

Must be made ahead.

Yield: 2 loaves, 12 servings each as a first course. 72 hors d'oeuvres

1. Preheat oven to 350°. Butter two 8½ x 4½ x 2½-inch loaf pans. Line with foil; butter foil.

2. Sauté shallots in butter for about 5 minutes. Place with spinach in food processor. Add cream, nutmeg, eggs, bread crumbs, cheese and salt. Process for 20 to 30 seconds. Spoon into loaf pans, smoothing surface.

3. Trim and clean mushrooms. Toss 6 perfect ones in lemon juice and set aside. Chop remaining mushrooms in clean food processor. Sauté whole mushrooms in butter; remove and center along length of spinach layer. Sauté chopped mushrooms with onion in same pan. Stir in sherry, salt and pepper; remove from heat. Add eggs and bread crumbs. Spoon mixture over spinach layer and whole mushrooms.

4. Purée carrots in food processor. Melt butter in saucepan; stir in flour, cream, salt, curry and carrots. Cook, stirring constantly, until mixture comes to a boil. Remove from heat; beat in eggs. Spoon mixture over mushroom layer.

5. Cover pans with wax paper, then foil. Set in a larger pan; fill with hot water to a depth of 1½ to 2 inches. Bake at 350° for 2 hours or until paté feels firm.

6. Place loaf pans on a wire rack; cool for 1 hour. Refrigerate overnight or up to three days.

7. When ready to serve, loosen paté around sides of pan; unmold onto serving platter. Carefully peel off foil.

8. Garnish with fresh mushrooms and dill. Serve with French bread or firm crackers.

Mustard Sauce for Cream Cheese   Yield: about 2 cups

A nice gift in a pretty jar or mustard pot.

1 1½-ounce can (8 tablespoons) dry mustard
1 cup cider vinegar
2 eggs
1 cup sugar
1 8-ounce package cream cheese

Try mustard sauce with Kielbasa slices on toothpicks for dipping or as a sauce for ham.

Must be made ahead.

1. Mix together mustard and vinegar in a ceramic or glass bowl; let stand overnight.
2. Next day, mix remaining ingredients with mustard-vinegar mixture. Cook in glass or enamel pan for 20 minutes, stirring frequently. Cool and refrigerate. (Will keep in refrigerator for several weeks.)
3. Serve poured over block of cream cheese and accompany with crackers.

Pita Crisps   Yield: 8 crisps

4 1-ounce pita rounds (3½-inch size), split (or 2 3-ounce pitas, quartered)
¼ cup (½ stick) melted butter
2 garlic cloves, minced
¼ teaspoon oregano
¼ teaspoon basil
¼ teaspoon thyme
¼ teaspoon dried parsley

Recipe may be doubled or tripled easily: serve with cocktails or with soup.

1. Preheat broiler. Arrange pita on baking sheet.
2. Mix herbs with melted butter and garlic. Brush generously onto pita.
3. Broil, 4 inches from element, until brown and bubbly, about 4 to 5 minutes. (Watch carefully, but do allow to "crisp".)
4. Serve hot.

Spinach Spread

**Serve in hollowed-out red cabbage.
A universal favorite.**

1 package (10-ounce) frozen chopped spinach, thawed, drained well
1 cup mayonnaise
1 cup sour cream
1 can water chestnuts, drained and chopped
1 small onion, chopped
1 package Knorr's dry Vegetable Soup and Recipe Mix

Must be made ahead.

1. Combine all ingredients. Cover and refrigerate overnight.
2. Serve in hollowed-out red cabbage or hollowed bread with crackers.

Pesto Layered Torte

Festive—out of this world!

Yield: 16 to 20 servings

¾ cup pesto
8 ounces cream cheese, softened
8 ounces unsalted butter, softened
three-cup mold
cheesecloth

This can be doubled.
Pesto is generally made in summer with fresh basil and frozen for winter use. However, you will note we have included a special recipe for Winter Pesto. (See page 231)

1. Torte is layered green and white. Choose mold accordingly. A slightly tapered bowl works fine.
2. Dampen cheesecloth and lay in mold allowing overhang.
3. Beat butter and cheese together.
4. Divide cheese into sixths, Lay one portion over bottom of mold spreading carefully to cover.
5. Continue process by using about 2 tablespoons pesto to form second layer.
6. Continue to layer cheese and pesto, using 2 to 4 tablespoons pesto as necessary. Lay mixture around edges first to form clean layers. End with cheese layer. Cover with overhanging cheesecloth. Refrigerate several hours.
7. To unmold, invert onto serving plate, remove cloth. Garnish as desired. Serve with crackers.

Poor Man's Boursin

A wonderful, garlicky spread

Yield: about 2 cups

½ pound (2 sticks) unsalted butter, softened
2 8-ounce packages (1 pound) cream cheese, softened
2 cloves garlic, minced
½ teaspoon oregano
¼ teaspoon marjoram
¼ teaspoon thyme
¼ teaspoon basil
¼ teaspoon white pepper
¼ teaspoon dill weed

Spread is excellent used on broiled fish or lamb chops.

Must be made ahead.

1. In food processor, or with electric mixer, combine softened butter and cheese with spices. Process, or mix, until smooth and well blended.
2. Pack into containers; cover with foil or plastic wrap. Refrigerate. Will keep for several weeks. (Best made well ahead)
3. Serve with crackers, vegetable crudities, or sliced French bread.

Salmon Paté

Yield: 6 cups spread

1 1-pound can salmon
2 envelopes unflavored gelatin
2 cups mayonnaise
½ cup bottled chili sauce
2 tablespoons lemon juice
2 tablespoons Worcestershire sauce
1 tablespoon dried dill weed
¼ teaspoon EACH black pepper, Tabasco
1 7-ounce can tuna, drained and flaked
4 hard-boiled eggs, finely chopped
½ cup pimento-stuffed green olives, chopped
⅓ cup minced onion (or 3 tablespoons
  dried minced onion)

Garnish: sliced olives, pimento strips,
parsley, assorted crackers

Especially attractive made in a fish mold.

Must be made ahead.

1. Drain salmon; reserve liquid. Add water to reserved liquid to make ½ cup. Bone and finely flake salmon; set aside.

2. In a heatproof measuring cup combine gelatin and reserved salmon liquid. Place cup in a pan of hot water and stir to dissolve gelatin.

3. Transfer dissolved gelatin to mixing bowl; slowly blend in mayonnaise. Stir in chili sauce, lemon juice, Worcestershire sauce, dill weed, pepper and Tabasco.

4. Fold in flaked salmon, tuna, chopped egg, olives, and onion. Turn into a greased 6-cup mold.

5. Chill till firm, about 3 hours.

6. Unmold paté onto platter. Garnish with sliced olives, pimento, parsley. Serve with crackers.

Soufflé Crackers

Originated at The White House.

Yield: 36 crackers

36 saltine crackers
½ cup (1 stick) butter (not margarine)
ice water

Options: Clove garlic, mashed; dill weed,
caraway, sesame, or poppy seeds, or choice
of herbs

**Makes a wonderful canape base
if the family doesn't find them first.**

1. Preheat oven to 400° and butter 2 cookie sheets.

2. Put ice water in shallow dish or pie plate. Using several at a time, put crackers into water in a single layer pushing just below surface. Let them stand about 30 seconds. Corners will be softening. Carefully remove crackers with slotted spatula to prepared cookie sheets, placing about ½ inch apart.

3. When sheets are filled, tip to drain excess water. With pastry brush and melted butter (mixed with garlic, if desired). VERY gently coat each cracker. Sprinkle with dill and sesame or other herb.

4. Bake at 400° for 15 minutes, then at 300° for 25 minutes. Cool on rack. Serve or store tightly covered.

Shrimp Spread

Popular and colorful.

Yield: 2 cups

8 ounces cream cheese, softened
½ pound cooked salad shrimp or
 finely chopped shrimp, well-drained
1 teaspoon Worcestershire sauce
1 clove garlic, crushed
2 teaspoons lemon juice
dash salt, white pepper

lettuce, watercress

Cocktail Sauce:

1 cup ketchup
1 tablespoon lemon juice
1 teaspoon onion juice
½ teaspoon Worcestershire sauce
Few drops Tabasco sauce
1 tablespoon sugar
1 tablespoon horseradish
½ teaspoon salt

This is an excellent sauce for any seafood cocktail.

Must be made ahead.

1. Combine all ingredients except sauce. Mix well and form into a cheese wheel, 1 inch high. Cover with plastic wrap and refrigerate several hours or overnight.
2. Combine ingredients for sauce and refrigerate to blend flavors.
3. To serve, place a bed of bibb or red lettuce on serving plate. Set wheel on top. Frost with sauce and garnish with watercress. Pass with crackers.

Asparagus Fingers

Yield: 24 servings

24 slices good quality white sandwich bread
 (about one loaf)
12 ounces Jarlsberg, Swiss or
 Monterey Jack cheese
¾ cup grained Pommery mustard
24 fresh asparagus spears, cooked
 (or about 2 10-ounce boxes frozen
 asparagus spears cooked)
½ cup (1 stick) unsalted butter, melted

**By using frozen asparagus spears,
you can keep all the ingredients on hand for
unexpected holiday guests.**

1. Preheat oven to 450°.
2. Trim crusts from bread. Flatten slices of bread as thin as possible with rolling pin. Keep squares covered with damp paper towel as you work.
3. Cut cheese in thin strips about the size of asparagus spears.
4. Spread each bread square with mustard. Place an asparagus spear and a piece of cheese on each square; roll up. Place seam side down on buttered baking sheet.
5. Brush "fingers' with melted butter.
6. Bake for 10 minutes or till brown and bubbly. Serve while hot.

Baked Brie

Yield: 12 to 16 servings

1 pound (approximately) wheel of ripe brie.
(Mushroom brie is exceptionally good
served this way)
1 frozen puffed pastry sheet,
thawed but chilled
1 egg beaten with 1 tablespoon water

1. Preheat oven to 400°.
2. Cut off top of brie.
3. Roll pastry on floured cloth. (The size is
determined by the size of the brie. One
sheet should be enough to enclose the brie
if rolled properly.)
4. Cut one piece of pastry to fit top of brie
plus some to extend down the sides.
Press in place.
5. Place brie on remaining pastry; cut to fit
bottom, sides and beyond. Again press in
place. Place on ungreased baking sheet.
6. Brush top and seal seams with egg wash.
7. Bake at 400° for about 20 minutes or until
puffed and light golden. Watch carefully
as cheese can suddenly "explode"
through crust.
8. Serve warm, allowing each person to slice
own piece.

Cheese Puffs

Watch these disappear.

Yield: 60 or more appetizer cubes

1 loaf unsliced white bread
2 3-ounce packages cream cheese
8 ounces sharp Cheddar cheese, shredded
1 cup (2 sticks) butter
4 egg whites, beaten stiff

***TO FREEZE: place baking sheet with cubes in
freezer. When cubes are frozen, remove with a
spatula and put in plastic freezer bag. When ready
to use, put on baking sheet and bake as in step 5.**

Must be made ahead.

1. Cut crusts off bread; cube loaf into
bite-size cubes.
2. In the top of a double boiler over hot water,
melt butter, cream cheese and sharp cheese,
stirring to blend. Cool slightly.
3. Fold in egg whites; blend completely.
4. Dip cubes into mixture using a long 2-tine
fork, turning to coat. Place cubes on a
baking sheet. Refrigerate for 3 hours or
overnight, or freeze*.
5. Bake at 400° for 12 to 15 minutes,
watching carefully so as not to brown
too much.

Goat Cheese and Roasted Pepper Tart   Yield: 8 servings as a first course

Different and distinctive.

Crust:

2 cups flour
¼ cup confectioners' sugar
¾ cup (1½ sticks) butter
2 to 3 tablespoons ice water

Filling:

2 red bell peppers
10 ounces Chevré (goat cheese)
½ cup half-and-half
3 eggs
4 ounces Canadian bacon, finely chopped

1. Place peppers in hot oven (400°) until they blister. Remove from oven; immediately place in brown paper bag. Close bag; let sit about 15 minutes to soften skins. Meanwhile, prepare crust.

2. Place flour, sugar and butter in food processor bowl; process, adding water, a tablespoon at a time, until dough forms a ball. (Or prepare in your usual way for pastry.) Roll dough to fit 10-inch tart, quiche or similar pie pan.

3. Peel skins from peppers; remove seeds. Chop one pepper; cut other pepper into strips.

4. In food processor or with electric mixer, cream cheese, half-and-half and eggs until smooth. Add bacon and chopped pepper; stir to mix. Pour filling into crust; decorate top with pepper strips, forming a star-burst effect radiating from center.

5. Bake at 375°, approximately 45 minutes, just until set and top has browned. May be served warm or at room temperature.

Marie's Roll-Ups   Yield: 3 dozen

You won't believe it till you've tried one!

8 slices extra-thin white bread
crunchy peanut butter
1 pound sliced bacon
wooden toothpicks

1. Using thin bread, make four peanut butter sandwiches. Spread peanut butter generously. Trim off crusts.

2. Cut each sandwich into thirds, both vertically and horizontally, to make 9 bite-size cubes.

3. Cut each slice of bacon into thirds. Wrap each sandwich cube with bacon; secure with a toothpick. (May be done ahead to here).

4. Place bacon-wrapped cubes on rack of broiler pan. Bake at 350° for 15 minutes, or until bacon is crisped to individual preference.

Italian Stuffed Mushrooms

Spicy good bites with cocktails or as first course.

Yield: 18 to 24 appetizers

5 links hot Italian sausage
1 clove garlic, minced
18 to 24 medium-size mushrooms, cleaned and wiped; stems removed and chopped
1 tablespoon chopped fresh parsley
2 tablespoons breadcrumbs
2 tablespoons grated Parmesan cheese
½ cup sherry or red wine

1. Preheat oven to 350°.
2. Remove sausage meat from casings. Brown, breaking up any chunks of meat, until half cooked. Add garlic and chopped stems of mushrooms; cook until meat is browned.
3. Remove meat from heat. Mix in parsley, bread crumbs and cheese. Add enough sherry to moisten well, approximately 2 tablespoons.
4. Stuff mushrooms with meat mixture, placing in baking dish. Pour remaining sherry into bottom of baking dish. Bake for 20 minutes. (Can be stuffed ahead, covered and refrigerated several hours. Add sherry just before baking).

Sausage Biscuit Bites

These always disappear quickly!

Yield: about 4 dozen

1 pound sharp Cheddar cheese, shredded
1 pound bulk sausage, mild or hot to taste
3 cups dry biscuit baking mix

May be frozen after baking: reheat in slow oven.

1. Preheat oven to 400°.
2. In a large saucepan heat together sausage and shredded cheese. Stir together with wooden spoon until cheese has melted.
3. Stir in biscuit mix until smooth. Cool. Chill for about 30 minutes for ease in handling.
4. Shape into small balls about the size of a quarter. Place on ungreased baking sheet.
5. Bake at 400° for 8 to 10 minutes. Remove; place on paper towels to drain. Serve warm.

Minted Cocktail Meatballs with Cucumber Dip

Yield: 48 small meatballs

Very unusual flavor.

Meatballs:
1 pound lean ground beef
¼ cup fresh bread crumbs
¼ cup onion, minced
2 cloves garlic, minced
1 tablespoon ground dry mint
1 tablespoon chopped fresh parsley
½ teaspoon pepper
1 teaspoon salt
1 egg
½ cup light cream
¼ cup sherry

1. Mix all ingredients together well.
2. Shape into bite-size balls; place on broiler tray (or place on baking sheet and freeze; put into sealed bags until needed.)
3. Bake in preheated 450° oven for 8 to 10 minutes (slightly longer if frozen). Serve hot with toothpicks.

Cucumber Dip:
1 3-ounce package cream cheese, softened
¼ cup plain yogurt
¼ teaspoon salt
1 garlic clove, crushed
1 cup peeled, seeded, finely chopped cucumber

Dip: Yield: 1½ cups

1. In small bowl of mixer, or in food processor, beat cream cheese and yogurt until smooth.
2. Stir in remaining ingredients (pulse once or twice in processor).
3. Refrigerate up to 24 hours.

Gingerbread Muffins with Smoked Turkey   Yield: 36 appetizers

A selection of unusual combinations.

1 recipe Gingerbread Muffins (see p. 59) prepared in miniature muffin pans.
1 pound fully cooked, hickory smoked turkey breast (such as Louis Rich) or leftover smoked turkey (see p. 79)*
chutney (bottled or favorite recipe)
marmalade
quince jelly
cranberry sauce

also good with ham

1. Slice Gingerbread Muffins horizontally.
2. Slice smoked turkey into thin slivers.
3. Assemble slivers of turkey on muffins with a teaspoon of any one of the spreads listed, as you would a sandwich. Serve either as a mixed platter or all with the same spread. Be sure to garnish platter, perhaps with watercress and kumquats or orange slices.

Merry, Merry, Merry Meatballs

Yield: 4 to 5 dozen meatballs

Three variations on a cocktail party basic.

Basic Meatball Ingredients

2 pounds extra-lean ground beef round
⅓ cup chopped fresh parsley
2 eggs
⅓ cup ketchup
I cup dry bread crumbs
2 tablespoons soy sauce
½ teaspoon garlic salt
¼ teaspoon black pepper
2 tablespoons grated onion

1. Preheat oven to 450°.
2. Combine all ingredients in a large bowl. Mix well (using hands is good). Form into walnut-size balls.
3. Place meatballs on rack of broiler pan. Bake 10 to 15 minutes until brown.

Piquant Cranberry Sauce

I I-pound can jellied cranberry sauce
I 12-ounce bottle chili sauce
2 tablespoons firmly packed brown sugar
I tablespoon lemon juice

Merry Sherry Sauce

I cup sherry
I cup ketchup
I½ teaspoons oregano
½ cup water

Spicy Molasses Sauce

I cup molasses
I cup vinegar
I cup ketchup
2 teaspoons butter
I teaspoon Tabasco sauce

Sauce:

1. Heat all ingredients for sauce of your choice in a large saucepan for 5 minutes.
2. Add cooked meatballs to saucepan and continue heating over medium heat for 15 minutes.
3. Transfer to chafing dish, if desired. Serve with toothpicks.

Marinated Mushrooms

Yield: 4 to 6 servings as a first course

A creamy approach.

1 pound fresh mushrooms, caps only
4 cups water
2 tablespoons lemon juice
½ cup sour cream
1 teaspoon salt
¼ cup onion, thinly sliced
1 teaspoon dill weed
white pepper

Must be made ahead.

1. Combine water and lemon juice. Bring to boil. Add mushrooms and cook 2 minutes. Drain mushrooms well.
2. Combine sour cream, salt, onion and dill. Toss with mushrooms. Add pepper to taste. Refrigerate overnight and stir occasionally.

Smoked Salmon Cheesecake

Elegant!

3 tablespoons fine bread crumbs
5 tablespoons freshly grated Parmesan cheese
⅔ cup chopped onion
½ cup chopped sweet green pepper
3 tablespoons butter
3½ 8-ounce packages (28 ounces) cream cheese, softened
4 eggs
½ cup heavy cream
5 ounces Nova Scotia salmon, cut into small pieces
½ cup grated Jarlsburg cheese
dash Tabasco sauce

Garnish: Cherry tomatoes, fresh dill weed

Must be made ahead.

1. Preheat oven to 300°.
2. Butter an 8-inch springform pan. Combine bread crumbs with 2 tablespoons Parmesan; sprinkle bottom and sides of pan with mixture; shake around pan to coat.
3. Sauté onion and green pepper in butter until tender. Set aside.
4. In food processor or with mixer, combine cream cheese, eggs, and heavy cream until smooth; add remaining 3 tablespoons Parmesan, Jarlsburg, and sautéed mixture and process. Stir in salmon. Add Tabasco to taste.
5. Pour batter into prepared pan; set pan in slightly larger pan. Pour boiling water into larger pan until it comes up 2 inches on the sides of the springform.
6. Bake for 1 hour and 40 minutes. Turn off oven; do not open oven door but let cake sit in oven 1 hour longer.
7. Lift cake out of larger pan; cool to room temperature on wire rack. Refrigerate.
8. To serve: remove from refrigerator 1 hour before. Loosen around edge with knife; unmold. Garnish with dill and sliced cherry tomatoes, if desired.

Norwegian Herring

A Christmas tradition.

Yield: 6 servings as a first course

1 pint herring (can use 2 8-ounce party snack jars)
1 medium onion, thinly sliced
2 dill pickles, thinly sliced
1 tablespoon capers
⅓ cup plain yogurt
⅓ cup sour cream
⅓ cup mayonnaise or salad dressing
¼ teaspoon sugar
⅛ teaspoon dry mustard
⅛ teaspoon pepper
paprika

Must be made ahead.

1. Drain herring, rinse and pat dry.
2. Place herring in flat dish and cover with pickles, onions and capers.
3. Combine yogurt, sour cream, mayonnaise, sugar, mustard and pepper. Pour over herring and onions, stirring in well. Cover and refrigerate overnight.
4. As first course, serve on a bed of lettuce and sprinkle with paprika.

Stuffed Canapes

Yield: 24 to 30 servings

1 baguette of French bread or 4 to 5 long hard rolls
1 cup (2 sticks) butter, softened
8-ounce package cream cheese, softened
2 teaspoons anchovy paste
1 teaspoon Worcestershire sauce
½ teaspoon curry powder
3 tablespoons capers
1 tablespoon sweet pickle relish, drained well
3 tablespoons grated onion
½ cup pecans, finely chopped
1 cup ground Genoa salami

Must be made ahead.

1. A day ahead of serving, cut off ends of bread and scoop out soft centers leaving a narrow crust. French bread will have to be halved or quartered first.
2. Cream butter and cheese. Blend in remaining ingredients. Stuff rolls tightly with mixture.
3. Wrap in plastic and refrigerate overnight or up to a week.
4. Cut into ¼ inch slices to serve.

An 8-ounce block of cream cheese can be paired success-fully for an hors d'oeuvre with chutney or hot pepper jelly. The latter comes in red and green and looks very seasonal at a holiday party.

Memorable Family Recipes

Recipe _____ Dates Served _____

Ingredients _____

_____

_____

_____

_____

Procedure _____

_____

_____

_____

_____

_____

_____

_____

_____

Comments _____

_____

Additional blank pages are provided for your use at the end of the book.

Inventive and thrifty housewives have been concocting splendid soups from cooking broths of various fowl and fish for centuries. They made judicious use of giblets, marrow bones, carcasses, vegetable scraps and almost anything tasty that was not destined for the table in another form. Add to these the old favorites made from scratch such as the English and American Victorian Christmas oyster soup (made effectively with salsify, if oysters happened to be too expensive or unavailable) and the variety is almost endless.

The soup course, however, was not accorded the attention it might have deserved during the nineteenth century. Publications mention soups in passing as a necessary preliminary to dinner. One reason for this dismissal may have been the custom of spreading the entire feast on the table to tempt the diners as they quickly ate the soup.

Soups

23

Carrot Soup
Yes, with peanut butter!

Yield: 6 servings

1½ quarts chicken broth, homemade or canned
1 small onion, minced
¼ teaspoon nutmeg
4 cups thinly sliced carrots
½ cup half-and-half
1½ tablespoons peanut butter
2 teaspoons Worcestershire sauce
Dash or two Tabasco sauce
1 clove garlic

1. Place broth, onion, nutmeg and carrots in tightly covered pan and cook carrots until tender.
2. Combine all ingredients in a food processor or blender in batches, if necessary and purée until smooth.
3. Keep warm, over low heat or cool and reheat gently.

Lynn's Seafood Bisque
**Easily available ingredients
for inland cooks.**

Yield: 10 to 12 servings

1 6½-ounce can minced clams
1 4½-ounce can tiny shrimp
1 7½-ounce can crabmeat or 8 ounces imitation crab and seafood mix
2 ounces salt pork or ¼ cup butter or margarine
1½ cups chopped onion
3 large potatoes, peeled and diced
1 10½-ounce can condensed cream of celery soup plus soup can of milk
1½ cups milk
2 cups boiling water
¼ teaspoon curry
2 cups cream (light or heavy or mixture)
3 tablespoons cornstarch
1½ teaspoons thyme (optional)
salt to taste
¼ teaspoon pepper
sherry (optional)

**If desired, add a spoonful of sherry to each bowl
before serving.**

1. Drain clams, shrimp and crabmeat; reserve liquids.
2. In a large pot or kettle, brown salt pork until fat is released; add onions and potatoes and sauté, stirring frequently, approximately 10 minutes.
3. Add soup with milk, additional milk, boiling water, reserved liquids and curry. Cover and simmer for 25 minutes over low heat.
4. Add clams, shrimp and crabmeat with thyme; cook 5 minutes.
5. Mix cream and cornstarch together; add to bisque stirring constantly, over medium high heat until just at boiling point. Do not boil. Season to taste. Lower heat and cook 5 minutes longer.
6. May be made ahead and reheated gently.

Cheddar Cheese Soup

Yield: 6 servings

½ cup EACH finely chopped carrots, celery, onion and green pepper
¼ cup butter
¼ cup flour
¼ teaspoon dry mustard
1 quart chicken broth
12 ounces (3 cups) sharp Cheddar cheese, shredded
2 cups evaporated milk, or part half-and-half

OPTION: Purée all or part of soup in blender or food processor.

1. Sauté vegetables in butter in heavy 3-quart pan for 5 minutes. Remove from heat.
2. Stir in flour and dry mustard. When mixed well, add broth and return to heat. Simmer 5 minutes, stirring occasionally.
3. Add cheese slowly; add milk. Stir and heat until cheese is melted and soup is hot. Do not cook or reheat over high-flame or bring near boil.

Cream of Crab-Broccoli Soup

Yield: 6 servings

Delicious but not complicated.

1 10-ounce package frozen chopped broccoli*
½ cup chopped onion
3 tablespoons butter
2 tablespoons flour
2 cups milk
2 cups half-and-half
2 chicken bouillon cubes
½ teaspoon salt, or to taste
⅛ teaspoon black pepper
⅛ teaspoon cayenne pepper
¼ teaspoon thyme
1 6- to 8-ounce package frozen crabmeat or
   1 7½-ounce can crabmeat or
   8 ounces imitation crab-seafood mix

*1½ cups cooked and chopped fresh broccoli may be used.**

1. Cook frozen broccoli according to package directions. Drain; set aside.
2. Sauté onion in butter until transparent; blend in flour. Add milk and half-and-half; stir and cook until thickened and smooth.
3. Dissolve bouillon cubes in hot soup. Add seasonings, crab and broccoli; heat through but do not allow to boil.

 Consider serving soups in attractive cups or mugs to guests before they are seated at the table.

Creamed Turkey Rice Soup

Yield: 6 to 8 servings

Hearty meal served with green salad and crusty bread.

3 10¾-ounce cans condensed chicken broth
2 cups water
½ cup wild or brown or white rice
½ cup green onions, finely chopped
4 carrots, finely sliced
2 tablespoons butter or margarine
¼ cup flour
¼ teaspoon poultry seasoning
⅛ teaspoon pepper
½ teaspoon salt
2 cups half-and-half
3 cups cooked turkey, cubed
1 tablespoon pimento, chopped
¼ pound bacon, cooked and crumbled
2 tablespoons dry sherry

1. In large stockpot, combine chicken broth and water. Add rice, onion and carrots. Bring to a boil, simmer until rice and carrots are tender.

2. In 1-quart pan, melt butter, stir in flour and seasonings. Add the half-and-half gradually, while stirring constantly. Cook until slightly thickened.

3. Stir cream mixture into rice mixture carefully. Add remaining ingredients. Heat gently but do not boil.

Hearty Beef-Vegetable Soup

Yield: 10 servings

A thick soup, almost a stew.

3 pounds stew beef, cut in 1½ inch cubes
1 cup chopped onion
2 garlic cloves, minced
2 tablespoons olive oil
1 teaspoon salt and ¼ teaspoon pepper
½ teaspoon EACH basil and oregano
3 13¾-ounce cans beef broth
2 cups water
1 1-pound can stewed tomatoes with liquid
1 14½-ounce can kidney beans, undrained
1 can ripe olives, pitted, sliced in half, and with 1 cup olive liquid
1 10-ounce box frozen sliced carrots
1 10-ounce box frozen sliced zucchini
1 10-ounce box frozen corn
1 cup small macaroni

1. Brown meat cubes, onions and garlic in olive oil. Season with salt and pepper.

2. Add broth, water, and seasonings; simmer for one hour.

3. Add tomatoes, beans, olives, carrots, zucchini, corn, and macaroni. Simmer for 45 minutes more.

4. Serve sprinkled with Parmesan cheese, if desired.

Cream of Mushroom Soup

Special.

Yield: 10 to 12 servings

1 pound mushrooms, sliced
1 Spanish onion (5–6 ounces), sliced
1 cup fresh parsley tops, packed
2 tablespoons flour
6 tablespoons butter
1 quart beef broth
1½ cup sour cream
freshly ground black pepper
⅛ teaspoon nutmeg
1 tablespoon sherry

1. Melt butter in large frying pan. Add mushrooms, onions and parsley and cook over medium-high heat until juices have evaporated, about 5 minutes. Remove from heat.
2. Stir in flour and add beef broth. Return to medium heat and bring to boil, stirring.
3. Remove from heat and add pepper, nutmeg and sherry.
4. In blender or food processor, put a portion of mushroom mixture and some sour cream. Purée until smooth. Continue this procedure until all has been puréed.
5. Return to pan and keep warm or cover and refrigerate until needed. Do not bring to a boil when reheating.

Oysters Rockefeller Soup

Rich and creamy with a hint of anise.

Yield: 8 servings

1½ cups chicken broth
1 small onion, finely chopped
1 stalk celery, finely chopped
2 cloves garlic, minced
1 cup finely chopped fresh spinach
1 pint shucked oysters
¼ cup grated Romano or Parmesan cheese
1 pint half-and-half
2 tablespoons cornstarch
1½ teaspoons aniseed
salt and pepper to taste
4 to 5 drops Tabasco sauce
¼ cup anisette

1. In a large saucepan cook ½ cup of the chicken broth, the onion, celery, and garlic, covered, for 5 minutes.
2. Add the spinach; cover and simmer 5 minutes more.
3. Drain oysters, reserving liquid. Add the oyster liquid and the remaining chicken broth to mixture in saucepan. Simmer mixture for 10 minutes, stirring occasionally. Stir in cheese.
4. Combine the cream, cornstarch, aniseed, salt, pepper, and Tabasco; stir into the mixture in the saucepan. Cook and stir till thickened and bubbly. Cook, stirring, 5 minutes more. (May be done ahead to here; reheat.)
5. Stir in oysters and anisette; heat through. DO NOT BOIL. Serve.

Ham and Corn Chowder

A tummy-warming way to use up the last of the ham.

Yield: about 6 cups

2 cups diced cooked ham
1 cup chopped celery
½ cup chopped onion
½ cup (1 stick) butter
2 16-ounce cans cream-style corn
1 cup milk
1 tablespoon grated onion
1 teaspoon celery salt
½ teaspoon thyme
½ teaspoon pepper

1. Sauté ham, celery and onion in butter in a large pot or Dutch oven.
2. Stir in remaining ingredients; bring to a boil. Reduce heat; simmer 20 minutes.

Chesapeake Oyster Stew

A rich, buttery stew

Yield: 10 servings

1 quart oysters with liquid
¼ cup (½ stick) butter
1 quart milk
½ pint heavy cream
1 teaspoon salt, or more to taste
pepper to taste

Stew keeps well over low heat, stirring occasionally (may even improve!)

1. Place oysters with liquid, butter, salt and pepper in a large saucepan; heat until oysters curl. Do not boil.
2. Heat milk and cream together until just below boiling point. Do not boil.
3. Pour milk-cream mixture into oysters; stir gently. Heat over low heat for 5 to 10 minutes, or until hot, but do not boil. Serve in bowls with oyster crackers.

Super Soup

This unusual "soup" should be served in demitasse portions

Yield: twelve 3-ounce servings

2 cans Campbell's consommé with gelatin
6 ounces cream cheese, softened
2 tablespoons curry powder or to taste

Garnish: parsley or watercress

1. Blend cheese, curry and 1¾ cup consommé. Pour into serving cups. Chill until firm. Leave remaining consommé at room temperature.
2. When set, spoon remaining consommé on top. Return to refrigerator until serving.

Mushroom Soup

Snappy!

Yield: serves 4 to 6 servings

2 tablespoons butter
¼ cup finely chopped onion
3 tablespoons flour
1 teaspoon salt
freshly ground pepper to taste
¼ teaspoon oregano
⅛ teaspoon cayenne pepper
1 quart chicken or turkey stock
1 pound mushrooms, cleaned and sliced
1 bay leaf
½ cup heavy cream

1. In large pan, melt butter over medium heat. Add onion and heat until translucent but not brown. Remove pan from heat and stir in flour and seasonings.
2. Gradually stir in stock to avoid lumps. Add mushrooms and bay leaf.
3. Bring to a boil, stirring constantly. Reduce to low, cover and simmer 30 minutes; uncover and stir in cream. Heat through but do not boil. Discard bay leaf before serving.

Pumpkin Soup in Pumpkin Shell

Yield: 6 to 8 servings

1 small can pumpkin (15-ounce size)
¼ cup butter
1 small onion, finely chopped
¼ teaspoon ginger
¼ teaspoon nutmeg
3 cups chicken broth
1 cup light cream
1 ounce brandy
salt and pepper
4-pound pumpkin, top cut, scooped and hollowed, to form bowl

1. Melt butter and sauté onion until soft. Add spices and broth and bring to a boil. Add pumpkin and return to boil.
2. Lower heat and slowly add cream. Do not boil. When thoroughly heated, add brandy. Adjust seasoning. Pour into pumpkin to serve.

Memorable Family Recipes

Recipe _____ Dates Served _____

Ingredients _____

_____

_____

_____

_____

Procedure _____

_____

_____

_____

_____

_____

_____

_____

Comments _____

_____

Additional blank pages are provided for your use at the end of the book.

Beverages

Beverages

The Wassail Bowl

"Wassail", which comes from the Anglo-Saxon "wes hal" and the Norse "ves heill", both meaning "to be whole" or "good health", has always been seen as a formal affirmation of friendship. The contents of the English wassail bowl were hot spiced ale and toasted apples. Known as "lamb's wool", it has pieces of toast floating on it – hence our term, "to toast". Often carolers carried cups to be filled at each house along the way,

Old Recipe for Wassail

Into a bowl is first placed ½lb sugar in which is placed one pint of warm beer; a little nutmeg and ginger are then grated over the mixture, and four glasses of sherry and five pints of beer added to it. It is then stirred, sweetened to taste and allowed to stand for two or three hours. Roasted apples are then floated on the creaming mixture and the wassail bowl is ready.

from The Curiosities of Ale and Beer
by John Bickerdyke c.1860

33

Bishop's Wine Cup

A hot, spiced wine drink.

Yield: 12 6-ounce servings

2 quarts apple cider
4 cinnamon sticks
6 whole cloves
1 orange, quartered but not peeled
½ teaspoon nutmeg (fresh or ground)
1 liter bottle port wine

1. Pour apple cider into a metal pot that may also be used for serving. Add cinnamon sticks, cloves and orange. Sprinkle in nutmeg. Simmer for 30 minutes.
2. Stir in port wine. Heat until steaming hot but do not boil. Serve from pot. (Place pot inside a wreath on table top, if desired.)

Carolyn's Wassail

Yield: 10 to 12 servings

4 cups apple cider
½ cup packed dark brown sugar
½ cup dark rum
¼ cup brandy
1 tablespoon Grand Marnier
¼ teaspoon cinnamon
¼ teaspoon ground cloves
⅛ teaspoon ground allspice
salt to taste
½ lemon (thinly sliced)
½ orange (thinly sliced)
Grand Marnier flavored whipped cream
freshly grated nutmeg

1. Heat apple cider and brown sugar together in a large saucepan or pot to boiling; stir until sugar dissolves.
2. Remove from heat; add rum, brandy, and Grand Marnier. Stir in spices and salt to taste. Add lemon and orange slices.
3. Heat over medium heat, stirring, for 2 minutes. Do not boil.
4. Pour into wine glasses; top each glass with Grand Marnier flavored whipped cream and freshly grated nutmeg.

Irish Cream Nog

A new flavor for egg nog.

Yield: 2 quarts

6 eggs
½ cup sugar
3 cups milk
1½ cups Irish cream liqueur
½ teaspoon ground nutmeg
½ cup heavy, or whipping cream, whipped
ground nutmeg

Must be made ahead.

1. Beat eggs until foamy at medium speed of an electric mixer. Gradually add sugar, beating 5 minutes or till thick and lemon colored.
2. Reduce speed to low; gradually add milk, liqueur, and ½ teaspoon nutmeg, beating until combined.
3. Chill thoroughly.
4. To serve: stir in whipped cream and sprinkle with additional nutmeg.

The Cooke Family's Wassail

Yield: about 30 servings

This wassail is best if made 3 to 5 days before serving.

1 gallon apple cider
1¾ cups firmly packed light brown sugar
6 2-inch cinnamon sticks
1 tablespoon whole cloves
1 tablespoon powdered allspice
2 pieces mace (or ¼ teaspoon powdered)
½ teaspoon salt
pinch crushed red pepper
¼ cup lemon juice
2 cups brandy (not fruit-flavored)

Must be made ahead.

1. Combine all ingredients except lemon juice and brandy. Bring to a boil; reduce heat and steep 30 minutes on low, covered.
2. Strain mixture twice through cheesecloth. Refrigerate.
3. Before serving, reheat. Add lemon juice and brandy. Heat but do not allow to boil.

Traditional Old English Wassail

Yield: 12 servings

All the ingredients of Mr. Bickerdyke's 1860 recipe have been adjusted for modern palates.

4 cups ale (or beer)
1 stick cinnamon
2 teaspoons powdered ginger
6 whole cloves
6 allspice berries
1 tablespoon ground nutmeg
2 cups sherry wine
juice and finely slivered rind of one lemon
½ cup sugar (or more to taste)
2 slices toasted bread
6 to 8 roasted crabapples or 2 to 3
   roasted large apples

Variation: A dozen well-beaten eggs may be beaten into hot wassail before adding apples.

1. Heat ale in an enameled saucepan until just at boiling point. Do not boil.
2. Stir in spices, sherry, lemon juice, rind and sugar. Stir until sugar dissolves; cover and steep over low heat for 20 to 30 minutes. Do not boil at any time.
3. Pour into a heated punch bowl. Add toast and apples. Ladle into warm punch cups.

Swedish Glögg

**For the Christmas Eve Smörgasbord—
wicked good!**

1 dozen blanched almonds (halved)
1 pound raisins
¾ pound prunes
peel of 1 orange, quartered
1 dozen whole cloves
2 sticks cinnamon
1 piece ginger root
1 dozen cardamon pods
1 quart water
1 4-liter bottle port wine
1 750-ml bottle brandy
1 750-ml bottle grain alcohol
¾ cup sugar

**Glögg may be saved after cooling by pouring into
bottles with some raisins and almonds in each.
Reheat before serving, but do not boil.**

1. Combine first 9 ingredients in a large pot. Cover; simmer 45 minutes.
2. Add wine. Cover tightly; heat but do not boil. Remove from heat; add grain alcohol and brandy. Cover again; heat to just below boiling. Cool, covered for 5 to 10 minutes.
3. Light a long-stemmed match and, carefully, hold over glögg until surface lights. Recover after a couple of seconds to put out flame. Repeat. Add the sugar; stir until dissolved.
4. Serve warm in small mugs in which you have put a few raisins and almonds.

The Professor's Glögg

Proceed with caution: a lethal beverage!

2 quarts dry red wine
2 quarts muscatel
1 pint sweet vermouth
2 tablespoons Angostura bitters
2 cups raisins
peel of 1 orange cut into fine slivers
10 whole cloves
12 whole cardamons, bruised by covering
   with towel and crushing with rolling pin
1 piece fresh ginger
1 cinnamon stick
1½ cups Aquavit
1½ cups sugar
2 cups whole almonds, blanched and peeled

Must be made ahead.

1. In a large, 6- to 8-quart pot, mix together red wine, muscatel, vermouth, bitters, raisins, orange peel, cardamons, whole cloves, ginger and cinnamon. Cover; let mixture stand at least 12 hours so flavors will develop and mingle.
2. Shortly before serving, add Aquavit and sugar. Stir well; bring to a full boil over high heat. Remove at once; stir in almonds.
3. Serve very warm in very small amounts!

Bayou Syllabub

A very old recipe from a family in Texas.

Yield: 12 to 16 servings

1 quart heavy cream
1 cup whole milk
1 cup French brandy
1 cup confectioners' sugar
grating of fresh nutmeg

1. Chill all liquid ingredients well.
2. Pour milk and brandy into chilled punch bowl; add sugar and stir until dissolved.
3. Whip cream lightly; add to punch bowl; whip again.
4. Serve in syllabub cups or punch glasses with fresh nutmeg grated over top of each serving.

Cam's Egg Nog

The best you've ever tasted!

Yield: 24 4-ounce servings

1 dozen eggs, separated
1 pint heavy cream
1 cup light rum
1 cup peach brandy
2 cups brandy (not fruit-flavored)
1 pound confectioners' sugar
3 cups whole milk
grated rinds of one orange and one lemon
grated nutmeg

If making several batches for a large crowd, store in clean plastic garbage can in a snowbank outside!

1. Separate eggs while still cold. Allow egg whites to come to room temperature and then beat until stiff.
2. Whip cream until softly mounded.
3. Beat egg yolks in a large bowl or container (a large, clean plastic dishpan is ideal); add liquor, sugar, milk, whipped cream and rinds. (Placing container in an ice-water bath in sink is helpful).
4. Fold in egg whites
5. If possible, chill several hours.
6. Serve topped with grated rinds and nutmeg.

Brandy Crusta

An Australian favorite.

Yield: 2 servings

extra fine sugar
orange juice
3 ounces brandy
1 ounce Curaçao
3 ounces orange juice

1. Prepare two glasses by dipping rims in orange juice then in sugar.
2. Shake remaining ingredients with ice or place in blender with an ice cube or two and mix well. Pour and enjoy.

Kentucky Egg Nog

Thick and velvety

Yield: about 5 pints

1 dozen egg yolks
1¼ cups granulated sugar
9 ounces Kentucky bourbon
3 ounces rum
1 quart heavy cream

Must be made ahead.

1. Beat egg yolks until thick in electric mixer.
2. Slowly add the sugar, beating well.
3. Slowly add 3 ounces of bourbon. Cover bowl and set in refrigerator over night.
4. Next day, whip the heavy cream until stiff. Beat remaining 6 ounces of bourbon and rum into egg yolk mixture. Fold into heavy cream.
5. Store in covered jars in refrigerator until needed. Allow several days to ripen. Keeps several weeks.
6. To serve, stir egg nog before pouring into small serving cup or glass. Sprinkle with nutmeg and serve with a spoon so as not to miss a drop!

Fish House Punch

**May be doubled easily for 90.
Beware: highly potent.**

Yield: 45 4-ounce servings

2 6-ounce cans frozen limeade
1 6-ounce can frozen lemonade
2 quarts water
1 750-ml bottle white rum
1 liter bottle dark rum
3 ounces peach brandy
4 ounces Southern Comfort
2 cups unsweetened pineapple juice
juice of 2 fresh limes

Garnish: lemon and orange slices, pineapple chunks, whole frozen strawberries

Must be made ahead.

1. Mix all ingredients in large pot. Chill for at least two hours.
2. To serve: pour over a block of ice into a punch bowl and garnish.

Loy Family Egg Nog

1 dozen fresh, large eggs
1 pint light cream
1 ⅓ cups brandy
1 ⅓ cups dark Jamaican rum
1 teaspoon ground nutmeg
½ cup sugar, or more to taste

Must be made 1 week ahead.

1. Use a blender or food processor (in lieu of a churn) to mix. (If using a blender, mix in two batches). Blend eggs and cream until thoroughly mixed. Add brandy, rum, nutmeg and ¼ cup sugar; blend until mixed. Taste and add more sugar if preferred.
2. Refrigerate, well-covered; stir every other day.
3. After one week, serve, but in very small portions.

This version of egg nog seems quite mild on drinking, but it packs quite a wallop. The recipe remained little changed for over a century except that today one mellows it in the refrigerator instead of the spring house.

Cranberry Daiquiris

Yield: 6 servings

Frosty and festive.

1 8-ounce can jellied cranberry sauce.
2 individual drink packets of dry daiquiri mix (comes 8 to a box)
¾ cup light rum
1 ½ tablespoons sweetened lime juice
ice cubes

1. Put first 4 ingredients in blender container; mix until blended.
2. Add ice to near the top. Process until frothy. Pour into 6 glasses, about 6 ounces to each.

Hot Buttered Rum

Yield: 25 servings

Sensational, but dangerous!

1 cup brown sugar
2 cups confectioners' sugar
½ pound (2 sticks) butter
1 pint vanilla ice cream, softened
½ teaspoon EACH cinnamon, nutmeg and allspice
dash mace
rum
boiling water

Must be made ahead.

1. Cream butter, spices and sugars; blend with softened ice cream. Mix well.
2. Pack into covered container and store in freezer.
3. To serve: Put generous spoonful into mug. Add 2 ounces rum and mix well. Add boiling water to fill. Adjust ice cream mixture to taste. Serve immediately. Drink slowly!

Phyllis' Coffee Bourbon Punch

Yield: 25 servings

8 cups (64 ounces) brewed coffee, cooled
½ gallon vanilla ice cream, softened
2 liters bourbon

Must be made ahead.

1. Combine softened ice cream with coffee and bourbon; cover and refrigerate overnight.
2. Pour into punchbowl and post a warning.

Cranberry Cocktail

Yield: 6 cups

Refreshing!

4 cups fresh or frozen cranberries
1 quart water
2 cups sugar
½ cup orange juice
2 tablespoons lemon juice

Must be made ahead.

1. Cook cranberries in water until they pop.
2. Add sugar and bring to a boil, stirring to dissolve sugar.
3. Press fruit through sieve or colander, and add juices.
4. Cover and refrigerate until chilled and thickened.

Spiced Percolator Punch

Yield: about 24 servings

This can be served with or without the addition of alcohol.

2 32-ounce bottles cranberry juice cocktail
1 46-ounce can unsweetened pineapple juice
1 cup packed brown sugar
4 teaspoons whole cloves
12 inches stick cinnamon, broken
peel of ¼ orange, cut into strips
1 750-ml bottle light rum (optional)

1. In 24-cup electric percolator combine juices and brown sugar.
2. In basket of coffee maker, place spices and orange peel.
3. Assemble coffee maker; plug in and percolate. Just before serving, remove basket and stir in rum. Keep hot.
4. To serve: float lemon slices in warmed mugs.

Add a few drops of Chambord to a glass of champagne for a colorful, worthy deviation from tradition.

"Just Like Store-Bought" Egg Nog

Yield: 6 to 8 servings

Kids' choice.

6 fresh eggs
6 tablespoons sugar
½ teaspoon nutmeg
1 pint good quality vanilla ice cream, softened
1 pint milk

1. Beat eggs with sugar until thick. Add nutmeg.
2. Beat in ice cream, then milk. Pour into serving cups or store covered in the refrigerator. Will keep a couple of days. Stir again before pouring.

Hot Mulled Cider

Yield: 10 servings

Make this warm drink in your crock pot!

½ cup brown sugar
¼ teaspoon salt
2 quarts apple cider
cheesecloth bag containing:
½ teaspoon allspice
1 teaspoon whole cloves
dash nutmeg
cinnamon stick

1. Bring all ingredients to a boil in a large saucepan; reduce heat and simmer 20 minutes.
2. Remove bag of spices. Serve with cinnamon stick stirrer.

To make in crockpot: Put ingredients into pot and cook on "Hi" for 30 to 40 minutes. Remove spice bag; reduce heat to "Lo" until ready to serve. May be kept on "Lo" for many hours.

Hot Spiced Fruit Punch

Yield: 24 servings

A non-alcoholic punch that smells wonderful while simmering.

1 gallon apple juice
1 quart orange juice
2 cups lemon juice
1 heaping cup sugar
1 16-ounce can frozen pineapple juice, thawed
2 cinnamon sticks
2 teaspoons whole cloves

1. Put all ingredients in a large saucepan or stockpot; heat to boiling.
2. Reduce heat; simmer for one hour. Serve in warmed mugs with cinnamon stick stirrer.

Memorable Family Recipes

Recipe _____ Dates Served _____

Ingredients _____

_____

_____

_____

_____

Procedure _____

_____

_____

_____

_____

_____

_____

_____

Comments _____

_____

Additional blank pages are provided for your use at the end of the book.

Breads

Breads

The Victorian Christmas was replete with breads of various shapes and rich ingredients. While everyday bread was plain fare, Christmas breads were lavish in their use of nuts, spices and fruits making it difficult to separate the fancy, traditional breads from the popular holiday cakes and cookies. Breads were baked in shapes such as crescents, stars, trees and yule logs and were often embossed with these shapes as well as animals.

Breads

Many of the traditional shapes can be traced to pre-Christmas pagan rituals of Europe and the British Isles. Animal shapes harken back to their original use as sacrificial offerings in place of actual animals and the beautiful braided breads may once have signified braided hair, symbolic of ancient human sacrifice. These cooking traditions, long forgotten by the nineteenth century, were still practiced for their festive associations with Christmas.

45

German Fruit Stöllen

Yield: 2 loaves

¼ cup EACH light and dark raisins
½ cup dried currants
8 ounces mixed chopped candied fruit
  and peel
½ cup candied red cherries
½ cup dark rum
2 packages dry yeast
1 teaspoon plus ¾ cup sugar
¼ cup warm water (110°)
2 tablespoons plus 5 to 6 cups flour
1 cup (2 sticks) butter
1 cup milk
½ teaspoon salt
2 large eggs, beaten
½ teaspoon almond extract
½ teaspoon grated lemon rind
confectioners' sugar

Garnish: candied cherries and angelica,
if desired

1. Reserve a few cherries to garnish finished loaves. Soak remaining fruits in rum, covered, for 1 hour.
2. Dissolve yeast and 1 teaspoon sugar in warm water. Let stand 5 minutes.
3. Drain fruit (reserve rum); pat dry. Toss with 2 tablespoons flour and set aside.
4. Melt ¾ cup butter (reserving ¼ cup). Add milk; heat until warm (110°).
5. In large bowl, combine milk mixture, rum, yeast mixure, ½ cup sugar, salt, eggs, almond extract and lemon rind. Stir in 5 cups flour.
6. Knead on floured board 8 to 10 minutes, adding enough extra flour from remaining 1 cup to make dough smooth and elastic. Knead in reserved fruit ⅓ at a time. Put dough in greased bowl; turn greased side up; cover and let rise in warm place until doubled in bulk, 1½ to 2 hours.
7. Punch down dough; divide into two; let rest 10 minutes.
8. Roll each half into a 12 x 18-inch oval. Brush each oval with reserved ¼ cup melted butter; sprinkle with sugar. Fold long sides over center, overlapping 1 inch. Press gently to seal. Taper ends and mound center.
9. Place loaves on greased baking sheets. Brush with butter. Cover; let rise 1 hour. Bake at 375° for 40 minutes.
10. Cool loaves on racks; dust with confectioners' sugar (or a light glaze may be used). Decorate with candied cherry halves and candied angelica.

Quick breads and yeast breads freeze well. Any glaze should be added after they are warmed slightly.

Grandma's Christmas Bread

Yield: 2 loaves

A German breakfast loaf.

2 cups milk
2 tablespoons shortening
2 packages active dry yeast
1 cup raisins (golden or regular
   or ½ cup each mixed)
2 tablespoons sugar
1 tablespoon salt
12 cardamon seeds, crushed
   (or 1 teaspoon ground cardamon)
5 to 6 cups flour, separated

1. Heat milk and shortening until very warm (between 120° to 130°).

2. Combine remaining ingredients using 2½ cups of flour. Add heated milk mixture. Mix at low speed for 1 minute.

3. Scrape down bowl; mix again for 3 minutes at medium speed.

4. With wooden spoon, stir in all but 1 cup of remaining flour; stir until dough sticks to spoon. Cover and let rest 5 minutes.

5. Knead dough using remaining flour as needed, until smooth and elastic.

6. Place dough in greased bowl; cover and allow to rise until doubled in size, 30 to 45 minutes.

7. Turn dough onto board. Do not punch down. Cut into two equal parts; place each piece in a greased 8½ x 4 x 2½-inch pan. Allow to rise in warm, draft-free place until 1½ inches above pan.

8. Bake at 375° for 45 minutes. Bread is done when it pulls away from sides of pan. Remove from oven; cool slightly and remove from pan. Cool on wire rack. While still warm, brush crusts with melted butter.

Danish Ring

Tender and buttery—worth the effort.

Yield: 2 rings

4 cups flour
1 teaspoon salt
3 tablespoons sugar
1 teaspoon cardamon
¾ cup water
¼ cup butter
1 package yeast
2 eggs
1½ cups (3 sticks) butter
1 to 1½ cups filling of choice for each ring
   Suggestions: almond, apricot, date,
   cinnamon-nut

Must be made a day ahead.

1. In food processor with steel blade, combine flour, salt, cardamon and all but 1 teaspoon of sugar.
2. Heat ¼ cup butter with ½ cup water to melt butter. Cool to lukewarm. Beat eggs and add.
3. Dissolve yeast in ¼ cup of lukewarm (110°) water, adding reserved sugar.
4. With food processor running, pour in egg mixture then yeast mixture. Let it run until thoroughly mixed. Remove dough to a greased bowl, cover, and refrigerate 20 to 30 minutes.
5. Whip 1½ cup butter.
6. Roll dough onto floured surface, into a rectangle ¼ inch thick. Using ¼ of the butter, spread it over ⅔ of the dough. Lap unbuttered dough over center and remaining third over that.
7. Turn the dough ¼ turn, roll, butter, and lap again.
8. Repeat step 7 twice more. Wrap dough in plastic wrap and refrigerate overnight.
9. Cut dough in half and roll each to approximately 10 x 14 inches. Trim edges if they prevent rolling properly. Cover with filling. Roll jelly roll fashion onto a greased cookie sheet. Form into ring and slash halfway through at one inch intervals. Twist each cut piece slightly on its side.
10. Let rise covered until doubled. Preheat oven to 375°.
11. Bake 25 minutes or until golden. Cool on rack. Glaze with confectioners' icing if desired.

Stöllen

Food Processor Method.

1 to 2 packages active dry yeast
¼ cup water, lukewarm (110°)
1 teaspoon sugar
3¾ cups flour
⅔ cup sugar
¾ teaspoon salt
½ teaspoon cinnamon
⅛ teaspoon mace
⅛ teaspoon cardamon
⅔ cup milk
½ cup butter, in chunks
1 egg, beaten
1 cup candied fruit, diced
¼ cup raisins
½ cup pecans, chopped

Frosting:
1 cup confectioners' sugar
1½ tablespoons butter, melted
½ tablespoon corn syrup
½ teaspoon vanilla
1–1½ tablespoons milk

Garnish: Red and green cherries and pecans

1. Add yeast to water with 1 teaspoon sugar. Let sit 10 minutes.
2. In processor bowl place all dry ingredients. Pulse to combine.
3. Scald milk and stir in butter to melt it. Cool.
4. With processor running, pour milk mixture into feed tube. Add egg and finally yeast mixture. Dough should be soft but not sticky. Add a bit more flour if necessary.
5. Put dough into a greased bowl and cover. Let rise in warm place until doubled. Punch down.
6. On floured board, knead fruits and nuts into dough. Form into a long oval on greased cookie sheet. Lap one half lengthwise over the other. Cover and let rise again. Preheat oven to 375°.
7. Bake about 40 minutes or until golden and hollow-sounding when tapped. Cool on rack. Freeze if desired.
8. Combine frosting ingredients adding milk to desired consistency; frost before serving.

Apricot Nut Bread

1 cup dried apricots
2 cups flour
1 cup sugar
2 teaspoons baking powder
1 teaspoon salt
¼ teaspoon baking soda
¼ cup shortening
1 egg
¾ cup orange juice
1 cup nuts, chopped

1. Preheat oven to 375° and grease 9 x 5-inch loaf pan.
2. In small bowl cover apricots with warm water. Let stand 15 minutes. Drain and coarsely chop.
3. In large bowl, mix flour, sugar, baking powder, salt and baking soda.
4. With mixer stir in shortening, egg and juice. Blend well. Add apricots and nuts and pour into prepared pan. Bake 45 to 55 minutes or until tester comes out clean.
5. Cool on rack. Serve with cream cheese.

Pecan Rolls

Rich and luscious—use food processor.

Dough:

1 cup sour cream, heated to 110°
1 package yeast
1 teaspoon sugar
2 cups flour
½ cup butter, cut into 6 pieces
1 tablespoon sugar
1 teaspoon salt
3 yolks of large eggs, beaten

Syrup:

½ cup light brown sugar
¼ cup (½ stick) butter, melted
1 tablespoon light corn syrup
36 pecan halves

Filling:

¼ cup brown sugar
1 teaspoon cinnamon
½ cup chopped raisins (optional)
1 cup chopped pecans
¼ cup (½ stick) butter, melted

Dough must be refrigerated before forming rolls.

1. In small bowl combine yeast, teaspoon sugar and sour cream. Let stand 10 minutes.

2. In food processor with steel blade, combine flour, butter, tablespoon sugar and salt. Pulse until mixture is crumbly. Add yolks and yeast mixture and pulse until just combined. Do not over-process. Cover and refrigerate several hours or overnight.

3. Prepare Tins: combine syrup ingredients. Put 1½ teaspoons into 18 muffin tins (or ¾ teaspoon into 36 mini tins). Place 2 pecans (or 1) in each tin.

4. Divide dough in two. Roll each into 6 x 9-inch rectangle. Combine brown sugar, cinnamon, raisins and pecans. Spread 2 tablespoons of butter on each rectangle. Top each with half the sugar mixture. Roll jelly-roll fashion. Cut each into 9 (or 18) pieces and put in prepared tins. Cover with damp cloth and let rise until doubled.

5. Preheat oven to 375°. Bake in upper part of oven about 15 minutes or until done. (Less for minis). Invert immediately onto racks. (Use waxed paper under rack.) May be frozen when completely cooled and warmed to serve.

 Yeast breads are time-consuming for last-minute preparation. Prepare them a week or more in advance and freeze without glaze or frosting. Remove from freezer the night before using. Prior to serving, warm slightly and glaze.

Poppyseed Bun

Special addition to sweet bread collection.

3 cups flour
1 package active dry yeast
1 cup milk
¼ cup shortening
¼ cup sugar
1 egg, slightly beaten
1 teaspoon salt
¼ teaspoon nutmeg or mace
grated rind of 1 orange, (2 teaspoons)

Filling:

1 can poppyseed filling
1 egg
¼ teaspoon vanilla
½ teaspoon cinnamon
2 to 4 tablespoons butter
egg white for top

Yield: 1 large coffee cake

Traditional method:

1. In a large bowl combine 1¼ cups flour and yeast. In a saucepan heat together milk, sugar, shortening and salt just until warm (115°–120°) stirring constantly until shortening almost melts. With electric mixer beat this into flour-yeast mixture.

2. Add egg, nutmeg, orange rind and remainder of flour. Beat with wooden spoon 5 minutes. Knead on lightly floured board adding flour as needed. But do not make dough too stiff. Put in greased bowl, cover and let rise until doubled. Proceed to step 3.

Food Processor Method:

1. Place all flour, sugar (minus 1 teaspoon) salt, nutmeg and orange in bowl with steel blade. Heat ¼ cup milk to 110° and add yeast and 1 teaspoon sugar. Let stand until dissolved and activated (5–10 minutes).

2. Heat remaining milk with shortening to lukewarm. Beat egg and add to milk mixture. With processor running, pour in egg-milk mixure then yeast mixture. Mix thoroughly. Place in greased bowl, cover and let rise.

3. Combine filling ingredients. Melt butter. Preheat oven to 375°.

4. On floured surface roll out dough ¼ inch thick. Brush with butter, spread with filling. Roll up lengthwise and form into ring, if desired, on greased cookie sheet. Brush dough with egg white. Bake 25 to 45 minutes or until it sounds hollow when tapped.

Two packages of yeast will help dough rise faster.

Saffron Bread

An old English recipe for tea bread.

Yield: 2 loaves

½ teaspoon shredded saffron, lightly packed
2 cups milk
½ cup (1 stick) butter, melted
1 package active dry yeast
2 tablespoons warm water (110°)
1 cup sugar
¼ teaspoon salt
½ teaspoon nutmeg
6 to 7 cups flour
½ cup candied lemon peel, chopped
2 cups dried currants

1. Steep saffron in ½ cup boiling water for at least 30 minutes; strain, saving liquid.
2. Scald milk; pour into large mixing bowl. Add saffron liquid; stir in melted butter. Cool to 110° to 115°.
3. Dissolve yeast in 2 tablespoons warm water; stir into warm milk.
4. Add sugar, salt and nutmeg; spoon in flour. Mix in candied peel and currants thoroughly. Dough should be quite stiff.
5. Cover with tea towel; let rise in warm spot away from draughts until doubled, about 1½ hours.
6. Punch down dough; knead on floured board until smooth. Divide in half; shape into loaves and place in two greased loaf pans. Let rise a second time until doubled in size.
7. Bake in preheated 350° oven for 45 minutes to 1 hour. Remove and brush with melted butter. Cool in pans 10 minutes before turning out. Slice when completely cool.

Cornbread Muffins

Yield: 1 dozen muffins

1 cup flour
¼ cup sugar
3 teaspoons baking powder
½ teaspoon salt
1 cup yellow corn meal
1 egg, well-beaten
1 cup milk
5 tablespoons sweet butter, melted

1. Preheat oven to 375°.
2. Mix together flour, sugar, baking powder and salt. Add corn meal.
3. Add to mixture: egg, milk and melted butter. Beat until smooth; do not overmix.
4. Bake in well-greased muffin pans at 375° for 12 to 15 minutes or till lightly browned.
5. Cool slightly; serve or store in plastic bags when cooled. Reheat wrapped in foil at 350° for 10 minutes.

Country French Bread

Walnuts and onions—wonderful.

Yield: 2 loaves

1 envelope yeast
½ cup lukewarm water (110°)
1 teaspoon sugar
½ cup (1 stick) butter, melted
1½ cup milk
2 teaspoons salt
6 cups flour (part may be whole wheat)
¾ cup onion, minced
1 cup walnuts, chopped

1. Proof the yeast in water and sugar.
2. Add melted butter and salt to milk.
3a. **No Knead: Food Processor Method:**
    Place flour in bowl with steel blade. With processor running slowly pour in milk, then pour in yeast. When it forms a ball, stop.
3b. **Traditional Method:**
    Combine yeast sponge with milk in large mixing bowl. Add flour a cup at a time, stirring to mix well. Knead slightly, if necessary, to combine thoroughly.
4. Place dough in greased bowl, cover with plastic wrap or damp towel and let rise until doubled.
5. After dough has risen, knead in the onions and nuts. Butter two 8 or 9-inch round cakepans. Preheat oven to 400°.
6. Divide dough in 4ths. Form into ovals. Place two side-by-side in each pan; cover again and let rise again until nearly doubled.
7. Bake 40–45 minutes or until nicely browned and bread sounds hollow when tapped. Cool on a rack. Serve warm.

Corn Spoonbread

Easy version of an old Southern favorite.

Yield: 18 to 20 servings

2 eggs, lightly beaten
1 16-ounce can cream-style corn
1 7½-ounce can whole kernel corn (with liquid)
1½ cups sour cream
½ cup (1 stick) butter, melted
1 16-ounce package corn muffin mix
4 ounces (approximately 1 cup) shredded Swiss or Cheddar cheese

1. Preheat oven to 350°. Grease a 16 x 10 x 3-inch baking pan.
2. Combine all ingredients, except shredded cheese. Pour into prepared pan. (Refrigerate if making ahead). Bake 35 minutes.
3. Top bread with shredded cheese; bake an additional 10 to 15 minutes. Cut into squares to serve.

Sweet Bread

May be the sweetest ever!

Yield: 2 loaves

1½ cup milk
1 cup sugar
1½ teaspoons salt
4 tablespoons shortening or butter
1 to 2 packages of yeast
⅓ cup lukewarm water (110°)
2 eggs, beaten
6 cups flour

Options: Brown sugar, raisins, walnuts

1. Scald milk. Combine with sugar, salt and shortening. Let it cool to lukewarm.
2. Dissolve yeast in water. Let rest 10 minutes.
3. Add yeast and eggs to milk mixture. One cup at a time stir in flour. Knead until smooth; cover and let rise until doubled.
4. Punch down and knead again. Shape into two loaves and place in greased pans. Or roll into two 9 x 12-inch rectangles and cover with brown sugar, raisins and walnuts. Roll as for jelly roll and slice, putting into 24 greased muffin tins. Let rise again until nearly doubled.
5. Preheat oven to 350°. Bake bread 30 minutes or until done. Rolls will take about 20 minutes.

Corn Popovers

Crunchy and memorable.

Yield: 6 large popovers

1 cup whole milk
1 tablespoon butter, melted
¾ cup flour
¼ cup corn meal
½ teaspoon salt
2 eggs

Can be made ahead. Reheat slightly in oven before serving.

1. Have ingredients at room temperature.
2. Preheat oven to 450°.
3. Butter well 6 glazed pottery custard cups. Sprinkle each with additional corn meal, shaking out excess.
4. In small bowl combine everything but eggs. Beat with whisk until smooth.
5. Add eggs one at a time, beating just until combined.
6. Divide batter among custard cups. Place in lower half of oven. Bake 15 minutes.
7. Without opening oven, lower heat to 350° and continue to bake about 30 minutes longer. When lifted from cup, sides will not collapse. For drier inside, pierce each to allow steam to escape. Remove from cups while cooling slightly.
8. Serve warm with plenty of butter.

Herbed Spirals

¼ cup sugar
1 teaspoon salt
1 package active dry yeast
3 cups flour, divided
1 cup water
¼ cup butter, cut into pieces
1 egg, at room temperature

Filling:

4 tablespoons melted butter
⅓ cup chopped fresh parsley
2 tablespoons toasted sesame seeds

1. Combine sugar, salt, yeast and 1¼ cups flour in large bowl of electric mixer.

2. In saucepan heat water and butter until very warm (125°) and butter is melted.

3. With mixer at low speed beat liquid into yeast mixture. Add egg; beat 2 minutes. Add ¾ cup flour ; beat 2 minutes. With wooden spoon, stir in remaining 1 cup flour until all is well combined.

4. Cover and refrigerate up to 24 hours.

5. Lightly oil 24 2½-inch muffin-pan cups. Roll out dough to an 18 x 12-inch rectangle using a floured rolling pin on a floured surface.

6. Brush dough with 2 tablespoons melted butter; sprinkle with parsley. Roll up jelly-roll fashion from the longest side. Cut into 24 uniform slices using a foot-long piece of string placed under roll and drawn up, crossed and pulled through dough. Place each slice, cut side up, in a muffin-pan cup. Cover; let rise until double in bulk, about 1½ hours.

7. Preheat oven to 400° Bake 10 to 12 minutes, or until golden brown. Remove from pan; brush immediately with mixture of remaining 2 tablespoons melted butter and toasted sesame seeds.

Breakfast Puffs

Yield: 12 muffins

Quick and worthy enough for Christmas morning preparation.

⅓ cup soft white shortening
½ cup sugar
1 egg
1⅓ cup flour
1½ teaspoon baking powder
½ teaspoon salt
¼ teaspoon nutmeg
½ teaspoon lemon peel
½ cup milk
½ cup (1 stick) butter, melted
½ cup sugar
1 teaspoon cinnamon

1. Preheat oven to 350°. Grease a muffin tin. Do not use muffin liners.
2. Cream shortening, sugar and egg.
3. Combine next 5 dry ingredients and add alternately with milk to creamed mixture. Spoon into prepared tins and bake about 20 minutes or until done.
4. Cool slightly. Combine cinnamon and sugar in small bowl. Put melted butter in another. One by one dip warm puffs into butter then sugar, coating bottom and sides. Serve immediately.

Cranberry Almond Coffee Cake

Yield: one 10-inch tube cake

Wonderful almond flavor!

2 cups flour
1 teaspoon baking powder
1 teaspoon baking soda
½ teaspoon salt
½ cup (1 stick) butter, softened
1 cup sugar
2 eggs
2 teaspoons almond extract
1½ cups sour cream (¾ pint)
1 16-ounce can whole cranberry sauce
½ cup chopped almonds

1. Preheat oven to 350°. Grease and flour well a 10-inch tube pan.
2. Mix together flour, baking powder, baking soda, and salt.
3. Cream together butter and sugar; beat well. Add eggs, beating well after each addition. Mix in almond extract.
4. Stir in flour, alternating with sour cream.
5. Spoon half the batter into tube pan; spoon half the cranberry sauce over batter and swirl. Spoon in remaining batter; cover with remaining cranberry and swirl. Sprinkle with nuts.
6. Bake for 45 to 55 minutes. Cool 5 to 10 minutes; remove from pan. Glaze.

Glaze:

¾ cup confectioners' sugar
2 tablespoons warm water
½ teaspoon almond extract

Glaze:

Mix together all ingredients; pour over top of cake.

Cranberry Bread

Moist, orange-flavored bread.

Yield: one large, or two small loaves

2 cups flour
1 cup sugar
1½ teaspoons baking powder
1 teaspoon salt
½ teaspoon baking soda
¾ cup orange juice
1 teaspoon freshly grated orange peel
2 tablespoons salad oil
1 egg
1¼ cup cranberries, chopped or halved
½ cup chopped walnuts

1. Preheat oven to 350°. Grease bottoms of two 7½ x 3½-inch loaf pans (or one 9 x 5-inch
2. Combine all dry ingredients in large bowl.
3. Separately mix egg, oil and juice and add to dry ingredients, mixing until thoroughly combined.
4. Quickly stir in berries and nuts and pour into pans. Bake for 45 minutes (or about an hour for one loaf) or until toothpick into center comes out clean.
5. Remove bread from pans. Cool on a rack.

Cranberry Pineapple Bread

Moist when fresh or delicious toasted.

Yield: one 3-inch loaf

2 cups flour
1 cup sugar
1 teaspoon baking powder
½ teaspoon salt
1 cup raisins
½ cup chopped nuts
1 cup coarsely chopped cranberries
1 egg, beaten
1 tablespoon melted butter
2 teaspoons vanilla
1 cup crushed pineapple (undrained)
1 teaspoon baking soda

1. Preheat oven to 350°. Grease a 9 x 5 x 3-inch loaf pan.
2. Sift together flour, sugar, baking powder and salt into bowl. Add raisins, nuts and cranberries; mix well.
3. Combine egg, butter and vanilla. Add to flour mixture.
4. Dissolve soda in crushed pineapple; mix. Add to batter. Stir until blended.
5. Pour batter into loaf pan. Bake about 1 hour, or until tester inserted in center comes out clean. Cool 10 minutes before removing from pan. Cool completely before slicing. Keeps well wrapped and refrigerated.

Baking powder begins to act when mixed with liquid ingredients. Therefore act promptly in getting such batter into pans and into oven.

Filled Muffins

Your choice of filling.

Yield: 12 muffins

1⅔ cup flour
½ cup sugar
2 teaspoons baking powder
½ teaspoon salt
¼ teaspoon nutmeg, cinnamon or mace
⅓ cup butter or margarine, melted
¾ cup milk
1 egg, beaten
¼ cup mincemeat or jam
   (apricot and raspberry are favorites)

1. Preheat oven to 400°. Line muffin tins or grease them.
2. Combine dry ingredients in medium bowl.
3. Combine egg, milk and butter. Gently stir into dry ingredients mixing only until dry ingredients are moistened.
4. Quickly spoon most of batter into tins (leaving about ½ cup for tops). Put one teaspoon of filling on each muffin, top each with remaining batter.
5. Bake for 20 minutes or until tops spring back.

Sweet Potato Muffins

Old-fashioned goodness.

Yield: 24 muffins

1¼ cups sugar
1¼ cups mashed cooked sweet potatoes
   (fresh or canned)
½ cup (1 stick) butter, softened
2 large eggs, at room temperature
1½ cups flour
2 teaspoons baking powder
1½ teaspoons cinnamon
¼ teaspoon nutmeg
¼ teaspoon salt
1 cup milk
½ cup dried currants
¼ cup nuts, chopped

1. Preheat oven to 400°. Thoroughly grease two muffin pans.
2. Beat sugar, sweet potatoes and butter until smooth. Add eggs; blend well.
3. Sift together flour, baking powder, spices and salt. Add alternately with milk to sweet potato mixture, stirring just to blend; do not overmix.
4. Fold in currants and nuts. Spoon batter into muffin cups.
5. Bake 25 to 30 minutes, or until muffins test done. Serve warm.

Try making muffins in miniature (1½ inch diameter) pans. Your diet-conscious guests will thank you. (Don't forget to reduce cooking time.)

Gingerbread Muffins

Yield: 24 large muffins or 36 small

Good for breakfast with marmalade; outstanding as an hors d'oeuvres (see p. 18).

2½ cups flour
1 cup light molasses
½ cup sugar
½ cup shortening
1½ teaspoons baking soda
1 teaspoon cinnamon
1 teaspoon ginger
½ teaspoon cloves
2 teaspoons grated lemon rind
1 egg

1. Preheat oven to 375°. Grease and flour two standard muffin pans or three miniature muffin pans.
2. In large bowl of mixer, combine all ingredients, mixing at low speed until just blended. Increase speed to medium and beat for about 2 minutes, scraping sides of bowl with rubber spatula.
3. Fill muffin cups halfway-full with batter. Bake 20 to 25 minutes. Cool muffins on wire rack for 10 minutes; remove from pans. (Bake miniature muffins 10 minutes less.)
4. Serve warm or when cool store in plastic bags or in freezer. Thaw at room temperature about 2 hours.

Pumpkin Bread

Yield: 2 tea loaves

Spicy and moist.

1¾ cups flour
1 teaspoon baking soda
½ teaspoon EACH cloves, ginger, cinnamon and nutmeg
½ teaspoon salt
½ teaspoon baking powder
1 cup canned pumpkin
¾ cup sugar
⅓ cup buttermilk or sour milk
⅓ cup oil
1 egg
3 to 4 tablespoons orange marmalade
½ cup raisins, optional
½ cup nuts, chopped

1. Preheat oven to 350°.
2. Grease two small 7 x 3-inch loaf pans.
3. Combine dry ingredients.
4. Cream sugar, oil, milk, egg, pumpkin and marmalade.
5. Stir in dry ingredients, then nuts (and raisins).
6. Pour into prepared pans and bake about 45 minutes or until tester shows it is done.
7. Cool on rack. Slice and serve as is or with whipped cream cheese.

Holiday Banana Bread

Nice for gift-giving.

Yield: one loaf

½ cup shortening
¾ cup sugar
2 eggs
3 bananas, mashed
1¾ cups flour
¼ teaspoon baking soda
¼ teaspoon salt
1 cup mixed glazed fruit
½ cup chopped nuts

1. Preheat oven to 350°. Grease an 8½ x 4½-inch loaf pan.
2. Beat together shortening and sugar until well mixed. Add eggs; beat well. Add bananas.
3. Sift together flour, baking soda and salt. Add to banana mixture.
4. Fold in fruit and nuts.
5. Bake for 50 to 60 minutes, or until tester inserted in center comes out clean. Cool completely before slicing.

Whipped Cream Biscuits

Whipped cream supplies liquid and shortening!

Yield: 16 to 20 small biscuits

1½ cups flour
4 tablespoons baking powder
½ teaspoon salt
1 cup heavy cream, whipped

1. Preheat oven to 425°.
2. Sift together dry ingredients into mixing bowl.
3. Blend in whipped cream with a fork till dough is stiff.
4. Turn dough onto a floured board and knead slightly.
5. Roll or pat dough to about ¾-inch thickness. Cut with a round cookie-cutter, approximately 2 inches in diameter.
6. Place well apart on an ungreased baking sheet. Bake at 425° for approximately 10 minutes or till golden brown.

Sifting flour, with the exception of cake flour, is no longer necessary. Simply stir the flour gently, spoon it into a dry measure, and level the top.

Yorkshire Pudding

A must with roast beef.

Pan drippings from a beef roast
2 eggs
1 cup whole milk
1 cup flour
½ teaspoon salt

Pans:

Either muffin tins, or 9-inch oven proof skillet or 8- to 9-inch cake pan

Yield: 9 servings

1. Preheat oven to 400°.

2. Remove roast to a platter and keep warm.

3. Prepare pans by pouring in drippings, about 1 tablespoon per muffin tin (use 9), or ¼ cup for skillet. Place in oven and heat 5 minutes.

4. Combine eggs and milk in blender or with an electric mixer. Add flour and salt and blend about 10 seconds, scraping once. Immediately pour into hot tins. Bake muffins 25 to 30 minutes. (Skillet 45 to 50 minutes.) Do not open oven before time is up. Puddings should be puffed, firm, crisp, not soggy. Serve immediately.

Memorable Family Recipes

Recipe _____ Dates Served _____

_____

Ingredients _____

_____

_____

_____

_____

Procedure _____

_____

_____

_____

_____

_____

_____

_____

Comments _____

_____

Additional blank pages are provided for your use at the end of the book.

Main Dishes

Main Dishes

The Boar's Head Tradition

The glorious centerpiece of early Christmas feasts in England was the boned and stuffed head of a wild boar conveyed into the great hall aboard an elaborate silver platter. The head, when reassembled, was surrounded by garlands of rosemary and holly. In its jaws was a large red apple. The long tables in the hall were piled high with immense haunches of beef, meat pies, roast ducks, geese and pigs. As the wild boar became extinct in England, noble families substituted the roast pig complete with apple or the peacock, goose and finally the imported American turkey. In New England the turkey became Victorian America's favorite Thanksgiving and Christmas dish.

This December 1857 recipe from Godey's Lady's Book shows that the tradition and drama of serving a seemingly intact wild animal's head was not lost in Victorian America. — "Wash well a lamb's head and pluck; take out the brains, blanch them by themselves and boil the head and take out the tongue, trim the head, score it, then place before the fire. Cut up the tongue, liver, heart and lights; fry in a little parsley, shallot and mushroom; dry up the butter with flour, add some stock; season with lemon, cayenne pepper, salt and a dust of sugar; put the émincées under the head, and serve."

Filet of Beef

Timing is the essence.

Yield: 3 to 4 servings per pound

Tenderloin of beef, whole or part
Butter, up to 4 tablespoons
⅛ teaspoon garlic powder
¼ teaspoon dry mustard
½ teaspoon onion salt
¼ teaspoon ginger
1 teaspoon rosemary
2 teaspoons seasoning salt
1 teaspoon salt
½ teaspoon freshly ground black pepper

Garnish: parsley or watercress, cherry tomatoes or tiny red Christmas ornaments for a festive touch.

1. Have filet rolled and tied if neccessary to keep uniform.
2. Combine seasonings and rub into meat.
3. Preheat oven to 425°.
4. For small filet use electric frying pan set at 350° or frying pan over medium heat. For large tenderloin use roasting pan over 2 burners at medium heat.
5. Melt butter and slowly brown roast on all sides. Turn with tongs rather than piercing with forks. Browning takes 15 to 20 minutes.
6. Place in preheated oven and roast EXACTLY 19 minutes.
7. Remove and let stand 20 minutes to serve warm. It should be perfectly medium-rare.
8. While roast is standing, make Yorkshire pudding if desired.

Ragout of Beef with Cranberries

Yield: 6 servings

Super flavor combination.

1 to 2 tablespoons unsalted butter
1 to 2 tablespoons oil
2 pounds lean stew meat in 1-inch chunks
¾ teaspoon salt
pepper
2 large cloves garlic, minced
2 onions (12 ounces total), chopped
½ pound mushrooms, sliced
¾ cup port or red wine
¾ cup beef broth
2 tablespoons red wine vinegar
1 tablespoon tomato paste
1½ cups cranberries, coarsely chopped
⅓ cup light brown sugar
2 tablespoons flour

This ages well although cranberries are only distinctively red when first cooked.

1. Melt 1 tablespoon butter and oil in Dutch oven. Brown meat well on all sides. Add oil as needed. Add seasonings, garlic and onions. Add mushrooms, wine, broth, vinegar and tomato paste. Bring to boil, reduce heat and simmer covered about 2 hours or until meat is tender.
2. Combine flour and sugar and toss with cranberries. (Or chop berries with flour and sugar in food processor.) Add to stew and cook another 10 minutes. Serve with noodles.

Rib Roast of Beef with Mushroom Madeira Sauce

Standing rib roast, trimmed, with chine
   tied to roast
1 to 2 cloves garlic, sliced
½ to 1 teaspoon thyme
salt and pepper
½ pound mushrooms, sliced
2 teaspoons lemon juice
2 tablespoons butter
a double recipe of Madeira Sauce (see below)

1. Preheat oven to 550°.
2. Rub cut garlic over entire roast. Discard pieces. Salt and pepper roast generously and sprinkle with thyme. Insert meat thermometer.
3. Place meat in roasting pan, fat side up. Put in oven and reduce temperature to 350°.
4. Sprinkle mushrooms with lemon juice and sauté them in butter until liquid evaporates.
5. Make a double recipe of Madeira Sauce, add mushrooms and set aside.
6. When roast is done, remove to platter and let stand 15 to 20 minutes before carving. Meanwhile, if desired, make Yorkshire Pudding (see p. 61).

Madeira Sauce

Yield: 1½ cups

¼ cup shallots, chopped
3 tablespoons butter
½ cup Madeira wine
1 10¼-ounce can beef gravy
3 tablespoons Madeira wine

1. Sauté shallots in 1 tablespoon butter until golden. Add ½ cup Madeira and cook until liquid is reduced by half.
2. Add gravy and cook over low heat for 10 minutes.
3. Add remaining butter, stirring until melted; add remaining Madeira. Keep warm or reheat gently. Do not boil.

Allow ½ to 1 pound of rib roast per person. It is possible to cook two ribs but generally better to cook a larger roast of 3 or more ribs. Let meat stand at room temperature at least an hour before roasting. A meat thermometer is the only reliable measure of doneness. However, based on the above method, a medium-cooked roast should take about 20 minutes per pound.

Stuffed Filet of Beef

Ready in minutes, yet very elegant!

Yield: 6 to 8 servings

4 pounds tenderloin of beef
garlic salt and freshly ground pepper
½ cup (I stick) butter
¾ pound mushrooms, chopped
I garlic clove, chopped
I cup scallions, chopped
I cup packaged herb-seasoned stuffing mix
2 teaspoons Worcestershire sauce
red wine or water
bacon slices

Madeira Sauce if desired (see p. 67).

1. Preheat oven to 450°. Make lengthwise cut along filet, about 2½ inches deep. Season well inside and out with garlic salt and pepper.
2. Melt butter in large skillet over medium heat; add mushrooms, garlic and scallions. Sauté about 5 minutes, stirring often.
3. Remove from heat; stir in stuffing mix and Worcestershire. Add enough red wine or water to bind mixture.
4. Spread open filet along cut. Fill with stuffing; secure with skewers or string, as needed. Wrap slices of bacon around stuffed filet. Insert meat thermometer.
5. Place filet on rack in roasting pan. Roast about 25 minutes for medium, or until thermometer reads 160°.

Christmas Crown

Spectacular!

6- to 8-pound crown roast of pork,
  backbone removed
rosemary, about 1½ teaspoons
salt and pepper

Sausage Cornbread Stuffing:

8 ounces cornbread stuffing mix
butter or margarine
I pound mild country or
  breakfast style sausage
½ cup minced celery
2 tablespoons chopped green onion
I apple, chopped
½ cup pecans, chopped
½ cup raisins
spiced applesauce

Garnish: spiced crabapples, parsley
watercress or paper frills

1. Preheat oven to 325°.
2. Rub salt, pepper into meat.
3. Prepare stuffing according to package directions, first sautéing celery and onions in some of the butter and adding to cornbread.
4. Cook crumbled sausage thoroughly. Drain and add to stuffing along with apples, pecans and raisins.
5. Fill roast cavity to the top. Spread with applesauce. Wrap bone ends in foil. Roast uncovered for 3 hours.
6. Garnish with crabapples, parsley and paper frills.

Phyllo Wrapped Tenderloin

Yield: 6 servings

Elegant but not intimidating!

3 pounds tenderloin of beef, trimmed of fat
1 teaspoon salt
¼ teaspoon Beau Monde
pinch each, thyme, garlic
4 tablespoon butter
1 pound mushrooms, sliced
4 shallots, chopped
1 package frozen phyllo, thawed
   according to directions
½ cup (1 stick) butter, melted

1. Preheat oven to 400°.

2. Combine seasonings and rub into meat.

3. Sear meat in 2 tablespoons butter over high heat until brown on all sides.

4. Sauté mushrooms and shallots in 2 tablespoons butter and set aside.

5. Prepare area to butter phyllo; keep waiting phyllo covered with plastic wrap.

6. Remove 1 sheet of phyllo onto floured pastry cloth and brush phyllo surface with melted butter. Cover buttered sheet with a second sheet of phyllo, lining it up carefully because once it is in place it can't be moved. Butter this layer and continue this layering process until butter is used (6 to 8 sheets). Return unused dough to package and save for another use.

7. Spread half of mushroom mixture onto dough. Place beef on top, then cover with remaining mushrooms. Wrap phyllo around roast, lapping it underneath.

8. Bake on buttered serving dish or platter for 40 to 45 minutes.

9. Let stand 10 minutes before slicing. If desired, pass Madeira Sauce separately (see p. 67).

Crown Roast of Pork with Wild Rice Stuffing   Yield: 8 to 10 servings

A dramatic entrée reminiscent of the boar's head of traditional Christmas feasts.

1 crown roast of pork (about 7 pounds)*

Wild Rice Stuffing:

1 package (6 ounces) long grain and wild rice mix
1 medium-size onion, chopped (about ½ cup)
⅓ cup celery, chopped
2 cloves garlic, chopped
¼ pound ground pork*
½ cup chopped pecans
8 ounces dried apricots, chopped
6 tablespoons chopped, drained preserved ginger**
½ teaspoon ground allspice
½ teaspoon ground ginger

Gravy:

6 whole cloves
2 bay leaves
¾ cup to 1 cup Marsala wine
1 13¾-ounce can beef broth

Garnish: whole kumquats and watercress

*Order roast from butcher several days ahead. He will assemble crown and usually fill cavity with ground meat.

**Available packed in syrup at gourmet shops.

1. Preheat oven to 400°. Place roast on rack in large shallow roasting pan.
2. Cook rice according to package directions.
3. Brown ground pork with onion, celery and garlic till vegetables are tender and meat loses pink color, about 5 minutes. Drain off excess fat.
4. Combine sautéed meat and vegetables, rice, pecans, apricots, gingers and allspice in bowl; mix well. Spoon lightly into center of roast. Cover ends of bones and top of stuffing with foil.
5. Roast in 400° oven for 10 minutes. Lower oven temperature to 325°. Roast for 30 minutes per pound, 3 to 3½ hours, or till meat thermometer registers 170° when inserted in thickest part of roast.
6. Remove roast to heated serving platter. Keep warm while making gravy.
7. For gravy: Skim off fat from pan drippings. Add cloves, bay leaves, Marsala and broth to juices in pan. Cook over medium heat, scraping up browned bits from pan. Increase heat to high and cook until gravy is reduced by a third. Strain into gravy boat. Serve with roast.
8. To garnish: decorate ends of bones with whole kumquats (fresh or canned) and small bunches of watercress—a dramatic and festive presentation!

Definition of eternity: two people and a ham.

Roast Pork with Mustard-Herb Crumb Crust   Yield: 28 servings

A delicious yet simple way to glorify a fresh ham.

1 14-pound pork leg (fresh ham), whole
¼ teaspoon pepper
salt or garlic salt, as preferred
½ cup prepared mustard
3 teaspoons Worcestershire sauce
1 teaspoon ground ginger
½ cup (1 stick) melted butter
6 slices good quality bread, crumbed
½ cup chopped fresh parsley

To serve pork leg with an elegant flair, wrap a clean white napkin around end to conceal shank bone.
Try mustard-crumb mixture another time as pork chop stuffing.

1. Preheat oven to 325°. With a sharp knife, remove skin and excess fat from pork leg; leave only a thin layer of fat.

2. Place pork leg, fat-side up, on a rack in a large open roaster. Rub pork with pepper and 1 teaspoon (garlic) salt. Having inserted a meat thermometer into the thickest part of the pork, roast for about 5½ hours or until thermometer reads 170° to 185°. Remove from oven.

3. Meanwhile, in a small bowl, mix mustard, Worcestershire and ginger. In another bowl, combine melted butter, bread crumbs and parsley; mix well.

4. Skim off 2 tablespoons fat from drippings in roaster; add to mustard mixture. Spread mustard mixture generously onto pork leg using pastry brush. Gently but liberally pat bread crumb mixture onto pork.

5. Return pork to oven; bake 15 minutes longer or until bread is lightly browned. Remove from oven and place on large platter or carving board; let stand 15 minutes before carving.

Baked Ham in Champagne Sauce Yield: 12 servings

Make this New Year's Day with leftover champagne!
A moist, tender method of cooking.

6- to 8-pound smoked ham
½ bottle champagne (14 ounces)
½ cup ham broth
¼ cup prepared Dijon mustard
3 tablespoons dark brown sugar
½ cup raisins

1. Place ham in a large pot, add water to cover. Bring to a boil, reduce heat and simmer for 1 hour.

2. Preheat oven to 450°.

3. Remove ham from pot and place in a large ovenproof casserole. Pour champagne and ½ cup of ham broth from pot over meat. Spread mustard over ham; sprinkle with brown sugar, add raisins to the pan. Bake for 20 minutes or until golden brown.

4. Serve with sauce from pan on the side. (If a thicker sauce is desired, thicken with 2 to 3 tablespoons cornstarch, dissolved in ¼ cup cold water, heated with sauce.)

Crabapple-Glazed Baked Ham with Mustard-Green Peppercorn Gravy

Yield: 28 servings

Try the Raisin Sauce (following) **if you prefer a milder accompaniment than the zesty mustard.**

1 fully-cooked boneless ham, about
  7 pounds
½ cup lightly packed brown sugar
½ cup crabapple jelly (or apple or quince)
1 tablespoon apple cider vinegar

Garnish: spiced crabapples and watercress
Mustard-Green Peppercorn Gravy (below)

1. Place ham on rack in shallow roasting pan. Score top in diamond pattern. Bake at 325° for 1½ hours.
2. Meanwhile, combine sugar, jelly and vinegar in small saucepan. Heat, stirring constantly, until sugar melts and mixture bubbles. Brush glaze over ham several times during last 30 minutes of baking time.
3. Transfer ham to serving platter or cutting board. Surround with crabapples and greens to garnish. Serve with Mustard-Green Peppercorn Gravy.

Mustard-Green Peppercorn Gravy

4 tablespoons butter
¼ cup flour
½ cup milk
½ cup white wine
1 cup heavy cream
¼ cup prepard Dijon mustard
3 tablespoons green peppercorns, rinsed
  and drained

Gravy:

1. Melt butter in medium-size saucepan. Gradually add flour. Cook, stirring constantly, over medium heat until bubbly; cook 1 minute more, stirring.
2. Gradually add milk, wine, cream and mustard. Cook, stirring over medium heat, until sauce thickens, about 5 minutes. Stir in green peppercorns. Serve with ham.

Raisin Sauce for Ham

Yield: 3 cups

Ideal for Crabapple-Glazed Ham.

1 cup sugar
1 cup water
1 cup raisins
2 tablespoons butter
2 tablespoons cider vinegar
⅛ teaspoon cloves
⅛ teaspoon cinnamon
pinch salt
¾ cup grape jelly
2 teaspoons cornstarch
1 teaspoon cold water

1. Bring sugar and water to boil in a 1-quart saucepan.
2. Add raisins, butter, vinegar, spices and grape jelly. Stir over low heat until jelly is dissolved.
3. Dissolve cornstarch in water. Add to sauce and heat until raisins are plump and sauce thickens slightly.
4. Serve warm with baked ham.

Peacock, swan, goose and many smaller birds graced the nobles' tables of fifteenth century England. Gilded peacock was a specially prized and spectacular dish. The skin, with feathers still attached, was stripped from the bird, which was boned, roasted and stuffed into the skin to look like the original bird. The beak and sometimes the whole bird was gilded with gold leaf. A wick was dipped in oil, placed in the golden beak and lighted. The tradition dictated that a noble woman of great beauty enter the dining hall bearing the gilded bird on a silver tray.

Godey's Lady's Book of December 1857 gave this recipe for turkey roast. "The turkey roast is stuffed with sausage meat, filet of veal... or truffles. (the truffles) must be peeled, chopped and pounded in a mortar... half a pound will be sufficient... Rasp the same weight of fat bacon and mix it with the truffles. This stuffing is placed over the breast. Roast but keep the heat well to the breast; baste well, serve with gravy in the dish and bread sauce in the tureen."

Chicken Breasts in Pastry

Yield: 6 servings

Enjoy the raves.

3 whole chicken breasts, skinned, boned
  and split
½ cup butter, clarified
salt and pepper
lemon juice
small can liver paté
Duxelles
1 package frozen puff pastry,
  thawed but chilled,
    or 2 packages patty shells
Madeira Sauce (see p. 67)

Duxelles:

12 ounces fresh mushrooms, finely chopped
3 tablespoons chopped shallots
2 tablespoons butter
2 tablespoons olive oil
generous ¼ teaspoon nutmeg
dash salt and pepper

1. Make Duxelles: enclose mushrooms in a clean cloth or linen towel; squeeze as much moisture as possible from the mushrooms by twisting hard. When this is done the worst part is over!

2. Over medium heat, lightly brown the shallots in butter and oil. Add the mushrooms and seasonings. Over high heat, cook until any remaining moisture has disappeared. Set aside.

3. Clarify butter by heating until milky substance surfaces. Skim this and use the remaining butter (clarified) to sauté the breasts for 1 minute on each side. Sprinkle each with salt, pepper and a dash of lemon juice. Cover and refrigerate.

4. Roll each sheet of puff pastry to approximately 12 x 18 inches (or patty shells to about 6-inch diameter). Place breast on dough. Top with 1 teaspoon paté and 2 tablespoons Duxelles. Cover with pastry; seal edges with water and pinch together. Refrigerate each as it is made. Use scraps of pastry to decorate, if desired. May also be frozen at this point.

5. Preheat oven to 400°.

6. Make Madeira Sauce.

7. Place chilled breasts on a baking sheet and bake 6 minutes at 400° then without opening oven, reduce heat to 350° and bake 15 minutes longer. Pastry should be light golden and puffed.

8. Serve immediately; pass Madeira Sauce separately.

Saucy Chicken Breasts

Piquant and festive.

Yield: 6 to 8 servings

6 to 8 boned, skinned chicken breasts
  (3 to 4 whole)
bread crumbs
I egg mixed with I tablespoon water
salt, pepper, paprika
butter
I cup chili sauce
I cup red currant jelly
I cup dry sherry

1. Preheat oven to 400°.
2. Flatten each chicken breast by pounding with a rolling pin or an empty champagne bottle.
3. Dip each breast into egg mixture then into bread crumbs. Season with salt, pepper and paprika. Roll and secure with a toothpick. Season again.
4. Sauté in butter until light golden, turning gently with two forks or tongs to brown evenly. At this point you can refrigerate or freeze for later use. You can also remove the toothpick.
5. Make sauce by combining chili sauce, jelly and sherry in I-quart sauce pan. Heat over low/medium heat, stirring occasionally until thickened, 30 to 45 minutes. Set aside or refrigerate.
6. When ready to serve, place chicken in shallow pan or baking dish, cover with sauce and bake about 20 minutes or until done. Serve with a rice or wheat pilaf.

Duckling with Orange Sauce

Yield: 2 to 4 servings

Serve crisp duckling with separate sauce.

1 5- to 6-pound duckling, giblets and excess
  fat removed, rinsed and dried
3 oranges (7 to 8 ounces each)
  Add 1 orange for each additional duckling
  cooked up to 3 total
1 onion
celery top
poultry seasoning
1 carrot, finely chopped
bay leaf
3 cups chicken broth
salt and pepper to taste
¼ cup wine vinegar
3 tablespoons sugar
½ cup plus 2 tablespoons port wine
2 tablespoons cornstarch mixed with
  3 tablespoons water
1½ tablespoons orange liqueur

1. Peel zest (orange part only) from oranges
   with vegetable peeler. Cover zest with 3 cups
   of water. Boil then simmer 15 minutes.
   Drain. (This may be done a day or two ahead.)
2. Preheat oven to 325°. Season duck inside
   and outside with salt and pepper. Into cavity
   place a few onion slices, tops of celery stalk,
   the cooked peel from 1 orange and some
   poultry seasoning. Skewer shut.
3. Attack outside of bird with a sharp fork,
   piercing well all over, to drain fat while
   cooking. Roast on a rack in pan for 2½ to 3
   hours or until leg moves easily.
4. Meanwhile cook giblets with chopped onion,
   carrot, bay leaf, and chicken broth until
   tender, about 1 to 1½ hours. Strain liquid
   and reduce by boiling rapidly over high heat
   to 2 cups (about 10 to 15 minutes).
5. Separately boil vinegar and sugar until
   caramelized and add to giblet liquid.
   Set aside.
6. When duck is done, drain fat from inside
   and keep duck warm. Pour off all fat
   reserving the drippings. (A 5-pound duck
   can produce 2½ cups of fat!) Sliver the
   remaining orange peel.
7. Make orange sauce: add port to drippings in
   pan, stirring to free particles. Pour giblet
   broth into pan with slivered orange peel.
   Blend in cornstarch and heat to boiling.
   Add liqueur. Keep warm.
8. Slice duck lengthwise and lay skin-side up on
   ovenproof platter. Run under broiler to crisp
   skin just before serving.
9. Serve with rice and pass orange sauce
   separately. To retain crispness, decorate
   platter, not duck, with glazed orange slices,
   if desired.

Glazed Orange Slices:

3 oranges from above
⅔ cup sugar
⅓ cup water

Glazed Orange Slices:

1. Slice off white part of oranges by cutting it from tops and bottoms then slicing it off lengthwise from top to bottom. Cut oranges crosswise into ¼ inch slices.
2. Combine sugar and water in pan, bring to boil and add slices, cooking 10 to 15 minutes. Cool and refrigerate.

Chicken in Brandy
Delightful flavor combination.

Yield: 4 to 6 servings

1½ pounds boned, skinned chicken breasts
¼ cup flour
1 teaspoon salt
½ teaspoon curry
¼ teaspoon pepper
⅛ teaspoon thyme
5 tablespoons butter
½ pound mushrooms, sliced
1 meduim onion, sliced
½ cup brandy
1 cup heavy cream

1. Preheat oven to 325°.
2. Cut chicken into 1 to 1½ inch pieces
3. Combine flour and spices in a plastic bag. Add chicken all at once and shake to coat thoroughly.
4. Melt 2 tablespoon butter in large skillet. Add mushrooms and onions. Cook until limp. Remove from pan to oven-proof casserole.
5. Add remaining butter to skillet, add chicken and brown lightly. Remove to casserole.
6. Pour brandy and cream into skillet. Scrape bits from pan, stirring into sauce, and heat until thickened a bit.
7. Pour over ingredients in casserole. Set aside in refrigerator or bake 20 to 30 minutes until heated through and chicken is done. It will take a bit longer if casserole has been refrigerated.

Roast Goose with Apple-Prune Stuffing   Yield: 10 to 12 servings

1 10- to 12-pound goose
salt

Apple-Prune Stuffing:

1 medium onion, finely chopped
¾ cup (1½ sticks) butter, melted
2 cups tart apples, peeled
  and coarsely chopped
2 cups cooked prunes, diced
6 cups day-old bread crumbs
1 cup walnuts, coarsely chopped
2 teaspoons salt
2 tablespoons lemon juice

Glaze:

½ cup honey
½ cup orange juice

Some people feel that because of the high fat content of goose, it should not be stuffed. If you concur, bake stuffing separately and roast the goose stuffed with apple quarters.

1. Prepare Stuffing: In a large skillet, sauté onion in butter until translucent. Add to remaining ingredients and combine well. If stuffing seems too dry, additional butter may be added. (Remember that stuffing will absorb fat from goose.)

2. Preheat oven to 400°.

3. Wipe bird well with damp paper towels and rub inside with 1½ teaspoons salt. Stuff with prepared stuffing. Rub outside with additional 2 teaspoons salt.

4. To truss, press wings to body and tie down by running twine around entire upper portion of goose; turn neck skin backward; tuck under twine. Tie legs together. Prick goose all over at 1 inch intervals with two-tined fork to allow fat to be released.

5. Place goose on rack in an open roasting pan. Immediately reduce oven temperature to 350°, and proceed to roast goose for 25 minutes per pound (approximately 4½ to 5 hours), draining fat from pan several times as it accumulates. Baste frequently. During last 30 minutes glaze with honey-orange juice mixture.

6. When done, skin should be very crisp and meat tender and juicy. Remove from oven; remove twine and any skewers used. Serve on heated platter.

Smoked Stuffed Turkey Breast

Ideal for buffet, easier than you'd guess.

Yield: 12 to 16 servings

7-to 8-pound turkey breast,
  boned by butcher
covered charcoal grill
charcoal
hickory chips, available packaged
seasoning (below)
baste (below)
stuffing (below)

Seasoning:

1 tablespoon salt
½ teaspoon seasoning salt
¼ teaspoon poultry seasoning
¼ teaspoon dry mustard
dash nutmeg

Baste:

½ cup (1 stick) butter, melted
¼ cup lemon juice
¼ teaspoon rosemary
¼ teaspoon thyme
¼ teaspoon paprika

Mushroom Stuffing:

1½ pounds mushrooms, sliced
½ cup fresh parsley tops,
  chopped firmly packed
½ teaspoon poultry seasoning
⅓ cup onions, chopped
4 tablespoons butter
2 teaspoons lemon juice
¼ cup almonds, chopped
dash nutmeg
salt and freshly ground pepper, to taste

1. Soak hickory chips in water according to package directions
2. Combine seasoning ingredients.
3. Prepare stuffing by sautéing mushrooms and onions, sprinkled with lemon juice, in butter. Remove from heat and add seasoning and parsley. Set aside.
4. Preheat grill using the indirect method of cooking.
5. On counter or board spread turkey breast skin side down. Salt and pepper meat; cover with stuffing. Form into a "package," securing skin around meat with skewers. Rub seasoning into skin.
6. Place on grill, attractive side up, when coals are ready. Add several soaked hickory chips to each bed of coals. Cover.
7. Prepare baste and brush meat occasionally.
8. A 7-pound breast takes about 2 hours over medium coals. May have to add more charcoal and more hickory chips.
9. Rest turkey 10 to 15 minutes before removing skewers and carving.

This method for smoked turkey breast can be used for a whole turkey. Season it well; stuff if desired. A meat thermometer is helpful but allow about 13 minutes per pound, adding chips and charcoal as necessary to maintain temperature. The bird tends to look mahogany-colored, almost black, when done but don't despair, the flavor is wonderful.

Roast Turkey

Uniquely American.

A few thoughts to consider:
- 1 to 1½ pounds of bird weight per person provides for enough leftovers.
- Hen turkey will generally have more white meat proportionally than toms.
- The best turkeys (for moistness and flavor) seem to be locally grown. A fresh turkey from a distance may not be as "fresh" as a properly thawed flash frozen one.
- Defrosting should be done in the bag in the refrigerator and may take up to 5 days depending on size.
- Never stuff a turkey until just prior to roasting. After roasting remove extra stuffing and refrigerate separately.

**Seasoning: for 12 pound bird
(double for 22–24 pounds)**

2 tablespoons salt
1 teaspoon seasoning salt
  (Lawry's or Season-All)
½ teaspoon poultry seasoning
⅛ teaspoon nutmeg
½ teaspoon dry mustard
¼ teaspoon paprika

*Some preparation must be done ahead.

Preparation of fresh or thawed turkey:

1. Remove giblets. Rinse bird thoroughly inside and out in cold water. Remove large chunks of fat. Dry thoroughly with paper towels.

* 2. Rinse giblets, place in covered saucepan with water to cover, some celery tops, few slices of onion, poultry seasoning, salt and pepper. (If not intending to use giblets in gravy omit this step. If needed for stuffing, do this the night before.) Simmer until giblets are tender. Set aside.

* 3. Prepare stuffing of choice. Try two—one in each cavity.

4. Prepare seasoning.

5. Rub seasoning well into the inside and outside of dry bird. Preheat oven to 325°.

6. Stuff both cavities but allow room for expansion. Do not pack tightly. Skewer closed. (Heat any remaining stuffing in the oven before serving). Place turkey on a rack in a roasting pan. Make a tent of several (2 to 3) layers of aluminum foil; anchor one end to tips of drumsticks, the other to edge of pan, being certain that foil does not touch bird anywhere else.

7. Timing is the most elusive part. Cooks have their own methods and their peculiar ovens. What has worked with the above procedure is 18 minutes per pound. A 21-pound turkey will take about 6 hours. The most security you can get is with a properly placed meat thermometer. Let it peek out from the tent. The movable drumstick is also a good indicator.

8. Remove turkey from oven and remove to a large platter. Rest it from 20 to 30 minutes before carving while preparing gravy.

9. Make Gravy: Pour off all visible fat. (There will be enough invisible fat!) Retain the juices and roast particles. Allowing about 2 tablespoons flour for 1½ cups gravy, measure flour into roasting pan, stirring well into the particles at bottom. Slowly add, while stirring, reserved giblet liquid, vegetable cooking liquid or water. You will need two burners set at medium heat under your roasting pan. Stir until thickened. Add more liquid as desired. (To thicken, add water to a little flour, then add to gravy.) Strain gravy into warm serving dish or saucepan and keep warm. Add chopped giblets if desired.

The seasonings make this gravy naturally very dark, not pasty.

Cranberry Cornbread Stuffing

A fruity favorite.

¼ cup (½ stick) butter or margarine
½ cup celery, finely chopped
½ cup onion, finely chopped
2 large apples, unpeeled and chopped
1 8-ounce can whole cranberry sauce,
   broken up
¼ cup raisins
1 8-ounce package cornbread stuffing mix
orange juice, optional

Yield: enough for chicken or for
   small end of turkey

1. Sauté celery and onion in butter until soft. Mix well with remaining ingredients. Add a bit of orange juice to moisten, if desired.

2. Pack lightly into bird, or cook separately in casserole. (Be certain to add juice, about ½ cup, if cooking this way.)

Stuffed Boned Turkey Breast with Mustard Cream Gravy

Yield: 12 servings

Easy top-of-the-stove preparation method and easy carving.
Use your favorite stuffing or try Florentine Stuffing (see p. 84)

1 whole turkey breast, about 6½ to 7 pounds, thawed, if frozen, or fresh, boned by butcher, but ask for bones.
4 to 6 cups prepared stuffing
cheesecloth and string
2 13¾-ounce cans chicken broth
1½ cups dry white wine
1 large onion, quartered and studded with 8 whole cloves
2 cloves garlic
2 stalks celery, quartered
2 carrots, quartered
1 teaspoon crushed red pepper flakes
1 large bay leaf

1. Spread out boned breast, skin side down, on cutting board. Flatten out with hands.
2. Spoon stuffing mixture down center of boned turkey. Fasten overlapping meat with skewers to help roll. Wrap rolled and skewered turkey breast tightly in cheese cloth. Tie with string at 1-inch intervals Remove skewers.
3. Place rolled and wrapped turkey breast atop turkey bones in Dutch oven or roasting pan. Add chicken broth, wine, onion, garlic, celery, carrots, pepper flakes, and bay leaf. Bring to a boil, lower heat, cover. Simmer, turning once or twice, for 2 to 3 hours, or until juices from meat run clear and are not pink when pierced with a fork. Cool in broth for one hour.
4. Remove turkey from broth; remove cheesecloth. Slice and serve with Mustard Gravy; garnish with whole mushrooms.

Mustard Cream Gravy:

4 tablespoons (½ stick) butter
¼ cup flour
1 cup milk
1 cup heavy cream
¼ cup prepared Dijon mustard
1 teaspoon paprika

Mustard Cream Gravy:

1. Melt butter in a medium-size saucepan. Gradually add flour. Cook, stirring constantly, over medium heat until bubbly; cook 1 minute more.
2. Gradually add milk, cream and mustard. Continue cooking over medium heat, stirring constantly, until sauce thickens, about 5 minutes. Stir in paprika. Serve with turkey. Makes about 2 cups.

Brandied Chestnut Stuffing

The Rolls Royce of Stuffing ...
Rich and elegant!
Try this in a boned turkey breast.

Yield: 8 cups, enough for a
10 to 12 pound turkey

2 cups finely chopped mushrooms
5 tablespoons butter
1 large onion, finely chopped
1 cup finely chopped celery
1 pound bulk sausage
4 cups crumbled, day-old bread
   (about 8 slices)
1 cup turkey or chicken broth
1 15½- or 16-ounce can whole chestnuts,
   rinsed, drained and coarsely chopped
   (or 2 cups coarsely chopped, peeled,
   cooked fresh chestnuts)
¼ cup brandy
¼ cup chopped parsley
1 teaspoon crumbled thyme leaf
½ teaspoon salt
¼ teaspoon pepper

1. Sauté mushrooms in 2 tablespoons butter
   in a large skillet. Transfer with slotted spoon
   to bowl.

2. Sauté onion and celery in remaining
   3 tablespoons butter. Add sausage, breaking
   up chunks with wooden spoon as it cooks;
   cook about 5 minutes. Remove from heat;
   drain excess fat.

3. Add bread and broth to skillet; stir to
   moisten. Stir in chestnuts, brandy, parsley,
   thyme, salt and pepper. Return to heat and
   stir to mix well a couple of minutes. Remove
   from heat; stir in reserved mushrooms.

Crabmeat Stuffing

A very special stuffing for Cornish hens
or a small chicken: also good for stuffing
fish fillets or lobster tail.

Yield: 2½ cups

1 7½-ounce can crabmeat, rinsed, drained,
   and flaked or 8 ounces imitation sea
   sticks, flaked
2 eggs, slightly beaten
¼ cup (½ stick) butter
½ cup minced onion
¾ cup finely chopped celery
1 to 2 teaspoons minced fresh dill or
   1 teaspoon dried dill weed
1 cup fine fresh bread crumbs (or substitute
   1 cup fresh dill bread crumbs for bread
   crumbs and dill)
salt and pepper to taste

1. Combine crabmeat and eggs in mixing bowl.

2. Melt butter in skillet, add onion and celery;
   sauté a few minutes; cool. Add to crab
   mixture; mix in dill and bread crumbs.

3. Mix well; season to taste with salt and pepper.

Florentine Stuffing

An extra-rich stuffing for special occasions.

Yield: about 6 cups

2 medium onions, finely chopped
2 garlic cloves, finely chopped
3 tablespoons olive oil
2 tablespoons margarine or butter
1 pound fresh mushrooms, chopped
1 10-ounce package frozen chopped
   spinach, thawed
1 package plain stuffing crumbs
¼ cup chopped fresh parsley
¼ teaspoon poultry seasoning
1 teaspoon salt
½ pound sausage meat, browned
2 cups chicken broth
1 egg, beaten

1. Sauté onions and garlic in olive oil and butter until soft. Add mushrooms and spinach; cook lightly. Cool slightly.
2. In mixing bowl, combine bread crumbs, seasoning, cooked sausage and broth. Add mushroom-spinach mixture; stir in egg.
3. Use to stuff boned turkey breast (see p. 82), or bake in casserole in a 350° oven for 25 to 30 minutes, or until nicely browned.

Mrs. Moore's Sage Stuffing

Very traditional.

Yield: enough for 12 to 16 pound bird.

Loaf of white bread, dried out slightly
1 medium onion, finely chopped
1 cup celery, finely chopped
⅓ cup butter
cooked giblets, optional
cooking liquid from giblets
1 egg, lightly beaten
salt and pepper
2 to 3 teaspoons Bell's Poultry Seasoning
   (sage is in the poultry seasoning)

Must be made ahead through step 1.

1. The night before bird is to be stuffed, cook giblets and prepare bread crumbs. Bread should be crumbed, not cubed into ¼ inch pieces. This takes awhile by hand. It can be done CAREFULLY in a food processor. Do not crumb the bread too much! You want 12 cups of light bread crumbs. Let them stand overnight.
2. Next day, sauté onion and celery in butter.
3. Grind or finely chop giblets and mix with celery and onions. Add these to bread crumbs. Add poultry seasoning, egg and enough giblet liquid to lightly moisten the bread. Stuffing should be more dry than wet. Add salt and pepper to taste.
4. Stuff bird loosely.

Cooking Giblets:
Rinse giblets, cover with water. Add some onion, celery leaves, salt. Cook until tender.

Wild Rice Stuffing

Yield: 8 cups or enough for 4 Cornish hens
      a duckling or goose (double for a turkey)

1 1-pound box wild rice
1 pound bulk sausage meat
2 carrots, finely diced
3 stalks celery, finely diced
1 green pepper, diced
1 medium onion, diced
1 cup coarsely chopped mushrooms
  (optional)
2 tablespoons chopped fresh parsley
1½ teaspoons salt
¼ teaspoon pepper
¼ teaspoon sage
¼ teaspoon poultry seasoning
½ teaspoon thyme

1. Cook rice according to package directions; drain. Set aside.
2. Sauté sausage meat; breaking up chunks with side of spoon. Gradually add all remaining ingredients; sauté until vegetables become soft.
3. Remove from heat; toss with rice. Stuff bird.

Fruit and Nut Stuffing

Yield: 8 cups

A fruity stuffing good with goose, duckling or pork.

1½ cups soft, pitted dried prunes, cut up
¾ cup dried apricots, cut up
6 cups day-old bread cubes
2 cups diced apple
¾ cup diced orange sections
¼ cup golden raisins
¼ cup raisins
½ cup chopped pecans or other nuts
1 teaspoon salt, or to taste
¾ teaspoon poultry seasoning
½ cup orange juice
¼ cup (½ stick) butter, margarine
  or other fat

1. Pour boiling water over prunes and apricots; drain
2. Add remaining ingredients; toss all together well.

Whole wheat bread adds a nice flavor to this stuffing.

 Dried fruits are easier to chop if put in the freezer for two hours before cutting up. Rinse your knife or kitchen shears frequently in hot water.

Memorable
Family Recipes

Recipe _____ Dates Served _____

Ingredients _____

_____

_____

_____

_____

Procedure _____

_____

_____

_____

_____

_____

_____

_____

Comments _____

_____

Additional blank pages are provided for your use at the end of the book.

Many traditional holiday fish dishes cooked in America were brought from Europe where fish remains an important dish at Christmastime. In Victorian America these dishes were often served on Christmas Eve – a remembrance of a time when there were religious restrictions on the eating of meat the day before Christmas. There is a scarcity of fish dishes on published menus of the time. They were eclipsed by the tukeys, roasts and hams. Only oysters, as soups, stews or on the half shell found their way to the Christmas table. The following is a simple recipe for oyster stew taken from Godey's Lady's Book for December 1890.

Seafood

"Remove all particles of shell before cooking the oysters. Into a granite saucepan pour one gallon of oysters and their liquor. Add salt and pepper and three quarters of a pound of very nice butter. Oysters require a quantity of butter if you want them in perfection. Stir them frequently and when they are heated through, stir into them one teacupful of fresh cracker dust, pounded finely. As soon as they are done, which is as soon as they plump out, remove them from the fire. Too much cooking, like too little butter, will ruin the oyster. While cooking, stir often, otherwise they will burn."

Block Island "Turkey"

Flavorfully seasoned "turkey-of-the-sea".

Yield: 4 servings

1 pound cod fillets
dry bread crumbs
2 eggs
1 heaping teaspoon dried, crushed rosemary
¼ teaspoon EACH basil and thyme
¼ cup (½ stick) butter
1 cup half-and-half
12 small, new potatoes, boiled and quartered
salt and pepper to taste

1. Cut fillets into serving portions. Put bread crumbs in a dish; in another dish beat eggs together with herbs. Dip pieces of cod first in egg mixture and then in crumbs.
2. Heat butter in a large, heavy skillet. Brown cod in butter, on both sides, just until golden. Add half-and-half; simmer over low heat for 10 minutes.
3. Serve fish and potatoes on a plate drenched in cream/butter "gravy" from pan. Use salt and pepper to taste.

Coquilles

Simple elegance for Christmas Eve.

Yield: 4 servings

1½ pounds scallops
1 cup milk
½ cup bread crumbs
¼ pound mushrooms, sliced
2 large cloves garlic, crushed
½ cup (½ stick) butter, melted
1½ tablespoons lemon juice.
4 scallions (green onions) finely chopped
¼ cup finely chopped parsley
salt and freshly ground pepper, paprika

1. Preheat oven to 450°.
2. If using sea scallops, cut into smaller pieces.
3. Heat milk in small pan. Add scallops and bring to boil. Remove from heat and cover for 5 minutes. Drain scallops, reserving some liquid. Cover to keep warm and set aside.
4. Mix garlic, lemon juice, butter and bread crumbs.
5. Combine scallops, mushrooms and scallions in shallow baking dish. Cover with butter and bread crumbs; sprinkle with parsley, salt and pepper and paprika.
6. Bake 5 to 10 minutes, until sizzling. Serve immediately.

Every time the oven door is opened, the temperature drops 25 to 30 degrees. Try to resist the temptation to peek to ensure even cooking.

Lobster Newburg

Yield: 8 servings

A classic! Shows off lobster to its best advantage.

½ cup (1 stick) butter
4 tablespoons flour
½ teaspoon salt, or to taste
½ teaspoon ground nutmeg
1 teaspoon paprika
3 cups light cream
6 egg yolks, slightly beaten
4 cups coarsely chopped, cooked
   lobster meat
¼ cup sherry
6 cups hot cooked rice

1. Melt butter in large heavy saucepan; remove from heat and stir in flour to make a smooth paste. Add salt, nutmeg and paprika. Gradually stir in cream.

2. Cook mixture, stirring constantly, until thick and bubbly. Reduce heat and cook, stirring, 3 more minutes.

3. In a bowl, beat egg yolks lightly. Add ¼ to ⅓ cup of hot mixture into eggs, stirring. Pour back into saucepan. Add lobster; cook, stirring constantly, until mixure thickens and lobster is hot. DO NOT BOIL.

4. Remove from heat; add sherry and stir to blend (If sauce becomes too thick, thin with milk). Serve over hot rice.

Shrimp and Artichoke Casserole

Yield: 6 servings

Shrimply delicious!

6½ tablespoons butter
4½ tablespoons flour
¾ cup milk
¾ cup heavy cream
½ teaspoon salt and pepper to taste
1 20-ounce can artichoke hearts, drained
1½ pounds large shrimp, cooked
½ pound fresh mushrooms, sliced
½ cup dry sherry
1 tablespoon Worcestershire sauce
½ cup freshly grated Parmesan cheese
paprika

1. Preheat oven to 375°. Butter an oblong baking dish.

2. Melt 4½ tablespoons of the butter; blend in flour; add milk and cream, and cook stirring constantly, until thickened. Add salt and pepper to taste; set aside.

3. In remaining 2 tablespoon of butter, sauté mushrooms gently for about 5 minutes.

4. Arrange artichokes in a single layer on the bottom of prepared baking dish; scatter shrimp over artichokes; cover shrimp with a layer of mushrooms.

5. Stir sherry and Worcestershire sauce into cream sauce and pour over contents of baking dish; sprinkle with cheese and paprika. Bake 20 to 30 minutes, or until bubbly. (Or refrigerate several hours; bake 45 minutes.)

Seafood Lasagne

Outstanding! Perfect for Christmas Eve.

Yield: 10 to 12 servings

1 tablespoon butter
1 tablespoon finely chopped onion
1 garlic clove, minced
¾ pound raw shimp, peeled
1 pound scallops
salt and freshly ground pepper
½ cup dry white wine or vermouth
2 cups thinly sliced mushrooms
2 cups béchamel sauce (below)
1 cup crushed canned tomatoes
½ cup heavy cream
¼ teaspoon crushed hot red pepper flakes
3 tablespoons finely chopped parsley
¼ teaspoon oregano
¼ teaspoon basil
9 lasagne strips,
   cooked according to package directions
4 small skinless, boneless flounder fillets,
   about 1 pound total
1 cup grated Swiss cheese

1. Melt the butter in a large skillet; add onions and garlic, cooking about 30 seconds. Add the shrimps and scallops (cut into bite-size if large) and sprinkle with salt and pepper.

2. When shrimp begins to turn pink, add wine; cook, stirring briefly, just until wine comes to boil. As soon as wine boils, turn off heat. Transfer the seafood to a bowl using a slotted spoon.

3. Bring the cooking liquid to simmer; add mushrooms and cook about 5 minutes. Add Béchamel sauce, stirring to blend.

4. Add tomatoes; simmer about 5 minutes. Add cream, pepper flakes, salt and pepper to taste, parsley, oregano and basil. Finally, pour off any lquid which may have accumulated in bowl of seafood and add to sauce.

5. Preheat oven to 375°; butter bottom and sides of a lasagne pan or baking dish which is 9½ x 13½ x 2-inches.

6. Spoon a layer of sauce over bottom; add half the shrimps and scallops. Cover with some more sauce. Cover with 3 lasagne strips.

7. Add a layer of flounder; add salt and pepper and a thin layer of sauce. Cover with 3 strips of lasagne.

8. Scatter remaining shrimps and scallops over; spoon a light layer of sauce over this; cover with 3 strips of lasagne.

9. Spoon final layer of sauce over top. Sprinkle with cheese. (May be covered and refrigerated.)

10. Bake 30 to 45 minutes, or until hot and bubbly. (Allow more heating time if refrigerated.)

Béchamel Sauce:

4 tablespoons butter
4 tablespoons flour
2 cups milk
salt and freshly ground pepper

Béchamel Sauce:

1. Melt butter in saucepan; add flour, stirring with wire whisk, until blended. Slowly add milk, stirring briskly with whisk. Add salt and pepper to taste. Stir until thick and smooth.

2. Lower heat; cook, stirring occasionally, about 5 minutes.

Salmon Loaf

Light and flavorful.

Yield: 6 servings

1 16-ounce can salmon, juices
  drained and reserved
1 cup fine bread crumbs
½ cup celery, finely cut
¼ cup onion, finely chopped
¼ cup green pepper, finely chopped
1½ teaspoons lemon juice
1 large can evaporated milk
1 egg, beaten
dash salt
freshly ground pepper, to taste

1. Preheat oven to 325°.

2. Remove bony pieces from salmon, breaking up with fork.

3. In large bowl combine salmon, bread crumbs, celery, onion and green pepper.

4. Separately mix lemon juice, evaporated milk, egg, salt and pepper. Mix with spoon into salmon mixture.

5. Pack into greased loaf pan and bake for 45 minutes.

Sauce:

¼ cup mayonnaise
1 tablespoon flour
¼ teaspoon salt
small can evaporated milk
½ cup reserved juices plus water if necessary
¼ cup stuffed green olives, sliced
¼ cup almonds, chopped

Sauce:

1. Combine mayonnaise, flour, reserved juices, salt and milk in small saucepan. Cook, stirring constantly, until thickened.

2. Add olives and almonds. Serve separately with salmon loaf.

Russian Salmon Loaf in Pastry

Yield: 10 to 12 servings

⅔ cup dry rice
1½ cups water
1 chicken bouillon cube
4 medium onions (10 to 12 ounces total)
½ pound mushrooms, sliced
2 16-ounce cans salmon
3 hard-boiled eggs, coarsely chopped
½ teaspoon salt
1 teaspoon dill weed
1 package frozen puff pastry, thawed

1. Cook rice in water and bouillon until done.
2. Sauté onions in half of the butter until soft. Add to rice.
3. Add remaining butter to pan and sauté mushrooms. Add to rice.
4. Flake salmon, removing skin and cartilage, and reserve juice.
5. Combine salmon with rice and remaining ingredients except pastry.
6. Preheat oven to 425°.
7. Roll pastry slightly. Place one sheet on ungreased baking sheet.
8. Cover with salmon mixture, then with remaining pastry, sealing edges with water, and flute.
9. Place in preheated oven, reducing temperature to 400°. Bake about 40 minutes or until puffed and light golden.
10. Serve slices with cream sauce if desired.

Cream Sauce, Optional:

2 tablespoons butter
2 tablespoons flour
1 cup chicken broth (or juice from salmon plus water)
½ cup light cream
2 teaspoons lemon juice
⅛ teaspoon nutmeg
salt and pepper to taste

Sauce:

1. Melt butter, add flour to make paste.
2. Add salmon liquid slowly, stirring to make a smooth sauce. When thickened, add lemon, seasonings and cream, keep over low heat. Do not boil.

Shrimp de Jonghe

Yield: serves 4 to 6

2 pounds raw medium shrimp, cleaned, drained
1 cup butter, melted
2 cloves garlic, minced
1½ cups soft bread crumbs (about 3 slices)
¼ cup chopped fresh parsley
½ teaspoon paprika
½ cup dry sherry

1. Preheat oven to 325°.
2. Prepare bread slices in food processor or blender.
3. Combine butter with ingredients other than shrimp.
4. Place shrimp in shallow baking dish. Cover with crumb mixture.
5. Bake 20 to 25 minutes or until crumbs are brown and shrimp is pink.

Shrimp Etouffé

A New Orleans-style specialty.

1 medium onion, finely chopped
2 green onions, finely chopped
2 cloves garlic, finely minced
½ cup celery, finely chopped
1 green pepper, finely chopped
½ cup butter
3 tablespoons flour
1¾ cups water
1 10½-ounce can tomato pureé
2 bay leaves
1 tablespoon Worcestershire sauce
4 to 5 drops Tabasco sauce
1 teaspoon salt
1 tablespoon sugar
½ teaspoon black pepper
½ teaspoon crushed dried thyme
3 cups cleaned, raw shrimp
   (or approximately 1 12-ounce bag frozen
   medium shrimp, thawed and drained)
sautéed sliced mushrooms (optional)
3 to 4 cups hot cooked rice

Yield: 6 to 8 servings

1. In a large skillet or saucepan, sauté onions, garlic, celery, and green pepper in butter until tender; do not brown.
2. Add flour; stir to make smooth paste; cook 1 or 2 minutes. Add water, pureé, bay leaves, Worcestershire, Tabasco and other seasonings. Simmer over low heat, stirring, until sauce thickens to desired consistency. (May be made ahead to this point. Reheat before proceeding.)
3. Add raw shrimp; cook 15 minutes over low heat, stirring occasionally.
4. Serve over hot cooked rice. Sprinkle with sautéed mushrooms if desired.

Variation:

To make Shrimp Gumbo, add one 10-ounce package frozen sliced okra to sauce; cook 10 minutes before adding shrimp. ("Gumbo" is an African word for okra.)

Shrimp Maison Cointreau

Perfect for an intimate champagne dinner.

12 jumbo shrimp, shelled, deveined,
   and butterflied
½ cup heavy cream
¼ cup melted butter
¼ cup Cointreau (orange liqueur)
2 large cloves garlic, minced
¼ cup chopped fresh parsley
1 teaspoon paprika
salt and pepper

Try serving on a bed of hot rice to which 1 teaspoon of grated orange peel and chopped parsley have been added.

Yield: 4 servings

1. Preheat oven to 400°.
2. Arrange shrimp in oven-proof dish. Combine other ingredients; pour over shrimp.
3. Bake uncovered for 12 to 15 minutes.

Seafood Crepes

Yield: 16 crepes, 8 servings

Basic Entrée Crepes:

1¾ cups flour, sifted before measured
4 large eggs
1 cup milk
1 cup water
¼ teaspoon salt
¼ cup (½ stick) unsalted butter,
  melted and cooled

When making crepes. consider doubling recipe and freezing them for use with turkey leftovers such as Turkey Curry Crepes (see pg. 105)

Seafood Filling:

½ pound flounder fillets
½ pound bay scallops
¼ pound small shrimp
½ pound crabmeat
  (cut into bite-size pieces)
milk
¼ cup dry sherry
¼ pound (1 stick) butter
3 green onions, minced
2 tablespoons flour
½ teaspoon salt
¼ teaspoon pepper
1 cup shredded Cheddar cheese
1 cup shredded Swiss cheese
¼ cup grated Parmesan cheese (optional)
lemon, bay leaf, peppercorns

Crepes:

1. In electric blender, place flour, eggs, milk, water and salt, in that order. Cover blender and blend at medium speed, stopping to scrape sides with rubber spatula.

2. When batter is smooth, add butter and blend again. Let stand at room temperature 30 minutes to 2 hours. (May be made ahead and refrigerated, but return to room temperature before using.)

3. Brush bottom of a 6 to 7-inch crepe pan with melted butter; place over medium heat. Pour a scant ¼ cup batter into hot pan, tipping pan to coat bottom. Cook until top of crepe is set, turn; cook other side about 30 seconds. Layer between sheets of waxed paper until ready to use. Continue until all batter is used. Set aside 16 crepes.

Filling:

1. Place flounder, scallops, and shrimp in 1 cup water, to which 1 thin slice lemon, a bay leaf and 4 peppercorns have been added. Simmer gently 5 to 10 minutes, covered, over low heat, until fish flakes easily. Do not overcook.

2. With slotted spoon, remove seafood to plate; cover and refrigerate. Strain broth into 2 cup measure; add enough milk to make 1½ cups. Add sherry. Set aside.

3. Melt butter in saucepan and sauté green onions until tender but not brown. Blend in flour, salt and pepper. Gradually add milk-sherry mixture; cook until sauce thickens slightly. Stir in ½ cup each Swiss and Cheddar cheese, stirring until melted. Pour off 1 cup sauce; reserve. Add fish, scallops, shrimp and crabmeat to remaining sauce.

4. Preheat oven to 325°. Spoon about ¼ cup filling onto the center of each crepe; fold sides over filling; place filled crepe, seam side down, in a 9 x 13-inch baking dish. Continue until all 16 crepes are filled.

To make ahead:

Prepare as directed but do not bake. Freeze. To reheat, thaw wrapped dish overnight in refrigerator. Thawed dish can be baked in preheated 325° oven for 45 to 50 minutes.

5. Add ¼ cup milk to cup of reserved sauce; whisk smooth. Pour over crepes in baking dish. Combine remaining cheeses; sprinkle over top of sauced crepes. Bake 25 minutes until hot and bubbly. (To microwave, cover and cook on medium for 8 minutes, rotating dish halfway through.)

Sole Gratin

Perfect make-ahead fish entrée.

2 pounds sole fillets
½ cup dry white wine
2 tablespoons lemon juice
½ pound mushrooms, sliced
¼ cup (½ stick) butter
3 tablespoons flour
1 cup light cream
⅛ teaspoon nutmeg
3 ounces Swiss cheese, shredded

Yield: 6 servings

1. Preheat oven to 400°.
2. Layer fillets in shallow baking dish, keeping thickness as uniform as possible.
3. Cover with wine and 1 tablespoon lemon juice.
4. Cover with foil and bake until fish flakes (10 to 20 minutes.)
5. Drain fish, reserving juices. cover fish and refrigerate.
6. Cook mushrooms, and 1 teaspoon lemon in half the butter over high heat until juices have evaporated.
7. Make a white sauce with remaining butter, flour, reserved fish broth (plus water to make 1 cup), cream and nutmeg. Cool.
8. Cover fish with mushrooms, then white sauce, then grated cheese. Cover and refrigerate until serving.
9. Preheat oven to 400°. Bake 15 minutes or until bubbling and cheese is slightly browned.

Stuffed Squid

Good served with hot fettucini.

Yield: 6 to 8 servings

2 pounds cleaned squid (chopped tentacles may be added to sauce if desired)
8 to 10 slices bread, crumbed
4 large eggs
salt and pepper to taste
2 cloves garlic, minced
2 tablespoons chopped fresh parsley
⅓ cup packed Parmesan cheese
¼ cup olive oil
2 15-ounce cans tomato sauce
¾ teaspoon oregano
½ cup Marsala wine

1. Mix together bread crumbs, eggs, salt and pepper, garlic, parsley and cheese. Stuff each squid and secure with toothpick (do not pack stuffing too tightly).

2. Heat oil in a large skillet; brown squid lightly, turning fequently, until browned on all sides.

3. Add tomato sauce, marsala and oregano. Stir gently. Lower heat, cover and simmer slowly for 30 minutes

Leftovers and Light dishes

Leftovers and Light Dishes

Barbara's Baked Omelet

Yield: 25 servings

A brunch buffet recipe to serve a crowd!

½ cup (1 stick) butter
3 dozen eggs
2 cups sour cream
2 cups milk
4 teaspoons salt
½ cup green onions, chopped
½ pound mushrooms, sliced
½ pound Cheddar cheese, shredded
½ pound bacon, cooked, drained,
   and crumbled

1. Heat oven to 325°.
2. In oven, melt ¼ cup butter in each of two 13 x 9 x 2-inch baking dishes. Tilt dish to coat bottom with butter.
3. In large mixing bowl, beat eggs, sour cream, milk and salt until blended. Stir in remaining four ingredients, or any other combination of extras you desire. Pour into baking dishes.
4. Bake until eggs are set but still moist, about 35 minutes. Cut into squares to serve.

Christmas Straw and Hay

Yield: 4 to 6 servings

A rich light-supper dish or first course.

4 ounces uncooked white linguine
4 ounces uncooked green linguine
½ cup (1 stick) butter or margarine
½ cup cooked ham, in thin strips
¾ cup cooked peas
⅓ cup pitted black olives, sliced
small can sliced mushrooms, drained
small jar sliced pimento, drained
2 egg yolks, well-beaten
1 cup whipping cream
1 cup grated Parmesan cheese
parsley

1. Cook linguine in boiling salted water until tender. Drain and return to pot.
2. Stir in butter and add ham, peas, olives, mushrooms, and half the pimento.
3. In small bowl combine eggs and cream. Slowly add this mixture to warm linguine, stirring well. Add half the Parmesan. Stir over medium high heat until mixture thickens slightly. Don't let eggs curdle.
4. Serve garnished with remaining pimento, cheese and parsley.

Duck and Wild Rice Casserole

Yield: 6 servings

Good made with any leftover poultry.

1 5-pound duck
1 apple, quartered
1 medium onion, quartered
4 strips bacon
1 cup orange juice
1 pound mild sausage, cooked and drained
1 6-ounce package long grain and wild rice, cooked according to package directions
2 cups thick cream sauce (or 1 can condensed mushroom soup)
½ pound mushrooms, sliced and sautéed

1. Wash duckling thoroughly. Sprinkle body cavity with salt; stuff with apple and onion. Place breast-side up on a rack in a roaster pan. Lay strips of bacon across the breast; pour orange juice over all. Cover and bake at 300° for 1½ to 2 hours.

2. Cool and remove meat from duck, cutting in bite-size pieces.

3. To assemble casserole: mix cut-up duck with cooked sausage, cooked rice, cream sauce (or soup), and sautéed mushrooms. Top with buttered bread crumbs, if desired. Cover and bake at 350° for 40 minutes; uncover and bake 20 minutes longer or until top browns.

Egg and Sausage Quiche

Yield: 6 to 8 servings

A nice addition to Christmas morning brunch buffet.

Pastry for 1-crust 9-inch pie
8 ounces bulk pork sausage
4 hard-boiled eggs, chopped
1 cup (4 ounces) natural Swiss cheese, shredded
1 cup (4 ounces) natural Cheddar cheese, shredded
3 eggs, beaten
1¼ cups light cream or evaporated milk, undiluted
¾ teaspoon salt
⅛ teaspoon pepper
paprika

1. Preheat oven to 350°.

2. Line 9-inch pie plate with pastry; flute edges. DO NOT PRICK. Bake for about 7 minutes.

3. In skillet, cook sausage, breaking up large chunks. Drain well on paper toweling.

4. Sprinkle hard-boiled egg in bottom of pie shell; top with sausage and shredded cheeses.

5. Combine eggs, cream, salt and pepper; pour over all. Sprinkle with paprika.

6. Bake at 350° for 30 to 35 minutes or until set. Let stand 10 minutes before serving. (Reheats well if made ahead.)

Best-Of-The-Dinner Sandwiches

From turkey leftovers.

1 English muffin or 2 slices rye or
    pumpernickel bread per person
turkey
dressing
cranberry sauce
cheese: American, Cheddar or Swiss
bacon, cooked and crumbled
"Sauce" made from 1 part chili sauce to
    2 parts salad dressing or mayonnaise

1. Preheat oven to 400°.
2. Lightly toast bread or muffin. Spread with a little "sauce". Layer turkey, a thin layer of stuffing, a thin layer of cranberry sauce and slice of cheese.
3. Place sandwiches on cookie sheet and heat about 10 minutes until cheese melts and turkey warms. (You can also do this step in a microwave.)
4. Spread second slice of toast with "sauce". Remove sandwiches from oven, top with crumbled bacon and toast.

Creamy Turkey Enchiladas

Not sure about Mexican food? Try these!

Yield: 6 to 8 servings

3 cups cooked turkey, diced
1 large Spanish onion (about 7 ounces),
    thinly sliced
1 jar sliced pimento, drained
2 tablespoons butter or margarine
1 8-ounce package cream cheese,
    in 1-inch chunks
salt and pepper to taste
12 soft corn tortillas
oil
½ cup whipping cream
½ pound Monterey Jack cheese, shredded

1. In a medium skillet, cook onions in butter until they just begin to brown. Remove from heat and stir in turkey, pimento and cream cheese. Stir to melt cheese slightly, adding salt and pepper to taste. This is your filling.
2. Ready a 13 x 9-inch pan or baking dish.
3. In small, tortilla-sized skillet, heat about ¼ inch salad oil over medium heat. When it begins to sizzle drop in a tortilla and fry a few seconds until it blisters. Remove from oil to paper towels. (Use tongs.) It should be soft enough to roll. Lay about ½ cup filling down center of tortilla and lap edges over it. Place seam side down in pan. Repeat procedure for all tortillas and filling. May cover and refrigerate at this point.
4. Preheat oven to 375°. Pour cream over tortillas to moisten. Cover completely with shredded cheese. Bake 20 to 30 minutes or until cheese bubbles. Should cover during first half of cooking.

Friand

A rich, filled pastry for Christmas Eve or brunch.

2 sheets (1 pound) puff pastry, chilled
½ pound fresh mushrooms, sliced
½ pound Gruyère or Swiss cheese, grated
½ pound ham, chicken or seafood
8 ounces cream cheese, cut into pieces
3 tablespoons butter
4 tablespoons flour
1 cup chicken broth
⅛ teaspoon nutmeg
freshly ground pepper
1 egg beaten with 1 tablespoon water

1. If pastry is frozen, thaw but keep chilled.
2. Sauté mushrooms in 1 tablespoon butter. Set aside.
3. Slice ham or chicken into bite-size pieces. Set aside.
4. Preheat oven to 400°.
5. Make a thick sauce by melting 2 tablespoons butter, adding flour to make a paste. Slowly add broth, stirring over medium heat until smooth and thick. Blend in chunks of cream cheese, Gruyère, ham and mushrooms. Set aside.
6. Roll out pastry into two 12 x 14-inch rectangles or join to form one 14 x 24-inch rectangle. Lay filling along centers but well within ends. Wrap to enclose filling completely, sealing seams with a little water.
7. Place on ungreased baking sheet. Brush with egg wash and bake for 35 to 45 minutes or until puffed and light golden.
8. Let stand 5 to 10 minutes; slice to serve. Salad and fruit or light dessert complete the meal.

Mary Katherine's French Ham Bake   Yield: 6 servings

Satisfying . . .

1 pound baked ham, thinly sliced
6 to 7 medium potatoes, thinly sliced
1 cup whipping cream
¾ cup sour cream
2 rounded tablespoons Dijon mustard
6 ounces Monterey Jack
  cheese, grated (1½ cups)

1. Preheat oven to 325°.
2. Starting and ending with potatoes, layer with ham in a 2-quart baking dish.
3. Combine creams and mustard. Pour over layers. Bake 1 hour and 20 minutes.
4. Cover with cheese and bake an additional 10 minutes or until cheese melts.

Holiday Brunch Casserole Eggs

Yield: 6 to 8 servings

Rich and cheesy and surprisingly easy!

4 slices bacon, cooked and crumbled
¼ cup chopped green onions
1 pound fresh mushrooms, cleaned
  and sliced
1 to 2 tablespoons butter
8 eggs
dash of Tabasco sauce
½ teaspoon salt
pepper to taste
2½ cups shredded Monterey Jack cheese
1 cup milk

1. Preheat oven to 350°. Grease 2-quart casserole.

2. Sauté onion and mushrooms in butter.

3. Combine all ingredients in a large bowl. Pour into casserole.

4. Bake at 350° for 40 to 45 minutes, or until golden on top and set. Eggs will seem runny in center, but this is only melted cheese. Let sit at room temperature 5 minutes before serving.

Pepperoni Stuffed Loaf

Yield: 1 loaf

**Main dish, snack, appetizer
—a universal favorite.**

1 1-pound loaf frozen bread dough, thawed
1 small green pepper, sliced
1 medium onion (about 3 ounces), sliced
4 ounces fresh mushrooms, sliced
oil, vinegar
salt and pepper
1 egg, beaten
1 teaspoon Italian seasoning
1 10-inch stick pepperoni, peeled and
  thinly sliced
⅓ cup grated Parmesan cheese
sesame seeds

1. Sauté green pepper, onion and mushrooms in 2 to 3 tablespoons oil. Sprinkle over them a dash or two of vinegar and season with salt and pepper. Set aside.

2. Preheat oven to 375°.

3. On greased 15 x 10-inch jelly roll pan, spread the dough with hands nearly to the edges.

4. Mix egg with seasoning and spread half over dough. Cover with pepperoni, then with green pepper mixture, then with cheese.

5. Roll lengthwise, stretching dough at the end to pull over and seal. (This seems an impossible feat. It does work.) Place seam side down, form a ring and lap one end inside other.

6. Glaze with remaining egg wash. Sprinkle with sesame seeds. Bake for 25 minutes.

7. Serve hot or at room temperature.

Lasagne Tomaso

Smoked turkey and three cheeses!

Yield: 10 to 12 servings

9 lasagne noodles (half of a 1-pound box),
  cooked according to package directions
1 onion, finely chopped
2 cloves garlic, finely chopped
6 tablespoons butter
4 tablespoons flour
⅛ teaspoon white pepper
3 cups whole milk
1 10-ounce package frozen chopped spinach,
  cooked and well drained
1 15-ounce container ricotta cheese
½ cup freshly grated Parmesan cheese
¼ teaspoon freshly ground pepper
¼ teaspoon nutmeg
½ teaspoon salt
12 ounces mozzarella cheese, grated
12 ounces smoked turkey, cut into
  julienne strips

May be doubled easily for crowd of 24.

1. Cook lasagne according to package directions; drain. Rinse in cold water; drain in a single layer on paper towels.

2. In a large saucepan melt butter and sauté onion and garlic until onion is soft. Remove from heat; stir in flour and white pepper. Cook over medium heat 1 minute until smooth and bubbly. Gradually stir in milk; cook, stirring constantly, until mixture comes to a boil. Boil 2 minutes. Remove from heat.

3. Drain spinach, squeezing out excess moisture. In food processor fitted with steel blade, finely chop spinach. Add ricotta, Parmesan, pepper, nutmeg and salt; process until smooth.

4. Add spinach-cheese mixture to white sauce; stir to combine. Taste for seasoning. Set aside one cup of sauce.

5. Butter a 13 x 9-inch baking dish. Line bottom with 3 noodles, cover with sauce. Place half of turkey on sauce; sprinkle with ⅓ of mozzarella cheese. Repeat layer. Cover with a third layer of noodles. Sprinkle remaining mozzarella on top and cover with reserved sauce. Cover dish with foil (Can be made ahead up to here and refrigerated; let stand at room temperature 2 hours before baking.)

6. Bake in preheated 350° oven 35 to 40 minutes, until hot and bubbly. Let stand 15 minutes before serving. Garnish with rings of sweet red pepper for a holiday touch.

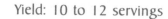

When cooking pasta, such as lasagne or shells, which require waiting before being used, drain off half of cooking liquid, replacing it with cold water. This stops the cooking but keeps pasta warm and separated. Drain each as it is used.

Smoked Salmon with Pasta

Yield: 20 servings

An excellent choice for a buffet table or light meal.

Salad:

1½ pounds medium (No. 22) pasta shells
3 tablespoons olive oil
4½ cups coarsely chopped scallions
¾ cup finely chopped fresh parsley
1¼ cup coarsely chopped black olives
¼ cup capers, drained
1½ pounds smoked salmon, cut into
  julienne strips

Dressing:

¾ cup olive oil
¼ cup red wine vinegar
3 tablespoons lemon juice
½ teaspoon anchovy paste
¾ teaspoon salt
¾ teaspoon freshly ground black pepper

1. Boil shells in a large pot of salted boiling water for 10 to 12 minutes, or until al dente. Drain; toss immediately with olive oil in a large serving bowl. Add the remaining salad ingredients; toss to mix.

2. In a screw-top jar, combing dressing ingredients; shake well to mix. Pour over salad and toss to coat.

3. May be made ahead and refrigerated. Serve at room temperature.

Turkey Curry Crepes

Yield: 6 servings

Perfect for using up the leftover bird.

12 Basic Entrée Crepes (see p. 94)
2 cups cubed cooked turkey (or chicken)
½ cup chutney, cut-up
2 slices bacon
¼ cup thinly sliced celery
¼ cup chopped onion
1 clove garlic, minced
2 tablespoons flour
1½ cups milk
½ cup applesauce
3 tablespoons tomato paste
1 tablespoon curry powder
2 teaspoons instant chicken
  bouillon granules

Garnish: toasted coconut and
  chopped peanuts

1. Preheat oven to 375°; grease a 13 x 9 x 2-inch baking dish.

2. On each crepe, spread chutney and sprinkle with a handful of cubed turkey. Roll up crepe and place, seam side down, in baking dish.

3. Prepare Sauce: Cook bacon; drain and crumble. Reserve drippings.

4. In bacon dripings, sauté celery, onion and garlic. Blend in flour; add milk, applesauce, tomato paste, curry and bouillon granules. Cook and stir until bubbly.

5. Pour sauce over turkey filled crepes in dish. Top with bacon. Bake 15 to 20 minutes. Sprinkle with coconut and peanuts.

105

Stuffed Monsieurs

Perfect for leftovers: a thick sandwich related to Croque Monsieur.

Yield: 4 sandwiches

4 thick slices (1½-inches thick) Italian
  or French bread
4 thick slices baked ham (or turkey)
4 slices Gruyère cheese
4 eggs
½ teaspoon salt
1 cup milk
butter
Sauces (optional, depending on
  what's left over)
Raisin sauce
Chutney or Cranberry Relish
Mustard sauce

1. Make a slit vertically through crust of bread, as though slicing each 1½-inch slice into two ¾-inch slices, but do not cut all the way though.
2. Place 1 slice of ham and 1 slice of cheese inside slit of each piece of bread.
3. Prepare batter: whisk together eggs, salt and milk in a shallow baking dish.
4. Butter a hot griddle, over medium high heat. Carefully dip sandwiches into batter, coating both sides. Brown on each side until golden.
5. Serve hot, accompanied by leftover sauces or relishes, if desired.

Turkey-Wild Rice Casserole

Party-fare from leftovers

Yield: 8 servings

1 cup wild rice (or 1 package long grain
  and wild rice)
1 pound fresh mushrooms, sliced
½ cup chopped onion
¼ cup (½ stick) butter
½ teaspoon salt
⅛ teaspoon pepper
3 cups diced cooked turkey
½ cup sliced almonds, toasted
3 cups canned chicken broth
1¼ cups heavy cream

May be doubled and casserole may be frozen before baking.

1. Wash wild rice thoroughly. Cover rice with water. Bring to boil. Remove from heat and soak 1 hour. Drain. Preheat oven to 300°.
2. Sauté mushrooms and onions in butter. Mix with remaining ingredients. (Including herb package if using long grain and wild rice.)
3. Turn into a 2-quart buttered casserole. Cover and bake 20 minutes. Uncover and bake until rice is tender. (About 40 minutes longer for wild rice, less for the other.)

 Freeze suet before grinding in food processor.

Venison Fettucine Cerullo

Yield: 6 to 8 servings

Veal may be substituted for venison in this superb pasta dish.

1 pound fettucine
1 cup olive oil
1 clove garlic, crushed
8 ounces mushrooms, cut in julienne strips
  (use straw mushrooms if available)
3 tablespoons chopped fresh basil
  (about 20 leaves) or 2 tablespoons
  dried basil if fresh is unavailable
2 ounces sun-dried tomatoes, cut in
  julienne strips
⅔ cup sliced black olives
crushed red pepper flakes to taste
1½ pounds venison (use any tender cut or
  tender veal), cut in julienne strips
¼ cup flour, seasoned with salt and pepper
juice of one lemon

1. Cook fettucine according to package directions, approximately 10 to 12 minutes, drain and keep warm. While fettucine is cooking, prepare sauce.
2. In a large skillet, heat olive oil over medium heat; add garlic and mushrooms and cook about 3 minutes. Add half of basil, tomatoes, olives and crushed red pepper flakes. Cook about 5 minutes more. Remove from skillet with slotted spoon. Discard garlic.
3. Dredge meat in seasoned flour.
4. Increase heat under skillet. To oil in skillet add half of meat; brown and then remove with slotted spoon. Brown second half of meat.
5. Return mushroom mixture to skillet with all of meat; heat thoroughly. Squeeze juice of lemon over sauce. Toss sauce with fettucine. Sprinkle with remaining basil. Serve hot.

Turkey with Artichokes

Yield: 8 servings

Elevates leftovers to new heights.

4 cups cut-up cooked turkey or chicken
3 15½-ounce cans artichoke hearts
¼ cup flour
¼ cup (½ stick) butter, melted
½ teaspoon nutmeg
2 cups chicken broth
3 cups (12 ounces) mild Cheddar, shredded
2 tablespoons butter, melted
½ cup bread crumbs
¼ teaspoon savory
¼ teaspoon thyme

May also be made with 4 whole chicken breasts.

1. Place meat and drained artichokes in large casserole. Preheat oven to 350°.
2. Blend flour and nutmeg with ¼ cup butter in medium saucepan. Add chicken broth and stir until thick. Add cheese. Pour over turkey.
3. Combine 2 tablespoons butter with herbs and bread crumbs. Sprinkle over top.
4. Bake 20 minutes or until bubbly.

Ham and Cheese Baked Fondue

Yield: 16 to 20 servings

With variations, may be halved.

2 loaves French bread, cubed (approximately
   10 cups, or use 16 slices white bread)
2 pounds ham, sliced
1 pound Cheddar cheese, shredded
1 pound Swiss cheese, diced
1½ teaspoons dry mustard
8 eggs
3 cups milk
1 cup dry white wine

Variation: Crab and Swiss

Use 1 pound crab, flaked and 1 pound
   Swiss cheese to replace ham and cheese.
Use ½ cup butter mixed with 2 cloves garlic,
   crushed to butter bread before cubing.
Use ½ teaspoon dry mustard and
   2 teaspoons paprika mixed with 3 cups
   wine and 1 cup light cream.

Variation: Cheese and Bacon

Omit ham.
Substitute Old English American cheese,
   cubed for Swiss cheese.
Butter the bread.
Use 4 cups milk, no wine.
Add dash Worcestershire sauce to eggs.
Cook and crumble 1 pound bacon,
   adding just before baking

**Half of recipe may be baked in 9-inch square pan
for 1 hour.**

Must be made ahead.

1. Butter 4- to 5-quart baking dish or a
   13 x 9-inch pan.
2. Layer ham, cheeses and bread, repeating
   until all is used.
3. Beat eggs, mustard, milk and wine together.
   Pour over casserole. Cover and refrigerate
   overnight.
4. Bake uncovered in preheated 350° oven for
   one hour.
5. Cool slightly and cut to serve.

Vegetables

Vegetables

Vegetables

were definitely subordinate to the magnificent main course and spectacular desserts at a traditional Victorian Christmas dinner. Published menus from nineteenth century American publications are consistent in their recommendations of the same basic list of vegetables, which could be easily stored until December 25th. The Ladies Home Journal of December 1890 suggested—"...potatoes that are roasted, boiled and mashed, vegetables in butter, vegetables with egg, with a flavoring of ham or bacon... turnips, beets, cole-slaw and fried celery." Earlier in the century Godey's Lady's Book varied its list only slightly for the December issues from 1857 to 1861. All of the lists included stewed beets, cole slaw, turnip, salsify, winter squash, celery sauce and fried celery.

Gnocchi Parisienne

A good substitute for potatoes or rice for a buffet.

Yield: 6 to 8 servings

Choux Pastry:

1 cup water
½ cup (1 stick) butter
1 cup flour
5 large eggs

Sauce:

⅓ cup butter
½ cup flour
½ teaspoon salt
1 pint light cream
½ cup grated Parmesan cheese
paprika

Pastry:

1. Bring water and butter to rapid boil; when butter is melted, add all the flour at once. Beat well until dough forms ball and pulls away from sides of pan.
2. Remove pan from heat; beat in eggs, one at a time, beating well after each addition.
3. Drop dough by teaspoonsful into boiling salted water. Cook until dumplings float to surface and expand, about 5 minutes.
4. Remove from water with slotted spoon; put into cold water (gnocchi will shrink). Remove from cold water; refrigerate until ready to use.

Sauce:

1. Melt butter in saucepan; stir in flour, making a smooth paste; cook 1 minute, stirring.
2. Add cream slowly to make a thick sauce. Mix in ⅓ cup grated cheese. (This may be stored in refrigerator until ready to use.)

To assemble:

1. Preheat oven to 375°. Grease a flat casserole or baking dish.
2. Put gnocchi in dish; cover with sauce. Sprinkle with remaining cheese and paprika. (At this point, casserole may be covered and refrigerated several hours or overnight.)
3. Bake at 375° for 15 to 20 minutes, or until hot and bubbly. (Gnocchi will expand again.)

Broccoli with Sour Cream and Cashews   Yield: 6 servings
Wonderful combination of flavors.

large head of fresh broccoli or 2 10-ounce
   packages frozen broccoli florets
1 8-ounce container sour cream
4 ounces sharp process American cheese,
   grated
½ teaspoon freshly grated lemon peel
1 tablespoon lemon juice
¼ teaspoon salt
dash white pepper
3 ounces salted cashews, chopped

1. Cook the fresh broccoli as follows: break off heavy stems from flower heads. This will leave the more tender stalk attached to the florets. With a knife peel the outer layer from the bottom toward the floret. Cut any large florets into smaller pieces. Cook about 5 to 6 minutes in boiling salted water. Drain. OR, cook frozen broccoli according to package directions and drain.

2. Place broccoli in shallow ovenproof serving dish and keep warm. Heat broiler.

3. Combine remaining ingredients except for the cashews. Spoon over the broccoli. Sprinkle nuts over all.

4. Run under the broiler until heated thoroughly, taking care not to burn cashews. Serve immediately.

Hot Broccoli Mold

Yield: 6 to 8 servings

2 10-ounce packages frozen chopped
   broccoli, cooked and drained well
¼ cup chicken broth
3 tablespoons butter
¼ cup chopped scallions
3 tablespoons flour
1 cup sour cream
3 eggs, lightly beaten
⅓ cup grated Swiss cheese
1 teaspoon salt
¼ teaspoon black pepper
½ teaspoon nutmeg
¼ cup finely chopped toasted almonds
3 tablespoons chopped pimento

1. Preheat oven to 350°. Grease well a 5-cup ring mold.

2. Add chicken broth to well-drained, cooked broccoli; set aside.

3. Melt the butter in large saucepan; add scallions and sauté until tender. Stir in flour and cook, stirring, about 1 minute.

4. Blend sour cream into flour mixture; cook, stirring constantly, until thick, but do not boil. Remove from heat; stir in eggs.

5. Stir in broccoli-broth mixture, cheese, seasonings, nuts and pimento. Pour into mold. Set in a shallow pan of boiling water; bake 45 minutes or until knife inserted in center comes out clean.

6. Let stand 5 minutes. Run knife around edges; unmold.

Broccoli-Cauliflower Medley

Yield: 10 to 12 servings

A colorful mix.

1 10-ounce package frozen chopped
   broccoli, cooked and drained
1 10-ounce package frozen cauliflower,
   cooked and drained
1 16-ounce poly-bag frozen small whole
   onions, cooked and drained
2 tablespoons butter
3 tablespoons onion, minced
2 tablespoons flour
¼ teaspoon salt
⅛ teaspoon pepper
2 cups milk
3 tablespoons chopped pimento
1 inner bag stack of buttery rich crackers,
   crushed
½ cup (1 stick) butter, melted
paprika

1. Preheat oven to 350°.
   Grease a 2-quart casserole.
2. Combine cooked, drained vegetables
   in casserole.
3. Prepare a white sauce: melt butter in
   saucepan; add onion and sauté until tender.
   Stir in flour, salt and pepper; cook, stirring,
   until smooth and bubbly. Slowly stir in milk.
   Heat until thick and bubbly, stirring
   constantly. Remove from heat; add chopped
   pimento. Pour over vegetables in casserole;
   toss lightly to mix.
4. Combine crushed crackers, melted butter
   and paprika. Sprinkle over top of casserole.
   Bake for 30 to 45 minutes, or until
   heated through.

Elegant Celery Casserole

Yield: 6 servings

A crunchy treat.

2 cups celery, diagonally sliced in
   ½-inch slices
1 8-ounce can sliced water chestnuts,
   drained
¼ cup slivered almonds, toasted
¼ cup chopped pimento
¼ cup (½ stick) butter or margarine
3 tablespoons flour
⅔ cup half-and-half
⅔ cup chicken broth
¼ teaspoon salt
½ cup bread crumbs
¼ cup (½ stick) melted butter
¼ cup grated Parmesan cheese
paprika

**A 10-ounce can of condensed cream of celery soup
may be substituted for cream sauce (step 2) for a
quick version.**

1. Cook celery in boiling water 4 minutes;
   drain. Combine celery, water chestnuts,
   almonds, and pimento; spoon into a greased
   1½-quart baking dish.
2. Melt butter in heavy saucepan over low heat;
   add flour, stirring until smooth. Cook
   1 minute, stirring constantly. Gradually add
   half-and-half and chicken broth; cook,
   stirring constantly, until thickened and
   bubbly. Add salt.
3. Pour sauce over celery mixture. Mix bread
   crumbs, melted butter and Parmesan;
   sprinkle over casserole. Sprinkle on paprika.
4. Bake at 350° for 30 minutes, or until hot
   and bubbly.

Brussels Sprouts with Chestnuts Yield: 6 servings

1 quart Brussels sprouts
1½ teaspoons salt
1 tablespoon finely chopped onion
1½ cups chicken broth
¼ cup (½ stick) butter
1 cup cooked chestnuts

1. Wash and trim sprouts. Soak in 4 cups cold water, in which one teaspoon salt is dissolved, for 20 minutes. Drain.
2. Place sprouts in saucepan with onion, broth and ½ teaspoon salt. Bring to a boil; cook, uncovered, for 5 minutes.
3. Cover and cook for 10 to 12 minutes longer, or until tender. Drain.
4. Melt butter; add chestnuts and cook until butter is golden brown. Pour over sprouts and toss lightly to mix.

To cook chestnuts:

1. With a paring knife cut a cross on the flat side of the shell of each chestnut. Cover chestnuts with water; bring to a boil. Simmer about 5 minutes. Drain.
2. Peel chestnuts. If they are hard, add water to cover, bring to a boil and simmer about 5 minutes more until tender. (Cooking time varies with age of chestnuts.) Peel off brown skins.

Yule Red Cabbage Yield: 4 to 6 servings

A traditional Scandinavian Christmas dish, excellent with goose, duckling or pork.

4 cups shredded red cabbage
  (about 1 medium-size head)
2 tablespoons butter or bacon drippings
½ teaspoon salt
¼ cup water
¼ cup wine vinegar
1 apple, cored and sliced thinly
3 tablespoons red currant jelly
1 tablespoon caraway seeds
¼ cup raisins (optional)

1. Melt butter or bacon fat in a large skillet; add cabbage, water and vinegar. Cover pan and simmer, stirring occasionally, approximately 15 minutes.
2. When cabbage is soft, add apple slices, currant jelly, salt, caraway and raisins. Stir gently; heat about 2 more minutes. Serve hot.

Carrots with Grapes

Yield: 10 to 12 servings

2 pounds fresh carrots
2 teaspoons dried basil
½ cup (1 stick) butter
1 teaspoon crushed chervil
1 clove garlic
pinch celery salt
2 cups seedless white grapes, halved
2 tablespoons freshly squeezed lemon juice
dash of salt and white pepper.

1. Clean carrots; cut into julienne strips; place in saucepan with basil, garlic clove stuck with a wooden toothpick, and water to cover; cook until tender; drain. Remove garlic.
2. Meanwhile, combine butter, chervil, and celery salt in a small saucepan. Stir until butter is melted. Toss with drained carrots.
3. Just before serving, add grapes; heat over medium heat, tossing all lightly, just until grapes are warmed. Serve.

Zesty Carrots

Yield: 6 to 8 servings

A colorful side dish with unexpected flavor.

6 large carrots, scraped and cut julienne style
2 tablespoons grated onion
½ cup mayonnaise
2 tablespoons prepared horseradish
¼ teaspoon pepper
¼ cup dry bread crumbs
2 tablespoons butter, melted

1. Place carrots in a medium saucepan; add boiling water just to cover and a pinch of salt. Cook, covered, 6 to 8 minutes.
2. Preheat oven to 350°.
3. Drain carrots, reserving ½ cup of liquid. Place carrots in a 1½-quart baking dish.
4. Combine onion, mayonnaise, horseradish, pepper and reserved liquid. Pour over carrots.
5. Toss bread crumbs with melted butter; sprinkle over sauced carrots.
6. Bake 15 minutes at 350°.

Morotspudding

Yield: 6 servings

Swedish Carrot Pudding.

½ cup (1 stick) butter, softened
½ cup brown sugar
2 eggs
1 cup carrots, grated
2 teaspoons grated lemon rind
1⅓ cup flour
1 teaspoon baking soda
¾ teaspoon baking powder
1 teaspoon cinnamon
½ teaspoon ginger

1. Preheat oven to 325°.
2. Cream butter and sugar. Add eggs, beating well after each addition. Add carrots and rind.
3. Combine dry ingredients and add to first mixture. Turn into a buttered 1-quart casserole and bake 40 to 45 minutes.
4. Serve hot.

Aunt Thelma's Corn Pudding

Yield: 6 servings

Simple, old-fashioned goodness.

2 tablespoons butter
3 tablespoons flour
¾ teaspoon salt
⅛ teaspoon pepper
1 cup milk
1 16-ounce can cream-style corn
3 eggs, well beaten

1. Preheat oven to 350°.
2. In a saucepan over low heat, melt butter. Blend in flour and salt; cook, stirring, for one minute. Gradually stir in milk. Cook over medium heat, stirring frequently, until thick.
3. Remove from heat. Add corn; blend. Mix in well-beaten eggs. Turn into a greased 1-quart baking dish.
4. Bake for one hour. Serve hot.

Green Beans in Mustard Sauce

Yield: 6 servings

An easy dress-up for beans.

1 pound whole green beans, trimmed (or 1 16-ounce box frozen whole green beans)
1 tablespoon prepared grained mustard
salt and pepper
juice of one lemon
2 to 3 tablespoons melted butter (or try 3 tablespoons olive oil for a change)

1. Cook whole beans in a large pot of boiling, salted water for 5 minutes or till crisp-tender.
2. While beans cook, combine remaining ingredients in a small bowl, stirring to blend well.
3. Drain beans. Add mustard sauce to beans and toss to coat. Serve hot in heated serving dish.

Marinated Vegetables

Most vegetables are suited to this "treat"ment.

2 pounds green beans cooked to crisp-tender and drained
½ medium onion, in rings
12 ounces fresh mushrooms, blanched and drained
good Italian dressing or vinaigrette

Dressing:

¾ cup mayonnaise
¼ cup chili sauce
2 tablespoons dried dill weed
1 tablespoon lemon juice
salt to taste

Must be made ahead.

1. Combine vegetables and marinate in refrigerator overnight. Stir occasionally.
2. Next day make dressing.
3. Drain marinade from vegetables and toss with dressing.
4. Mix well; chill until serving. Serve on a bed of lettuce.

Baked Mushrooms

Yield: 6 servings

1 pound small white mushroom caps
2 tablespoons lemon juice
1 tablespoon onion, finely chopped
3 tablespoons butter
¼ teaspoon salt
⅛ teaspoon pepper
1 tablespoon flour
2 tablespoons Parmesan cheese
1 cup light cream or half-and-half
2 egg yolks, lightly beaten
2 tablespoons bread crumbs
paprika

1. Preheat oven to 425°.
2. Sprinkle mushrooms with lemon juice. In medium skillet, sauté mushrooms with onion in butter. Sprinkle with flour, salt, pepper, and cheese. Cover and simmer 3 minutes. Put mushrooms into baking dish.
3. Combine cream and egg yolks. Pour over mushrooms. Cover with bread crumbs and touch of paprika. Bake until golden, 10 to 20 minutes.

Mushrooms Florentine

Yield: 6 to 8 servings

1 clove garlic, chopped
½ cup (1 stick) butter
1 pound mushrooms, sliced
3 packages frozen chopped spinach, thawed and drained
¼ cup chopped onion
1 teaspoon salt
pepper to taste
1 cup (4 ounces) Cheddar cheese, shredded

1. Sauté garlic in ¼ cup butter. Remove garlic and sauté mushrooms.
2. Combine spinach, onion and remaining ¼ cup melted butter. Salt and pepper to taste.
3. With this mixture cover the bottom of a 10-inch shallow casserole. Sprinkle with half the cheese. Cover with mushrooms, and then remaining cheese. Refrigerate, if desired.
4. Preheat oven to 350°. Bake casserole 20 to 30 minutes or until heated through and cheese melts.

Creamed Onions with Almonds

Yield: 6 servings

3 1-pound cans small onions, drained
½ cup seasoned white sauce or canned cream of mushroom soup concentrate
4 ounces Swiss cheese, grated
2 tablespoons dry sherry
⅓ cup sliced almonds, lightly toasted

Can be doubled.

1. Place onions in buttered casserole.
2. Combine sauce or soup with cheese and sherry. Pour over onions tossing lightly. Can refrigerate at this point.
3. Preheat oven to 350°. Sprinkle almonds over top and bake uncovered for 25 to 30 minutes or until bubbly.

Yuletide Scalloped Onions

Yield: 8 to 12 servings

2 pounds small white onions, freshly cooked
  or equivalent net weight in canned onions,
  drained (about 4 1-pound cans)
¼ cup (½ stick) butter or margarine, melted
¼ cup flour
2 cups milk
½ teaspoon salt
¼ teaspoon pepper
1 cup sharp Cheddar cheese, grated
¼ cup pimento, chopped
¼ cup parsley, chopped
½ cup bread crumbs
1 tablespoon butter, melted

1. Make basic white sauce with butter, flour, milk, salt and pepper. Bring to boil and heat 3 minutes to cook flour, stirring constantly. Stir in cheese until melted. Add pimento and parsley. Preheat oven to 375°.
2. Put onions in 1½-quart casserole. Cover with sauce. Combine butter and bread crumbs and sprinkle on as a border. Bake 15 to 20 minutes or until bubbly.

Festive Peas and Squash

Yield: 6 to 8 servings

3 pounds butternut or other winter squash
2 tablespoons butter
1 cup sour cream
½ cup onion, chopped
1 teaspoon salt, or to taste
¼ teaspoon pepper, or to taste
1 10-ounce package frozen peas
dash nutmeg, if desired

1. Preheat oven to 350°.
2. Peel and cut butternut squash. Do not wash. Place in covered casserole. Season well with salt and pepper and dot with butter. Cover and bake 35 to 45 minutes or until tender. Mash. Stir in remaining ingredients except peas. Keep covered and return to oven 10 to 15 minutes to heat through.
3. Cook peas according to package directions, drain and add nutmeg if desired.
4. Place squash in serving dish, creating a well in center. Fill with peas and serve immediately.

Pea Pods with Almonds

Yield: 6 servings

Accompanies beef nicely.

1 cup water
2 tablespoons soy sauce
1 tablespoon cornstarch
1 teaspoon chicken bouillon
¼ cup (½ stick) margarine
¼ cup slivered almonds
2 6-ounce packages frozen pea pods
½ pound mushrooms, sliced

1. Combine water, soy sauce, cornstarch and bouillon. Set aside.
2. Melt butter in large skillet. Add mushrooms. Stir to sauté a minute. Add pea pods and almonds. Stir a minute or two to heat pea pods. Add reserved liquid and stir just until thickened. Pea pods should still be green.
3. Serve immediately.

Christmas Snow Peas

Yield: 8 servings

A festive red and green mix.

2 6-ounce packages frozen pea pods
2 large sweet red peppers, roasted, seeded
   and peeled
2 tablespoons butter
1 clove garlic, minced
salt and pepper to taste

1. Roast peppers in a 450° oven until blisters form; immediately place in brown paper bag and close. Let sit for 15 minutes. Peel, seed and cut into strips.

2. Bring a large pot of salted water to boil; add pea pods, cover, and turn off heat. Let sit 2 minutes. Drain and rinse in ice water to stop cooking.

3. Melt butter in a large skillet or wok. Add garlic, pea pods and pepper strips. Sauté just until vegetables are heated through. Season to taste. Toss to mix before serving.

Hopping John (Black-eyed Peas and Rice)

Yield: 10 servings

4 strips bacon
½ cup chopped onion
2 10-ounce packages frozen black-eyed peas
   (or 2 cups freshly prepared)
½ cup uncooked long-grained white rice
2 cups water
salt and pepper to taste

1. Dice bacon and place in a Dutch oven over medium heat; add onion and cook until bacon is crisp and onions are yellow.

2. Add peas, rice and water. Cover and simmer over low heat 20 to 25 minutes, or until rice is tender. Add salt and pepper to taste.

In the South, not consuming a dish of Hopping John on New Year's Day, brings a year's bad luck or so the superstition goes. Some believe the name "Hopping John" may have derived from an old custom that children must hop once around the table before the dish is served (who knows why) while others claim it was named for a lively Southern waiter. Usually this dish accompanies pork ("black-eyed peas with 'hog-jowls'").

Chived Potatoes Au Gratin

Yield: 8 to 10 servings

3 pounds potatoes
1 large onion, chopped
⅓ cup butter
⅓ cup flour
1¼ teaspoons salt
¼ teaspoon pepper
3 cups milk
1 4-ounce jar chopped pimento
¼ cup chopped chives (fresh or frozen)
paprika

1. Peel potatoes, slice thinly. Cook in small amount of boiling salted water in a large saucepan for 5 to 8 minutes; drain.

2. Sauté onion in butter in medium-size saucepan until tender, about 3 minutes. Stir in flour, salt and pepper until smooth; cook until bubbly, 1 minute. Gradually stir in milk. Cook, stirring constantly, until mixture thickens and bubbles, about 3 minutes. Remove from heat.

3. Stir pimentos and chives into sauce.

4. Turn potatoes into buttered 2-quart casserole; pour sauce over top; stir carefully to mix. Sprinkle top with paprika.

5. Bake in 350° oven for 30 to 45 minutes, or until brown and bubbly. (45 to 60 minutes if refrigerated.)

Potato-Turnip Casserole

Yield: 8 to 10 servings

A German-style casserole which can be prepared ahead.

3 cups diced potatoes
3 cups diced yellow turnips
1½ teaspoons salt
1 tablespoon butter
1 tablespoon flour
¼ teaspoon salt
⅛ teaspoon pepper
1 cup whole milk
6 to 8 slices bacon, cooked, drained
  and crumbled
paprika

1. In a large saucepan, cook potatoes and turnips together in boiling water, with 1½ teaspoons salt, until tender, about 20 minutes. Drain.

2. Prepare white sauce: in medium saucepan, heat butter over low heat until melted; blend in flour, salt and pepper. Cook over low heat, stirring constantly, until smooth and bubbly; remove from heat. Stir in milk slowly. Heat to boiling, stirring constantly. Boil 1 minute.

3. Combine sauce with drained vegetables; pour into 1½-quart buttered casserole. Top with bacon and sprinkle with paprika. (Refrigerate until ready to use.) Bake at 350° until hot and bubbly, about 30 minutes.

Company Potatoes

**A do-ahead cheesy casserole
—ideal for a buffet.**

Yield: 8 to 10 servings

6 large potatoes
2 cups sour cream
1 cup milk
2 cups grated sharp cheese
½ cup (1 stick) butter
⅔ cup onion, chopped
salt and pepper to taste
paprika

1. Boil potatoes in skins in salted water until cooked. Chill until cold. Peel and shred on grater or in food processor.
2. In the top of a double-boiler over hot water, melt butter; add cheese, a little at a time, reserving 2 tablespoons. Mix together sour cream and milk; add to cheese mixture. Add onions and stir all together. Add to shredded potatoes.
3. Put potato mixture in a large, greased casserole. Bake, uncovered, at 350° for 45 minutes. Sprinkle top with reserved cheese and paprika; bake 5 more minutes.

Fluffed Sweets

Yield: 4 to 6 servings

1 pound sweet potatoes (not yams)
salt and pepper
¼ cup (½ stick) butter
milk
Marshmallow Fluff

1. Cook, drain, peel and mash potatoes. (If using canned potatoes, heat thoroughly then mash.)
2. With electric mixer whip potatoes with the butter, salt and pepper to taste, and enough milk to make a nice mashed potato consistency.
3. Add two generous spoonsful (about ¼ cup each) Marshmallow Fluff and whip until completely combined. Serve immediately or keep warm.

Glazed Sweet Potatoes

Yield: 6 to 8 servings

6 sweet potatoes, boiled or baked
¾ cup dark brown sugar
2 tablespoons orange juice
2 tablespoons butter
½ teaspoon grated lemon rind
½ cup walnuts, coarsely chopped, optional

1. Preheat oven to 350°.
2. Peel potatoes and slice in half lengthwise.
3. Combine sugar, juice, butter and rind. Bring to a boil.
4. Layer potatoes in shallow baking dish. Cover with syrup. Bake 15 to 30 minutes or until heated through. Baste occasionally.
5. Sprinkle with nuts when serving.

Sweet Potato-Apple Casserole

Yield: 8 to 10 servings

Delicious accompaniment to the holiday bird.

6 large sweet potatoes
6 large tart apples
½ cup brown sugar
½ cup honey
1 teaspoon allspice
½ cup (1 stick) butter, melted
2 teaspoons lemon juice
2 tablespoons brandy or cream sherry

1. Boil potatoes in skins until tender. Peel and slice about ¼ inch thick.
2. Peel and slice the apples. Preheat oven to 375°.
3. Combine remaining ingredients.
4. Butter a 1½- to 2-quart casserole and layer potatoes and apples, ending with potatoes, coating each layer with some of sugar mixture.
5. Bake 45 to 60 minutes.

Sweet Potato-Cranberry Casserole

Yield: 10 servings

2 large (17-ounce) cans sweet potatoes
2 16-ounce cans whole cranberry sauce
½ cup brown sugar
¼ cup (½ stick) butter or margarine, melted
2 cups coarse bread crumbs

1. Preheat oven to 350°.
2. Slice potatoes. Stir cranberry sauce. Layer potatoes with sauce in buttered 1½-quart casserole.
3. Combine butter and sugar. Toss with bread crumbs. Top the casserole with this mixture and bake about 35 minutes or until potatoes are hot.

Sweet Potatoes in Orange Shells

Yield: 8 servings

A striking, edible garnish when used to surround the roast or bird.

4 large navel oranges
6 medium-size sweet potatoes
  (2½ to 3 pounds)
6 tablespoons butter
¼ cup bourbon
2 tablespoons brown sugar
¼ teaspoon nutmeg
¼ teaspoon cinnamon

Garnish: parsley and chopped pecans
if desired

1. Cut oranges in half; scoop out pulp being careful not to tear skins. Scallop edges of orange shells using a small knife to make V-cuts.
2. Cook sweet potatoes in boiling salted water in a large saucepan for 30 minutes or until tender.
3. Drain potatoes; peel. Place in a large bowl and mash together with bourbon, brown sugar, nutmeg and cinnamon. Beat until smooth and fluffy. Spoon into orange shells. Refrigerate for baking later, if desired.
4. Bake in hot oven (400°) for 15 minutes or till heated through. Garnish with parsley and chopped pecans, if desired.

Mandarin Sweet Potato Casserole

Yield: 10 servings

A not-too-sweet casserole.

2 29-ounce cans cut sweet potatoes, drained
6 tablespoons butter, melted
½ cup brown sugar, firmly packed
¼ cup dark rum
½ teaspoon salt
1 11-ounce can mandarin oranges
¼ cup chopped pecans

1. Preheat oven to 375°. Grease a 2-quart casserole.
2. With mixer at low speed, or in food processor, whip together sweet potatoes, 2 tablespoons butter, 4 tablespoons brown sugar, rum, and salt.
3. Drain mandarin oranges reserving ¼ cup syrup. Add syrup to sweet potatoes; mix until smooth. Fold oranges into mixture, reserving several for top. Turn into casserole.
4. Arrange reserved orange sections attractively on top of sweet potatoes. Combine 4 tablespoons brown sugar, 4 tablespoons butter, and chopped pecans. Sprinkle over the top.
5. Bake for 30 minutes, (45 minutes if refrigerated).

Fresh Spinach Casserole

Yield: 6 servings

Fresh spinach is a must in this delicious dish.

1 10-ounce bag fresh spinach, washed and trimmed
1 cup fresh bread crumbs
1 cup heavy cream
1 egg, beaten
1 teaspoon salt
¼ teaspoon pepper
1 teaspoon Worcestershire sauce
½ cup grated sharp Cheddar cheese
paprika

1. Preheat oven to 350°. Grease a 2-quart casserole dish.
2. Tear spinach into bite-size pieces. Combine with bread crumbs.
3. Combine cream, egg, salt, pepper, and Worcestershire. Pour over spinach and mix. Pour all into casserole. Refrigerate, if desired.
4. Sprinkle with grated cheese and paprika. Place casserole in a pan full of hot water which comes 2 inches up the side of the casserole dish. Bake for 35 minutes or until set.

Rice and Cheese Casserole

Yield: 4 to 6 servings

A great way to use up leftover boiled rice.

2 cups cooked rice
2 eggs, beaten
2 cups milk
⅓ cup butter, melted
1 cup chopped fresh parsley
1 cup grated cheese
1 small onion, grated
1 teaspoon salt
pepper to taste

1. Preheat oven to 400°. Butter a 1½-quart casserole.
2. Combine all ingredients; mix well. Pour into buttered casserole. Refrigerate, if desired.
3. Place casserole inside large pan of hot water which comes halfway up the side of casserole. Bake for 45 to 50 minutes, or until brown on top and set.

Zucchini Casserole

Yield: 6 to 8 servings

2 pounds zucchini squash, washed and dried
1 green pepper, chopped
1 clove garlic, minced
2 small onions, chopped
½ cup (1 stick) butter
½ cup bread crumbs
½ cup parsley, chopped
3 eggs, beaten
½ cup Parmesan cheese, grated
salt and pepper to taste

1. Preheat oven to 350°.
2. Coarsely grate unpeeled zucchini.
3. Sauté pepper, garlic, and onions in butter.
4. Add zucchini, bread crumbs, parsley and eggs. Mix well.
5. Pour into greased 8-inch square or 1½-quart baking dish. Cover with Parmesan. Bake about 45 minutes.

BAKED SWEET POTATOES: Try baking Sweet Potatoes as you would white potatoes. Serve with salt, pepper and butter. It's a wonderful experience to have a sweet potato without added sugar!

FAVORITE TOPPING FOR BAKED, WHITE POTATOES: Sautéed chopped onions mixed with cooked crumbled bacon, with or without sour cream or butter.

BAKED POTATO SKINS: Scoop out most of the cooked potato, coat inside and outside with oil or oil and butter, season with salt, pepper, garlic, onion, paprika, or herbs of choice. Return to oven and heat 10 to 15 minutes at 400°. For brunch fill with scrambled eggs and top with some warm asparagus tips and hollandaise.

Memorable Family Recipes

Recipe _____ Dates Served _____

Ingredients _____

_____

_____

_____

_____

Procedure _____

_____

_____

_____

_____

_____

_____

_____

Comments _____

_____

Additional blank pages are provided for your use at the end of the book.

Salads

Salads

Vegetable

Molded

Fruit

Dressings

Accompaniments

• **Indicates items suitable for gift giving**

Bibb Lettuce, Kiwi and Cucumber Salad   Yield: 4 servings

**Another time substitute pears or
mandarin oranges for the Kiwi fruit.**

1 head Bibb lettuce, torn into bite-size pieces
3 Kiwi fruits, peeled and thinly sliced
1 seedless cucumber, thinly sliced
4 scallions, sliced
salt, freshly ground pepper

$100 Salad Dressing (see p. 137)

1. Place the lettuce, fruit, cucumbers and scallions in a salad bowl.
2. Toss lightly with $100 Salad Dressing and add salt and freshly ground pepper to taste.

Boston Lettuce with Grapes and Walnuts   Yield: 4 to 6 servings

2 to 4 small heads Boston or butter lettuce, washed and torn in bite-size pieces
⅔ cup walnut pieces
½ cup Feta cheese, crumbled (4 ounces)
1 cup seedless grapes, red or white, sliced in half
5 tablespoons walnut oil
3 tablespoons vegetable oil
2 tablespoons white wine vinegar
salt and pepper

1. In a large salad bowl toss together lettuce, walnuts, crumbled cheese and grapes.
2. In a small screw top jar combine oils, vinegar, and freshly ground black pepper to taste. Shake well until dressing appears creamy.
3. Drizzle dressing over salad and toss just before serving.

Curried Rice Salad   Yield: 6 servings

1 package Uncle Ben's chicken-flavored rice
2 green onions, chopped
½ green pepper, chopped
½ cup stuffed green olives, sliced
2 ounces marinated artichokes, chopped
¼ teaspoon curry powder
⅓ cup mayonnaise

1. Cook rice (omitting butter) according to directions.
2. Add vegetables reserving artichoke marinade.
3. Combine marinade with mayonnaise and curry. Fold into rice.
4. Serve warm or cold. Cooked chicken, turkey or seafood may be added.

Broccoli Avocado Salad

Yield: 6 servings

Pretty colors mingled together.

1 bunch broccoli
½ cup sliced ripe olives
2 sweet red peppers
¼ cup chopped green onion
2 ripe avocados

1. Cut broccoli into flowerets. Bring pot of salted water to boil. Add broccoli; cover; turn off heat and leave for 2 minutes. Drain and immediately rinse broccoli in cold water. Drain again. Put in glass salad bowl.
2. Core and seed red pepper. Slice into thin strips. Add with olives and green onions to broccoli. (May be done ahead to here, mixed with dressing below and refrigerated.) Add peeled, sliced avocado just before serving. Toss gently.

Dressing:
⅓ cup oil
1 tablespoon lemon juice
1 tablespoon vinegar
1 teaspoon herb seasoning salt
½ teaspoon dried basil

Dressing:
In a screwtop jar combine all ingredients. Shake well. Pour over salad and toss.

Oriental Pea Pod Salad

Yield: 6 servings

¾ pound pea pods (or 2 6-ounce packages frozen pea pods)
1 pint cherry tomatoes, halved
2 fresh water chestnuts*, peeled and sliced (or one 5-ounce can water chesnuts, sliced)
4 green onions, chopped

Dressing:
⅓ cup peanut oil
1 tablespoon rice vinegar
1 tablespoon lemon juice
¼ teaspoon roasted sesame oil
1 clove garlic, finely minced
½ teaspoon salt
1 tablespoon sugar

*available in oriental food stores. Fresh water chestnuts have a sweet, crisp, apple-like flavor.

Cooked white rice may be added to stretch recipe.

1. In a large pot bring salted water to boil. Add pea pods, immediately turn off heat and cover pot. Let stand for 1 to 2 minutes. Drain. Rinse pea pods in cold water. Drain.
2. Add tomatoes, water chestnuts and green onion. Set aside.
3. In a screwtop jar, combine all dressing ingredients. Shake well.
4. Pour dressing over pea pod mixture in a large bowl. Toss lightly to coat.
5. Chill a couple of hours before serving.

Pickled Beet Salad

Yield: 4 servings

1 bunch fresh beets
¼ cup cooking water
⅓ cup wine vinegar
¼ cup light brown sugar
½ teaspoon cinnamon
¼ teaspoon EACH allspice, cloves, salt
red onion
lettuce
sour cream

Must be made ahead.

1. Cook fresh beets by cutting off stems and tips and cooking until tender in boiling salted water. Cool.
2. Slip off outer skin and slice beets thinly. Set aside.
3. Reserve ¼ cup cooking water and combine with remaining ingredients in small saucepan. Heat until boiling.
4. Add beets, cover and simmer 5 minutes. Chill overnight.
5. To serve: drain pickled beets; place on bed of lettuce and top with onions and sour cream.

Creamy Spinach Salad

Yield: 6 servings

1 16-ounce package fresh spinach
½ pound bacon
½ cup scallions, chopped
2 hard-boiled eggs, chopped
¼ pound mushrooms, sliced
¾ cup herbed croutons, optional

Dressing:
½ cup mayonnaise
½ cup salad oil
¼ cup lemon juice
1 tablespoon tarragon vinegar
1½ teaspoons prepared mustard
¼ teaspoon sugar
salt and pepper to taste

1. Wash, trim and dry spinach leaves. Break into bite-size pieces and put into plastic bag with some paper toweling to keep crisp. Refrigerate.
2. Cook bacon until crisp. Drain and crumble.
3. Combine dressing ingredients and store in refrigerator until needed.
4. Assembly: Put spinach in large bowl. Decoratively arrange other ingredients over top. Bring to table. Add dressing just before tossing.

Spinach-Chutney Salad

Yield: 6 servings

1 pound fresh spinach, washed, dried, torn
   into smaller pieces
¼ pound fresh mushrooms, sliced
½ cup walnuts, coarsely chopped
¼ pound bacon, cooked, drained, crumbled
2 apples, cored, sliced
1 ripe avocado, peeled and sliced
2 ounces Gruyeré cheese, grated

Dressing:
¼ cup red wine vinegar
3 tablespoons Chutnut or chutney
1 clove garlic, crushed
2 tablespoons coarse mustard
2 teaspoons sugar
⅓ cup salad oil

1. Place all dressing ingredients except oil in blender. Blend well. Add oil slowly until well mixed.
2. Store in covered container in refrigerator, but serve at room temperature.
3. Combine salad ingredients. Toss with dressing.

Zucchini and Hearts of Palm

Yield: 6 servings

An ideal salad when advance preparation is desired.

3 large (or 4 small) zucchini
2 14-ounce cans hearts of palm
juice of 3 lemons
½ teaspoon marjoram
½ teaspoon oregano
2 cloves garlic, minced
¼ teaspoon pepper
1 teaspoon salt
3 tablespoons peanut oil (no substitute)

Note: Peanut oil is essential for delicate flavor combination.

Must be made ahead.

1. Trim ends of zucchini, scrub, but do not peel. Cut into thin, pencil-like strips. Place in a large glass salad bowl.
2. Rinse hearts of palm in cold water; pat dry, cut into similar-size thin strips. Add to bowl. Toss gently with zucchini.
3. In a small screwtop jar put remaining ingredients. Shake well. Drizzle over vegetables; toss lightly, mixing well.
4. Chill well before serving, allowing flavors to marry.

Cranberry-Port Wine Salad

Yield: 8 servings

1 3-ounce package raspberry jello
1 cup boiling water
¼ cup cold water
¼ cup port wine
1 16-ounce can whole cranberry sauce
1 small can crushed pineapple in own juice, drained well
1 11-ounce can mandarin oranges, drained
¼ cup walnuts or pecans, chopped

1. Dissolve jello in boiling water. Add cold water and port. Refrigerate until partially set.
2. With a fork, break up cranberry sauce. Add pineapple, oranges and nuts.
3. Pour into 6-cup mold and refrigerate several hours or overnight. Unmold onto a bed of lettuce to serve.

Frozen Cranberry Salad

Yield: 12 servings

1 cup heavy cream
¼ cup sugar
2 tablespoons mayonnaise or salad dressing
1 16-ounce can whole cranberry sauce
½ 6-ounce can (about ⅓ cup) frozen orange juice concentrate, thawed

Must be made ahead.

1. Whip cream and sugar to soft peaks.
2. Break up cranberry sauce with fork.
3. Combine orange juice and mayonnaise.
4. Fold orange juice mixture into cream, then cranberries into cream.
5. Line 12 muffin tins with foil baking cups. Fill cups and freeze. When solid, store in plastic bags.
6. To serve: remove from cups and place on lettuce on individual plates. Serve immediately.

Molded Beet Wreath

Smooth texture, beautiful color!

Yield: 6 to 8 servings

1 16-ounce can sliced beets
1 3-ounce package lemon gelatin
1 can consommé
1 cup sour cream
¼ of a fresh lemon, peeled and seeded
½ teaspoon salt
½ small onion, quartered

Must be made ahead.

1. Grease a 5- to 6-cup ring mold.
2. Drain beets, reserving liquid. Measure liquid in measuring cup; add enough consommé to make one cup (save the rest of consommé for another use). Heat liquid just to a simmer.
3. In a blender or food processor, combine hot liquid with gelatin; blend at low speed for 20 seconds. Add remaining ingredients and blend on high for 10 to 20 seconds.
4. Pour into mold and chill until firm.
5. To serve: unmold on bed of salad greens and serve with sour cream.

133

Christmas Layered Aspic

Red tomato layers alternate with green avocado layers.

Yield: two 8-cup molds, 20 servings
    May be halved

Tomato Aspic:

1 46-ounce can tomato juice
4 dashes Tabasco sauce
2 tablespoons prepared horseradish
1 tablespoon lemon juice
¼ cup catsup
1 teaspoon salt
1 tablespoon liquid from dill pickles
    or ½ teaspoon dried dill weed
1 teaspoon Worcestershire sauce
2 tablespoons tarragon vinegar
½ teaspoon garlic salt
1 tablespoon sugar
4 envelopes unflavored gelatin

1. Heat all ingredients together in a large saucepan, stirring frequently until gelatin dissolves. Cool.
2. Chill until a spoonful will mound.

Avocado Aspic:

1 cup mayonnaise
2 cups canned chicken broth
2⅔ cups milk
4 envelopes unflavored gelatin
1½ large avocados, peeled, pitted and cubed
½ cup lemon juice
3 tablespoons prepared hot mustard
1 tablespoon caper juice
3 dashes Tabasco sauce
1 teaspoon salt
1 cucumber, peeled, seeded and finely chopped
1 cup thinly sliced scallion
½ green pepper, minced
1 cup diced celery

Garnish:

½ large avocado, sliced
lemon juice
watercress

Must be made ahead.

1. Mix mayonnaise, chicken broth, 2 cups milk and gelatin, heat together until gelatin dissolves. Cool.
2. In blender, or food processor, purée avocado with lemon juice. Mix in mustard, caper juice, Tabasco, ⅔ cup milk and salt and process until smooth and creamy.
3. Combine mayonnaise-gelatin mixture with avocado mixture. Fold in chopped vegetables.
4. Chill until a spoonful will mound.

To Mold:

1. Grease two 8-cup ring molds. Alternate layers of tomato aspic with avocado for a ribbon effect. Or marbelize by placing alternate spoonsful of red and green around bottom of mold; reverse spoonsful in second layer and alternate until mold is full. Then carefully, with spatula, draw three concentric rings through mixture.
2. Chill molds until firm.
3. Unmold on large round platter. Garnish with avocado crescents, which have been dipped in lemon juice, and watercress sprigs.

Gingered Cranberry Mold

Yield: 10 to 12 servings

A subtle hint of ginger adds spark.

4 cups raw cranberries
2 cups sugar
juice of 3 medium-sized oranges
2 envelopes unflavored gelatin
½ cup cold water
½ cup boiling water
½ cup pineapple juice
1 teaspoon ground ginger
1 cup finely chopped pecans
½ cup canned crushed pineapple
3 tablespoons finely chopped ginger crystals

Garnish: whipped cream,
chopped ginger crystals

Must be made ahead.

1. In food processor or food grinder, coarsely grind cranberries. Mix with sugar and orange juice; let stand about 3 hours.
2. Soak gelatin in cold water to soften. Add boiling water, pineapple juice and ground ginger. Refrigerate until gelatin just begins to thicken.
3. Add cranberries, nuts, pineapple, and ginger crystals. Pour into an oiled 8-cup mold. Refrigerate until firm.
4. To serve: unmold on a platter decorated with salad greens. Accompany with whipped cream dressing into which chopped crystallized ginger has been mixed.

Red Pepper Jelly Aspic

Yield: 10 to 12 servings

A piquant, but not-too-hot taste compliments a roast.

4 cups V-8 juice
3 tablespoons confectioners' sugar
1 tablespoon dried tarragon
½ cup mild vinegar (or tarragon vinegar)
3 tablespoons lemon juice
4 tablespoons (4 packets) unflavored gelatin, softened in ½ cup cold water
5 ounces red pepper jelly*

Garnish: arugula or other salad greens

*Available in gourmet or specialty food departments, or use recipe on page 228.

Must be made ahead.

1. Oil 12 individual aspic molds or a 6-quart ring mold.
2. Heat 1½ cups juice with sugar and tarragon. Add vinegar and lemon juice. Add gelatin; stir until dissolved. Add jelly; stir until dissolved. Add remaining V-8 juice.
3. Pour into molds. chill until set, at least 3 hours of overnight.
4. To serve: unmold on bed of arugula or watercress; accompany with Green Goddess dressing, if desired.

Snappy Aspic

Yield: 4 to 6 servings

A surprising combination, great with beef.

2 cups tomato-vegetable juice
1 3-ounce package strawberry gelatin
½ of a 5-ounce bottle prepared horseradish

Must be made ahead.

1. Heat vegetable juice in a saucepan to a boil. Remove from heat.
2. Stir gelatin into heated juice until dissolved. Add horseradish; stir well.
3. Pour into oiled 4-cup mold. Refrigerate until set, at least three hours.
4. To serve, unmold on bed of greens.

Cranberries 'n Cream Salad

Yield: 6 to 8 servings

Serve this in a clear glass or crystal bowl to show off its lovely color.

1 12-ounce package fresh cranberries
1 cup sugar
1 cup red grapes, halved and seeded
1 cup chopped apple with peel
1 cup drained pineapple chunks
½ cup chopped pecans
1 cup heavy cream

Must be made ahead.

1. Wash and pick over cranberries. Grind up coarsely in food processor or meat grinder. Stir in sugar; allow to sit several hours or overnight.
2. Drain juice from cranberries. Combine all fruits and nuts.
3. Whip cream; fold into fruit mixture. Chill.

Five Cup Salad

Yield: 10 to 12 servings

5 apples, unpeeled and chopped
5 bananas, sliced
1½ cups purple grapes, halved and seeded or seedless red grapes, halved
1 cup pecans, broken
1 20-ounce can unsweetened pineapple chunks, reserve juice
1 cup heavy cream

Sauce:

2 eggs, beaten
juice of 1 lemon (3 tablespoons)
reserved pineapple juice
½ cup sugar
2 tablespoons cornstarch

Many varieties of fruits can be used with this dressing. Perishable fruits such as bananas or apples should be added just before serving.

1. In small pan, combine sauce ingredients. Heat gently stirring until thickened. Cool.
2. Combine fruits and nuts. Whip cream and fold into sauce. Fold cream mixture into fruits and refrigerate until serving.

$100 French Dressing

Yield: 1 pint

So-called because that's what someone had paid the Waldorf-Astoria's chef for the recipe over 50 years ago.

1 teaspoon salt
1 teaspoon dry mustard
1 teaspoon paprika
1 teaspoon celery seed
1 tablespoon grated onion
¼ cup + 2 tablespoons sugar
¼ cup vinegar
1 cup vegetable oil

1. Put all in double boiler and stir well over hot water until lukewarm.
2. Remove from heat and beat until slightly thickened.
3. Cover and store in refrigerator.

Blue Cheese and Chive Dressing

Yield: 3 cups

1 pint mayonnaise
½ tablespoon Worcestershire sauce
½ cup cider vinegar
2 tablespoons chives, chopped
¼ cup sugar
4 ounces blue cheese, crumbled

1. Combine all ingredients except cheese. Mix well with whisk or beater.
2. Add blue cheese. Mix in but leave small pieces of cheese visible.
3. Store in covered container in refrigerator.

Cranberry-Pear Relish

Yield: 8 cups

A spiced fruit accompaniment with a little zip of orange liqueur.

2 pounds fresh cranberries
3 pears, cored and diced
2 apples, cored and diced
2 cups golden raisins
1½ cups sugar
1 cup fresh orange juice
2 tablespoons grated orange peel
2 tablespoons cinnamon
¼ teaspoon freshly ground nutmeg
½ cup Cointreau

Must be made ahead.

1. Heat all ingredients, except liqueur, in a large saucepan to boiling; reduce heat.
2. Simmer, uncovered, stirring frequently, until mixture thickens, about 45 minutes.
3. Remove from heat; stir in liqueur. Refrigerate, covered 4 hours or overnight. Serve slightly chilled.

Cranberry Sherbet

Yield: 10 to 12 servings

**An alternative to cranberry sauce.
A rich red sorbet.**

2 12-ounce packages fresh cranberries
1 pint water
2 cups sugar
1 large navel orange, juice and grated rind

Must be made ahead.

1. Bring cranberries and water to boil then simmer until berries pop and become soft.
2. Press through sieve. Add sugar and rind to fruit and heat again until sugar dissolves. Add orange juice and cool.
3. Freeze in tray until firm. Break up and beat with electric mixer or process in food processor.
4. Pack in freezer container and store in freezer to use at moment's notice.

Cheese Custards

Yield: 6 servings

4 eggs
1 cup milk
¼ teaspoon baking soda
1 teaspoon cornstarch
2 tablespoons butter
6 tablespoons grated Cheddar cheese
pepper to taste
1 teaspoon salt

1. Preheat oven to 450°.
   Grease 6 custard cups.
2. Beat eggs until light and fluffy.
3. Heat milk with soda and cornstarch, just to boiling point. Stir into eggs. Add butter, cheese, pepper and salt. Beat well.
4. Pour into custard cups. Bake for approximately 15 minutes.

Ginny's great-grandfather was from New Bedford. At the age of 18, in the 1860's, he set sail on a whaling ship, eventually ending up in Puget Sound. There he met Ginny's great-grandmother. This recipe comes from a handwritten collection compiled by their daughter, Mabel, Ginny's grandmother. And Ginny? She lives on the Connecticut coast, back in New England. We present the recipe in the original and with modern instructions.

"Beat the eggs very light and pour upon them the heated milk (with a pinch of soda) having thickened with cornstarch. While warm add butter, pepper, salt and cheese. Beat well and pour into greased custard cups. Bake in a quick oven about 15 minutes or until high and brown. Serve at once as a separate course with bread and butter after soup or before dessert."

Curried Fruit

Yield: 6 cups

A lightly curried accompaniment for ham, roast pork or lamb.

⅓ cup butter
¾ cup brown sugar
4 teaspoons curry powder
1 16-ounce can pear slices, drained
1 16-ounce can peach slices, drained
1 17-ounce can apricot halves, drained
1 20-ounce can pineapple chunks, drained
5 or 6 maraschino cherries, sliced (optional)

Must be made ahead.

1. Preheat oven to 325°.
2. Melt butter in small saucepan, add brown sugar and curry; mix well.
3. Spread drained fruit on paper towels to dry. Place fruit in a 1½-quart casserole. Add butter mixture.
4. Bake, uncovered, for 1 hour. May be reheated.

Glazed Apricot Garnish

An attractive garnish for poultry or pork.

1 1-pound can whole apricots, drained
½ cup apricot juice (drained from above)
1 cup brown sugar
¼ cup (½ stick) butter
whole cloves

Must be made ahead.

1. Put all ingredients, except cloves, in large saucepan or skillet and heat slowly at a simmer, turning apricots often to glaze all over.
2. Drain apricots and stick each apricot with about 9 whole cloves in a decorative arrangement.

Hot Fruit Compote

Yield: 10 to 12 servings

Deliciously simple accompaniment to ham, turkey or chicken.

1 16-ounce can sliced peaches
1 16-ounce can sliced pears
1 17-ounce can apricot halves
1 20-ounce can pineapple chunks
1 21-ounce can cherry pie filling
½ cup dry white wine

1. Drain syrup from all canned fruits. Add cherry pie filling and wine; mix well. Pour into a 2-quart casserole; cover.
2. Bake at 350° for 25 minutes. Serve hot.

Pear Sauce

A pleasant change from applesauce.

Yield: 1½ cups

6 pears (not too ripe), peeled, cored,
   and quartered
1 lemon, peeled, seeded, and quartered
1½ cups sugar, or more to taste
½ teaspoon nutmeg

**Store as you would applesauce or ladle into hot
sterilized jars and seal with melted paraffin.**

1. In the bowl of a food processor, process
   half the pears and lemon; pour into a large
   saucepan. Process remaining pears
   and lemon.

2. Add sugar and nutmeg to pears. Cook,
   covered, on low heat for about 30 minutes.
   Add more sugar, if necessary. Continue
   cooking about an hour more, or until sauce
   is the thickness of thick applesauce.

Pineapple Sorbet

**Refreshing as a first course or
between courses.**

Yield: 8 to 10 servings

2 large (20-ounce) cans pineapple slices,
   in own juice
Champagne, optional

1. Drain pineapple, reserving juice.
2. Place rings on cookie sheet and freeze.
3. When pineapple is solid, break into smaller
   pieces and, a third at a time, purée in the
   food processor.
4. Add some of the reserved juice while
   processing (up to ½ cup total). Final product
   should be smooth and creamy, but will hold
   its shape.
5. With ice cream scoop, form balls of sorbet
   and place on cookie sheet. Freeze until firm.
   Remove from sheet and store in plastic bag
   in freezer until needed.
6. To serve: put sorbet into sherbet or wine
   glasses and pour over it a little champagne,
   if desired.

**Save the unused portion of a jar of pimentos or olives by
covering them with a little white vinegar and water.
Cover tightly and refrigerate.**

Pineapple "Spoonbread"

Yield: 8 to 10 servings

A different accompaniment for ham or pork main dishes.

½ cup sugar
1 tablespoon flour
¼ teaspoon salt
3 eggs, lightly beaten
1 20-ounce can crushed pineapple, undrained
4 slices good white bread, cubed
½ cup (1 stick) butter, melted

1. Preheat oven to 350°. Grease a 2-quart casserole.
2. Mix sugar, flour and salt together. Beat in eggs. Add pineapple with juice.
3. Pour into casserole. Toss together bread cubes and melted butter; place on top of pineapple mixture.
4. Bake for one hour.

Spiced Cranberries in Sherry

Yield: 2 pints

Fills kitchen with a wonderful aroma.

2½ cups sugar
½ cup water
2 sticks whole cinnamon
1 teaspoon ground cloves
juice and grated rind of 1 lemon
16 ounces fresh cranberries
⅓ cup cream sherry

1. In medium pan, combine all ingredients except cranberries and sherry. Simmer 5 minutes.
2. Add cranberries and cook slowly until most of the skins pop. Remove from heat and stir in sherry.
3. Cool and refrigerate. Keeps well.

Memorable Family Recipes

Recipe _____ Dates Served _____

Ingredients _____

_____

_____

_____

_____

Procedure _____

_____

_____

_____

_____

_____

_____

_____

_____

Comments _____

_____

Additional blank pages are provided for your use at the end of the book.

Desserts

Desserts

• **Indicates items suitable for gift giving**

Athole Brose

Yield: 8 servings

Fashioned after a Scottish New Year's drink.

½ cup fine scotch
⅔ cup honey
1 pint (2 cups) heavy cream

Make a day ahead.

1. In small bowl combine honey and scotch. Stir together until thoroughly combined.
2. Whip cream to stiff peaks.
3. Fold scotch mixture gently but thoroughly into whipped cream.
4. Pour into serving dishes and place in freezer. When firm, cover with plastic wrap and leave overnight.
5. Serve directly from freezer. Sprinkle with nutmeg or grated chocolate, if desired.

"Blue Nose" Torte

Yield: 8 to 9 servings

Named for the ship that serves this while sailing from Maine to Nova Scotia.

2 cups crushed vanilla wafers
   (about 4 cups uncrushed)
2 cups chopped fresh cranberries
⅔ cup granulated sugar
½ cup (1 stick) butter
2 eggs
1 cup confectioners' sugar
1 cup heavy cream
½ cup pecans or walnuts, chopped

Must be made ahead.

1. Mix cranberries with sugar and set aside for half an hour.
2. Cover the bottom of an ungreased 8-inch square pan with 1 cup vanilla wafer crumbs.
3. Cream butter and confectioners' sugar. Add eggs and beat thoroughly. Spread over crumbs
4. Top with cranberries, then with nuts.
5. Whip cream and spread over nuts. Top with remaining crumbs.
6. Refrigerate several hours or overnight. Cut into squares to serve.

Black and White Dessert

Yield: 8 servings

The best of both chocolate worlds.

6 ounces semi-sweet chocolate
8 ounces white chocolate
4 ounces unsalted butter, softened
4 ounces (½ cup) heavy cream
8 foil muffin liners

Garnish: Pistachios, coarsely chopped

**It is necessary to use high quality chocolates.
Must be made ahead.**

1. Melt semi-sweet chocolate. Spoon into foil liners, taking care to cover bottom and sides evenly. Place in muffin tins and refrigerate until firm. Peel away the foil and set aside.
2. Melt white chocolate. Cool.
3. Whip cream and refrigerate.
4. With electric mixer cream butter until soft and fluffy. Beat in the cooled white chocolate. Fold in the whipped cream. Spoon into the chocolate cups. Garnish with pistachios and refrigerate.
5. Remove from refrigerator 30 minutes before serving.

Christmas Macaroon Torte

Yield: 6 to 8 servings

1 cup flaked coconut
½ cup graham cracker crumbs
⅓ cup chopped nuts
½ cup chopped red and green
 candied cherries
4 egg whites, room temperature
dash salt
1 teaspoon almond or vanilla extract
1 cup sugar

1. Preheat oven to 350°.
2. Grease a 9-inch pie plate.
3. Combine coconut, crumbs, nuts and cherries. Set aside.
4. In a large mixing bowl, free of grease, beat egg whites and salt until soft peaks form. Slowly add sugar, one tablespoon at a time, beating until stiff. Add almond.
5. Fold in first mixture thoroughly. Spread in prepared pie plate and bake for 30 to 35 minutes until lightly browned. Cool on wire rack.
6. Serve with whipped cream, garnished with additional chopped cherries.

**Save lemon and orange rinds; freeze and grate as needed.
Or candy them for holiday use.**

Chocolate Mousse-cake in Hazelnut Meringue   Yield: 8 to 10 servings

Merry Christmas to Chocolate-Lovers!

Meringue Crust:

3 egg whites, room temperature
¼ teaspoon cream of tartar
pinch of salt
1 cup sugar
30 2-inch saltine crackers, ground to
    fine crumbs
1 cup chopped hazelnuts
    or other chopped nuts

Chocolate Filling:

½ cup (1 stick) butter
2 ounces unsweetened chocolate
2 eggs
1 cup sugar
¼ cup flour
2 teaspoons vanilla extract

Vanilla ice cream

Must be made ahead.

Crust preparation:

1. Preheat oven to 350°. Butter 10-inch
   ovenproof glass pie plate.
2. In large bowl of mixer beat egg whites,
   cream of tartar, and salt at high speed to soft
   peaks. Gradually add sugar; beat until stiff
   but not dry.
3. Fold in cracker crumbs and nuts. Spoon into
   prepared pie plate, spreading up sides. Bake
   until light golden, about 12 minutes.
4. Cool to room temperature. Press down
   gently with palm of hand to create a well.

Filling preparation: Keep oven at 350°.

1. Melt butter and chocolate in double boiler
   over simmering water. Stir until smooth.
   Cool slightly but do not allow mixture to set.
2. Beat eggs and sugar together at high speed
   until slowly dissolving ribbon forms when
   beaters are lifted.
3. Add flour; beat until smooth. Add chocolate
   mixture and vanilla extract; beat 1 minute.
4. Pour into crust. Bake at 350° until set,
   about 35 minutes. Cool to room temperature.
5. Serve topped with a scoop of vanilla
   ice cream.

Cranberry Almost Pie   Yield: 8 servings

Great served warm with ice cream.

2 cups fresh cranberries
½ cup sugar
⅓ cup chopped walnuts or pecans
2 eggs
1 cup sugar
1 cup flour
¾ cup (1½ sticks) butter, melted

1. Preheat oven to 325°. Grease well a 10-inch
   pie plate.
2. Spread dry cranberries over bottom of pie
   plate. Sprinkle with nuts and ½ cup sugar.
3. In small bowl of electric mixer, beat eggs
   well; add 1 cup sugar and beat until well
   mixed. Add flour and melted butter, beat
   well. Pour over cranberries.
4. Bake for about 1 hour or until golden brown.

147

Dolce Maddalena

Yield: 8 servings

A ravishingly rich, frozen dessert.

2 packages ladyfingers, or enough to line a
  1-quart Charlotte mold or bowl
¼ cup Marsala
2 eggs, separated
½ cup sugar
¾ cup ricotta cheese
16 double Amaretti macaroons, crushed
4 ounces mini chocolate chips
½ cup candied fruit
¼ cup finely chopped toasted almonds

Must be made ahead.

1. Sprinkle lady fingers with Marsala. Line sides and bottom of mold with ladyfingers, browned side to the outside.

2. Beat the egg yolks with the sugar until thick and heavy. Mix in the ricotta. Stir in crushed macaroons, chocolate chips, candied fruit and almonds.

3. Beat egg whites until they hold stiff peaks. Fold into ricotta mixture; spoon into prepared mold. Tap mold to get rid of any air pockets. Cover top with more Marsala-soaked ladyfingers. Cover mold with plastic wrap and freeze.

4. Unmold by dipping mold quickly into hot water. Serve in thin slices.

Egg Nog Mousse with Scarlet Sauce

Yield: 8 servings

A light and delicate ending to a heavy meal.

Egg Nog Mousse:
2 envelopes unflavored gelatin
½ cup cold water
1 quart prepared egg nog
¼ teaspoon nutmeg
2 tablespoons rum
16 to 18 double ladyfingers, split
1 cup walnuts, chopped

Mousse preparation:
1. In a small saucepan, soften gelatin in ½ cup cold water. Meanwhile, line bottom of 8-inch springform pan with ladyfingers cut to fit; stand others around sides. Sprinkle liberally with rum.

2. Add 1 cup egg nog to saucepan with softened gelatin; heat until gelatin is dissolved. Remove from heat. Add remaining egg nog, nutmeg and rum. Chill.

3. When egg nog is partialy set, beat with beater or electric mixer until light and fluffy. Add nuts. Pour into springform pan; refrigerate until set. Unmold; serve with sauce.

Scarlet Sauce:
1 10-ounce package frozen raspberries
  in syrup
½ cup currant jelly
2 teaspoons cornstarch
1 tablespoon cold water

Must be made ahead.

Sauce preparation:
1. Heat raspberries until soft. Press through a sieve to remove seeds.

2. Add jelly to strained berries; heat to dissolve.

3. Add cornstarch mixed with water; cook until thick and clear.

English Trifle

Fruit-filled, layered classic.

1 16-ounce butter pound cake in ½-inch slices, crust removed
1 16-ounce package frozen sweetened strawberries, thawed
1½ cups unsweetened blueberries, frozen or fresh
1½ cups unsweetened blackberries or raspberries, frozen or fresh
3 ounces pecans, chopped and toasted
¼ cup brandy, cream sherry or liqueur of choice

Custard:

4 egg yolks
¾ cup sugar
scant ½ cup flour (lightly spooned then measured)
1½ cup milk, scalded
2 tablespoons of liquor chosen for trifle
1 teaspoon vanilla extract
butter

1 cup heavy cream, whipped and lightly sweetened

Must be made ahead.

1. Make custard: in top of double boiler beat egg yolks with sugar until thick. Beat in flour. Gradually add milk, stirring constantly.

2. Put custard over boiling water and cook stirring until thick. Reduce heat and cook an additional 2 to 3 minutes to cook flour.

3. Remove from heat and stir in flavorings. Spread a little butter over surface to prevent skin from forming. Set aside.

4. In medium bowl, combine fruits, nuts and liquor.

5. Using a straight-sided, 2½-quart glass bowl, make single layer of pound cake. (Cut pieces to fit shape of bowl.) Top cake with half the fruit mixture. Layer cake and fruit once again. Top fruit layer with custard and then whipped cream.

6. Refrigerate several hours to mingle flavors. Garnish with additional toasted pecans, if desired.

Frozen Nesselrode Mousse

Yield: 8 to 12 servings

Delicate, luscious for holidays.

5 egg whites, room temperature
¼ teaspoon cream of tartar
1 cup sugar
5 egg yolks
⅛ teaspoon salt
⅓ cup golden dark rum
2 teaspoons lemon juice
2 cups (1 pint) heavy cream
4 ounces finely chopped mixed candied fruit
  or use 1 part chopped slivered almonds
  to 3 parts fruit

Must be made ahead.

1. Whip heavy cream until stiff and refrigerate.
2. Add cream of tartar to egg whites, and beat to soft peaks. Gradually, 2 tablespoons at a time, add ¾ cup sugar and beat to stiff peaks.
3. In a small bowl beat egg yolks and salt until thick. Gradually add remaining ¼ cup sugar and beat well. Add rum and lemon juice.
4. Fold rum mixture, fruit-nut mixture and whipped cream into egg whites.
5. Pour into 2-quart serving bowl and freeze. Cover with plastic to store. This will not become as hard as ice cream.
6. To serve, garnish with additional candied fruit and spoon into individual dishes.

Frozen "Plum Pudding"

Yield: 10 servings

For ice cream lovers and chocoholics.

¼ cup kirsch (cherry brandy)
¼ cup EACH golden raisins and
  dried currants
½ cup diced mixed candied fruits
¼ cup blanched whole toasted almonds
3 tablespoons EACH thin-sliced dates
  and dried figs
10 candied red cherries, halved
1 quart rich chocolate ice cream

Garnish: whole candied cherries
chocolate curls

Must be made ahead.

1. Except for the ice cream and garnish, marinate all the ingredients together in the kirsch in a medium-sized bowl for at least 12 hours.
2. Put ice cream into a large bowl and let stand at room temperature until soft enough to stir. Stir in fruit mixture.
3. Pour into a lightly oiled 6-cup deep decorative mold. Cover and freeze at least one day to marry flavors.
4. Before serving, unmold on a high-rimmed plate (a pedestal-style is nice for this) after briefly dipping the mold in very hot water. Refreeze until ready to serve.

Georgia's Christmas Pudding

Yield: 6 to 8 servings

Sherry and rum-flavored meringue with custard sauce.

½ cup pecans, chopped
½ cup golden raisins, chopped
½ cup cream sherry
¼ cup rum
1 teaspoon lemon juice
6 egg whites, at room temperature
½ cup sugar

Custard:

6 egg yolks
¼ cup brown sugar
⅛ teaspoon salt
1½ cups milk, scalded
½ teaspoon vanilla extract

Fruit must be marinated overnight.

1. Soak raisins and pecans overnight in sherry, rum and lemon juice.
2. Prepare Custard: beat egg yolks until thick. Add sugar and salt. Put in top of double boiler over hot, not boiling, water and slowly add scalded milk, stirring until mixture thickens slightly and coats the spoon, about 7 minutes. Strain, flavor with ½ teaspoon sherry and ½ teaspoon vanilla. Chill until serving.
3. Next day, preheat oven to 350°. Beat egg whites until stiff with electric mixer; gradually add sugar. Mixture should be stiff and shiny. Fold in raisins, nuts, sherry and rum.
4. Pour into buttered 8-cup souffle dish. Set in pan of hot water, bake in pan of hot water for 45 minutes or until pudding is puffed and dark golden brown.
5. Serve immediately with chilled custard.

Grandma's Indian Pudding

Yield: 10 to 12 servings

¼ cup corn meal
1½ quarts (48-ounces) milk
⅛ teaspoon salt
3 tablespoons molasses
⅔ cup sugar
3 beaten eggs
2 cups sliced apples
¼ teaspoon ginger
1 large teaspoon cinnamon
1 cup raisins

1. Preheat oven to 325°.
2. In top of double boiler, combine corn meal, 2 cups milk and salt. Heat, stirring to prevent lumps, until slightly thickened, about 20 minutes. Cool.
3. In 2- to 3-quart baking dish (bean pots work nicely), combine the remaining ingredients; add the corn meal mixture and bake in moderate oven for about 3 hours. Stir occasionally.
4. Depending on size of baking dish, you may want to add 2 cups of milk at the beginning, adding another cup at end of first hour and another at the end of second.
5. Serve warm with cream or ice cream. May be reheated.

Nantucket Cranberry Dumplings with Cinnamon Sauce

Yield: 8 servings

Delightful contribution from an old Nantucket family.

4 cups fresh cranberries
pastry for a 9-inch double crust pie

Sauce:
2 cups sugar
2 cups water
2 tablespoons butter
4 teaspoons cinnamon

1. Wash and drain cranberries.
   Preheat oven to 425°.
2. Roll dough to make 8 pieces, 4 to 5 inches square.
3. Drape dough over cupped hand and fill with ½ cup berries. Seal edges with a little water, if necessary, to form pastry into little packages, enclosing berries completely.
4. Arrange in pie pans. Bake 45 minutes or until crust is nicely browned.
5. Serve warm or cold with warm sauce ladled over.
6. To make sauce: bring all ingredients to boil in small saucepan.

Pavlova

Yield: 8 to 10 servings

An Australian creation for visiting ballerina, Pavlova.

6 egg whites, room temperature
2 cups extra-fine sugar
1½ teaspoons white vinegar
1½ teaspoons vanilla
1 tablespoon cornstarch
2 cups whipping cream

Garnish: kiwi fruit and strawberries

In lieu of extra-fine sugar, measure granulated sugar, then process a few seconds in a blender.

1. In grease-free non-metallic bowl, beat egg whites until they reach stiff peaks. Gradually add 1 tablespoon sugar at a time, beating until all sugar has been added and whites are shiny. This process takes 15 to 20 minutes. Fold in vanilla, vinegar and cornstarch.
2. Preheat oven to 300°. Line baking sheet with foil. Butter the foil and outline a 7-inch circle. Heap egg whites onto circle, molding sides higher with a slight depression in the center.
3. Place Pavlova in bottom of preheated oven and bake 45 minutes. Turn off heat and leave until oven is cold.
4. To serve, whip cream and fill center. Top decoratively with Kiwi fruit, strawberries or fruit of choice. Slice to serve. May pass a bowl of crushed strawberries.

Instant Berry Ice Cream

Yield: 8 to 10 servings

This could be the reason to buy the necessary food processor!

1 16-ounce package individually quick frozen raspberries, cranberries, strawberries, or blueberries. DO NOT DEFROST
1 tablespoon lemon juice
1 14-ounce can sweetened condensed milk
8 ounces (half-pint) heavy cream
optional but preferable: ¾ cup nuts

1. With metal blade in place, put FROZEN berries in food procesor. Add lemon juice. Pulse about 5 times.
2. Add condensed milk. Run until just mixed, scraping bowl once or twice.
3. Add cream, mix well. Add nuts and pulse 6 to 8 times until nuts are slightly chopped.
4. Immediately spoon into serving dishes or store in covered freezer container, if made just before dinner.

Peanut Brittle Torte Victoria

Yield: 8 to 10 servings

Light, creamy confection with crunch.

1 cup egg whites, room temperature (use at least 3 days-old eggs)
2 cups granulated sugar
1 tablespoon cider vinegar
1 pint heavy cream
peanut brittle

Must be made ahead.

1. Preheat oven to 325°.
2. Line the bottom and sides of two 8- or 9-inch round cake pans with waxed paper.
3. Beat egg whites in large bowl with electric mixer until VERY stiff. This take about 2 to 3 minutes.
4. Gradually add sugar, about 2 tablespoons at a time. This takes about 6 to 8 minutes.
5. Fold vinegar into egg white mixture.
6. Pile egg whites into prepared pans, covering bottom but leaving some peaks.
7. Bake 45 minutes in middle of 325° oven. Turn off oven and leave for an additional 20 minutes. Cool in pans on a rack.
8. Whip the cream until stiff. Remove meringues from pans and paper from meringues. Place one layer on serving plate. Frost with some cream. Cover with second layer, top sides facing each other; lightly press layers together, and use remaining cream to cover top and sides.
9. With rolling pin crush about 5 ounces of peanut brittle. Sprinkle over top and sides. Refrigerate several hours or overnight. Slice to serve.

Snowball

Delicate, citrus-flavored, and delightful.

Yield: 12 servings

1 large angel food cake
1 tablespoon unflavored gelatin
¼ cup cold water
1 cup boiling water
2 tablespoons lemon juice
1 teaspoon grated orange rind
¼ cup orange marmalade, finely chopped
  if necessary
1 cup granulated sugar
1 pint whipping cream
coconut
a large round-bottomed bowl

Must be made ahead.

**This makes a colorful Easter Egg
when molded in an oval bowl.
Use food coloring to tint the coconut.**

1. Dissolve gelatin in cold water. Stir in boiling water, then sugar, juices, rind and marmalade. Mix well and refrigerate until mixture BEGINS to gel (about 2 hours or ½ hour in freezer).
2. Whip 1 cup of cream and fold into gelatin mixture.
3. Line a 4-quart bowl with plastic wrap. Break angel cake into 1- to 1½-inch pieces. (Avoid heavy crust.) Layer cake and syrup in bowl, beginning and ending with a few tablespoons of syrup. Cover with plastic wrap pressing down gently to coat every piece of cake with syrup and remove air holes. Refrigerate several hours or overnight until firm.
4. Remove from bowl, place flat side down on serving plate. Remove all plastic.
5. Whip remaining cream with a little sugar. Frost cake and cover with coconut. Refrigerate until serving.

Royal Cranberry Torte

Tangy and refreshing.

Yield: 12 servings

Crust:

1½ cups graham cracker crumbs
½ cup chopped pecans
¼ cup sugar
6 tablespoons butter, melted

Filling:

1½ cups ground FRESH cranberries
  (2 cups whole berries; do not use
  previously frozen berries)
1 cup sugar
2 egg whites, at room temperature
1 tablespoon frozen orange juice
  concentrate, thawed
1 teaspoon vanilla extract
⅛ teaspoon salt
1 cup whipping cream

Crust:

Combine graham cracker crumbs, pecans, ¼ cup sugar and melted butter. Press into bottom and sides of an 8-inch springform pan. Chill.

Filling:

1. In food processor chop whole berries until coarse; add 1 cup sugar and let stand for 5 minutes.
2. Add unbeaten egg whites, orange juice concentrate, vanilla and salt. Whirl in processor until thick.
3. With electric mixer, whip cream. Fold into berry mixture. Turn into crust; freeze firm.

Cranberry Glaze:

½ cup sugar
1 tablespoon cornstarch
¾ cup fresh cranberries
⅔ cup water

Garnish:

1 orange, cut into circular slices
  and then quartered

Must be made ahead.

Glaze: (make same day as serving torte):
Combine all ingredients in a saucepan. Cook just until berries pop; cool to room temperature. (Do not chill.)

To Serve Torte: Slice a whole, unpeeled orange into slices like wheels, then into fourths. Place oranges on top of torte with points of quarters pointing toward center. Spread center with glaze.

Spanish Flan

A flavorful version of the Spanish custard.

Yield: 8 servings

1½ cup sugar
1½ cups milk
1½ cups heavy cream
1 2-inch piece vanilla bean
4 eggs, lightly beaten
3 egg yolks
½ teaspoon grated lemon rind
¼ cup freshly squeezed orange juice
½ teaspoon salt
1 tablespoon dark rum
1 teaspoon almond extract

Must be made ahead.

1. Preheat oven to 350°. Grease a 4-cup ring mold.
2. In a small, heavy skillet heat ¾ cup sugar over low heat, stirring constantly with a wooden spoon. When sugar melts, is smooth, and turns a light golden brown, pour immediately into warmed, prepared mold; rotate to coat mold.
3. In top of double boiler heat milk, cream and vanilla bean over hot water.
4. In a small bowl, combine eggs, egg yolks, lemon rind and orange juice; add ¾ cup sugar and salt. Mix well.
5. Add ½ cup hot milk mixture to egg mixture; return all to milk mixture in top of double boiler. Cook 2 minutes over hot water.
6. Stir in rum and almond extract; remove vanilla bean.
7. Pour custard mixture over caramel in mold. Set mold in pan of hot water, 1-inch deep. Bake 30 minutes, till set.
8. Cool custard at room temperature; refrigerate several hours or overnight.
9. To serve, unmold by running a knife around the edges of pan to loosen. Place plate over mold; quickly invert.

Speyside Cream

"Creme caramel" with marmalade

Yield: 6 servings

½ cup sugar
1 cup heavy cream
1 cup whole milk
1-inch piece vanilla pod or
   1 teaspoon vanilla extract
1 cup sweet orange marmalade
1 tablespoon scotch whiskey
3 eggs
2 egg yolks

Try ginger marmalade or traditional caramel topping: boil ½ cup water with 1 cup sugar until golden brown.

1. Preheat oven to 325°.
2. Scald cream and milk with vanilla pod. Let it cool slightly.
3. Put whiskey and marmalade in small pan and stir over low heat until marmalade melts; bring to a low boil. Pour into 1-quart souffle dish or divide among 6 individual molds.
4. Beat eggs, egg yolks and sugar together; pour gradually into cooled milk, stirring constantly. Add vanilla extract, if desired. Strain through fine sieve into prepared dish.
5. Place dish in pan of hot water and bake 45 minutes for one dish or 25 minutes for individual molds, or until knife inserted half way between center and outer edge comes out clean.
6. Cool, then chill in refrigerator several hours or overnight. Run knife around edge and unmold to serve. May be garnished with almonds, and/or heavy cream, poured or whipped.

Tirrell Christmas Pudding

Yield: 2 oblong baking dishes

A one-hundred-fifty year old recipe originating in New Hampshire, this pudding has the old-fashioned flavor of the best bread pudding you ever ate.

1 1-pound loaf white bread
2 quarts milk
3 eggs, beaten
½ cup molasses
½ pound suet, ground
½ cup sugar
½ teaspoon salt
½ teaspoon cloves
1 teaspoon cinnamon
1 pound raisins

1. Preheat oven to 325°. Grease two oblong glass baking dishes.
2. In a large bowl, tear bread slices into large chunks; pour milk over bread and let soak until bread softens. Beat fine.
3. Add eggs and remaining ingredients. Mix well. Pour into baking dishes.
4. Bake approximately 2 hours, stirring often, scraping sides of dish, and adding more milk, if necessary, to maintain consistency of Indian pudding. Once pudding becomes bubbly, lower heat to 300° for remainder of cooking.
5. Serve warm with whipped cream or ice cream.

Plum Pudding

Both the English and the Scots claim to have invented the rich and delectable plum pudding in the tenth or eleventh century and it appears to have been a Christmas mainstay ever since. By the nineteenth century in America we find nineteen different recipes for various kinds of plum pudding recounted in the December 1856 issue of Godey's Lady's Book along with a detailed analysis of the differences and their effects on the outcome.

"One pound of flour, two pounds of suet, one pound of currants, one pound of plums, eight eggs, two ounces of candied peel, almonds and mixed spice according to taste. Boil gently in pudding cloth for seven hours."

Captain Cooke's Plum Pudding

Yield: two 6-cup molds

From Devon, England, comes this recipe from the granddaughter of Captain Cooke; a golden, not-too-sweet, steamed pudding made with dark ale.

1 pound raisins
1 pound dried currants
¼ pound sultanas (extra-large raisins)
1 pound suet, finely chopped
¾ pound fresh bread crumbs
¼ pound flour
½ pound brown sugar
rind of one lemon, grated
½ pound candied peel
½ of a whole nutmeg, grated
½ teaspoon ginger
a few drops almond extract
6 eggs, beaten
½ pint flat dark ale
pudding charms, if available

Must be made ahead.

1. Mix all ingredients together in a very large bowl or pot. Stir carefully to thoroughly mix.

2. Have each child in family stir pudding by turn for good luck. Each child should whisper his Christmas wishes as he stirs.

3. If desired, add small silver charms to batter to bring luck throughout the coming year. (This is an old tradition.)

4. Grease two 6-cup pudding molds; fill both molds leaving one inch at top. Cover tightly with foil and mold lid.

5. Steam in hot water for 4 to 5 hours (Place molds on rack inside pot of hot water which comes halfway up sides of molds; cover pot. Simmer.)

6. Remove molds from pot. Cool pudding completely in molds. Remove from molds; wrap pudding in cheesecloth which has been soaked in brandy; wrap again in foil. Store in cool, dry place for several weeks.

7. To serve: reheat or steam for 3 additional hours. Serve with hard sauce.

Virtually everything, except for whipping cream and egg whites, can be done in a food processor. Old fashioned fruitcakes and steamed puddings become new fashioned when it comes to chopping candied or dried fruits, nuts and suet. Be sure to add a little of the recipe's flour or sugar to these ingredients in the bowl to prevent their sticking to the blade.

Grandma Latham's Fig Pudding   Yield: one pudding

Bring us the figgy pudding!
Not a heavy fruited pudding, but a simply and nicely
flavored one. Now into the 5th generation.

1 cup molasses
1 cup milk
2½ cups flour
¼ teaspoon nutmeg
1 teaspoon baking soda
1 cup beef suet, finely chopped
1 cup English walnuts, chopped
½ cup dried figs, chopped

Sauce:

2 eggs
1 cup confectioners' sugar
½ pint whipping cream
½ teaspoon vanilla

1. Combine milk and molasses. Combine dry ingredients. Mix the two well and add suet, fruit and nuts. Pour into 5-cup greased pudding mold or "lard bucket" or coffee can. Cover. Use waxed-paper tied on if necessary. Steam 3 hours. Serve warm with sauce.

2. Make sauce: beat eggs and sugar until thick. In separate bowl beat cream until stiff. Fold egg mixture into cream. Add vanilla. Serve with warm pudding.

New England Plum Pudding   Yield: 12 servings

Rich and fruity.

7 ounces beef suet, finely chopped
1 cup bread crumbs, finely ground
scant ½ cup flour
1 cup sugar
¼ teaspoon salt
½ teaspoon allspice
1 teaspoon cinnamon
3 eggs
1 cup seedless raisins
1 cup dried currants
1 cup candied citron, chopped if desired
1 tablespoon grated lemon rind
1 cup candied orange peel, diced
2 cups raw apples, diced
½ cup milk
½ cup brandy

Make about a month in advance.

1. Mix beef suet, bread crumbs and scant ½ cup flour. Blend in sugar, salt, allspice and cinnamon. Beat in eggs.

2. Combine raisins, currants, citron, lemon rind, orange peel and raw apples and add to above.

3. Grease a 2-quart mold or use 2 coffee cans. Cover with lid or foil and steam in large covered pot on a rack. Water should be halfway up molds and be replenished as needed. Cook about 3 hours.

4. Remove cover, then remove pudding from mold when cool. Wrap in cheesecloth and hang two weeks in a cool place to dry out. Then wrap in foil until used.

5. An hour or more before serving, heat pudding in foil in double boiler. Serve with hard sauce.

Grand Marnier Plum Pudding

Yield: 10 to 12 servings

1¾ cups golden raisins
2 cups chopped pecans
1¾ cups dried currants
¼ cup chopped candied ginger
¾ cup chopped candied orange peel
¾ cup chopped candied lemon peel
½ cup chopped candied citron
½ cup chopped dried dates
1 cup flour
1 teaspoon salt
1 teaspoon ground allspice
½ teaspoon ground ginger
3 to 4 slices fresh bread, toasted and
  crumbed in food processor to make
  2 cups dry crumbs
1 cup firmly packed light brown sugar
3 eggs, lightly beaten
⅓ pound ground suet
1 cooking apple, cored and finely chopped
1 carrot, peeled and grated
¼ cup freshly squeezed orange juice
¼ cup Grand Marnier

¼ cup brandy

½ cup brandy
1 teaspoon sugar

1. Preheat oven to 400°. Butter 10-cup pudding mold; line sides with wax paper and butter paper.
2. Combine first 8 ingredients in large bowl. Mix in flour, salt, allspice and ginger. Add bread crumbs, brown sugar, eggs, suet, apple, carrot, orange juice and Grand Marnier; mix well.
3. Pack batter tightly into prepared mold. Cover with wax paper and mold lid. Set mold in roasting pan. Add enough boiling water to pan to come halfway up sides of mold. Cover pan. Bake 5 hours, adding more boiling water to pan as needed to maintain water level.
4. Remove mold from pan; uncover, cool on rack. Run a knife along sides of mold; carefully remove pudding. Soak a 16-inch length of cheesecloth in ¼ cup brandy. Wrap pudding in cheesecloth; pour remainder of ¼ cup over pudding. Wrap tightly in foil. Refrigerate for at least 3 days, for flavor to mellow, or up to 3 months.
5. To reheat: preheat oven to 300°. Unwrap pudding and remove cheesecloth; rewrap in foil. Place in oven and reheat for approximately 2 hours.
6. Place pudding on platter. Heat ½ cup brandy and sugar in a small saucepan over low heat till warm. Ignite with match; pour over pudding. Bring flaming pudding to table. Serve with sauce passed separately.

Grand Marnier Hard Sauce:

1 cup (2 sticks) unsalted butter,
  at room temperature
3 cups powdered sugar, sifted
¼ cup Grand Marnier
1 teaspoon grated orange rind
1 egg yolk

Must be made ahead.

Sauce preparation:
Cream butter and sugar till light and fluffy (about 1 minute in processor). Add Grand Marnier, rind and yolk and beat till smooth. Put in serving bowl; refrigerate till firm. Bring to room temperature to serve.

Old English Plum Pudding with Fairy Breath Sauce

Yield: 2 medium puddings

Recalls the age of Dickens and merry Christmases past —shared for wider enjoyment in Christmases present and yet-to-come.

1 pound suet, in chunks
1 pound raisins
1 pound dried currants or chopped dates
¼ pound figs, cut-up
½ pound mixed candied peel
½ pound blanched slivered almonds
1½ cups flour
2 cups soft bread slices (no crusts)
1 cup molasses (or 1 pound
　light brown sugar)
½ cup brandy or sherry
8 eggs
4 teaspoons nutmeg (or 1 nutmeg grated)
¼ teaspoon mace
¼ teaspoon ground cloves
½ teaspoon cinnamon
½ teaspoon ginger
2 teaspoons salt
pudding charms, if you have them

1. With metal blade in place, put bread into bowl of food processor and chop fine. Put bread into large pot.
2. Finely chop suet with some of recipe's flour. Add to pot.
3. Put raisins, figs and nuts into processor with more flour. Chop and add to pot with currants. May also process candied fruit to make finer. Add to pot.
4. Process eggs to make a light foam. Add to pot along with remaining ingredients. Mix thoroughly. Get eveyone to stir it (even the postman!) as they come and go, for good luck.
5. Prepare 2 molds of about 6 cups each, by greasing insides including covers. Pour pudding into molds. Add pudding charms if desired. Cover tightly. Place on a rack in large pot of boiling water. Steam 4 to 6 hours, renewing water as needed. Keep water halfway up molds.
6. Cool with cover off. Replace cover and store in cool place.
7. To serve, reheat 1 or more hours as it was cooked. Flame with brandy, if desired, and serve with a whisper of a fairy's breath.

Fairy Breath Sauce:

½ cup (1 stick) unsalted butter
1 cup or more confectioners' sugar
1 egg yolk
1 egg white
1 teaspoon orange or lemon juice
small amount brandy (1 to 2 tablespoons)

Make before Thanksgiving for Christmas.

Directions given are for food processor.

Sauce preparation:

In processor, cream butter, slowly adding sugar; add yolk, then white; add juice and brandy. Chill and serve cold on warm pudding. Make 1 to 2 days ahead.

Brown Sugar Hard Sauce

Yield: about 3 cups

2 cups dark brown sugar
1 cup (2 sticks) unsalted butter
2 tablespoons hot water
1 ounce sherry
1 ounce brandy
1 teaspoon vanilla
grated nutmeg

1. Cream sugar and butter until light and fluffy. (This step is important.)
2. Add flavorings drop by drop, beating continuously.
3. Shape into mound on a serving dish and cover lightly with nutmeg.
4. Chill thoroughly.

Rum Sauce

Yield: about 2 cups

2 eggs
1 cup confectioners' sugar
½ pint heavy cream, stiffly whipped
1 teaspoon rum (more to taste)

1. Beat eggs with sugar until thick and smooth.
2. Fold in stiffly whipped cream. Just before serving, stir in rum to taste. (May be made ahead several hours and refrigerated.)

Wine Sauce

Yield: about 3 cups

A thin, sweet, syrup-like sauce.

½ cup (1 stick) butter, softened
2 cups granulated sugar
1 cup hot water
1 egg yolk, beaten
1 teaspoon vanilla
2 tablespoons white wine

Must be made ahead.

1. Cream butter and sugar; add hot water. Cool slightly.
2. Add beaten egg yolk, vanilla, and wine. Beat until smooth. Refrigerate.

Though it is best to beat egg whites at room temperature, it is easier to separate the whites and the yolks while eggs are cold.

Twelfth Cake

To two pounds of flour—well sifted—united
    Of loaf sugar, ounces sixteen;
Two pounds of fresh butter, with eighteen fine eggs,
    And four pounds of currants washed clean;
Eight ounces of almonds, well blanched and cut small,
    The same weight of citron sliced;
Of orange and lemon-peel, candied, one pound,
    And a gill of pale brandy, united.
A large nutmeg grated; exact half an ounce
    Of allspice, but only a quarter
Of mace, corriander, and ginger well ground,
    Or pounded to dust in a mortar.
An important addition is cinnamon — which
    Is better increased than diminished —
The fourth of an ounce is sufficient. Now this
    May be baked four good hours till finished.

Godey's Lady's Book - Dec. 1857 & 1859

163

Bishop's Cake

Yield: one 9 x 5-inch loaf cake

Chocolate chips distinguish this from others.

3 eggs, well beaten
1 cup sugar
1½ cups flour
1½ teaspoons baking powder
¼ teaspoon salt
6 ounces chocolate chips
2 cups coarsely chopped walnuts
1 cup pitted dates, cut up
1 cup candied cherries, halved

1. Preheat oven to 325°. Grease a
   9 x 5 x 3-inch loaf pan and line it with
   waxed paper; grease waxed paper.
2. Cream together eggs and sugar, beating
   until thick and pale.
3. Sift together flour, baking powder, and salt
   over bowl of fruit, nuts and chips. Mix well.
4. Add egg and sugar mixture to flour and
   fruit mixture. Mix well.
5. Bake for approximately 1¼ to 1½ hours, or
   until tester is clean when inserted into
   center. Cake will have a crusty top. Cool on
   wire rack. Remove from pan when
   completely cool.

Bourbon Pecan Cake

Yield: one 10-inch tube cake and one loaf.

A "white" fruitcake of Southern origins.

2 cups whole red candied cherries
2 cups golden raisins
2 cups bourbon whiskey (good quality)
2 cups (4 sticks) butter, softened
2 cups sugar
2 cups packed dark brown sugar
8 eggs, separated
5 cups sifted flour
4 cups pecan halves
1½ teaspoons baking powder
1 teaspoon salt
2 teaspoons ground nutmeg

Glaze: (optional)

1½ cups confectioners' sugar
2 tablespoons hot milk
¼ teaspoon vanilla extract
candied cherries for garnish

Must be made ahead.

1. Combine cherries, raisins and bourbon in a
   large bowl. Cover tightly and refrigerate
   overnight. Drain fruits and reserve bourbon.
2. In a large bowl, beat butter at medium speed
   till light and fluffy. Add sugars, gradually,
   until well blended. Add egg yolks, beating
   until well blended.
3. Combine ½ cup of the flour with pecans.
   Sift remaining flour with baking powder,
   salt, and nutmeg.
4. Add 2 cups of flour mixture to creamed
   mixture and mix thoroughly. Add reserved
   bourbon and the rest of the flour mixture
   alternately, ending with flour. Beat well after
   each addition.
5. Beat egg whites until stiff but not dry; fold
   gently into cake batter. Add drained fruits
   and floured pecans to cake batter;
   blend thoroughly.

6. Grease a 10-inch tube cake pan; line bottom with wax paper. Pour cake batter into pan within 1 inch of the top. (Prepare a small loaf pan in the same way for remaining batter).

7. Bake in a preheated 275° oven: bake tube cake for about 4 hours and loaf cake about 1½ hours, or until cake tester inserted in the center comes out clean.

8. Cool cakes in pans on racks about 2 to 3 hours. Remove cakes from pans; peel off wax paper. Wrap cakes in cheesecloth which has been soaked in bourbon; then wrap in foil or plastic wrap and store in a tightly covered container in the refrigerator for several weeks. Periodically resoak cheesecloth in bourbon.

9. If desired, just before serving cake, beat together glaze ingredients and spread over top of cake, allowing some to run down side. Decorate with cherries.

The Buell's Fruitcake

Batter enough to hold together luscious chunks of fruit and nuts.

1½ pounds pitted dates, halved
1 pound candied pineapple, cut up, (a few rings reserved for tops of cakes)
1 pound candied cherries, halved
½ pound citron, chopped
2 cups sifted four
½ teaspoon salt
2 teaspoons baking powder
4 eggs, medium-size, beaten
1 cup sugar
2 pounds pecan halves

Ingredients can be halved for 2 loaf cakes.
Must be made ahead.

Yield: 3 to 4 loaves

1. Grease 8½ x 5-inch loaf pans, lining bottoms with greased brown paper, cut to fit.

2. Combine flour, salt and baking powder in sifter and add to the fruit, mixing with fingers, until each piece is coated. (A large roasting pan is the right size for this operation.)

3. Don't give up. It gets messier, but it's worth it.

4. Beat eggs; add sugar and beat. Mix into above ingredients with fingers.

5. Add pecans; continue mixing by hand.

6. Using hands, firmly press mixture into prepared pans. Garnish top with whole fruit. Bake in preheated oven at 275° for 1¼ to 1½ hours. Immediately remove from pans and peel off paper. Cool completely. Wrap well and store in a cool, dry place at least a month before Christmas.

Christmas Fruitcake

Yield: one 10-inch tube cake

**An old recipe that has served as wedding cake—
spices, fruit, applesauce with a hint of chocolate.**

½ cup shortening
¾ teaspoon salt
½ teaspoon cinnamon
½ teaspoon cloves
½ teaspoon nutmeg
½ teaspoon allspice
2 tablespoons cocoa
1½ cups sugar
2 eggs
1½ teaspoons baking soda
2 cups sifted flour
¾ cup dates, chopped
¾ cup raisins
¾ cup nuts, chopped
1½ cups unsweetened applesauce

1. Grease and flour a 10-inch tube pan (or a 10-inch square pan). Preheat oven to 350°.
2. In large bowl with electric mixer, blend shortening, salt, spices and cocoa. Add sugar and cream well. Add eggs one at a time beating well after each addition.
3. Mix baking soda with flour. Sprinkle fruit and nuts with 2 tablespoons of the flour.
4. Add remaining flour to batter alternately with applesauce. Fold in fruit and nuts.
5. Pour into pan and bake about an hour or until cake tests done.
6. Frost with a white butter frosting and decorate top if desired.

Double-Frosted White Fruitcake

Yield: one 9-inch square cake

**A delicate, almond flavored fruitcake handed down
by one of Mystic Seaport Museum's first volunteers.**

1¼ cups sugar
¾ cup (1½ sticks) butter
1 tablespoon lemon juice
1 teaspoon vanilla extract
1 teaspoon almond extract
1 teaspoon orange flavoring
3 eggs, separated
⅔ cup milk
1¼ cups flour
1 cup golden raisins
½ cup dried currants
½ cup candied cherries, halved
½ cup angelica or candied citron, chopped
¾ cup walnuts, chopped
white buttercream frosting (below)
bitter chocolate glaze (below)

Must be made ahead.

1. In large bowl of mixer, cream together sugar and butter; add flavorings and beat until light and fluffy.
2. Combine beaten egg yolks with milk; add to creamed mixture in small amounts alternately with 1 cup flour.
3. Mix together fruits and nuts, tossing to coat with ¼ cup flour. Add to batter.
4. In small bowl of mixer, beat egg whites until stiff. Fold into batter.
5. Pour batter into a greased 9-inch square baking pan which has been lined with waxed paper and greased again. Bake in a preheated 350° oven for 1 to 1¼ hours.
6. Cool 5 minutes; invert on wire rack and remove from pan. Remove waxed paper. Cool completely; wrap tightly in foil and store in cool, dry place. May be made several weeks ahead; do not frost until day cake is served.

166

White Buttercream Frosting:

8 ounces confectioners' sugar
¼ cup (½ stick) butter, softened
1½ tablespoons milk
¼ teaspoon vanilla extract
¼ teaspoon almond extract
¼ teaspoon orange flavoring

Bitter Chocolate Glaze:

1 square unsweetened chocolate
1 square semi-sweet chocolate

White frosting:

1. Cream together all ingredients with mixer. Beat until of spreading consistency.
2. Frost top and sides of fruitcake. Refrigerate cake.

Chocolate Glaze:

1. In top of double boiler, melt chocolate squares together over hot water. Cool slightly.
2. Remove cake from refrigerator. Spread chocolate across top of cake. Garnish top, if desired, by making "holly leaves and berries" using red and green candied cherries and pineapple pieces.

Gates' Blackberry Jam Cake
Yield: 13 mini loaves

Perfect for gift-giving if made at Thanksgiving time.

¾ pound dates, cut up
1½ pounds raisins
3 cups pecans
¾ cup bourbon
9 large eggs
3 10-ounce jars blackberry jam
1½ cup (3 sticks) butter or margarine
3 cups sugar
1½ teaspoons baking soda
¾ cup buttermilk
4½ cups flour
1 teaspoon salt
1 tablespoon nutmeg
1 tablespoon cinnamon

Must be made ahead.

1. Soak dates, raisins and nuts in bourbon for several hours or overnight.
2. Grease and flour 13 mini-loaf tins. (Disposable tins measure 5¾ x 3¼ x 2-inches.) Preheat oven to 275°.
3. Blend sugar and butter in food processor or electric mixer. Beat in eggs and jam.
4. Combine dry ingredients in large bowl; mix baking soda and buttermilk.
5. In overly large bowl, perhaps a punch bowl, combine flour, jam and milk mixtures thoroughly. Add fruit and nut mixture.
6. Fill each loaf tin about ¾ full. Stagger on two shelves in oven. (Perhaps switch some partway during baking). Bake for 1⅓ hours.
7. Leave in disposable tins to store. Sprinkle each with about ½ tablespoon bourbon every few days to keep moist and "age." Keep in plastic bags or sealed tins.

English Fruitcake

Yield: two 9½ x 5½ x 3-inch loaf cakes

A very moist, dark fruitcake which keeps well.

2 cups dried currants
2 cups seedless raisins
2 cups seeded raisins (sultanas)
1 cup candied cherries
1½ cups candied orange peel,
  or 2 cups mixed candied fruit
1 cup coarsely chopped walnuts
1 cup cider, burgundy, sherry or Madeira
1 cup (2 sticks) butter
1¼ cups firmly packed brown sugar
6 eggs
½ teaspoon cinnamon
½ teaspoon nutmeg or mace
¼ teaspoon ground cloves
¼ teaspoon lemon juice
2 teaspoons grated lemon rind
½ cup light molasses (or dark corn syrup)
3 cups sifted flour
1 teaspoon baking soda
¼ teaspoon salt
honey for glaze
¼ cup brandy or rum

Must be made ahead.

1. Place fruit and nuts in large mixing bowl; toss to mix well. Add cider or wine and marinate several hours or overnight.

2. Grease two 9½ x 5½ x 3-inch loaf pans or one 10-inch tube pan; line pan with waxed paper and grease waxed paper.

3. In large bowl of mixer, cream butter and sugar until light and fluffy; add eggs, one at a time, mixing well after each addition. Stir in spices, lemon juice and rind, and molasses.

4. Sift flour with baking soda and salt. Beat into butter mixture a third at a time; mix well.

5. Turn batter over marinated fruits and nuts. Mix together well using large spoon or hands.

6. Divide batter between pans. Level tops.

7. Bake in preheated oven at 275°, allowing 2 to 2½ hours for loaf cakes, 3 to 3½ hours for tube cake. When cake is done, it will pull away from sides of pan and center will spring back when lightly pressed.

8. While still warm, glaze tops by spreading with honey. Cool completely in pans on wire rack before removing from pans.

9. Wrap in cheesecloth soaked in brandy or rum, if desired. Store in tight tins, or sealed freezer bags, for at least a week at room temperature before refrigerating for further keeping.

It is rumored that there's really only one fruitcake in the entire world . . . and each year it just keeps getting passed from one friend to another!

Irish Christmas Cake

Yield: three 8 x 4-inch loaves

This rich raisin cake is traditionally baked with a ring inside of it. The one who receives the piece of cake containing the ring will marry within the year.

1 pound raisins
1 pound sultanas
1 pound brown sugar
1½ cups strong brewed tea
1½ cups Irish whiskey
3½ cups flour
1 tablespoon ground cinnamon
1 tablespoon nutmeg
3 eggs, beaten lightly
1 tablespoon baking powder
honey to glaze

Must be made ahead.

1. In a large glass bowl, soak fruit and brown sugar in tea and whiskey overnight.

2. The next day set the oven at 300°. Grease well three 8 x 4 x 3-inch loaf pans.

3. Mix together flour and spices; add to soaking fruits, alternating with beaten eggs. Add baking powder last. Mix all well.

4. Pour into prepared pans. Bake about 1½ hours. When cool, brush tops with honey to glaze. Cakes keep well, wrapped in foil and refrigerated, for several weeks. (May also be prepared in one 10-inch tube pan: bake approximately 3 to 3½ hours.)

Old South Christmas Cake

Yield: one 10-inch tube cake

Rich and good, with pecans and mincemeat.

1 28-ounce jar prepared mincemeat
1 15-ounce box seedless raisins
2 cups chopped pecans
1 tablespoon vanilla
2 tablespoons rum or brandy (optional)
½ cup (1 stick) butter, melted
2 cups sugar
3 eggs, separated
1½ teaspoons baking soda
¼ cup water
3 cups flour

1. Preheat oven to 275°. Grease and flour a 10-inch tube pan.

2. In a large bowl, combine mincemeat, raisins, nuts, vanilla and liquor. Set aside.

3. In large mixer bowl, combine butter, sugar and egg yolks; beat well. Combine baking soda and water; add to mixture.

4. Sift flour over mincemeat mixture; stir to mix well. Combine contents of both bowls; mix well. (Batter will be stiff.)

5. In small bowl of mixer, beat egg whites until stiff but not dry. Fold into batter.

6. Spoon batter into prepared pan. Bake at 275° for 2 to 2½ hours, or until done (Cake will pull away from sides of pan slightly; a cake tester may appear moist from mincemeat; check carefully.)

7. Cool slightly; remove from pan. Cool completely. Wrap to store. Cake keeps well.

Italian Fruitcake

Yield: 4 cakes

Chocolate and honey make a candy-like cake—outstanding!

1 pound shelled walnuts
½ pound whole blanched almonds (or slivers)
½ pound shelled hazelnuts
¾ pound raisins
⅔ cup flour (plus about 2 cups)
¼ cup (heaping) grape jelly
3 1.45-ounce milk chocolate bars
6 ounces citron
3 ounces candied orange peel
3 ounces mixed candied fruit
1 pint honey plus additional for glaze

A kitchen scale eases preparation of this recipe, but is not necessary; approximations are fine.

1. Preheat oven to 300°.
2. Combine nuts and fruits in a very large bowl. Coat all well with flour, using about ⅔ cup.
3. In a medium saucepan over medium heat, dissolve jelly, stirring occasionally. Lower heat; add chocolate and honey; stir until melted and smooth.
4. Remove from heat; pour over floured ingredients, mixing well. (This may be accomplished best by using hands.) Add additional flour, as needed, until mixture holds together (about 2 to 2½ cups).
5. Shape mixture into 4 balls, about 6 to 8 inches in diameter, or slightly larger than a grapefruit, and flatten on the bottom. Place on ungreased cookie sheet (2 per sheet) and bake for 40 minutes.
6. Brush fruitcakes with honey while still hot. When completely cooled, wrap in foil and store in cool, dry place. Make well before Christmas. Serve at room temperature.

Pecan Christmas Cake

Yield: 12 to 16 servings

Buttery with a hint of citrus.

2 cups (4 sticks) butter
2 cups sugar
6 eggs
1 tablespoon lemon juice
1 tablespoon vanilla
1½ cups golden raisins
4 cups pecans
3 cups flour
1 teaspoon salt
1 teaspoon baking powder

Glaze:
¼ cup orange juice
¼ cup lemon juice
¼ cup sugar

1. Grease and flour a 10-inch tube pan. Preheat oven to 300°.
2. Cream butter and sugar until fluffy. Beat in eggs, one at a time. Add lemon juice and vanilla.
3. Mix raisins and nuts with ¼ cup flour. Mix remaining flour with salt and baking powder. Add to creamed mixture. Fold in the fruit and nuts. Pour into prepared pan and bake 1 hour and 40 to 50 minutes or until tester comes out clean.
4. In small saucepan, combine glaze ingredients and heat just to dissolve sugar. Pour over hot cake. Cool cake thoroughly then remove from pan.

Orange Slice Fruitcake

Not only the children's favorite.

Yield: 12 servings

8 ounces dates, cut-up
16 ounces orange slice candy, cut-up
2 cups pecans, broken
4 ounces shredded coconut
1 cup (2 sticks) butter or margarine, melted
4 eggs
1½ cups sugar
½ cup buttermilk
2 cups flour
1 teaspoon baking soda

1. Combine dates, candy, nuts, and coconut. Pour melted butter over and let stand while proceeding.
2. Beat eggs with electric mixer; gradually add sugar.
3. Add baking soda to flour. Add flour alternately with buttermilk to egg mixture.
4. Stir in fruit-nut mixture and blend well.
5. Pour into greased and floured 10-inch tube pan. Put into COLD oven, set at 300°, and bake about 2 hours or until toothpick comes out clean.

Steamed Fruitcake

Moist and fruity.

Yield: two 8 x 4 x 3-inch loaves

1½ pounds raisins
½ pound dates, chopped
½ pound figs, chopped
½ pound chopped pecans
1½ pounds chopped candied fruit
¼ cup flour
1 cup (2 sticks) butter
1 cup sugar
6 eggs, well beaten
½ cup apple jelly
½ cup brandy
1 cup flour
1 teaspoon baking powder
⅛ teaspoon baking soda

Must be made ahead.

1. Preheat oven to 400°. Grease and line with wax paper two 8 x 4 x 3-inch loaf pans. Grease wax paper.
2. Combine fruits and nuts. Coat well with flour, using approximately ¼ cup.
3. Cream butter and sugar until light and fluffy. Add eggs; beat well. Add jelly, brandy and dry ingredients; mix well. Fold in fruits and nuts.
4. Pour batter into prepared pans; cover tightly with foil. Place pans on rack inside a large roasting pan. Fill roaster with enough hot water to come half-way up sides of loaf pans; cover with roaster lid. Steam in oven for approximately 3 hours. CAREFULLY remove lid (steam can burn and boiling water in roaster is hazardous!) Remove loaf pans and uncover.
5. Cool cakes in pans about 10 minutes. Invert on wire racks and remove from pans; remove wax paper. Cool completely.
6. Wrap fruitcakes in cheesecloth which has been soaked in brandy. Wrap again in foil. Store in cool place. Make several weeks ahead

Almond Butter-Crusted Pound Cake   Yield: 2 cakes

Moist, delicious; smells divine while cooking.

Almond Butter Crust:
⅓ cup butter, softened
½ cup light brown sugar, packed
¾ cup flour
1 cup (4-ounces) almonds, chopped

Pound Cake:
⅔ cup butter, softened
6 ounces cream cheese, softened
1 cup sugar
4 eggs
2 cups flour
1 teaspoon baking powder
½ teaspoon salt
4 teaspoons vanilla (or part almond) extract

1. Preheat oven to 350°. Prepare crust: in small bowl combine flour and brown sugar. Cut in butter until mixture is crumbly. Add almonds. Divide mixture and press evenly into 2 loaf pans measuring 7½ x 3½ inches.

2. Prepare Cake: with electric mixer, cream butter, cream cheese, and sugar in large bowl. Blend in eggs. Combine dry ingredients and add to batter with vanilla. Pour into prepared pans. Bake about 45 minutes or until tester comes out clean.

3. Cool on rack. Insert knife between cake and pan. Invert then turn top side up onto serving plate.

Favorite Spirited Cake   Yield: 12 servings

1 cup chopped pecans
1 18½-ounce regular yellow cake mix
1 3¾-ounce vanilla instant pudding mix
4 large eggs
¾ cup water
½ cup vegetable oil
¼ cup rum or bourbon
½ teaspoon nutmeg

Glaze:
½ cup (1 stick) butter
2 tablespoons water
1 cup sugar
½ cup rum or bourbon

1. Preheat oven to 350°. Grease and flour tube pan.

2. Sprinkle nuts over bottom.

3. Combine remaining cake ingredients in food processor or mixer. Mix well and pour batter into prepared pan.

4. Bake 50 minutes or until done. Remove pan to rack.

5. Make glaze by combining butter, water and sugar in saucepan. Bring to boil; cook 2 to 3 minutes. Remove from heat and stir in rum.

6. Prick top of cake with skewer. Pour warm glaze over. When completely cool, remove from pan to serving plate.

Christmas Angel

Formerly the family birthday cake, now a Christmas Eve tradition.

Cake:
5 eggs, separated
½ cup orange juice
¼ teaspoon salt
1 cup sugar
½ teaspoon vanilla
¼ teaspoon almond extract
1 teaspoon lemon peel
1½ cups sifted cake flour
1 teaspoon baking powder
¾ teaspoon cream of tartar

Cake is very versatile and foolproof.

Cake preparation:
1. Add orange juice to egg yolks in large mixing bowl. Add salt and beat with electric mixer until foamy.
2. Add sugar and flavorings and beat until thick and smooth.
3. Mix flour and baking powder well in separate bowl.
4. In grease-free bowl, add cream of tartar to egg whites and beat until they stand in moist peaks.
5. Add flour mixture to sugar and egg yolk mixture and beat 2½ to 3 minutes with electric mixer.
6. Fold egg whites into flour mixture. Pour into ungreased 10-inch tube pan with removable bottom.
7. Put in COLD oven set at 325°. Bake 30 minutes then raise to 350° and bake an additional 15 minutes.
8. Let cake cool in pan upside down.
9. Serve slices with oranges spooned over, topped with lightly sweetened whipped cream and caramelized sugar.

Oranges:
6 oranges
¾ cup water
¼ cup sugar
zest of 1 orange
2 tablespoons Grand Marnier

Orange preparation:
1. Remove zest (orange skin—no white) from 1 orange. Combine with sugar and water in small pan and cook over low-medium heat 10 minutes. Remove zest. Set aside.
2. Prepare oranges: slice off tops and bottoms then slice off skin from top to bottom all around the orange. Section with knife.
3. Add oranges to syrup and add liqueur. Stir well. Cover and refrigerate.

Caramelized Sugar:
1 cup sugar

1 pint whipping cream, whipped and sweetened

Caramelized Sugar preparation:
1. Place sugar in small frying pan over medium heat; shake rather than stir as it heats. When completely melted and light golden, pour immediately onto foil-lined cookie sheet or pie plate.
2. When completely cool peel away foil, and break into small pieces.

Christmas Cassata

2 small all-butter pound cakes, slightly frozen
2 cups whole-milk ricotta cheese
½ cup red and green cherries,
   finely chopped (optional)
⅔ cup mini chocolate chips
1 ounce orange liqueur
1 12-ounce jar red raspberry jam

Frosting:
6 ounces unsweetened chocolate
¾ cup (1½ sticks) butter
1 pound confectioners' sugar
6 tablespoons brewed coffee
2 eggs
2 teaspoons vanilla extract
pinch salt

Garnish: candied cherries, toasted almonds

Make at least one day ahead.

Yield: two cakes, 6 to 8 servings each

1. Slice each cake into 4 layers while slightly frozen.

2. Drain any liquid from ricotta. Process in blender or food processor until smooth; mix in the cherries if desired.

3. Combine chips and liqueur with jam.

4. Spread about ⅓ cup cheese on 2 bottom cake layers. Top with about the same amount of jam. Top with cake and continue layering, ending with cake.

5. Wrap in plastic wrap, gently pressing layers together. Refrigerate overnight. (Can also be frozen at this point.)

6. Next day prepare frosting. Melt chocolate and butter in double boiler. Stir in remaining ingredients, mixing well. Put top of double boiler over a bowl of ice water and beat with electric mixer until spreadable.

7. Clean sides of chilled cakes and frost. Make bark-like designs with tines of fork. Decorate with candied cherries or toasted almonds if desired. Refrigerate until half an hour before serving, or freeze one for future use.

Fig Cake

Similar to Lane Cake, the Fig Cake has a moist fig filling.

Yield: one 2-layer cake

Cake:
3 egg whites, at room temperature
½ cup (1 stick) butter
1 cup sugar
½ cup milk
1½ cups flour
2 teaspoons baking powder
¼ teaspoon salt
½ teaspoon vanilla extract
½ teaspoon almond extract

1. Preheat oven to 350°. Grease and flour two 9-inch round cakepans.

2. In small bowl of mixer, beat egg whites until soft peaks form; add ½ cup sugar and beat until stiff. Set aside.

3. Cream butter; add ½ cup sugar and beat until fluffy.

4. Sift together dry ingredients. Add to butter mixture alternately with milk, ending with flour.

5. Fold in egg whites. Add flavorings.
6. Divide batter evenly between 2 pans. Bake for about 25 minutes, or until tester in center comes out clean. Cool 10 minutes; remove from pans and cool completely.
7. Spread filling between layers. Frost sides and top. Garnish with figs and chopped nuts, if desired.

Fig Filling:
½ pound dried figs, finely chopped
⅓ cup sugar
⅓ cup boiling water
1 tablespoon lemon juice

Frosting (see Lane Cake p. 177)

Filling preparation:
1. In top of double boiler, mix together all ingredients in order given. Cook over boiling water until mixture thickens to spreading consistency.
2. While mixture is still hot, spread between cooled cake layers.

Cranberry Cream Cake

A variation on the Fig Cake.

2-layer white cake (see Fig Cake opposite)

Cranberry Filling:
1 16-ounce can whole cranberry sauce
½ cup cranberry juice drink
½ cup sugar

1 cup heavy cream, whipped with
¼ cup sugar and 1 teaspoon vanilla extract

Yield: one 4-layer cake

1. Prepare 2-layer white cake early in day. Cool. Carefully split each cake horizontally to form 4 layers.
2. Filling preparation: combine cranberry sauce, juice and sugar in saucepan. Bring to a boil over medium-high heat, stirring constantly; boil for 3 minutes.
3. Assemble when ready to serve: alternate cranberry filling and whipped cream, spreading top of bottom layer with cranberries, next layer with cream, third layer with cranberries. Frost top and sides with whipped cream. Serve immediately or refrigerate briefly. Cake may also be frosted with seven-minute frosting (see Lane Cake).

 Your nose is often reliable as an indicator of a cake's readiness. It's just about that time when you REALLY become aware of the aroma from the oven.

Holiday Chocolate Cake

Yield: 8 to 10 servings

Every day should be a holiday with this prize winner!

½ cup (1 stick) butter
1 cup sugar
4 eggs
1 16-ounce can Hershey's chocolate syrup
  (1½ cups)
1 tablespoon almond extract
1 cup flour

Glaze:

⅓ cup seedless raspberry jam

Frosting:

¼ cup heavy cream
4 ounces semisweet chocolate
½ teaspoon instant coffee powder

Garnish:

¼ cup sliced almonds, toasted

**This cake tends to change shape after being
removed from pan. Do not be concerned.**

1. Preheat oven to 350°.
2. Line the bottom of an 8- or 9-inch round pan with waxed paper. Grease sides of the pan.
3. FOOD PROCESSOR METHOD: Put all ingredients in bowl and run until thoroughly mixed. Go to step 5.
4. MIXER METHOD: Cream butter and sugar. Beat in eggs, then remaining ingredients.
5. Pour into prepared pan and bake 40 to 45 minutes or until center of cake is high, firm and no longer looks sticky. Cool on cake rack, although total cooling isn't necessary. It always seems to come out the same.
6. Remove cake from pan and onto cake rack. Place rack on sheet of waxed paper.
7. In small pan heat jam to boiling over medium heat. Lower heat and cook 2 minutes.
8. Pour jam over cake, spreading to coat top.
9. In small pan cook frosting ingredients over low heat, stirring constantly. When chocolate is melted and frosting is smooth pour over cake, spreading over top and sides.
10. By carefully lifting off of rack with fingers, place cake onto serving plate. Coat sides with almonds if desired. Let frosting set.
11. Serve small slices topped with freshly whipped and lightly sweetened cream.

176

Lane Cake

**THE cake of the Deep South:
a spectacular 3-tiers.**

1 cup (2 sticks) butter, softened
2 cups sugar
3¼ cups flour
1 tablespoon baking powder
¾ teaspoon salt
1 cup milk
1 teaspoon vanilla extract
½ teaspoon almond extract
8 egg whites, stiffly beaten
Filling (follows)
Frosting (follows)

Garnish: Pecan halves and stemmed
   maraschino cherry

1. Preheat oven to 325°. Grease and flour three 9-inch round cakepans.
2. Cream butter; gradually add sugar, beating well. Combine dry ingredients; add to creamed mixture alternately with milk, beginning and ending with flour mixture. Mix well after each addition. Stir in flavorings.
3. Carefully fold egg whites into batter.
4. Pour batter equally among the 3 pans. Bake for 25 minutes, or until tester inserted in center comes out clean. Cool in pans 10 minutes; remove and cool completely.
5. Spread filling between layers and on top of cake; spread sides with frosting. Garnish with cherries and pecan halves, if desired.

Filling:
8 egg yolks
1½ cups sugar
½ cup (1 stick) butter
1 cup chopped pecans
1 cup raisins
1 cup flaked coconut
¼ to ½ cup Southern Comfort (or bourbon)
½ cup sliced maraschino cherries

Filling preparation:
1. Combine egg yolks, sugar and butter in a 2-quart saucepan. Cook over medium heat, stirring constantly, about 20 minutes or until thickened.
2. Remove from heat; stir in remaining ingredients. Cool completely.

7-Minute Frosting:
¾ cup sugar
2 tablespoons + 2 teaspoons water
1 egg white, at room temperature
½ tablespoon light corn syrup
dash of salt
½ teaspoon vanilla

Frosting preparation:
1. Combine first 5 ingredients in top of double boiler; beat 30 seconds at low speed of electric mixer.
2. Place over boiling water; beat constantly on high speed for 7 minutes or until stiff peaks form. Remove from heat; add vanilla and beat 1 minute more. Yield: frosts sides of 3-layer cake; top and sides of 2 layer cake.

Amaretto Cheesecake

Velvety, delicately flavored.

Yield: 10 to 12 servings

4 whole graham crackers (8 squares), crushed
1½ pounds cream cheese, softened
1 14-ounce can sweetened condensed milk
  (not evaporated)
3 large eggs
¼ teaspoon salt
¼ cup amaretto
1 teaspoon vanilla extract
½ teaspoon almond extract

Topping:

1 cup sour cream
1 tablespoon amaretto
1 tablespoon brown sugar
¼ teaspoon almond extract

Optional: ¼ cup sliced almonds, toasted.

Must be made ahead.

1. Preheat oven to 300°.
2. Grease a 9-inch springform pan and coat with graham cracker crumbs. Set aside.
3. Beat cream cheese at high speed until fluffy, about 3 minutes. Add remaining ingredients and beat until smooth, scraping bowl occasionally.
4. Pour into pan and bake for 65 minutes. Turn off oven.
5. Combine topping ingredients. Spread over top of cheesecake. Sprinkle with almonds if desired. Return to turned-off oven and let topping firm up for 15 minutes.
6. Cool and refrigerate covered. Remove springform to serve. Make 1 or 2 days in advance.

Chocolate Cheesecake

The ultimate!

Yield: 12 to 16 servings

¼ cup water
8 ounces semisweet chocolate
20 chocolate wafers, crushed to make 1 cup
¼ cup (½ stick) butter, melted
3 8-ounce packages cream cheese,
  at room temperature
1 cup sugar
2 eggs
1 cup sour cream
1 teaspoon vanilla extract

Garnish: chocolate "Holly" leaves and frosted cranberries

Chocolate "Holly" Leaves:

½ cup semisweet chocolate chips
2 teaspoons shortening
4 or more small lemon leaves (or other non-toxic leaves)

1. Preheat oven to 350°.
2. Heat water and chocolate over low heat, stirring until chocolate is melted. Cool.
3. In small bowl combine crushed wafers and butter. Press into a 9-inch springform pan.
4. In large bowl with electric mixer (or in food processor) beat cream cheese until light. Add sugar and eggs, then beat in sour cream and vanilla. Add melted chocolate. Mix thoroughly and pour into prepared pan.
5. Bake 55 to 60 minutes or until firm.

Chocolate Leaves preparation:

1. In a heavy saucepan over low heat, heat together chocolate and shortening until chocolate is melted and smooth, about 5 minutes. Stir occasionally.
2. Spread a layer of chocolate mixture on underside of lemon leaves. Place coated

leaves, chocolate-side up, on plate; refrigerate 20 minutes or until firm.

3. Carefully peel off lemon leaves. Refrigerate chocolate leaves until ready to use.

4. Arrange two chocolate leaves with a cluster of 3 frosted cranberries so as to resemble holly leaves and berries.

Frosted Cranberries:
3 to 6 cranberries
corn syrup to coat
sugar to coat

Frosted Cranberry preparation:
Roll 3 to 6 cranberries in corn syrup; toss in sugar to coat.

Ginger Cheesecake

Yield: 18 servings

Three types of ginger, five-star rating!

Gingersnap Crust:
1 cup ground pecans
½ cup ground gingersnaps (about 2 ounces)
¼ cup sugar
¼ cup (½ stick) butter, room temperature

Filling:
4 8-ounce packages cream cheese, softened
¾ cup sugar
4 eggs
½ cup heavy cream
1 teaspoon vanilla extract
½ cup preserved ginger with syrup
2 teaspoons ground ginger
1 to 2 tablespoons finely grated
  fresh gingerroot

Garnish: finely chopped candied ginger
chopped pecans

Must be made ahead.

Pass a dish of crystallized ginger as you serve the cheesecake if you wish. For a whimsical holiday touch, garnish top with miniature (2-inch) Gingerbread People (see p. 202), hands touching to form circle around cake.

Crust preparation:
1. Combine ingredients in food processor; process for 30 seconds.

2. With damp fingers, press mixture evenly over bottom and 2 inches up sides of a lightly greased 9-inch springform pan.

Filling preparation:
1. Preheat oven to 300°.

2. Combine all ingredients in bowl of food processor. Process for about 3 minutes, or until smooth, stopping occasionally to scrape down sides of bowl with rubber spatula. Pour into prepared crust.

3. Bake for 1 hour and 40 minutes. Turn off oven; let cake stay in oven for 1½ hours. Cool cake on wire rack to room temperature. Refrigerate overnight.

4. Garnish top of cheesecake with finely chopped candied ginger and chopped pecans, if desired.

Tom's Pumpkin Cheesecake

Yield: one 10-inch cake

Enough for the entire clan.

Crust:
1⅓ cups flour
⅓ cup sugar
dash salt
1 egg, separated
½ cup (1 stick) butter, in pieces

Cheesecake:
2 pounds cream cheese, room temperature
1½ cups sugar
6 eggs
3 tablespoons flour
2 teaspoons cinnamon
1 teaspoon cloves
1 teaspoon ginger
½ teaspoon nutmeg
1 cup heavy cream
1 1-pound can cooked pumpkin
2 teaspoons vanilla extract

Spiced Whipped Cream:
1 cup heavy cream
¼ cup confectioners' sugar, or to taste
¼ to ½ teaspoon pumpkin pie spice
½ teaspoon vanilla extract

Topping is wonderful on gingerbread, apple pie, and simple puddings.

1. In food processor combine flour, sugar and salt. Add egg yolk and butter, pulsing to chop butter and make a fine crumbed dough.
2. Press evenly into 10-inch springform pan, bottom and sides. Brush with egg white.
3. Preheat oven to 425°. Put cheese, sugar and eggs in large food processor bowl or large mixing bowl. Mix well. Add remaining ingredients and combine thoroughly.
4. Pour into prepared pan and bake 15 minutes. Reduce heat to 300° and bake 90 to 105 additional minutes or until firm. Turn off oven leaving cake until cool. Store in refrigerator.
5. Slice into small pieces and, if desired, top with spiced whipped cream. (Whip cream with sugar and flavorings until stiff.)

Bûche de Noël

Rich, wonderful, chocolate through and through.

Cake:

½ cup flour
¼ teaspoon salt
¼ teaspoon orange peel
½ cup Dutch-process cocoa
6 eggs
1 cup sugar

Filling:

12 ounces semisweet chocolate, in pieces
4 ounces sweet chocolate, in pieces
1 cup heavy cream
¾ to 1 cup apricot jam
Orange-flavored liqueur

Bark:

8 ounces semisweet chocolate

confectioners' sugar

Must be made ahead.

1. Preheat oven to 350°.
2. Grease and flour 15 x 10-inch jelly-roll pan.
3. Combine flour, salt, peel and cocoa.
4. With electric mixer beat eggs and sugar until thick and it forms a ribbon as batter falls onto itself (5 to 10 minutes).
5. Fold cocoa mixture gently but thoroughly into eggs by thirds. Spread evenly into prepared pan and bake about 15 minutes or until top springs back when touched. Do not overbake. Watch carefully.
6. Turn cake out onto a linen towel. Roll cake lengthwise with towel inside. Cool on rack.
7. Strain apricot jam to get ½ cup of purée.
8. Prepare filling. Heat cream to boiling and pour over chocolate stirring until smooth. Remove from heat.
9. Unroll cooled cake. Sprinkle with liqueur (2 to 3 tablespoons). Spread with apricot. Spread half of chocolate mixture on top of jam, and roll lengthwise. Cover with plastic wrap and chill well.
10. Prepare bark: melt chocolate. Spread with the back of spoon onto waxed paper in strips 15 inches long. Let chocolate harden.
11. When chocolate bark is firm and Bûche is well chilled, gently reheat remainder of filling to make spreadable. Cover entire Bûche. Lay strips of bark on top, overlapping where necessary. Sprinkle log with confectioners' sugar. Refrigerate. Remove from refrigerator 20 to 30 minutes before serving. Serve on tray or platter decorated with fresh holly and additional confectioners' sugar.

Frozen Bûche de Noël

Yield: 10 servings

A frozen chocolate version of the French classic cake roll.

Cake:

5 eggs, separated, at room temperature
confectioners' sugar
3 tablespoons cocoa
dash salt
Mocha Cream
Chocolate Icing
Meringue Mushrooms

Must be made ahead.

Mocha Cream:

⅓ cup packed brown sugar
2 tablespoons instant coffee powder
2 cups heavy cream

Chocolate Icing:

1 cup heavy cream
1¼ cups sugar
5 ounces (5 squares) unsweetened chocolate,
  broken into small pieces
½ cup (1 stick) sweet butter
1 teaspoon vanilla

Cake:

1. Preheat oven to 400°. Grease 15½ x 10½-inch jelly-roll pan; line with wax paper; grease and flour paper.

2. In large bowl of mixer, beat egg whites at high speed until soft peaks form; beating at high, gradually sprinkle in ½ cup confectioners' sugar; beat until sugar is completely dissolved; set aside.

3. In small bowl with same beaters, on high, beat egg yolks until thick and lemon-colored; on low speed, beat in ½ cup confectioners' sugar, cocoa and salt. Gently fold yolk mixture into beaten whites until blended. Spread batter evenly in pan; bake 15 minutes or until top springs back when lightly touched with finger.

4. Sprinkle clean cloth towel with confectioners' sugar. When cake is done, immediately loosen edges from sides of pan; invert cake onto towel. Gently peel paper from cake. Roll cake and towel from a narrow end, jelly-roll style. Cool on wire rack.

5. When cake is cool, unroll. Trim crusts from cake. Spread Mocha Cream over cake almost to edges. Reroll cake (without towel); place, seam-side down, on chilled platter. Freezer-wrap and freeze. This part can be done up to 1 month ahead.

Mocha Cream preparation:

1. In medium bowl mix together all ingredients at medium speed of mixer just until soft peaks form. Spread as directed above.

Chocolate Icing preparation:

1. In a large, heavy saucepan stir cream and sugar to mix; heat over medium heat, stirring, until mixture comes to boil. Reduce heat; simmer for EXACTLY 6 minutes.

2. Remove cream mixture from heat; add chocolate and stir until melted; add butter and stir until melted. Add vanilla and stir.

On day of serving cakeroll, make icing.

This is a delicious icing suitable for any cake calling for a chocolate frosting.

Yield: 24 mushrooms

Meringue Mushrooms:

2 egg whites at room temperature
⅛ teaspoon cream of tartar
½ cup sugar
½ cup chocolate chips
1 tablespoon unsweetened cocoa

The mushrooms can be made well ahead and stored in an air-tight container.

TO SERVE: Remove frosted cakeroll from freezer and allow to sit at room temperature 15 to 20 minutes to soften mocha cream. Garnish with meringue mushrooms and small branches of real evergreens around platter, if desired. Dust all with confectioners' sugar "snow."

3. Fill sink about 3-inches full of ice water. Place saucepan of icing in sink and stir often until completely cool. Then stir constantly and vigorously until mixture thickens.

4. When icing begins to thicken, remove from sink and beat with wooden spoon until smooth and thick enough to spread.

5. Remove cakeroll from freezer; unwrap and place on serving plate. Working quickly and gently, spread frosting over top and sides of roll, being careful not to "tear" cake. Using a 4-tine dinner fork, make short vertical markings down frosting to resemble bark. Return cake to freezer.

Meringue Mushrooms:

1. Line a baking sheet with brown paper. Preheat oven to 200°.

2. In small bowl of mixer, combine egg whites and cream of tartar. Beat at high speed until foamy. Gradually add sugar, 2 tablespoons at a time, beating well after each addition.

3. Put meringue into large pastry bag with large plain tip, ½-inch in diameter. To make caps: press mounds of meringue, 1¼ inches each in diameter, onto brown paper, 2 inches apart. Smooth tops with spatula. To make stems: holding pastry tube upright, press out strips of meringue 1¼ inches long, 2 inches apart.

4. Bake 2 hours, or until dry. Remove from paper with spatula; cool on wire rack.

5. To assemble mushrooms: turn caps upside down; poke a small hole in center using a sharp knife tip (the stem will fit into this hole).

6. Melt chocolate in small saucepan over low heat. This will be used as "glue."

7. Spread a thin layer of melted chocolate over bottom of cap. Immediately insert smaller end of mushroom stem into hole.

8. Place "mushrooms" upside down on rack; let stand until chocolate hardens, about 1 hour. Sift cocoa lightly over tops of mushrooms.

9. Cover with waxed paper; store airtight at room temperature. Makes 24.

Pumpkin Cake Roll

Yield: 8 to 10 servings

3 eggs
1 cup sugar
⅔ cup cooked or canned pumpkin
1 teaspoon lemon juice
¾ cup flour
1 teaspoon baking powder
2 teaspoons cinnamon
1 teaspoon ginger
½ teaspoon nutmeg
½ teaspoon salt
1 cup finely chopped walnuts

1. Preheat oven to 375°.
2. In large bowl of mixer, beat eggs on high speed for 5 minutes. Gradually beat in sugar. Stir in pumpkin and lemon juice.
3. Mix together dry ingredients and fold into pumpkin mixture.
4. Line greased 10½ x 15½ x 1-inch cookie sheet with wax paper; grease paper. Spread batter in pan; sprinkle with nuts. Bake for 12 to 15 minutes.
5. Turn cake onto towel sprinkled with confectioners' sugar. Start at narrow end and roll up cake and towel together. While cake cools, prepare filling.

Filling:
1 cup confectioners' sugar
6 ounces cream cheese, softened
4 tablespoons butter, softened
1 teaspoon vanilla extract

Filling preparation:
1. Whip sugar with cheese, butter and vanilla until smooth.
2. Unroll cooled cake; spread with filling. Roll again. Place seam side down on serving platter. Trim ends. Serve in slices. (Freezes well.)

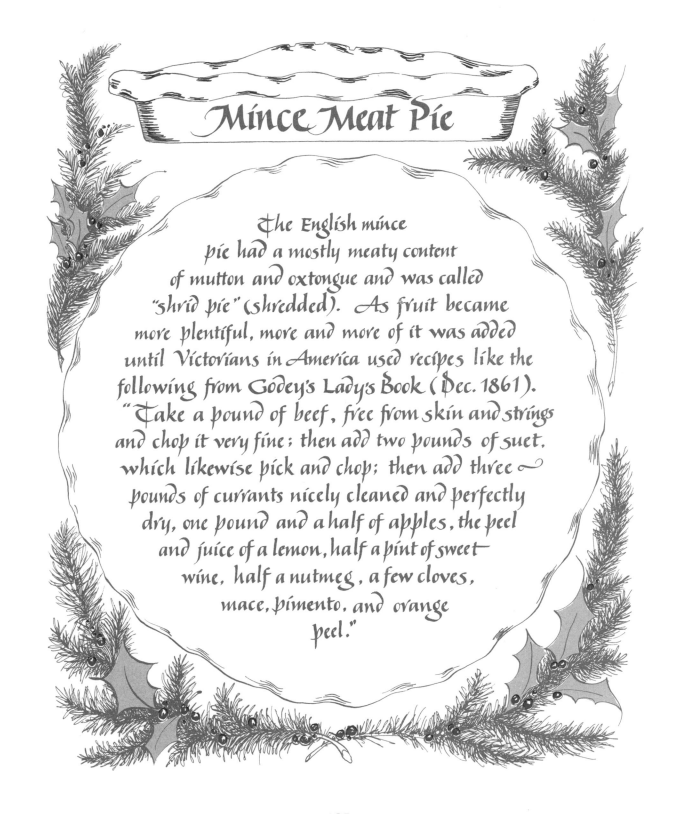

Mince Meat Pie

The English mince pie had a mostly meaty content of mutton and oxtongue and was called "shrid pie" (shredded). As fruit became more plentiful, more and more of it was added until Victorians in America used recipes like the following from Godey's Lady's Book (Dec. 1861). "Take a pound of beef, free from skin and strings and chop it very fine; then add two pounds of suet, which likewise pick and chop; then add three pounds of currants nicely cleaned and perfectly dry, one pound and a half of apples, the peel and juice of a lemon, half a pint of sweet wine, half a nutmeg, a few cloves, mace, pimento, and orange peel."

Cranberry Apple Pie

Slightly tart, perfect "a la Mode".

Yield: 6 to 8 servings

2 cups cranberries, coarsely chopped
3 cups apples, pared, sliced
1¼ cups sugar
1 tablespoon flour
½ teaspoon cinnamon
dash allspice
dash salt
2 tablespoons butter
double crust for 9-inch pie

1. Preheat oven to 400°.
2. Combine apples and berries.
3. Mix sugar, flour and spices. Mix with apples.
4. Line a 9-inch pie plate with pastry. Pour in the fruit. Dot with 2 tablespoons butter.
5. Make lattice crust on top.
6. Bake 40 to 45 minutes or until apples are tender and crust is golden.
7. Serve warm with vanilla ice cream.

French Silk Pie

Fudge in a pie crust.

Yield: 8 to 10 servings

9-inch baked pastry pie shell, cooled
¾ cup (1½ sticks) unsalted butter
1 cup lightly packed brown sugar
3 ounces unsweetened chocolate, melted
1 teaspoon vanilla extract
4 eggs
½ cup walnuts

Topping:
1 teaspoon unflavored gelatin
2 tablespoons cold water
2 cups heavy cream
½ cup confectioners' sugar
1 teaspoon vanilla extract

Most reliably made in a food processor. Cream butter and sugar well if doing conventionally.

1. Combine butter and sugar well in food processor. Add chocolate and vanilla. Mix well, scraping bowl occasionally.
2. Add eggs one at a time, processing thoroughly with each addition. Add nuts and pulse a few times to chop a bit. Pour into baked shell and refrigerate until firm.
3. Prepare topping: sprinkle gelatin over water. Let stand a minute or two, then place over hot water (or in microwave for 5 to 10 seconds) to dissolve gelatin. Reserve ¼ cup cream, whip remaining cream with sugar and vanilla to nearly soft peaks. Stir reserved cream into gelatin and immediately pour into whipped cream and continue beating to soft peaks.
4. Cover pie with cream and return to refrigerator until serving. Garnish with grated chocolate.

Mary Burns Pumpkin Pies

Yield: 2 pies

A definite headliner.

2 9-inch unbaked crusts
2 tablespoons melted butter
5 eggs
2 cups brown sugar
1 teaspoon salt
2 teaspoons cinnamon
1 teaspoon ginger
½ teaspoon nutmeg
3½ cups canned pumpkin
3 cups heavy cream
¼ cup cognac or Grand Marnier

1. Flute edges of crusts to make a high rim. Brush crusts with melted butter and chill for 30 minutes.
2. Preheat oven to 425°.
3. Beat eggs with sugar, salt and spices. Mix in the pumpkin, cream and cognac.
4. Pour mixture into prepared pie crusts. (Rather than overfilling, pour any extra pumpkin into small baking dish and bake as custard.)
5. Bake at 425° for 15 minutes, then lower heat to 350° and bake an additional 30 minutes or until knife comes out clean when inserted halfway between center and edge. Watch carefully. DON'T BURN.
6. Cool on rack. Pies may be frozen but they should be chilled before wrapping.

Pecan Chess Pie

Yield: one 9-inch pie

An old Deep South recipe which always gets raves.

1½ cups sugar
½ cup (1 stick) butter
3 eggs
1 tablespoon vinegar
1 teaspoon vanilla extract
1 tablespoon corn meal
1 cup whole pecan halves
Pastry for 1-crust 9-inch pie
whipped cream (optional)

1. Preheat oven to 300° to 325°.
2. Cream together sugar and butter; add eggs, one at a time.
3. Add remaining ingredients; stir well. Pour into an unbaked 9-inch pie shell.
4. Bake 1 hour or longer until set in center. Let pie remain in oven an additional hour or so with oven off and door slightly ajar after cooking. (If made ahead, reheat).
5. Serve topped with whipped cream, if desired.

Pumpkin Cream Pie

Yield: 8 servings

Light and easy with pudding "short-cut".

Baked 9-inch pie shell or Gingersnap Crust
  (see below)
1 quart vanilla ice cream, softened*
2 cups canned pumpkin
2 3½-ounce packages vanilla instant pudding
1 teaspoon cinnamon
whipped cream (optional)

***Be sure not to over-soften ice cream or it will
take longer for pie to firm up when chilled.**

Must be made ahead.

1. Blend ice cream and pumpkin. Add instant pudding mix and cinnamon; fold together as quickly and lightly as possible to prevent further softening of ice cream.
2. Pour into prepared pie crust and chill at least 8 hours or overnight.
3. Garnish with whipped cream before serving.

Pumpkin Ice Cream Pie

Yield: 8 servings

A refreshing alternative.

1 cup canned or cooked pumpkin
½ cup packed brown sugar
dash salt
½ teaspoon ginger
¼ teaspoon nutmeg
1 quart French Vanilla ice cream, softened

Crust:

1 cup ground nuts (pecans or walnuts)
½ cup ground gingersnaps
3 tablespoons sugar
¼ cup (½ stick) butter, melted

Must be made ahead.

1. Preheat oven to 450°.
2. Combine crust ingredients and press into 9-inch pie plate. Bake for 5 to 7 minutes, not until it is dark. Cool.
3. Combine pumpkin, sugar, spices. Mix with softened ice cream.
4. Pour into cooled shell and freeze several hours or overnight. Remove from freezer 15 minutes before serving.

Pumpkin Pecan Pie

Yield: 12 to 16 servings (2 pies)

2 deep 9-inch unbaked pie crusts
7 eggs, (3 whole, 4 separated)
3 tablespoons butter, melted
1¼ cups sugar
1 cup dark corn syrup
1 16-ounce can pumpkin or 2 cups
   fresh cooked pumpkin purée
1 cup half-and-half
2 cups pecans
½ teaspoon salt
¾ teaspoon pumpkin pie spice
1 teaspoon vanilla extract

1. Preheat oven to 350°. Divide pecans between two pie shells. Combine in medium bowl, 3 eggs, melted butter, ½ cup sugar, corn syrup and vanilla. Pour half into each pie shell, covering pecans. Bake 30 minutes.

2. Meanwhile, beat 4 egg whites until soft peaks form. Gradually add about half the remaining sugar, beating until stiff.

3. In another bowl, combine pumpkin, remaining sugar, spice, salt and half-and-half. Gently fold in the egg whites.

4. Divide pumpkin mixture between partly baked pies and bake an additional 30 minutes or until pumpkin layer is set. Test by inserting knife into pumpkin layer about halfway from center to outside edge.

5. Cool on racks. Serve with whipped cream.

Raisin-Nut Pie

Yield: 6 to 8 servings

pie pastry for single crust 9-inch pie
2 eggs
1½ tablespoons flour
⅔ cup packed brown sugar
½ teaspoon salt
1 teaspoon vanilla extract
1 cup heavy cream
½ cup golden raisins
1 cup pitted dates, chopped
1 cup coarsely chopped walnuts

1. Preheat oven to 350°

2. Line 9-inch pie plate with pastry.

3. Beat eggs until thick and lemon-colored.

4. Combine flour, brown sugar, and salt; add to eggs. Beat together well.

5. Stir in vanilla, cream, raisins, dates and walnuts. Spoon into prepared pastry.

6. Bake for 50 to 60 minutes, until a knife inserted into center comes out clean. Serve warm or cold.

Rum Cream Pie

Eggnog eaten with a fork.

Yield: 6 to 8 servings

1 9-inch baked pastry or
  graham cracker crust
1 envelope unflavored gelatin
½ cup cold water
1 cup sugar
5 egg yolks
⅓ cup dark rum
1½ cups whipping cream
unsweetened chocolate

1. Soften gelatin in cold water in small pan. Place over low heat, stirring until dissolved.
2. In large bowl, beat egg yolks and sugar with electric mixer until very light. Stir in gelatin gradually; then rum.
3. When egg mixture is cooled to room temperature, whip the cream until it stands in soft peaks. Fold into gelatin mixture. Pour into crust and chill until firm enough to cut.
4. Garnish with a little grated unsweetened chocolate.

Food Processor Pie Crust

Yield: 3 single crusts

3 cups flour, lightly spooned
  then measured
1½ teaspoons salt
1 cup Crisco shortening, frozen in small
  chunks on a plate for 20 to 30 minutes
½ cup chilled water

1. Place flour and salt in food processor with steel blade. Pulse several times to mix.
2. Put half the frozen shortening in the bowl and pulse on and off until the shortening is the size of peas.
3. Add remaining shortening and, with the same technique, cut in shortening until it is nearly of corn meal texture.
4. All at once add water and pulse until dough begins to form a ball. Do not over-process.
5. Let dough rest 10 minutes. Divide into thirds; wrap and store in refrigerator or freezer to roll out as needed, or roll on floured cloth to use immediately.

SECRET: Don't overdo handling of dough; roll once carefully and transfer to pie plate. Patch if necessary. Don't reroll. Too much handling makes crust tough.

Cookies and Candies

Cookies and Candies

• **Indicates items suitable for gift giving**

The age-old art of figurative cookies was imported to America with the first colonists, and immigrants from European countries have continued to bring their own favorite recipes, cookie molds, cutters and decorative techniques. During the nineteenth century, cookies were a most important decoration on the American tree for Christmas, as well as an essential edible ingredient of the holiday.

Christmas Cookies

Matzebaum – cakes of almond paste, sugar and egg whites

Marzipan – a thicker version of matzebaum that made wonderful rounded fruit and vegetable forms.

Springerle – white egg dough that formed cameo-like images, flavored with anise seeds

Tirggel – are thin, molded cookies of honey, flour, water and sugar with a browned relief on the top

Sandtart – rich cookies baked as thin as possible; made of egg, flour and sugar glazed with an egg mixture, sprinkled with sugar and cinnamon and decorated with half of a hickory nut

Gingerbread men – animal and flat cakes that sometimes had colored pictures pasted on with egg white and were at least a half inch thick

Pretzels and pretzel-shaped cookies represented hands in prayer.

Austrian Anise Drops

Yield: 2 dozen

A crispy, two-layer cookie.

2 eggs
1 cup sugar
⅛ teaspoon salt
1 cup flour
½ teaspoon baking powder
1 teaspoon anise extract

Must be made ahead.

1. With electric mixer, beat eggs on high for 10 minutes. Add sugar; beat 5 minutes more. Add remaining ingredients; beat 15 minutes with spoon by hand.
2. Drop by teaspoonsful onto well-greased cookie sheets at least one inch apart. Let stand overnight. Do not disturb.
3. In the morning, bake at 300° for about 10 minutes until lightly browned. Remove from cookie sheet immediately.

Chocolate Chip Meringues

Yield: 2 to 2½ dozen cookies

2 egg whites, at room temperature.
⅛ teaspoon cream of tartar
⅛ teaspoon salt
1 teaspoon vanilla extract
¾ cup sugar
1 6-ounce package chocolate chips

Variation: add ¼ cup each chopped candied cherries and finely chopped nuts along with the chocolate chips.

1. Preheat oven to 300°.
2. In large bowl of mixer, beat together egg whites, cream of tartar, salt and vanilla until stiff peaks form. Slowly add sugar, a tablespoon at a time, beating well after each addition, so egg whites remain stiff and do not become grainy.
3. Fold chocolate chips into egg whites.
4. Drop batter by the tablespoonful onto cookie sheets covered with brown paper (shopping bags can be cut to fit). Bake for 25 to 30 minutes until meringues are golden and can be lifted easily off of paper. Cool completely and store in air-tight containers.

Gingered Florentines

Yield: 24 to 30 cookies

A truly distinctive, five-star cookie.

¾ cup heavy cream
¼ cup (½ stick) unsalted butter
¾ cup sugar
1¾ cups finely chopped
   blanched almonds
½ cup flour
¼ teaspoon ground ginger
⅓ cup finely chopped candied ginger,
   packed into cup
4 squares (1-ounce each) semisweet chocolate

1. Preheat oven to 350°.
2. Combine cream, butter and sugar in heavy saucepan. Bring to boiling, stirring until sugar is dissolved and all ingredients are well blended. Remove from heat. Mix in almonds, flour, ginger and candied ginger.
3. Drop batter by heaping teaspoons 3-inches apart onto ungreased cookie sheet.
4. Bake for 10 to 12 minutes, or until well browned on edges. Watch closely: cookies should not be undercooked or overcooked.
5. Cool cookies briefly on sheets. If cookies stick to pan, return pans to oven for 15 seconds to soften. Carefully transfer cookies with spatula to wire rack to cool.
6. When cookies are completely cooled cover bottoms with melted chocolate. Place on rack, chocolate side up, until chocolate hardens. Store in airtight container.

Mrs. Claus's Cookies

Yield: 4 to 5 dozen

**Chewy, macaroon-type cookies
reputed to be Santa's favorites.**

½ cup (1 stick) unsalted butter softened
1 cup sugar
1 large egg, lightly beaten
1 teaspoon vanilla extract
½ teaspoon rum flavoring
1¼ cups flour
½ teaspoon baking soda
½ teaspoon salt
1 cup chopped walnuts or pecans
1 cup chocolate chips
1 cup sweetened grated coconut
1 cup finely chopped mixed candied fruit

1. Preheat oven to 350°. Grease baking sheets.
2. In large bowl of mixer, cream butter and sugar until light and fluffy. Add egg, vanilla and rum flavoring.
3. Sift together flour, baking soda and salt; add to egg mixture. Stir in nuts, chocolate, coconut and fruit.
4. Drop batter by heaping teaspoons 2 inches apart onto baking sheets. Bake for 13 to 15 minutes (less for chewy cookies, more for crispy) or until golden. Transfer to racks to cool.

"Mysterious" Wine Drop Cookies   Yield: 4 to 5 dozen

**A 100-year old recipe. The mystery is ours.
Who drank the wine?**

⅔ cup shortening
1 cup packed brown sugar
1 egg
4 cups flour
2 teaspoons baking soda
1 teaspoon cinnamon
1 teaspoon powdered ginger
1 teaspoon ground cloves
1 cup molasses
1 cup sour milk
¾ cup raisins, optional
confectioners' sugar

1. Preheat oven to 350°.
2. Cream well the shortening, sugar and egg in food processor or electric mixer.
3. In medium bowl, combine dry ingredients. In another bowl combine milk and molasses.
4. Add flour and milk mixture. Add raisins.
5. Drop by spoonsful onto lightly greased cookie sheet. Bake 10 to 15 minutes.
6. While still warm from the oven, dust with confectioners' sugar.

Pansy Ann Cookies   Yield: 6 to 7 dozen

A chewy French Christmas cookie.

3 cups light brown sugar, packed
1 cup (2 sticks) butter, softened
3 eggs
3½ cups flour
1 teaspoon baking soda
1 teaspoon cream of tartar
1 teaspoon vanilla extract
1 teaspoon almond extract

1. Preheat oven to 350°.
2. Cream butter and sugar; add eggs and beat until light.
3. Combine flour, soda and cream of tartar. Mix well with creamed mixture. Add flavorings. If dough is not stiff enough to drop add a bit more flour.
4. Drop by teaspoonsful onto greased cookie sheets. Bake about 10 minutes.
Cool on rack.

Pumpkin Drop Cookies

Yield: 4 to 5 dozen

Elisabeth's old-fashioned, irresistable spice cookie.

1 egg
1 cup canned pumpkin
½ cup shortening
¾ cup sugar
¼ cup molasses
1¾ cups flour
1 teaspoon baking soda
1 teaspoon cinnamon
½ teaspoon ground cloves
½ teaspoon salt
½ cup chopped nuts, optional
½ cup raisins, optional

These don't last long which is fortunate. They can get soggy. Try freezing if necessary.

1. Preheat oven to 350°.
2. With electric mixer in medium bowl, combine egg, pumpkin, shortening, sugar and molasses.
3. Combine dry ingredients and add to first mixture.
4. Add nuts and raisins if desired.
5. Drop by teaspoonsful onto lightly greased cookie sheet and bake 10 to 12 minutes.

Travis House Cookies

Yield: about 2 dozen

Chewy, butterscotch meringue cookies with pecans made famous by a Williamsburg restaurant in the 1940's.

1 egg white, at room temperature
1 cup brown sugar
pinch of salt
1 level tablespoon of flour
¾ cup chopped pecans

1. Preheat oven to 350°. Grease baking sheet well.
2. Beat egg white until stiff peaks form; gradually add brown sugar, a tablespoon at a time, beating well after each addition. Beat in salt and flour.
3. Stir in chopped pecans. Drop batter by teaspoonsful, 2 inches apart on baking sheet.
4. Bake approximately 15 minutes. Cool slightly; remove from pan.

Sentiments of many ruffled parents during the holiday season:

We like to give homemade gifts at Christmas. Which of our children would you like?

Almond Cut-Out Cookies

Yield: 4 to 5 dozen

Simple and chewy.

1 cup (2 sticks) butter
1¼ cups sugar
1 egg
¼ teaspoon almond extract
1¼ cups almonds with skins
1¾ cups flour
dash salt
confectioners' sugar glaze (see p. 199)

Dough must be chilled.

1. Grind almonds in food processor or blender. Do not let them become "butter." Set aside.
2. Cream butter and sugar. Add egg and extract. Beat thoroughly. Add nuts, flour and salt; mix well.
3. Cover and refrigerate dough, at least an hour.
4. Preheat oven to 325°. Roll out dough as thinly as possible on floured cloth. Cut into shapes. Bake on ungreased cookie sheet 8 to 10 minutes or until lightly browned. Cool on rack.
5. Make a thin confectioners' glaze flavored with almond. Apply to cooled cookies with a pastry brush.
6. When thoroughly dry, store cookies in tightly covered container or freeze.

Anise Cut-Out Cookies

Yield: 4 to 5 dozen

Rolls easily, stores well.

½ cup (1 stick) butter
¾ cup sugar
1 egg
1 teaspoon anise extract
½ teaspoon vanilla extract
1¾ cups flour
1 teaspoon baking powder
¼ teaspoon salt
confectioners' sugar glaze (see p. 199)
colored sugars, optional

Dough must be chilled.

1. Cream butter and sugar. Add egg, anise and vanilla; beat until light.
2. Mix dry ingredients and add to creamed mixture.
3. Cover and chill dough at least an hour or until firm enough to roll.
4. Preheat oven to 350°. Working with part of the dough at a time, roll to ⅛-inch thick on floured cloth. Cut into shapes and bake on lightly greased cookie sheet for 6 to 8 minutes, or until lightly browned at edges. Remove to rack to cool.
5. Make anise-flavored glaze and brush over tops of cookies. If desired, immediately sprinkle lightly with decorative sugars.
6. Dry thoroughly before storing in tightly covered tin or in freezer.

Brown Sugar Cut-Outs

Yield: approximately 6 dozen

A rolled cookie with rich butterscotch taste.

1 1-pound package brown sugar
2 cups (4 sticks) butter, softened
1½ teaspoons vanilla extract
4½ cups unsifted flour
confectioners' sugar glaze (see below)

Dough must be chilled.

1. Cream sugar and butter together until fluffy; add vanilla. Mix in flour. (Or place all ingredients in bowl of food processor fitted with steel blade and process until dough forms a ball.) Shape into a smooth ball, cover and chill. (May be stored up to a week.)
2. Preheat oven to 300°.
3. Pinch off about ⅙ of dough at a time; flatten and roll out on a floured surface to ⅛-inch thickness. Cut with cookie-cutters of desired shapes. Place on ungreased baking sheet. Bake approximately 12 to 15 minutes. Remove to wire rack and cool. Decorate as desired with frosting and sprinkles.

Chocolate Jumbles

Yield: about 6 dozen

A spicy, dark chocolate cut-out cookie

½ cup sugar
½ cup (1 stick) butter or margarine
1 egg
1 scant cup molasses
1 teaspoon vanilla extract
½ cup cocoa
3¾ cups flour
2 teaspoons ground cloves
¼ cup hot coffee
1 teaspoon baking soda
confectioners' sugar glaze (see below)

1. Preheat oven to 350°.
2. Beat together sugar, butter, egg, molasses and vanilla.
3. Combine cocoa, flour and cloves.
4. Dissolve soda in coffee. Add to egg mixture alternately with flour.
5. Roll dough on floured surface. Bake on lightly greased cookie sheets about 8 minutes or until puffed and firm. Cool.
6. Brush cookies with glaze.

Confectioners' Sugar Glaze

1 cup confectioners' sugar
2 to 3 tablespoons milk
¼ teaspoon extract of choice

Mix all ingredients together and brush over cooled cookies.

Cookie-Cutter Cookies

The absolutely BEST rolled cookie for children to cut into shapes.

Yield: depends on size of shapes!
(About 3 dozen)

1 cup (2 sticks) butter, at room temperature
½ cup sugar
2½ cups flour
(1 teaspoon almond or lemon extract may be
 added if desired)
confectioners' sugar glaze (see p. 199)

Dough must be chilled.

1. In large bowl of mixer (or food processor), cream together butter and sugar. Blend in flour. When dough is well mixed, pat into a ball and refrigerate for 2 hours.

2. When ready to make cookies heat oven to 300°. Roll cookies on floured board or between sheets of waxed paper dusted with flour, to about ¼-inch thickness. Cut with cutters dusted in flour. Place on ungreased cookie sheet. Re-roll dough until all is used.

3. Bake for 20 to 25 minutes until brown around edges. Cool for 15 minutes.

4. Decorate with frosting and sprinkles as desired.

Cream Cheese Cut-Out Cookies

Yield: 3 to 4 dozen

1 cup sugar
1 cup (2 sticks) butter, softened
3 ounces cream cheese, softened
¼ teaspoon salt
1 teaspoon vanilla (or half almond,
  or lemon) extract
1 egg yolk
2¼ cups flour
confectioners' sugar glaze (see p. 199)
colored sugars

Dough must be chilled.

1. Cream sugar, butter, cream cheese, salt, extract, and egg yolk until light. Add flour blending well. Chill dough several hours or overnight.

2. When ready to bake, preheat oven to 375°.

3. Using a section at a time, roll dough to ⅛-inch on a floured cloth. Cut into desired shapes and bake on ungreased cookie sheets for 7 to 10 minutes or until light golden. Cool on a rack.

4. Brush with confectioners' sugar glaze and sprinkle with colored sugars if desired.

Cut-out cookie batter can also be rolled into logs, wrapped and refrigerated to be sliced when needed. Saves time and fuss when you are not concerned about decorative shapes.

Chocolate Scotch Shortbread Cookies   Yield: 3 dozen

Traditionally rich, thick and buttery; untraditionally, very chocolate.

2 cups flour
½ cup unsweetened cocoa powder
I cup confectioners' sugar
¼ teaspoon salt
½ teaspoon mace
I cup (2 sticks) unsalted butter, cut into chunks.
½ teaspoon vanilla extract

1. Preheat oven to 300°.
2. In food processor or with electric mixer combine dry ingredients, butter chunks, and vanilla; mix well, until dough holds together.
3. By hand, work dough until smooth; shape into a ball and flatten.
4. Flour board and rolling pin. Roll dough evenly to ½-inch thickness.
5. Cut cookies into desired shape with floured cutter. Place on ungreased cookie sheet; prick in center with fork.
6. Bake 25 to 30 minutes, or until firm. Do not overbake. Cool on wire rack. Store in airtight container.

Cinnamon Stars   Yield: about 5 dozen

This crunchy almond and cinnamon flavored cookie from Germany is reminiscent of the matzebaum of Victorian days.

3 egg whites
1¼ cups sugar
2 tablespoons cinnamon
I pound ground unblanched almonds
I teaspoon almond extract
additional ground almonds for pastry board

1. Beat egg whites and, as they become foamy and stiff, beat in sugar a little at a time. Continue beating until whites form stiff peaks that retain the mark of a knife blade. Set aside ½ cup of beaten whites.
2. Sprinkle remaining egg whites with cinnamon. Stir in ground almonds and flavoring. Stir gently but thoroughly. Mixture should be thick and solid. Add more almonds if dough is too sticky to be rolled.
3. Preheat oven to 300°. Butter baking sheet.
4. Sprinkle pastry board with nuts; roll out dough to ¼-inch thickness. Cut into star shapes with cookie cutter.
5. Arrange on baking sheet; brush top of each cookie with reserved egg whites. Bake about 20 minutes or until golden brown.
6. Cool on wire rack; store in airtight container.

Frosted Christmas Cookies

Yield: about 4 dozen

Buttery, versatile cut-out cookie, somewhat fragile for storage.

1 cup (2 sticks) butter
1½ cup confectioners' sugar
1 egg
1 teaspoon vanilla extract
2½ cups flour
1 teaspoon baking soda
1 teaspoon cream of tartar
¼ teaspoon salt
confectioners' sugar glaze, if desired
  (see p. 199)

Dough must be chilled.

1. Cream butter and sugar; add egg and vanilla.
2. Combine dry ingredients thoroughly and add to creamed mixture.
3. Cover and refrigerate 2 hours.
4. Roll out on floured cloth and cut into shapes. Bake on ungreased cookie sheet at 400° for 6 to 8 minutes, or until lightly browned.
5. Frost if desired, with confectioners' sugar glaze.

Gingerbread People

Yield: depends on size of cutter

This recipe has been perfected for taste and ease of handling and produces a sturdy cookie for mailing and decorating packages or the tree.

2½ cups sifted flour
1 teaspoon salt
1½ teaspoons ginger
½ teaspoon cloves
1 teaspoon cinnamon
2 teaspoons baking soda
½ cup shortening
1 cup molasses
raisins
cinnamon candies

Decorative frosting:
1 cup sifted confectioners' sugar
1½ tablespoons light cream
½ teaspoon vanilla extract

Dough must be chilled.

1. Sift together flour, salt, spices and baking soda.
2. In a large saucepan, heat molasses until bubbly; add shortening and stir until melted. Remove from heat and cool slightly.
3. Add sifted ingredients to molasses. Mix well. Cover and refrigerate dough for several hours.
4. Preheat oven to 350°. Roll dough a little at a time, on floured surface. Cut with people cutters (or other desired shapes). Press raisins into cookies for eyes, cinnamon candies for mouth and buttons. Bake 8 to 10 minutes on ungreased cookie sheet. Cool thoroughly on wire rack before frosting.
5. To frost, mix all ingredients. Use outline tip of decorator tube, if desired.

Springerle (German Anise Cakes)

Yield: about 6 dozen

There are spingerle rolling pins but antique molds are lovely if you can find them. These cakes could also be used to decorate the tree.

1 pound confectioners' sugar
4 eggs
grated rind of 1 lemon (1 teaspoon)
4 cups flour
1 teaspoon baking powder
about ¼ cup anise seed

Must be made a day ahead.

1. In large bowl of electric mixer, beat eggs with sugar until thick and light, 15 to 20 minutes. Add lemon rind.

2. Combine flour and baking powder. At low speed of mixer, blend flour with eggs and sugar. Cover bowl and let rest 15 minutes.

3. Divide dough into thirds and roll to ¼-inch thickness (about an 8-inch square).

4. Prepare an out-of-the-way lightly floured surface.

5. Flour molds and press into dough. Cut and place cakes on prepared floured surface. Cover with a towel and leave overnight.

6. Lightly grease cookie sheets. Preheat oven to 325°. Sprinkle sheets with anise seed. Place cakes on top of seed and bake 20 to 25 minutes. They should not brown.

7. Store in tightly covered container or in freezer. These are a soft cookie/cake and should not become hard.

Carol's Sugar Plums

Yield: varies according to size

No-bake yummies the kids can make.

12 ounces vanilla wafers, crushed
¾ cup coconut
¾ cup confectioners' sugar
½ cup orange concentrate, thawed
sugar

1. Combine first three ingredients.

2. Mix in orange juice, combining well.

3. Form into 1-inch balls, roll in sugar and refrigerate or freeze.

Candy-Cane Cookies

Yield: about 4 dozen

Butter-cookie dough colored and shaped as candy-canes.

½ cup (1 stick) butter, softened
½ cup shortening
1 cup sifted confectioners' sugar
1 egg
1½ teaspoons almond extract
1 teaspoon vanilla extract
1 teaspoon salt
2½ cups flour
red food coloring
½ cup crushed peppermint candy
½ cup granulated sugar

1. Preheat oven to 375°.
2. In bowl of mixer or in food processor, combine butter, shortening, confectioners' sugar, egg, almond and vanilla extracts. Mix well.
3. Sift together salt and flour; stir into dough.
4. Divide dough into two halves. Blend ½ teaspoon red food coloring into half of dough. Roll about 1 teaspoon of each color dough into strips about 4 inches long. Place strips side-by-side, press lightly together, and twist like a rope. Place on ungreased cookie sheet; curve top down to form cane.
5. Bake about 9 minutes. Carefully remove from sheet with spatula while still warm; sprinkle with mixture of crushed candy and sugar.

Chocolate-glazed Shortbread Cookie

Yield: about 5 to 6 dozen

1 cup (2 sticks) butter
1 cup confectioners' sugar
2 cups flour
2 cups almonds or pecans, finely chopped
6 ounces semisweet chocolate

Dough must be chilled.

1. Cream butter and sugar; gradually add flour, stir in half the nuts. Chill dough 1 hour.
2. Preheat oven to 325°.
3. Form 1 tablespoon dough into a 2-inch long finger. Cut in half lengthwise and place cut side down on ungreased cookie sheet. Bake 15 minutes or until pale golden brown. Cool.
4. Melt chocolate. Dip one end of cookie into chocolate then into chopped nuts. Cool on waxed paper until set.

Chestnut Fingers

Delicious, unusual flavor.

Yield: 4 to 5 dozen

1½ cups (3 sticks) unsalted butter, softened
½ cup sugar
2 egg yolks
1 cup chestnut purée or canned chestnuts, drained and puréed
½ teaspoon vanilla extract
2 cups flour
½ teaspoon salt
¼ teaspoon ground cinnamon
2 egg whites, slightly beaten
sugar
1 cup semisweet chocolate pieces, melted

1. Preheat oven to 350°. Grease cookie sheets.
2. In mixer bowl, cream butter and ½ cup sugar; add egg yolk, and mix until light and fluffy. Beat in chestnut purée and vanilla.
3. Stir together flour, salt, and cinnamon; stir into creamed mixture.
4. Using about a tablespoon of dough for each cookie, roll into 2½-inch "fingers." Dip one side of each finger in egg white, then in sugar.
5. Place fingers, sugar side up, on greased cookie sheets.
6. Bake 20 minutes or until edges begin to brown.
7. Remove from sheet; cool on racks.
8. Dip one end of each finger in melted chocolate; place on waxed paper until set.

Italian Spice Cookies

Yield: approximately 30 slices

2 eggs
1 cup sugar
2 teaspoons water
⅓ cup oil
2½ cups flour
1 cup EACH white and brown sugar
2 teaspoons baking powder
½ teaspoon baking soda
2 teaspoons cinnamon
1 cup (5½-ounce package) chopped almonds
white of 1 egg, beaten

1. Preheat oven to 350°. Grease cookie sheet.
2. Beat together eggs, sugar, water and oil.
3. Sift together dry ingredients and add to egg mixture.
4. Add almonds and mix well.
5. Roll dough into 2 long rolls or "logs." Place parallel on greased cookie sheet, leaving about 2½ to 3 inches between logs. Bake for 30 minutes; brush tops of logs with egg whites. Continue baking for 20 minutes, being careful not to over cook or cookies will become hard.
6. Cool for 5 minutes. Cut horizontally into 1-inch slices.

Italian Christmas Cookies

Yield: about 4 dozen

Unique chocolate cookie brimming with filberts.

1 cup sugar
¾ cup flour
1½ teaspoons cinnamon
1 tablespoon orange rind
1 teaspoon baking powder
1 tablespoon rum
4 ounces sweet chocolate, melted
1 egg, beaten
8 ounces toasted chopped filberts

Dough must be chilled.

1. Mix first 5 ingredients in large bowl.
2. Add rum, chocolate and beaten egg, blending or kneading well as dough is stiff. Add toasted nuts.
3. Form into rolls about 1¾-inches in diameter. Wrap and refrigerate. Chill several hours.
4. To bake, cut ½-inch slices from roll and bake on ungreased cookie sheet for 10 minutes. Cookies are light, dry but chewy.

Kiss Cookies

Yield: 3 dozen cookies

This recipe is dedicated to very young cooks: Mom, make the cookie dough ahead, then let the pre-schoolers unwrap the kisses and help cover them.

1 cup (2 sticks) butter or margarine, softened
½ cup sugar
1 teaspoon vanilla extract
1¾ cups flour
1 cup walnuts, finely chopped
1 9-ounce package milk chocolate kisses (about 36)
confectioners' sugar (optional)

Dough must be chilled.

1. Preheat oven to 375°.
2. In a large bowl, cream butter, sugar and vanilla; add flour and walnuts. Beat on low speed with electric mixer until thoroughly mixed. Cover and chill.
3. Wrap each kiss with about 1 tablespoon dough, covering each candy completely. Roll each between palms to form a ball. Place about 2 inches apart on ungreased cookie sheets. Bake about 10 to 12 minutes, until centers of cookies look set and edges are beginning to brown.
4. Cool and store in tins or, cool slightly and roll in confectioners' sugar while still warm.

The Magi's Jewels

**A wonderful rich, butter cookie.
Children adore the jam!**

Yield: 2½ to 3 dozen

1 cup (2 sticks) butter at room temperature
½ cup sugar
2 egg yolks, slightly beaten
1 teaspoon vanilla extract
½ teaspoon salt
2 cups flour
strawberry or apricot preserves

1. Preheat oven to 350°.
2. Cream butter and sugar; add egg yolks, vanilla and salt and mix well. Stir in flour; combine well.
3. Using about a tablespoon of dough, roll into a ball, about one inch in size. Place balls on ungreased cookie sheet. Make an indentation with fingertip in top of each and fill with ½ teaspoon strawberry or apricot preserves.
4. Bake for 10 to 12 minutes. Remove from cookie sheet immediately and cool on wire rack.

Pfeffernuesse

Traditional German "pepper nut" cookie.

Yield: 4 dozen

3 cups sifted flour
2 teaspoons baking powder
2 tablespoons cinnamon
1 teaspoon cloves
½ teaspoon nutmeg
1 cup diced candied citron
grated peel of one lemon
4 eggs
2 cups sugar
confectioners' sugar
milk

1. Preheat oven to 350°. Grease cookie sheets.
2. Sift together flour, baking powder, and spices; add citron and lemon peel.
3. Beat eggs and sugar with electric mixer until very thick. Blend in flour mixture. If necessary, add additional flour to make a smooth dough.
4. With hands well floured, roll dough into balls a teaspoon at a time; place on greased cookie sheet.
5. Bake about 15 minutes. when cool, frost with a thick mixture of confectioners' sugar and milk.

Rudolph's Delights

Yield: about 4 dozen

Tell the little ones that the cherry halves are in honor of Rudolph's nose.

1 cup (2 sticks) butter, softened
½ cup sugar
½ cup light corn syrup
2 eggs, separated
2½ cups flour
2 cups finely chopped pecans
candied cherry halves

Dough must be chilled.

1. In large bowl of electric mixer, or in food processor, cream butter and sugar until light and fluffy. Add corn syrup, egg yolks and flour; mix well. Chill.
2. Preheat oven to 350°. Grease cookie sheets.
3. Lightly beat egg whites. Shape dough into one-inch balls; dip in egg whites and coat with nuts. Press cherry half, cut side down, into each cookie.
4. Place cookies 2 inches apart on cookie sheets. Bake for 20 minutes, or until edges are browned.

Snowball Cookies

Yield: about 4 dozen

1 cup (2 sticks) butter, softened
¼ cup confectioners' sugar
2 teaspoons vanilla extract
2 cups flour
1½ to 2 cups ground nuts
confectioners' sugar

Dough must be chilled.

1. Cream butter. Add remaining ingredients, mixing well. Chill dough.
2. Roll dough into 1-inch balls; place on ungreased baking sheets.
3. Bake in preheated 325° oven for 25 to 30 minutes.
4. Roll in confectioners' sugar while still warm. Cool and roll again.

Variations:

1. Substitute 1 teaspoon almond extract for 1 of vanilla and use ground almonds. Shape ball around candied cherry.
2. Use walnuts for ground nuts. Shape into crescents.
3. Substitute 1 teaspoon anise flavoring for vanilla.
4. Use pecans for ground nuts (often called "Mexican Wedding Cookies").
5. Add ½ teaspoon ground cloves and 1 teaspoon ground cinnamon to dough. Shape as crescents. Stick one whole clove in curve of crescent before baking.

Almond Puff Bars

Yield: 3 to 4 dozen

½ cup (1 stick) butter, softened
1 cup flour
2 tablespoons water

½ cup (1 stick) butter
1 cup water
1 teaspoon almond extract
1 cup flour
3 eggs

Frosting:

1 to 2 tablespoons water
2 tablespoons butter
1 teaspoon almond extract
1½ cups confectioners' sugar
toasted almond slices

1. Preheat oven to 350°.
2. Using a fork, mix together butter, flour, and water until a ball forms. Divide dough in half. Shape each half into a 3 x 12-inch strip on ungreased cookie sheet.
3. In a saucepan bring to a boil the other stick of butter and water; add almond extract and flour. Stir until dough forms a ball and leaves sides of pan. Add eggs, one at a time, beating well after each addition.
4. Evenly cover strips on sheet with dough in pan. Bake for one hour, until brown and hollow sounding.
5. Mix together frosting ingredients until smooth. Spread on baked strips; sprinkle with almonds
6. Cut each strip into diagonal slices and down center.

Date and Nut Bars

Yield: 2 dozen

Chewy, old-fashioned and yummy.

¼ cup (½ stick) butter, melted
1 cup sugar
2 eggs, well beaten
¾ cup flour
¼ teaspoon baking powder
1 cup dates, chopped
1 cup nuts, chopped
dash salt
confectioners' sugar

1. Preheat oven to 350°. Line 8-inch square pan with waxed paper.
2. Stir ingredients together in medium bowl in order given.
3. Spread batter into prepared pan. Bake 30 to 45 minutes or until cooked through.
4. Cut into bars, peeling away from waxed paper, remove bars while hot and roll in confectioners' sugar. Cool and store in tightly covered tin.

Creme de Menthe Brownies

Yield: 24 to 30 bars

A winning combination with eye appeal too.

Brownies:

2 cups sugar
4 eggs
1½ cups flour
1 teaspoon baking powder
½ teaspoon salt
2 teaspoons vanilla extract
1 cup (2 sticks) butter
4 squares (4 ounces) unsweetened
  chocolate, melted
1½ cups chopped walnuts

Brownies:

1. Preheat oven to 350°. Grease and flour two 8-inch square pans or one 9 x 11-inch pan.
2. In a large bowl, beat together sugar, eggs, flour, baking powder, salt and vanilla.
3. Melt butter and unsweetened chocolate together over low heat. Add to flour mixture; mix well. Add nuts. Pour into pan(s); bake 30 minutes or until tester inserted in center comes out clean.
4. Cool in pan. Frost with creme de menthe frosting, then chocolate topping. Cut into small squares.

Creme de Menthe Frosting:

¼ cup (½ stick) butter, softened
3½ cups confectioners' sugar
½ cup green creme de menthe liqueur

Creme de Menthe Frosting preparation:

1. Cream together all ingredients. Mixture should be smooth and spreadable.
2. Spread on cool brownies.

Chocolate topping:

½ cup heavy cream
8 ounces (8 squares) semisweet
  baking chocolate

Topping preparation:

1. In a small saucepan over low heat, melt chocolate and cream together. Cool.
2. Spread over frosted brownies.

Mincemeat Squares

Yield: 18 squares

1½ cups flour
1¼ cups uncooked oats
¾ to 1 cup brown sugar
½ teaspoon salt
¾ cup shortening
2 cups mincemeat or other filling

1. Preheat oven to 400°.
2. Combine dry ingredients. (Some fillings are sweeter than others. Thus, the range for sugar.)
3. Cut shortening into mixture with pastry blender until it reaches texture of coarse crumbs. Pat half into a 13 x 9-inch pan.
4. Spoon mincemeat or other filling over crust. Top with remaining crumbs. Bake 25 to 30 minutes, or until lightly browned.
5. Cool then cut in squares. If desired, serve with whipped cream.

"Elves"

Incredibly rich brownies.

½ cup (1 stick) butter, softened
1 cup sugar
3 eggs
1¼ cups flour
1 16-ounce can Hershey's chocolate syrup
1 cup nuts, chopped (optional)

Frosting:

1 cup sugar
6 tablespoons butter
6 tablespoons whole milk
½ teaspoon vanilla extract
1 6-ounce package semisweet
    chocolate chips

1. Preheat oven to 350°. Grease 15 x 10-inch jelly-roll pan.
2. Mix all ingredients except nuts with electric mixer. When thoroughly combined, add nuts and pour into prepared pan.
3. Bake 25 minutes. Cool on rack.
4. Make frosting: in small pan, boil sugar, butter and milk together for 1 minute. Remove from heat and stir in chips and vanilla. Stir until chips are melted.
5. Pour over brownies. Cool thoroughly before cutting. Elves seem to improve with age. (Mrs. Claus says the same about Santa.)

Frosty Fruit Bars

A soft, chewy fruitcake bar.

Yield: about 4 dozen

½ cup shortening
1 cup sugar
1 egg
1 tablespoon grated orange rind
¼ cup orange or pineapple juice
2½ cups flour
1 teaspoon baking powder
½ teaspoon salt
½ teaspoon cinnamon
½ teaspoon nutmeg
1 cup raisins
1 cup mixed candied fruit
½ cup chopped nuts

1. Preheat oven to 400°. Lightly grease baking sheet.
2. In large bowl of mixer, cream together shortening and sugar; add egg, orange rind, and juice. Mix well.
3. Sift together flour, baking powder, salt, cinnamon and nutmeg; add to creamed ingredients. Stir in raisins, fruit and nuts.
4. Divide dough in half. Shape each half into a strip roughly 7 x 12-inches on baking sheet.
5. Bake about 12 minutes or until browned. Remove from oven; cool slightly. Frost with glaze while still warm. Cut into strips for bars. (These freeze well.)

Glaze:

½ cup confectioners' sugar, sifted
1 tablespoon melted butter
1 tablespoon rum

Glaze preparation:

Mix together all ingredients until smooth.

Jean's Chocolate Squares

Yield: 3 dozen

A Canadian bittersweet, layered bar.

Crust:
3 tablespoons sugar
½ cup (1 stick) butter
¾ cup flour
¼ cup cocoa
pinch salt

Filling:
2 eggs, beaten
1 cup brown sugar
½ cup coconut
½ cup dates, chopped
½ cup walnuts, chopped
3 tablespoons flour
1 teaspoon baking powder
1 teaspoon vanilla extract

Frosting:
¼ cup water
2 tablespoons butter
½ teaspoon vanilla extract
2 1-ounce squares unsweetened chocolate
2 cups confectioners' sugar

1. Preheat oven to 350°.
2. Mix dry ingredients for crust and cut in butter. Press into an 8-inch pan. Bake 15 minutes.
3. Beat eggs and sugar. Add flour, baking powder, and vanilla. Stir in fruit and nuts. Pour over crust and bake 20 minutes or until firm.

Editors suggest that date, nut and coconut lovers might want to double those amounts.

Frosting preparation:
Heat water, butter, and chocolate over low heat. Stir until chocolate is melted. Add vanilla. Beat in sugar and spread on squares while still warm. When cool cut in squares.

Lemon Snow Bars

Yield: 36 to 48 bars

A Southern favorite!

Crust layer:
1 cup (2 sticks) butter, softened
2 cups flour
½ cup confectioners' sugar

Lemon filling:
4 tablespoons flour
1½ cups sugar
1 teaspoon baking powder
4 eggs, beaten
juice and grated rind of 2 lemons
confectioners' sugar

1. Preheat oven to 350°.
2. Combine butter, flour, and confectioners' sugar. Press into a 13 x 9-inch baking pan in an even layer. Bake for 20 minutes.
3. Meanwhile combine flour, sugar, and baking powder. In another bowl combine eggs, lemon juice, and grated rind. Add to flour mixture.
4. Pour lemon-flour mixture over crust. Bake an additional 25 minutes. Sprinkle with confectioners' sugar. Cool. Cut into bars.

Nutcracker Sweet Bars

Yield: 4 dozen bars

Rich shortbread crust with nutty confection topping.

Cookie Crust:
1 cup (2 sticks) butter
½ cup sugar
1 egg
1 teaspoon vanilla extract
2¼ cups flour

Topping:
1 cup sugar
2¼ cups chopped pecans
4 egg whites
1½ teaspoons cinnamon

1. Preheat oven to 350°. Lightly grease a jelly-roll pan (approximately 13 x 9 x 1-inch).

2. With electric mixer or in food processor, cream butter and sugar until light and fluffy; add egg and vanilla. Mix well. Add flour; mix until dough reaches good spreading consistency.

3. Spread dough in jelly roll pan. Bake 15 minutes. Remove from oven; cool slightly. Maintain oven heat at 350°.

4. Mix together all of topping ingredients by hand. DO NOT beat egg whites. Spread over cookie crust; bake 15 minutes more. Cool; cut into bars.

Shortbread

Yield: about 32 pieces

The challenge is in allowing it to age.

1 cup (2 sticks) BUTTER, cut into 8 pieces
1 cup confectioners' sugar
½ teaspoon salt
2 cups flour

Variation:
1 cup butter
¼ cup Dutch process cocoa
1¾ cups flour
1½ cups confectioners' sugar
½ teaspoon salt

1. Preheat oven to 250°. Lightly spoon flour into measuring cup and level off.

2. In food processor, combine flour, salt and sugar. Add butter pieces and mix until batter begins to form a ball.

3. Press evenly into 8- or 9-inch round cake pan. (Set another pan inside the first to help level the shortbread.) With a fork, prick shortbread all over, preferably radiating evenly out from center, spacing holes about ½-inch apart. Bake in preheated oven until lightly golden—about 60 to 65 minutes.

4. Remove from oven and again with fork, prick to divide into 32 pie-shaped pieces. When cool, remove from pan. Store in covered tin for several days, at least, before serving or giving. (This is the hard part. Shortbread improves with age—we think. Generally it doesn't last that long!)

Little Jack Horner's Christmas Tarts and Pastries

Yield: 24 pastries

A variety of fillings for a basic cream cheese pastry.

Cream Cheese Pastry:

1 3-ounce package cream cheese
½ cup (1 stick) BUTTER
1 cup flour
pinch of salt

Jam Tarts:

damson plum preserves or
  seedless red raspberry jam
1 recipe cream cheese pastry (above)

Pecan Tarts:

1 egg
⅓ cup dark corn syrup
⅓ cup sugar
1 teaspoon flour
1 tablespoon butter, melted
½ teaspoon vanilla extract
⅓ cup pecans, chopped fine or
  1 half nut per tart
1 recipe cream cheese pastry (above)

Chocolate Tarts:

1 egg
2 tablespoons sugar
¼ teaspoon vanilla extract
2 teaspoons butter
¼ cup chocolate chips
⅓ cup dark syrup
¼ cut nuts
1 recipe cream cheese pastry (above)

For Pastry: Cream together cream cheese and butter. Cut in flour and salt; blend with pastry blender (or put all ingredients in food processor and process until dough forms a ball.)

Jam Tarts:

1. Preheat oven to 450°.
2. Roll out pastry on floured board: use 2-inch, scalloped edge, round cookie cutter for tarts. Press pastry circle into cup of miniature muffin tins. Fill with filling (about 1 teaspoon). Use 1-inch cutter for top; press edges together. Make a small "x" with sharp knife.
3. Bake jam tarts for 10 minutes or until golden brown.

Pecan Tarts:

1. Preheat oven to 350°.
2. Beat together egg, corn syrup, sugar, flour, melted butter and vanilla.
3. Proceed with pastry for tarts as for jam tarts. Place a pecan half or a teaspoon of chopped nuts in each tart; fill with syrup mixture (about 1½ teaspoons). Do not top with pastry. Bake at 350° for 15 minutes.

Chocolate Tarts:

1. Preheat oven to 350°.
2. Mix together egg, sugar and vanilla. In saucepan over low heat melt together butter and chocolate chips. Remove from heat and stir in dark syrup and egg mixture. Add nuts.
3. Proceed with tart pastry, as for jam tarts, filling each tart with a generous 1½ teaspoons filling. Do not cover with pastry .
3. Bake for 15 minutes or until golden.

Mincemeat Foldovers:
1 recipe cream cheese pastry
½ cup prepared mincemeat

Glaze for Foldovers:
½ cup confectioners' sugar
1 tablespoon rum
1 teaspoon light corn syrup

Mincemeat Foldovers:
1. Preheat oven to 350°.
2. Prepare pastry; divide in half. Roll each half into a 10-inch circle. Use a 3-inch round cutter to cut circles.
3. Place ½ teaspoon mincemeat in center of pastry circle. Fold pastry in half over mincemeat. Seal edges with tines of fork.
4. Place on ungreased baking sheets. Bake for 20 to 25 minutes. When cooled, drizzle with glaze.

Glaze: combine all ingredients until smooth. Drizzle over cooled foldovers.

Toffee Cookies

Very simply delicious!

Yield: 4 dozen

24 2-inch graham cracker squares
  (or enough to cover jelly-roll pan)
1 cup (2 sticks) butter
1 cup light brown sugar
1 cup coarsely chopped walnuts

1. Preheat oven to 350°.
2. Cover bottom of a 15½ x 10½-inch jelly roll pan with layer of whole graham crackers touching one another.
3. In a saucepan over medium heat, melt butter; stir in brown sugar and bring to a boil to form caramel syrup.
4. Pour caramel over graham crackers. Sprinkle with chopped nuts.
5. Bake for 10 minutes. Remove from oven and cool 2 to 5 minutes, or until cookies begin to harden. Cut into halves or quarters while still warm. Cool completely. Store in airtight container.

Turtles

**Keep copies of this recipe handy—
everyone will ask for one.**

Yield: 48 squares

Crust:
2 cups flour
1 cup brown sugar
½ cup (1 stick) butter, at room temperature

Caramel:
1 cup (2 sticks) butter
1½ cup brown sugar
3 tablespoons corn syrup
2 cups chopped pecans

12 ounces chocolate chips

1. Preheat oven to 350°.
2. Mix crust ingredients in mixer bowl at medium speed until well mixed and dough forms fine particles. With hands pat dough into a 13 x 9 x 2-inch pan.
3. In a saucepan over medium heat, mix butter, syrup and brown sugar for caramel. Bring to a boil; boil for one minute, stirring constantly.
4. Sprinkle nuts over crust; pour caramel over all. Bake 18 to 22 minutes, until surface bubbles.
5. Immediately after removing pan from oven pour chocolate chips evenly over all. Let stand briefly to melt then spread chocolate. Cool; cut into squares.

Sugar Plums

while visions of sugar plums danced thro' their heads

"Sugar plums" were made of greengage plums, Seckel pears, apricots and crab apples, which were candied by boiling in a thick syrup of sugar and cornstarch until they became translucent and sugared through. They were attached to the branches of the Christmas tree by colored strings tied to their stems. "Comfits," "sweetmeats," and "confections" were also terms used for any of many sugared fruits or other candies. Chocolates wrapped in gold foil, candy canes and figurative clear candies of boiled sugar were also hung by strings or piled into paper cornucopias, which were tied to the tree branches.

Almond Butter Crunch

Yes, yes!

1 cup (2 sticks) butter
1 ⅓ cups sugar
1 tablespoon light corn syrup
3 tablespoons water
1 cup slivered almonds
8 ounces milk chocolate
  or semisweet chocolate
1 cup finely chopped almonds

Yield: about 2 pounds candy

1. Line a 10 x 15-inch jelly-roll pan with foil.
2. Melt butter in large heavy saucepan. Stir in sugar, corn syrup and water. Attach candy thermometer and cook without stirring to 300°.
3. Remove from heat and quickly stir in 1 cup slivered almonds. Pour immediately onto prepared jelly-roll pan. Cool.
4. Melt half of chocolate and spread over cooled toffee. Sprinkle with half of finely chopped nuts, pressing in slightly. When chocolate is hard, lift foil from pan and peel away from candy. Turn over and repeat procedure with melted chocolate and nuts.
5. When chocolate is completely hardened, break into pieces. Store in tightly covered container or freeze.

California Fudge

Chocoholics take note!

¼ cup (½ stick) butter
2 cups sugar
2 tablespoons unsweetened cocoa
¼ cup corn syrup
¼ teaspoon salt
½ cup evaporated milk
3 tablespoons Marshmallow Fluff
1 teaspoon vanilla extract
½ cup chocolate chips
1 cup chopped nuts

Editor got carried away with marshmallow and used 3 heaping spoonsful. Upon realizing what had happened, had to add an additional ½ cup chips to compensate. WONDERFUL!

Yield: about 1½ pounds

1. In 2-quart saucepan, bring butter, sugar, cocoa, corn syrup, salt and evaporated milk to a boil and boil rapidly for 4 minutes. Remove from heat and let stand 5 minutes.
2. Add marshamllow and vanilla. Stir well. Add chips, letting them melt. Beat until mixed and beginning to get firm. Stir in nuts and pour into greased 8-inch square pan. Cool and cut into squares.

Candied Orange Peel

Yield: about 2 cups

Dipped in chocolate—an impressive, appreciated gift.

5 large oranges
water
sugar
corn syrup
semisweet, bittersweet chocolate,
    or white chocolate, melted

1. Peel oranges and slice peel into lengthwise sections.
2. Cover with water, bring to boiling then simmer 20 minutes. Drain. (If you'd rather have a less bitter peel, drain peel and repeat the process of bringing to a boil and simmering.) Remove white part from peel, then cut orange zest into ¼-inch strips.
3. For each cup of peel combine ¼ cup water, ¼ cup sugar, and 1 tablespoon corn syrup in small pan. Cook peel slowly in this syrup until peel is transparent. Either roll in sugar and let dry or allow to dry on waxed paper, then dip in melted chocolate.

Chocolate Truffles

Yield: 3 to 4 dozen

Velvety morsels.

6 ounces semisweet chocolate
1 ounce unsweetened chocolate
½ cup whipping cream
2 tablespoons butter
¾ cup confectioners' sugar, sifted
2 egg yolks
1 to 2 tablespoons rum, brandy
    or favorite liqueur
cocoa, chopped nuts, colored non pareils,
    finely grated chocolate

Finely chopped raisins or nuts may be added to chocolate before chilling.

1. Place chocolate, cream and butter in top of double boiler. Stir over hot water to melt chocolate.
2. Remove from heat. Cover chocolate surface with sugar. Top with egg yolks. Whisk until smooth, returning to heat to thoroughly blend ingredients.
3. Remove from heat. Add liquor. Pour into flat dish and refrigerate until malleable.
4. Shape into small balls, roll in cocoa, nuts, etc. Refrigerate until shortly before serving. Serve in paper candy cups.

Golden Candy Caramels

Rich and buttery.

½ pound (2 sticks) butter
2 cups (1 pound) sugar
1 cup light corn syrup
1 can sweetened condensed milk
1 teaspoon vanilla extract

2 cups broken nut meats, optional

Yield: about 3 pounds candy

1. Melt butter in a 2-quart pan and add rest of ingredients. Stir constantly and cook to 240° on candy thermometer.
2. Remove from heat and add nuts. Pour into 8-inch square pan. Cool then cut into squares. Wrap individually in waxed paper and hide them.

Peanut Brittle

½ cup (1 stick) butter
2 cups sugar
1 cup light corn syrup
½ cup water
2 cups raw peanuts, with skins
2 heaping teaspoons baking soda

Try cashews or Macadamias as alternatives to peanuts.

Yield: 2 pounds

1. Mix sugar, butter and syrup in heavy pan. Boil to 235° (softball stage).
2. Add 3 tablespoons butter and peanuts. Cook to crack (295°).
3. Remove from heat and add baking soda. Stir quickly and pour onto buttered foil-lined jelly-roll pan (using remaining butter to coat foil). Pull apart from edges with fork and let cool.
4. Break apart and store in dry place tightly covered.

Spiced Pecans

A microwave quickie!

4 tablespoons peanut oil
1½ tablespoons Worcestershire sauce
1 teaspoon soy sauce
½ teaspoon ground ginger
5 to 6 dashes Tabasco sauce
2 cups pecan halves

Yield: 2 cups

1. Mix peanut oil and seasonings in 2-quart glass bowl or casserole. Add pecans; stir well to coat.
2. Microwave on high power for 4 minutes; stir. Continue microwaving for 2 to 4 minutes more, until light brown. Be careful not to burn.
3. Drain on paper towels. Store in airtight containers.

Peanut Butter Balls (or Bars)

Yield: 7 to 8 dozen

Reese's rival.

1²⁄₃ cups graham cracker crumbs OR
   1 sleeve of graham crackers, crumbed
scant 2 cups confectioners' sugar
1 cup crunchy peanut butter
1 cup (2 sticks) butter or margarine
6 to 12 ounces semisweet chocolate chips

**This is fast work in a food processor—
10 minutes, maximum, if you make into bars.**

1. Combine graham cracker crumbs and sugar.
2. In saucepan melt peanut butter and butter together, stirring until smooth. Stir into crumb mixture, blending throroughly.
3. Either form dough into 1-inch balls and chill or evenly press into a 13 x 9-inch pan.
4. Melt 6 ounces of chocolate and coat chilled balls placing on waxed paper to harden; OR spread on top of mixture in pan. (You will need the second 6 ounces of chocolate for making the balls.)
5. When chocolate topping has hardened, cut into 1-inch bars. Store either bars or balls tightly covered or freeze.

Sugar Plums

Yield: about 3 dozen

**Reminiscent of the confections of the past century
but appealing to the tastes of today.**

½ cup dried apricots
½ cup chopped pecans
¼ cup dried figs
¼ cup golden raisins
¼ cup flaked coconut
3 tablespoons Cointreau (or orange liqueur)
sugar

1. In a food processor, finely chop apricots, pecans, figs, raisins and coconut together. (This can also be done by hand.) Add liqueur and blend well.
2. Roll scant tablespoons of mixture into 1-inch balls; roll balls in granulated sugar to coat. Store in airtight container in refrigerator in pleated paper candy cups or waxed paper.

Toast nuts on tray in toaster oven or in shallow pan in regular oven preheated to 350°. Watch carefully as nuts change from golden to brown very quickly. Time varies with type and size of nuts, but generally toasting takes from 5 to 15 minutes.

221

Sweet Spiced Nuts

Yield: 1 pound

1 cup sugar
1½ tablespoons ground cinnamon
1 teaspoon ground cloves
1 teaspoon salt
1 teaspoon gound ginger
½ teaspoon ground nutmeg
1 egg white
1 tablespoon cold water
1 pound pecans or other whole, shelled nuts

Any kind of nut may be used but pecans seem to be the number one choice.

1. Preheat oven to 250°. Butter a large jelly-roll pan.
2. Mix together thoroughly all dry ingredients (may be done in food processor).
3. Beat egg white with cold water until frothy but not stiff. Add spiced sugar mixture; stir well.
4. Add nuts; stir well to coat nuts.
5. Spread nuts on pan; place in oven. Bake for 1 hour, stirring to separate every 15 to 20 minutes. Remove from oven when dry and toasty. Cool. Store in airtight container.

Potpourri

·Potpourri

• **Indicates items suitable for gift giving**

Apple Chutney

Yield: 6½ cups

Try over cream cheese with crackers for hors d'oeuvres.

4 apples, pared, cored, coarsely chopped
½ pound pitted dates, chopped
1 large onion, chopped
1 cup canned pineapple chunks, drained
1 cup raisins
¾ cup chopped drained preserved
   ginger root
2 tablespoons coconut
1 cup brown sugar
¼ cup lime juice
¾ cup apple cider vinegar
½ cup pineapple juice
1 tablespoon salt
¼ teaspoon chili powder
½ teaspoon nutmeg
½ teaspoon dry mustard
pinch cayenne pepper

Must be made ahead.

1. Place all ingredients in a large pot; cover and simmer for 45 minutes, stirring occasionally.
2. Pour into containers; cover tightly. Store in refrigerator for 4 to 6 weeks.

Cashew Butter/Almond Butter

Yield: about 1 cup

If you love peanut butter, wait'll ya taste these!

Cashew Butter:
2 cups (about 12 ounces) cashews
2 tablespoons butter
½ to 1 teaspoon salt

Almond Butter:
2 cups (about 12 ounces),
   whole blanched almonds
4 tablespoons butter, cut up
½ teaspoon almond extract

Cashew Butter:
1. With metal blade in food processor, add cashews to beaker of processor. Process, turning on and off rapidly, until cashews are very finely ground.
2. Add butter and salt; process until smooth. Taste and add more salt, if desired; process.

Almond Butter:
1. Process almonds as in step 1 above.
2. Add butter and almond extract through feed tube; process until smooth.
3. Store butters covered in refrigerator to prevent oil separation.

Chestnuts in Rum

Yield: 6 cups

Try this sauce over duck or on ice cream.

2 pounds fresh chestnuts
6 cups water

2 pounds brown sugar
1½ cups water
1½ cups light rum
1 orange, cut in paper-thin slices
1 tablespoon chopped candied ginger

Must be made ahead.

1. Bring 6 cups water to boil; add chestnuts and simmer until tender, about 1 hour.
2. Drain; remove shells and skins from nuts.
3. Combine brown sugar, water, rum, orange slices and ginger in saucepan. Cook, stirring often, until sugar dissolves and syrup thickens slightly.
4. Pack chestnuts into sterilized jars; pour syrup over. Cover tightly. Do not process.

Cranberry Chutney

Yield: 1½ pints

Special accompaniment to poultry.

1 cup water
1 cup sugar
2 cups cranberries
2 tablespoons vinegar
½ cup raisins
½ cup almonds, chopped
1 tablespoon brown sugar
¼ teaspoon ground ginger
¼ teaspoon cayenne pepper
¼ teaspoon garlic salt

1. Combine ingredients in saucepan and cook slowly for ½ hour or until thick.
2. Pour into jars and cover with paraffin to give as gifts. Keeps weeks in the refrigerator.

Cranberry Conserve

Yield: about 4 pints

A Mystic favorite.

4 cups fresh cranberries
1½ cups water
2⅔ cups sugar
1 cup raisins, chopped
½ to 1 cup walnuts, chopped
2 small oranges, grated rind and meat
1 teaspoon grated lemon rind

To use as garnish: serve on half a poached pear on lettuce leaf.

1. Wash cranberries then boil them in water until the skins pop. Add sugar, raisins, nuts, and orange and lemon rind.
2. Slice off white part of oranges. Chop remaining orange pulp and add to cranberries. Cook to dissolve sugar.
3. Pour into clean jars and cover with paraffin or store in refrigerator to keep several weeks.

Dad's Mincemeat

Yield: 5½ quarts

Homemade can convert the non-afficionado.

2 pounds lean beef round stew meat
8 cups water
1 pound suet, cut up
12 medium cooking apples,
  pared and cored
3 pounds seedless raisins
3 cups dried currants
1 cup candied orange peel, finely diced
4 teaspoons salt
4 teaspoons cinnamon
1 teaspoon powdered allspice
1 teaspoon ground cloves
2 cups granulated sugar
2 cups brown sugar
1 cup molasses
8 teaspoons lemon juice
2 cups apple cider

1. Boil beef in water. Cover and simmer 2 hours.
2. Remove meat and reserve 4 cups stock.
3. Put meat, suet, apples through a food chopper. Put in large (7- to 8-quart) pan.
4. Add remaining ingredients, except lemon juice and cider.
5. Add reserved stock and simmer uncovered 1 hour, stirring occasionally.
6. Add juices during last 5 minutes of cooking.
7. Pack while hot into sterilized jars. 1 quart will make a 9-inch pie (3 cups) with 1 cup left over for cookies or tarts.
8. Option: add brandy or rum to taste when making pie.

This recipe doubles the original. A jar of mincemeat makes a wonderful gift with suggested recipes included.

Homemade Vanilla Extract

Yield: 2 cups

A pungent vanilla for special flavor in holiday baking.

2 vanilla beans
1 pint brandy

Must be made three to four weeks ahead.

1. Slice vanilla beans down center to expose the seeds; drop into bottle of brandy. Shake, cover and allow to marinate for several weeks. Shake every few days. (It may be necessary to pour off small amount of brandy to accomodate beans: pour into snifter and sip slowly.)
2. Use homemade extract whenever extract is called for in a recipe. For gifts, pour into four 4-ounce bottles and cap; tie with ribbon.

Kahlúa

Yield: about 1 quart

**A home-brewed coffee liqueur
for a thoughtful gift.**

4 cups granulated sugar
2 ounces instant coffee granules
2½ cups boiling water
2 cups 100-proof vodka
1 vanilla bean, broken up

Must be made ahead.

1. Mix the sugar and instant coffee in a
   half-gallon jar.
2. Add boiling water, vodka and vanilla bean.
   Cap and shake well.
3. Let sit at least 30 days, shaking jar
   occasionally.
4. To serve: pour into liqueur glasses; top with
   whipped cream, or mix in other cocktails.

Pepper Jelly

Yield: about 5 pounds

**Christmas red or green!
Serve with cream cheese on crackers.**

8 green or red bell peppers
2 or 3 large hot chili peppers
7 cups sugar
1 cup vinegar
1 6-ounce package liquid pectin
green or red food coloring, optional

Must be made ahead.

Can be used in Red Pepper Jelly Aspic (see p. 135)

1. Separately grind bell pepper and chili
   peppers. Strain each and reserve juices.
2. Measure ¼ cup chili pepper juice. Measure
   2 cups of bell pepper juice (or add water to
   make 2 cups).
3. Combine juices and ground peppers and
   store in glass jar in refrigerator overnight.
4. Next day: sterilize jars. Pour peppers into
   8-to 10-quart kettle. Add sugar and vinegar.
   Bring mixture to rolling boil. (One that
   cannot be stirred down.) All at once add
   pectin and boil vigorously for 1 minute.
   Remove from heat and let stand 5 minutes.
   Melt paraffin.
5. Skim any foam from surface. Add coloring if
   desired. Pour into hot jars and seal with thin
   layer (⅛-inch) of paraffin. When cool add
   another thin layer of paraffin.

Memory-Making Aprons

An inedible gift idea perfect for Moms and Grandmas.

white chef's aprons* (100% plain cotton duck)
approximately 32 x 34-inches
permanent ink markers (El Marko by Flair)
in assorted colors, especially red and green
assorted children, ages 5 to 10

Garnish: wrapping paper and ribbon

*available from Williams-Sonoma

1. Cover work area to protect. Also be sure that children are in old clothes.
2. Give each child an apron and give them free-reign with the markers. Let them draw any picture on apron that they want. Be sure they sign and date the pictures—these are collector's items.
3. Have each child gift wrap completed apron.

Play Dough

To fill stockings or occupy would-be cooks.

1 cup flour
½ cup salt
2 teaspoons cream of tartar
1 cup water
1 tablespoon oil
food coloring

You may leave out coloring in step 1, adding different colors to small portions of dough once it is cooked. Be sure coloring is well mixed in before handling it. Food coloring stains.

1. Combine all ingredients in saucepan. Stirring constantly, cook over low-medium heat about 3 minutes until a dough is formed. Cool.
2. Can be used immediately though warm. Keeps well in plastic bags or covered container.

Plum Conserve

Yield: 5 pints

A cinch with a food processor. An appreciated gift.

48 Italian or prune plums
4 small oranges
3 cups seedless raisins
6 cups sugar
1¾ cups walnuts, chopped

1. Slice each plum in half and remove seed. Chop fruit coarsely. Put into large pot.
2. Coarsely chop whole oranges, removing any seeds. Add to plums.
3. Add raisins and sugar. Stir well.
4. Boil; then reduce heat to low and cook, uncovered, until thick, about 15 minutes. Stir in nuts.
5. Immediately pack into hot sterilized jars and seal with paraffin.

Sugar Plum Cottages

Easier and less tedious to make with young children than a traditional gingerbread house. A perfect project for a Brownie Troop.

1 to 2 boxes graham crackers
1 ½-gallon milk or juice carton per house (or per child)
1 or 2 recipes decorative "mortar" frosting
assorted candies and small cookies for decorating (Lifesavers, jujubes, gum drops, mints, chocolate wafers, spearmint leaves for shrubs)
1 10-inch square of cardboard per child's house, covered with foil, for base or one large tray or cardtable top covered with foil on which to cluster cottages for a village

1. Cut BOTTOMS off cartons, so that the remaining sides are the height of a double graham cracker. Cover carton with crackers using frosting "mortar" as glue. Cutting crackers to size is best accomplished by using a serrated knife and a metal ruler or straight edge.

2. When sides and roof are in place, proceed to decorate with candies in any imaginative way desired. Set on foil-covered cardboard base and create "snow mounds" around house, if desired, using more frosting. Surround with spearmint leaves and gumdrops tacked on toothpicks to create shrubs and trees. Candy canes or licorice sticks can be used for corner boards. Overlap cookies or mints for roof shingles, etc.

Decorative "mortar" frosting:

3 egg whites at room temperature
1 1-pound package confectioners' sugar
½ teaspoon cream of tartar

Frosting preparation:

1. Place egg whites, sugar and cream of tartar in large bowl. With mixer at medium speed, beat 7 to 10 minutes, or until mixture is very stiff.

2. Keep bowl covered with damp cloth as much as possible while using so frosting will not dry out and harden. Makes 2 cups.

 The sani-cycle, or its equivalent on your dishwasher, can usually sterilize jars and equipment. Check to be certain of water temperature if in doubt.

Winter Pesto

Yield: 2 cups

Make in food processor.

2 ounces Parmesan cheese, cut into
  1-inch cubes
1 ounce Romano cheese, cut into
  1-inch cubes
3 cups fresh spinach leaves, well packed
½ cup fresh parsley
1 tablespoon dried basil, or to taste
2 cloves garlic
2 tablespoons butter
1 teaspoon salt
¼ teaspoon pepper
½ to 1 cup olive oil
¼ cup pine nuts, optional

**If using nuts, roast a few minutes in a slow oven,
do not let burn.**

1. With steel blade of food processor in place
   and machine running, drop cheese cubes in
   and finely grate. Add other ingredients
   reserving half the oil. Process until
   finely chopped.

2. While machine is running, add enough oil to
   make a smooth paste.

3. Store in refrigerator or freezer. Serve over
   pasta; add to minestrone soup or use in
   Pesto Layered Torte (see p. 12).

231

Memorable Family Recipes

Recipe _____ Dates Served _____

_____

Ingredients _____

_____

_____

_____

_____

Procedure _____

_____

_____

_____

_____

_____

_____

_____

Comments _____

_____

Memorable Family Recipes

Recipe _____ Dates Served _____

_____

Ingredients _____

_____

_____

_____

_____

Procedure _____

_____

_____

_____

_____

_____

_____

_____

Comments _____

_____

Memorable Family Recipes

Recipe _____ Dates Served _____

Ingredients _____

_____

_____

_____

_____

Procedure _____

_____

_____

_____

_____

_____

_____

_____

Comments _____

_____

Memorable Family Recipes

Recipe _____ Dates Served _____

Ingredients _____
_____
_____
_____
_____

Procedure _____
_____
_____
_____
_____
_____
_____
_____

Comments _____
_____

Memorable Family Recipes

Recipe _____ Dates Served _____

Ingredients _____

_____

_____

_____

_____

Procedure _____

_____

_____

_____

_____

_____

_____

_____

Comments _____

_____

Memorable Family Recipes

Recipe _____   Dates Served _____

Ingredients _____

_____

_____

_____

_____

Procedure _____

_____

_____

_____

_____

_____

_____

Comments _____

_____

Memorable Family Recipes

Recipe _____ Dates Served _____

Ingredients _____

_____

_____

_____

_____

Procedure _____

_____

_____

_____

_____

_____

_____

Comments _____

_____

Memorable Family Recipes

Recipe _____ Dates Served _____

Ingredients _____
_____
_____
_____
_____

Procedure _____
_____
_____
_____
_____
_____
_____
_____

Comments _____
_____

Memorable Family Recipes

Recipe _____ Dates Served _____

Ingredients _____
_____
_____
_____
_____

Procedure _____
_____
_____
_____
_____
_____
_____
_____

Comments _____
_____

Memorable Family Recipes

Recipe _____ Dates Served _____

Ingredients _____

_____

_____

_____

_____

Procedure _____

_____

_____

_____

_____

_____

_____

_____

Comments _____

_____

Memorable
Family Recipes

Recipe _____ Dates Served _____

_____

Ingredients _____

_____

_____

_____

_____

Procedure _____

_____

_____

_____

_____

_____

_____

_____

Comments _____

_____

Memorable Family Recipes

Recipe _____ Dates Served _____

Ingredients _____

_____

_____

_____

_____

Procedure _____

_____

_____

_____

_____

_____

_____

_____

Comments _____

_____

Memorable Family Recipes

Recipe _____ Dates Served _____

_____

Ingredients _____

_____

_____

_____

_____

Procedure _____

_____

_____

_____

_____

_____

_____

_____

Comments _____

_____

Memorable Christmas Menus

Date- _____ Occasion - _____

Guests- _____

_____

Menu- _____   Recipe Source-

_____

_____

_____

_____

_____

_____

_____

Comments- _____

_____

_____

_____

_____

Memorable Christmas Menus

Date- _____ Occasion - _____

Guests- _____

_____

Menu- _____ Recipe Source- _____

_____

_____

_____

_____

_____

_____

Comments- _____

_____

_____

_____

_____

Memorable Christmas Menus

Date- _____ Occasion - _____

Guests- _____

_____

Menu- _____   Recipe Source-

_____

_____

_____

_____

_____

_____

Comments- _____

_____

_____

_____

Memorable Christmas Menus

Date- _____ Occasion - _____

Guests- _____

_____

Menu- _____   Recipe Source-

_____

_____

_____

_____

_____

_____

Comments- _____

_____

_____

_____

_____

Memorable Christmas Menus

Date- _____ Occasion - _____
Guests- _____
_____

Menu- _____ Recipe Source- _____
_____
_____
_____
_____
_____
_____

Comments- _____
_____
_____
_____

Memorable Christmas Menus

Date- _____ Occasion - _____

Guests- _____

_____

Menu- _____ Recipe Source- ____

_____

_____

_____

_____

_____

_____

Comments- _____

_____

_____

_____

_____

Memorable Christmas Menus

Date- _____ Occasion- _____

Guests- _____

_____

Menu- _____ Recipe Source-

_____

_____

_____

_____

_____

_____

Comments- _____

_____

_____

_____

_____

Memorable Christmas Menus

Date- _____ Occasion - _____

Guests- _____

_____

Menu- _____ Recipe Source- ____

_____

_____

_____

_____

_____

Comments- _____

_____

_____

_____

_____

Memorable Christmas Menus

Date- _____ Occasion- _____

Guests- _____

_____

Menu- _____ Recipe Source- _____

_____

_____

_____

_____

_____

_____

Comments- _____

_____

_____

_____

_____

_____

Memorable Christmas Menus

Date- _____ Occasion - _____

Guests- _____

_____

Menu- _____   Recipe Source-

_____

_____

_____

_____

_____

_____

Comments- _____

_____

_____

_____

_____

Index

Meals in Minutes

AS a busy professional dietitian, Janice MacLeod of Roanoke, Virginia appreciates quick-meal menus that are hearty *and* wholesome.

Her Orange-Glazed Pork Tenderloins with Quick Baked Potatoes combine both traits tastily—they can satisfy a man-sized appetite, but are suitable for calorie-conscious folks, too. And they can be ready to serve in just 30 minutes!

"I fix the potatoes first, since they take the longest time to cook," Janice explains. "Potatoes are a good source of carbohydrate, and—if you prefer—with this recipe they don't need gravy or sour cream. They're also pretty on the plate."

While the potatoes cook, Janice prepares the tenderloins in a sweet/tart sauce. "Pork tenderloin is perfect for a quick meal," she points out, "and it's nearly as lean as chicken. I use nonstick cookware and a minimum of oil for browning."

Steamed fresh vegetables complete the meal. A year-round favorite for its appealing color and natural good taste is broccoli. "I squeeze some fresh lemon juice over it just before serving," Janice says.

For a refreshing dessert, Janice uses frozen fruit to make a soft sherbet—also in seconds!

QUICK BAKED POTATOES

 4 large baking potatoes,
   scrubbed
 2 to 3 tablespoons butter *or*
   margarine, melted
Paprika
Salt to taste
 3 tablespoons grated
   Parmesan cheese

Cut the potatoes in half lengthwise. Brush each cut half with butter; sprinkle with paprika, salt and cheese. Place cut side down on oiled cookie sheet. Bake at 350° for 25-30 minutes or until potato is fork tender. **Yield:** 4 servings.

ORANGE-GLAZED PORK TENDERLOINS

 8 slices lean pork tenderloin
   cutlets (1/4 inch thick)
 2 teaspoons vegetable oil
Freshly ground black pepper to
   taste
 1/4 teaspoon garlic powder
 2 tablespoons Worcestershire
   sauce
 4 tablespoons orange juice
   concentrate
 4 green onions, sliced
Orange slices, optional

Heat oil in a heavy, nonstick skillet. Brown pork on both sides; sprinkle with pepper and garlic powder. Continue cooking pork while combining Worcestershire sauce and concentrate. Pour sauce over meat; add onions and cook over low heat until sauce is thick and glazed. Serve with orange slices, if desired. **Yield:** 4 servings.

CREAMY PEACH SHERBET

 2 cups frozen unsweetened
   peach slices*, partially
   thawed

 1/2 cup plain nonfat yogurt
 2 tablespoons orange juice
   concentrate
Freshly grated nutmeg to taste
   (1/8 to 1/4 teaspoon)
 1 teaspoon vanilla extract
 2 tablespoons sugar *or* 1 to 2
   packets sweetener

In food processor or blender, pulse/chop peaches. Add remaining ingredients; blend until creamy. May be served immediately or stored in freezer until serving time. **Yield:** 4 servings (3/4 cup each). *Other frozen fruits may be substituted for peaches.

HEARTY HASH BROWNS: Parboil *unpeeled* potatoes until just tender when tested with a fork, then refrigerate them whole overnight. Next morning, peel and shred potatoes. Heat oil in a skillet on high and cook the potatoes until golden brown on both sides.

FOOLPROOF POTATOES: For scalloped potatoes, layer sliced potatoes, sliced onions, ham pieces, flour, milk and *undiluted* cream of celery soup in a baking dish. Top with bread crumbs and Parmesan cheese; bake at 350° until sauce is bubbly and potatoes are tender.

Sun-splashed and spicy Southwestern foods delight the senses and warm both body and spirit, taking the edge off winter's chill.

Colorful regional staples like corn, tomatoes, beans and chilies brighten nearly every basic Southwestern dish, and the delicious spices will warm any palate!

This sensational sampler of dishes tempts the taste buds with innovations like snappy tortilla soup, sizzling steak with peppers and a crisp, citrus-flavored salad. Traditional tastes come through in tamales, guacamole and nachos. Let the bold colors and flavors of the Southwest bring some sunshine into your meals!

SOUTHWESTERN STARS: Clockwise from lower left—**Cheese/Blue Cornmeal Crackers**, Kay Langdon, Morrison, Colorado (Pg. 11); **Marc Ann's Tortilla Soup**, Marcia Ann Jones, Killeen, Texas (Pg. 11); **Southwest Salad**, Sharon Evans, Rockwell, Iowa (Pg. 12); **Super Nacho Appetizer**, Connie Bolton, San Antonio, Texas (Pg. 13); **Cuernavaca Casserole**, Joanne Jones, Refugio, Texas (Pg. 13); **Guacamole**, Anne Tipps, Duncanville, Texas (Pg. 11); **Marinated Flank Steak with Peppers**, Sandra Wright, Embudo, New Mexico (Pg. 11); **Mexican Tamales**, Marie Macy, Fort Collins, Colorado (Pg. 11).

Southwestern sweets reflect the region's rich cultural heritage—Mexican, Native American, even American cowboy!

Desserts like Flan are favorites in the Southwest, as are the nut-filled, sugarcoated cookies called Pastelitos De Boda (Mexican Wedding Cakes). For a traditional treat, serve these cookies with lightly spiced Mexican Hot Chocolate.

Sweet, airy confections like Navajo Fry Bread (or sopaipillas) also are indigenous to the Southwest.

DESERT DESSERTS: Clockwise from lower left—**Pastelitos De Boda**, Terri Lins, San Diego, California (Pg. 12); **Navajo Fry Bread**, Thelma Tyler, Dragoon, Arizona (Pg. 12); **Flan**, Kathy Gilligan; Phoenix, Arizona (Pg. 12); **Mexican Hot Chocolate**, Kathy Young, Weatherford, Texas (Pg. 12).

CHEESE/BLUE CORNMEAL CRACKERS
Kay Langdon, Morrison, Colorado

(PICTURED ON PAGE 8)

2 cups (8 ounces) shredded sharp cheddar cheese, room temperature
1/2 cup grated Parmesan cheese, room temperature
1/2 cup butter *or* margarine, softened
1/4 cup skim milk
1 teaspoon seasoned pepper
1 teaspoon garlic powder
1 teaspoon paprika
1 cup old-fashioned whole oats
1/2 cup all-purpose flour
1/2 cup blue cornmeal
2 tablespoons sesame seeds

Combine cheeses, butter, milk, pepper, garlic powder and paprika in mixing bowl. Mix in oats, flour, cornmeal and sesame seeds. Shape dough into 12-in. roll; wrap tightly in plastic wrap; refrigerate 4 hours or overnight. Slice in about 1/8-in. slices. Bake on cookie sheet (lightly greased or lined with parchment paper) at 400° for 8-10 minutes or until crisp. Remove immediately to cooling rack. **Yield:** about 7 dozen crackers.

MEXICAN TAMALES
Marie Macy, Fort Collins, Colorado

(PICTURED ON PAGE 8)

PASTRY:
1 package cornhusks*
3 cups Masa Harina flour*
1-3/4 cups water
1 cup lard *or* vegetable shortening
1 teaspoon salt
FILLING:
1 pound ground pork *or* beef
1/2 cup chopped onion
1 garlic clove, minced
1 can (10-1/2 ounces) tomato puree
1 hard apple, peeled and chopped
1/4 cup chopped fresh parsley
1/2 cup toasted almonds, chopped
1 tablespoon vinegar
1 teaspoon sugar
1/4 teaspoon ground cumin
1/2 teaspoon ground coriander
1/2 teaspoon ground black pepper
1/2 teaspoon chili powder
1 cup water *or* chicken broth

*Cornhusks and Masa Harina are avail-

able in some large supermarkets. Immerse husks in water; cover. Soak overnight. Mix flour and water to form dough; cover. Let stand 30 minutes. In large bowl, beat lard and salt until mixture resembles beaten egg whites (about 6 minutes). Add dough 2 tablespoons at a time, beating constantly. Brown meat, onion and garlic in large skillet; drain fat. Add remaining ingredients except last one and simmer 25 minutes, covered. Cool slightly. Pat husks dry with paper towels and spread about 2 tablespoons dough (1/8-1/16 in. thick) on each, leaving 1-in. border (see illustration). Top with 1 tablespoon filling. Roll up; tie in center. Place upright, folded end down, in Dutch oven with steam rack or oven-proof inverted plate on bottom. Add 1 cup water or chicken broth. Bring to boil; cover and steam 45 minutes, adding water as needed. When done, husk should peel back easily from dough. **Yield:** about 3 dozen.

GUACAMOLE
Anne Tipps, Duncanville, Texas

(PICTURED ON PAGE 9)

1 large ripe avocado
1-1/2 tablespoons lemon juice *or* lime juice
1/4 cup minced onion
1 tablespoon finely diced green chilies
1 small tomato, seeded and finely chopped
1 garlic clove, minced
1/4 teaspoon salt, optional

Peel and pit avocado. Place in bowl with lemon or lime juice; mash with fork. Stir in onion, chilies, tomato, garlic and salt, if desired. Cover; chill. **Yield:** about 1-1/2 cups.

MARINATED FLANK STEAK WITH PEPPERS
Sandra Wright, Embudo, New Mexico

(PICTURED ON PAGE 9)

1 beef flank steak (about 1-1/2 pounds)
MARINADE:
1 large garlic clove, minced
Juice of 1 lime with grated rind
2 teaspoons leaf oregano
1-1/2 tablespoons olive oil *or* vegetable oil
1 teaspoon salt, optional
Freshly ground black pepper

1 large green pepper
1 large sweet red pepper
1 large yellow pepper

Place steak in a heavy plastic bag. Combine marinade ingredients, whisking to blend. Pour marinade over steak; turn to coat. Seal bag and refrigerate overnight. Grill steak and char peppers over hot coals. Cook steak about 10 minutes per side for medium doneness. Turn peppers until skins are charred and blackened; place peppers in a paper sack, close and allow to steam for about 10 minutes. Remove skins; slice into strips and keep warm. Place steak on warm platter; let stand a few minutes before carving. **Yield:** 4 servings.

MARC ANN'S TORTILLA SOUP
Marcia Ann Jones, Killeen, Texas

(PICTURED ON PAGE 8)

1 small onion, chopped
1 hot chili pepper *or* 1 can (4 ounces) green chilies, seeded and chopped
2 garlic cloves, minced
1 tablespoon vegetable oil
1 large tomato, peeled and chopped
1 can (10-1/2 ounces) beef bouillon
1 can (10-3/4 ounces) chicken broth
1-1/2 cups water
1-1/2 cups tomato juice
1 teaspoon ground cumin
1 teaspoon chili powder
1/8 teaspoon pepper
2 teaspoons Worcestershire sauce
1 tablespoon bottled steak sauce
3 flour tortillas, cut in 1/2-inch strips
1/4 cup shredded cheddar cheese

Saute onion, chili pepper or chilies and garlic in oil until soft. Add tomato, bouillon, broth, water, tomato juice, cumin, chili powder, pepper, Worcestershire and steak sauces. Bring to boil; lower heat and simmer 45 minutes to 1 hour. Add tortillas; simmer 10 minutes. Serve in bowls; sprinkle with cheese. **Yield:** 6 servings.

FAST FINALE: Slice fresh peaches into a pretty glass bowl, add fresh raspberries, sprinkle with sugar and garnish with a sprig of mint.

11

SOUTHWEST SALAD
Sharon Evans, Rockwell, Iowa

(PICTURED ON PAGE 8)

3 heads Boston lettuce, washed and chilled
1 small cucumber, sliced thin
1 avocado, peeled and sliced crosswise
1 small red onion, sliced and separated into rings
1 can (11 ounces) mandarin oranges, drained *or* fresh orange sections

SALAD DRESSING:
1/2 teaspoon grated orange rind
1/4 cup fresh-squeezed orange juice
1/2 cup vegetable oil
2 tablespoons sugar
3 tablespoons red wine vinegar
1 tablespoon lemon juice
1/4 teaspoon salt

Combine dressing ingredients; mix well and set aside. Arrange lettuce, cucumber, avocado, onion and oranges on individual plates. Drizzle salads with dressing just before serving. **Yield:** 6 salads.

BREAKFAST BURRITOS
Linda Wells, St. Marys, Georgia

(PICTURED ON PAGE 4)

1 pound bulk pork sausage
1/4 cup diced onion
1/4 cup diced green *or* sweet red pepper
1-1/2 cups frozen Southern-style hash brown potatoes
4 eggs, beaten
12 flour tortillas (8-inch size)
1/2 cup shredded cheddar cheese
Picante sauce
Sour cream

Brown sausage in a large skillet. Add the onion and pepper; cook until tender. Drain off grease. Add potatoes; cook for 6-8 minutes or until tender. Add eggs; stir. Cook until eggs are set. Prepare tortillas by browning in hot oil in large skillet for 5 seconds on each side, or heating in microwave for 45 to 60 seconds. Divide filling mixture between 12 tortillas, placing filling down center. Sprinkle with cheese. Fold bottom of tortilla up and sides toward each other. Serve with picante sauce and sour cream on side. (Burritos can be made in advance and refrigerated or frozen. Reheat in microwave.) **Yield:** 12 burritos.

PASTELITOS DE BODA
Terri Lins, San Diego, California

(PICTURED ON PAGE 10)

3/4 cup butter, room temperature
1/2 cup confectioners' sugar
2 teaspoons vanilla extract
2 cups sifted all-purpose flour
1/4 teaspoon salt
1 cup finely chopped walnuts
1/4 cup heavy cream
Additional confectioners' sugar

Cream together butter and sugar; add vanilla. Add flour, salt and nuts. Add cream; knead lightly. Form into a roll 2-1/2 in. in diameter; roll up in plastic wrap. Chill several hours or overnight. With sharp knife, cut in 1/4-in. slices. Place on ungreased cookie sheets; bake at 375° for 15 minutes or until delicately browned around edges. Remove to wire cooling rack. While still hot, roll in confectioners' sugar. Serve with hot chocolate. **Yield:** about 3 dozen.

FLAN
Kathy Gilligan, Phoenix, Arizona

(PICTURED ON PAGE 10)

8 eggs
2/3 cup sugar
1/4 teaspoon salt
2 cans (12 ounces *each*) evaporated milk
2 teaspoons vanilla extract
1/2 cup packed brown sugar

Beat eggs slightly; add sugar and salt. Blend in milk and vanilla. Sift brown sugar into bottom of eight 5-oz. custard cups or a 1-1/2-qt. baking dish. Pour custard mixture over sugar. Place cups or baking dish in shallow baking pan of hot water. Bake at 325° for 30-40 minutes or until knife inserted near center comes out clean. Chill overnight. Sprinkle with additional brown sugar before serving or unmold to serve. **Yield:** 12 servings.

MEXICAN HOT CHOCOLATE
Kathy Young, Weatherford, Texas

(PICTURED ON PAGE 10)

1/4 cup unsweetened cocoa
2 tablespoons brown sugar
1 cup boiling water

Dash ground cloves *or* nutmeg
1/4 teaspoon ground cinnamon
3 cups milk
1 teaspoon vanilla extract
Whipped cream
Whole cinnamon sticks

Combine cocoa and sugar in a small saucepan; stir in water. Bring to a boil; reduce heat and cook 2 minutes, stirring constantly. Add cloves or nutmeg, cinnamon and milk. Simmer 5 minutes (do not boil). Whisk in vanilla. Pour into mugs; top with whipped cream. Use cinnamon sticks for stirrers. **Yield:** 4 1-cup servings.

NAVAJO FRY BREAD
Thelma Tyler, Dragoon, Arizona

(PICTURED ON PAGE 10)

FRY BREAD:
2 cups unbleached flour
1/2 teaspoon salt
1/2 cup instant dry milk powder
1 tablespoon baking powder
1-1/2 tablespoons solid shortening
2/3 to 3/4 cup water
Vegetable oil for frying
Butter, honey and fresh lemon juice, optional

TACO FILLING:
1 pound ground beef
1/2 cup chopped onion
1/2 teaspoon salt
Pepper to taste
2 cans (15 ounces) ranch- *or* chili-style beans, undrained
4 cups (16 ounces) shredded cheddar cheese
1 can (4 ounces) diced green chilies
2 tomatoes, chopped
Shredded lettuce
Salsa

Mix dry ingredients; cut in shortening as for pastry. Add water gradually, mixing to form a firm ball. Divide into 12 balls; let rest, covered, for 10 minutes. Roll each ball into 6-in. circle. Cut a 1/2-in.-diameter hole in center of each circle. Heat 1 in. oil in Dutch oven to 400°. Slip each circle into oil; fry each side about 1 minute or until puffed and golden. Drain. If desired, serve warm with butter, honey and lemon juice. Or, to make tacos, brown beef, onion, salt and pepper; drain. Stir in beans; cook 5 minutes. Place fry bread on baking pan; spread each with 1/2 cup taco mixture. Sprinkle with cheese and chilies. Bake at 350° until cheese melts. Serve with tomato, lettuce and salsa. **Yield:** 12 fry breads.

SUPER NACHO APPETIZER

Connie Bolton, San Antonio, Texas

(PICTURED ON PAGE 9)

1/2 pound ground beef
1/2 pound chorizo (Mexican sausage)
1 can (31 ounces) refried beans
1 can (4 ounces) diced green chilies, drained
3 cups (12 ounces) shredded cheddar cheese
3/4 cup bottled taco sauce
1 cup (8 ounces) sour cream
1 medium tomato, chopped
1/2 cup pimiento-stuffed green olives, sliced
Additional cheese for garnish

GUACAMOLE:
3 large ripe avocados
1 tablespoon fresh lemon juice
1/4 teaspoon garlic salt

Brown meats together; drain well. Layer the meat mixture, beans, chilies, cheese and taco sauce in 13-in. x 9-in. x 2-in. greased baking pan. Bake at 400° for 20 minutes. For guacamole, peel and pit avocados and mash with lemon juice and garlic salt. Remove nacho mixture from oven; let cool about 5 minutes. Top with layers of guacamole, sour cream, tomato, olives and cheese. Serve with tortilla chips. **Yield:** 30 appetizer servings.

CUERNAVACA CASSEROLE

Joanne Jones, Refugio, Texas

(PICTURED ON PAGE 9)

1 cup cornmeal
1-1/2 teaspoons salt
1/2 teaspoon baking soda
2 eggs, beaten
1 cup milk
4 drops hot pepper sauce
1/4 cup vegetable oil
2 cups cooked rice
2 cups (8 ounces) shredded cheddar cheese
1 can (8-3/4 ounces) or 1 cup creamed corn
1/2 cup chopped onion
2 tablespoons chopped green chilies

In a small mixing bowl, mix cornmeal, salt and soda. In a large mixing bowl, combine remaining ingredients; blend in cornmeal mixture. Pour into 12-in. x 7-1/2 in. x 2-in. greased baking dish. Bake at 350° for 35-40 minutes. **Yield:** 12 servings.

PORK CROWN ROAST WITH APRICOT/APPLE STUFFING

Mary Ann Taylor, Rockwell, Iowa

(PICTURED ON PAGE 4)

Pork rib crown roast (5-1/2 to 6 pounds, 12-16 ribs)
Salt and pepper to taste

STUFFING:
1 tablespoon sugar
1 teaspoon chicken bouillon granules
3/4 cup hot water
1/3 cup chopped dried apricots
4 cups cubed dry whole wheat bread (about 6 slices)
1 large apple, peeled, cored and chopped
1/2 teaspoon finely grated orange peel
1/2 teaspoon salt
1/2 teaspoon ground sage
1/4 teaspoon ground cinnamon
1/8 teaspoon black pepper
1/2 cup chopped celery
1/4 cup chopped onion
1/4 cup butter or margarine

GLAZE:
1/4 cup orange juice
1 tablespoon light corn syrup
1/2 teaspoon soy sauce
Apricot halves and fresh sage for garnish

Place roast, bone tips up, on rack in shallow roasting pan. Season with salt and pepper. Make a ball of aluminum foil and press into cavity to maintain shape. Wrap bone tips with foil. Insert meat thermometer, making sure the tip does not touch bone. Roast at 325° until thermometer reaches 150°. To prepare stuffing, dissolve sugar and bouillon in hot water; pour over apricots. Let stand 5 minutes. In a large bowl, combine bread, apple, orange peel, salt, sage, cinnamon and pepper. Add softened apricots. Cook celery and onion in butter until tender; add to bread mixture. Remove foil from roast center; pack stuffing lightly into roast. Combine the glaze ingredients; spoon over meat. Return roast to oven until thermometer registers 160° (total cooking time for roast will be about 2-1/2 to 3 hours). Transfer to warm platter; garnish with apricot halves and fresh sage. Slice between the ribs to serve. **Yield:** 12-16 servings.

TOMATO/SAUSAGE POLENTA

Carol Mead, Los Alamos, New Mexico

(PICTURED ON PAGE 5)

1 medium onion, chopped
1 garlic clove, minced
1/2 pound bulk pork sausage
1 can (16 ounces) tomatoes with juice, cut up
1 can (8 ounces) tomato sauce
1/2 teaspoon oregano
1/4 teaspoon salt
1/2 cup grated Parmesan cheese
1/2 cup all-purpose flour
1/2 cup cornmeal
2 tablespoons sugar
2 teaspoons baking powder
1/4 teaspoon salt
1 egg
1/2 cup milk
2 tablespoons vegetable oil
1 cup (4 ounces) shredded cheddar cheese

Brown onion, garlic and sausage together until sausage shows no pink; drain off grease. Add tomatoes, tomato sauce, oregano and salt; simmer, uncovered, for 5 minutes. Set aside. In a small bowl, stir together the Parmesan cheese, flour, cornmeal, sugar, baking powder and salt. Mix together egg, milk and oil; stir into dry ingredients just until mixed. Pour batter into greased 9-in.-square pan. Carefully pour tomato mixture over batter. Bake at 400° for 20-25 minutes until golden. Sprinkle with the cheddar cheese. **Yield:** 6 servings.

HAMSLAW SALAD

Marian Tammany, Sparks, Nevada

(PICTURED ON PAGE 6)

1 cup cooked diced ham
2 cups shredded cabbage

DRESSING:
1/2 cup sour cream
2 tablespoons honey
1 to 2 tablespoons Dijon mustard
1/4 cup finely chopped green onion, *divided*
1/2 cup toasted broken pecans

In a small bowl, combine dressing ingredients except for 1 tablespoon of green onion and the pecans. Mix well; cover; chill. Toss together ham and cabbage; add dressing, stirring gently to coat. Just before serving, sprinkle with reserved green onion and pecans. **Yield:** 4-6 servings.

BARBECUED PORK CHOPS WITH ROSEMARY/LEMON MARINADE

Peggy Gwillim, Strasbourg, Saskatchewan

(PICTURED ON PAGE 5)

✓ This tasty dish uses less sugar, salt and fat. Recipe includes *Diabetic Exchanges.*

    2 garlic cloves, minced
    1/2 cup lemon juice
Grated rind of 1 lemon
    2 tablespoons olive oil
    1 tablespoon chopped fresh
      rosemary or 1 teaspoon dried
    1/8 teaspoon dried basil
    1/8 teaspoon lemon pepper
      seasoning
    4 pork chops, cut 1 inch thick

Whisk together first seven ingredients. Place pork chops in a large plastic bag; pour in marinade, seal and refrigerate at least 2 hours or overnight, turning occasionally. Drain and reserve marinade; brush on the chops while cooking. Grill chops over medium coals about 6 minutes per side or until juices run clear. **Yield:** 4 servings. **Diabetic Exchanges:** 2-1/2 protein; also, 171 calories, 43 mg sodium, 99 mg cholesterol, 3 gm carbohydrate, 17 gm protein, 10 gm fat.

SWEET AND SOUR PORK KABOBS

Barbara Fossen, La Crescent, Minnesota

(PICTURED ON PAGE 4)

✓ This tasty dish uses less sugar, salt and fat. Recipe includes *Diabetic Exchanges.*

    2 medium carrots, bias cut into
      1-inch pieces
    1 can (8 ounces) pineapple
      chunks, juice pack
    1 tablespoon vegetable oil
    1 garlic clove, minced
    1/4 cup red wine vinegar
    1 tablespoon soy sauce
    1 teaspoon sugar
    3/4 pound boneless pork, cut
      into 1-inch cubes
Small green pepper, cut into 1-inch
      pieces
Small sweet red pepper, cut into
      1-inch pieces
Cooked rice

Cook carrots in boiling water for about 12 minutes; drain well. Drain pineapple and set aside, reserving 1/4 cup juice. Combine pineapple juice, oil, garlic, vinegar, soy sauce and sugar. Pour over cubed pork; let stand for 30 min-

utes. On four skewers, alternate pork, carrots, green and red pepper and pineapple. Grill kabobs over hot coals for about 12 minutes, turning once. Baste often with marinade/sauce. Serve with rice. **Yield:** 4 servings. **Diabetic Exchanges:** 3 protein, 1 bread; also, 238 calories, 278 mg sodium, 79 mg cholesterol, 17 gm carbohydrate, 25 gm protein, 8 gm fat.

INDONESIAN-STYLE PORK ROAST

Alice Vidovich, Walnut Creek, California

(PICTURED ON PAGE 6)

    1 boneless pork loin roast
      (2 pounds)
COATING:
    1/4 cup creamy peanut butter
    3 tablespoons soy sauce
    2 tablespoons ground
      coriander
1-1/2 teaspoons ground cumin
    1/2 teaspoon chili powder
    1 large garlic clove, minced
    1 tablespoon lemon juice
PEANUT SAUCE:
    1 cup soy sauce
    2 tablespoons pineapple juice
    1 garlic clove, minced
    1/4 cup dry sherry, optional
    1/2 teaspoon minced fresh
      gingerroot
    1/2 cup chopped unsalted
      peanuts

Combine coating ingredients in a bowl; mix until smooth. Rub coating over all exposed surfaces of the roast; let stand for 30 minutes. Place roast in greased baking dish; bake at 325° until meat thermometer inserted in center registers 160° (about 75 to 90 minutes). To make sauce, combine all ingredients except peanuts in saucepan; bring to boil. Let cool; add peanuts. Set aside. Remove roast from oven; let rest 15 minutes. Slice into serving portions and serve with sauce. **Yield:** 6 servings.

PINTO BEAN/HAM SOUP

Eva Greenman, Livonia, New York

(PICTURED ON PAGE 5)

    1 pound dry pinto beans
    6 large carrots, sliced 1/2 inch
      thick
    1 large onion, chopped
    6 stalks celery, bias cut into
      1/2-inch pieces
    1 large garlic clove, minced

3-1/2 to 4 pounds ham hocks
    2 teaspoons paprika
    1/2 cup sour cream, optional
    1 tablespoon fresh chopped
      parsley
    2 teaspoons vinegar
CSIPETKE:
    1 cup all-purpose flour
    1/2 teaspoon salt
    1 egg
    1 tablespoon vegetable oil

Wash and sort beans. Soak in cold water overnight; drain. In a large 8-qt. pot, combine beans, carrots, onions, celery, garlic, ham hocks and paprika. Add enough water to cover ingredients by 2 in. Simmer, partly covered, for 2-1/2 hours or until the beans are tender, adding more water as needed. When beans are tender; remove meat to side dish. To make Csipetke, mix all ingredients into stiff dough; let rest for 30 minutes. Divide into 4 parts. Flatten each part and pinch off pieces about the size of a cherry pit; roll between fingers and drop into hot soup. Cook 30 minutes. Blend in sour cream, if desired. Mix in parsley and vinegar; adjust seasoning. Cut reserved ham into bite-size pieces; stir into soup. **Yield:** 4 quarts.

PORK TENDERLOIN DIANE

Patsy Steenbock, Shoshoni, Wyoming

(PICTURED ON PAGE 5)

✓ This tasty dish uses less sugar, salt and fat. Recipe includes *Diabetic Exchanges.*

    1 pound fresh pork tenderloin,
      cut into 8 crosswise pieces
    2 teaspoons lemon pepper
      seasoning
    2 tablespoons butter or
      margarine
    6 teaspoons lemon juice
    1 tablespoon Worcestershire
      sauce
    1 teaspoon Dijon mustard
    1 tablespoon fresh minced
      parsley

Press each tenderloin slice to 1-in. thickness; sprinkle surfaces with lemon pepper. Heat butter in heavy skillet and cook tenderloin slices 3 to 4 minutes on each side; remove to a warm serving platter. In skillet, combine lemon juice, Worcestershire and mustard; cook, stirring with pan juices, until heated through. Pour sauce over meat; sprinkle with parsley. **Yield:** 4 servings. **Diabetic Exchanges:** 4 protein; also, 246 calories, 213 mg sodium, 121 mg cholesterol, 1 gm carbohydrate, 33 gm protein, 12 gm fat.

HAM AND VEGETABLE ROLL-UPS
Jody Steinke, Nekoosa, Wisconsin

(PICTURED ON PAGE 6)

2 cups seasoned croutons
1/4 cup melted butter *or* margarine
1 can (10-3/4 ounces) cream of chicken soup, undiluted
1 cup mayonnaise
2 tablespoons lemon juice
1 package (10 ounces) frozen chopped spinach, thawed and drained
1/3 cup plain yogurt *or* sour cream
1 teaspoon instant minced onion
1 teaspoon Worcestershire sauce
8 thin slices boiled ham
8 spears fresh asparagus
1/2 pound fresh mushrooms, sliced crosswise
2 tablespoons butter *or* margarine

Mix the croutons with melted butter; spread in bottom of 9-in. baking dish. Combine soup, mayonnaise and lemon juice. Spoon half of mixture over croutons; set remainder aside. Mix together spinach, yogurt or sour cream, onion and Worcestershire. Spread spinach mixture on each ham slice. Place an asparagus spear on top; roll up. Place rolls seam side down in baking dish; spoon remaining sauce over top. Saute mushrooms in 2 tablespoons butter; spoon on top. Bake at 350° for 25 minutes or until bubbly. **Yield:** 4-6 servings.

PORK PIPERADE
Hyacinth Rizzo, Buffalo, New York

(PICTURED ON PAGE 5)

1 pound boneless pork, cut thin into 1-in. x 1-1/2-in. x 1/8-in. strips
COATING:
1/4 cup all-purpose flour
1 envelope (1-1/4 ounces) taco seasoning mix, *divided*
2 tablespoons vegetable oil
PIPERADE:
3 tablespoons virgin olive oil
1 Spanish onion, thinly sliced
2 sweet red peppers, cut in julienne strips
2 green peppers, cut in julienne strips
2 cups canned plum tomatoes, juice drained and reserved

In a small paper bag, combine flour and half of taco seasoning mix. Add a few pork strips at a time and shake well to coat. Heat oil in a heavy 10-in. skillet; stir-fry pork strips until golden brown and tender. Remove pork to a platter; cover and keep warm. Wipe out skillet with paper towel. Pour in olive oil; heat until hot. Stir-fry onion and peppers until crisp-tender. Chop tomatoes; add to skillet. In small bowl, combine remaining taco seasoning and reserved tomato juice. Stir until blended; add to skillet mixture. Cook and stir until thickened. Return pork to skillet; heat through. **Yield:** 8-10 servings.

MARINATED PORK TENDERLOIN SANDWICH
Alice Gregory, Overland Park, Kansas

(PICTURED ON PAGE 6)

 This tasty dish uses less sugar, salt and fat. Recipe includes *Diabetic Exchanges*.

1 whole pork tenderloin (1 pound)
24 small dinner *or* Parkerhouse rolls, warmed
MARINADE:
1/2 cup soy sauce
1/4 cup packed brown sugar
2 tablespoons vegetable oil
1 teaspoon ground ginger
1/2 teaspoon dry mustard
2 garlic cloves, minced

In a shallow 1-1/2-qt. glass baking dish, mix marinade ingredients. Place tenderloin in dish; turn to coat surface. Cover and refrigerate for 12 hours or overnight, turning several times. Drain, reserving marinade for grilling. Grill tenderloin over hot coals or gas grill on medium-high, brushing occasionally with marinade. Grill *each side* about 6 minutes for medium doneness, or 7 to 8 minutes per side for well-done. Let stand for 10 minutes; carve in thin slices and serve on rolls. (Alternate cooking method: Bake tenderloin in 375° oven until meat thermometer registers 160°. Let stand for 10 minutes; carve in thin slices. Combine 1/4 cup reserved marinade and 1 cup water. Heat in chafing dish; add pork slices.) **Yield:** About 24 small sandwiches. **Diabetic Exchanges:** One serving equals 1 protein, 1 fruit; also, 112 calories, 435 mg sodium, 22 mg cholesterol, 13 gm carbohydrate, 7 gm protein, 4 gm fat.

ODOR EATER: Eliminate cooking odors by boiling a tablespoon of vinegar mixed with a cup of water. That's it!

HAM AND CREAMY POTATO SCALLOPS
Mabel Courtney, Wauseon, Ohio

5 pounds white potatoes, partially cooked
3 tablespoons butter *or* margarine
1/4 cup all-purpose flour
1/4 cup chopped onion
1/2 cup sliced celery
1 pound cooked ham, diced
1 can (14-1/2 ounces) chicken broth
1/4 cup mayonnaise
1 cup process cheese spread
Salt and pepper to taste

Cool and peel potatoes; slice 1/4 in. thick. Spread in greased 2-qt. casserole. In saucepan, melt butter and stir in flour until well blended. Add onion, celery, ham, broth, mayonnaise and cheese spread; cook until thickened. Season with salt and pepper. Pour ham and cheese mixture over potatoes and toss gently. Bake at 275° for 1 hour or until potatoes are tender. **Yield:** 6-8 servings.

HERBED HARVEST VEGETABLE CASSEROLE
Netty Dyck, St. Catharines, Ontario

4 new potatoes, cut in 1/4-inch slices
1/4 cup butter *or* margarine
1 tablespoon finely chopped fresh sage *or* 1 teaspoon dried sage
1 tablespoon finely chopped fresh tarragon *or* 1 teaspoon dried tarragon
3 sweet red peppers, seeded and diced
1 onion, thinly sliced
1/2 cup uncooked long-grain rice
3 medium zucchini, thinly sliced
4 medium tomatoes, sliced
1 cup (4 ounces) shredded Swiss cheese

Grease a 2-1/2-qt. casserole dish and arrange half the potato slices in overlapping rows. Dot with half the butter. Sprinkle with half the sage, tarragon, peppers, onion, rice and zucchini. Dot with remaining butter and repeat layering. Cover and bake at 350° for 1-1/2 hours or until potatoes are tender. Remove cover and top with tomato slices and cheese. Bake 10 minutes, or until tomatoes are warm and cheese is melted. Remove from oven; cover and allow to stand 10 minutes before serving. **Yield:** 6-8 servings.

CURRIED CHICKEN CANTALOUPE SALAD

Margaret Maurer, South Pasadena, California

✓ This tasty dish uses less sugar, salt and fat. Recipe includes *Diabetic Exchanges.*

2 cups cubed cooked chicken
   (cut in 1/2-inch chunks)
1 can (20 ounces) pineapple
   chunks, drained
1/2 cup sliced green onions
1/3 cup diced celery
1/3 cup unsalted peanuts
1/3 cup raisins
1/4 cup coconut
2 cantaloupe

DRESSING:
1 jar (4-1/2 ounces) strained
   apricots with tapioca (baby
   food)
3 tablespoons mayonnaise
2 to 3 teaspoons curry powder
1/4 teaspoon powdered ginger

In a large bowl, combine chicken, pineapple, onions, celery, peanuts, raisins and coconut; set aside. In separate bowl, mix dressing ingredients. Combine chicken mixture with dressing; mix well. Cover; refrigerate for 1 to 4 hours. Cut melons in half; remove seeds. Remove fruit by cutting into bite-size pieces or using a melon ball cutter. Combine melon with chicken mixture, dividing among the four melon halves. Serve chilled; refrigerate leftovers. **Yield:** 4 large individual salads. **Diabetic Exchanges:** One serving equals 3 protein, 2 bread, 2 fruit, 1 vegetable, 1-1/2 fat; also 486 calories, 169 mg sodium, 62 mg cholesterol.

CHICKEN/ASPARAGUS ROLL-UPS

Mrs. Wilbur Yates, Huntington, Indiana

4 chicken breasts, split, skinned,
   boned and pounded thin
Salt and pepper to taste
1 pound fresh asparagus,
   trimmed
2 tablespoons all-purpose flour
1 garlic clove, minced
1 teaspoon salt, *divided*
1/2 teaspoon leaf thyme, *divided*
1/4 teaspoon paprika
2 cups sliced white onions
   (cut 1/4 inch thick)
3 large tomatoes, sliced 1/2 inch
   thick
1/2 cup chicken broth

Season chicken breasts lightly with salt and freshly ground pepper. Place 2-3 asparagus spears on each chicken breast half. Roll up tightly; secure with toothpicks, if necessary. Set aside. Combine flour, garlic, 1/2 teaspoon salt, 1/4 teaspoon thyme and paprika. Roll chicken in this mixture. Place half of onions and tomatoes in bottom of 13-in. x 9-in. x 2-in. pan. Place chicken breasts over vegetables; top with remaining onion and tomato slices. Combine broth with remaining salt and thyme; pour around chicken. Cover pan loosely with foil. Bake at 350° for 30 minutes, basting every 10 minutes. Uncover and bake until tender, about 10-15 minutes. **Yield:** 8 servings.

WHOLE WHEAT PASTA CHEESE SALAD

Mildred Reedy, Sardinia, Ohio

SOY/GINGER DRESSING:
3 tablespoons soy sauce
3 tablespoons apple cider
   vinegar
3/4 teaspoon ground ginger
1 large garlic clove, minced
2 dashes hot pepper sauce
1/3 cup vegetable oil
2 tablespoons minced green
   onions

SALAD:
8 ounces whole wheat macaroni
   or spirals
2 cups small broccoli florets,
   cooked crisp-tender, drained
1 large sweet red pepper, cut in
   thin strips
8 ounces part-skim mozzarella
   cheese, cut in 1-1/2-inch x
   1/4-inch strips

In a large salad bowl, mix soy sauce, vinegar, ginger, garlic and hot pepper sauce until well blended. Beat in oil and onions; set aside. Cook pasta in boiling water 3-7 minutes; drain. In large bowl, combine pasta, prepared vegetables, cheese and dressing; toss. Serve immediately; chill leftovers. **Yield:** 4 servings.

SALMON POTATO SALAD

Brenda Piester, Coats, Kansas

✓ This tasty dish uses less sugar, salt and fat. Recipe includes *Diabetic Exchanges.*

1 can (16 ounces) red salmon,
   drained, boned and skin
   removed *or* 2 cans (6-1/2
   ounces *each*) tuna, flaked
2 cups diced boiled salad
   potatoes
1/2 cup diced celery

1/2 cup grated carrot
3/4 cup chopped onion
1 hard-cooked egg, chopped

DRESSING:
1 cup cottage cheese
2 tablespoons milk
1 tablespoon vinegar
1/2 cup creamy salad dressing
1 teaspoon dill weed
3/4 teaspoon salt
Dash freshly ground pepper
Fresh dill for garnish, optional

Combine salmon or tuna, potatoes, celery, carrot, onion and egg; set aside. For dressing, mix all ingredients except fresh dill in blender or food processor. Add half of dressing to salmon and potato mixture; cover and refrigerate. Serve chilled. Remaining dressing can be added to salad later or offered on the side. Garnish with fresh dill, if desired. Refrigerate leftovers. **Yield:** 6 servings. **Diabetic Exchanges:** One serving equals 3 protein, 1 bread, 1 fat; also, 316 calories, 890 mg sodium, 89 mg cholesterol, 15 gm carbohydrate.

DELUXE EGG SALAD SANDWICHES

Audrey Ulmer, Pulaski, Wisconsin

1 package (3 ounces) cream
   cheese with chives, softened
2 tablespoons butter *or*
   margarine, softened
2 tablespoons finely chopped
   celery
3 tablespoons mayonnaise *or*
   salad dressing, *divided*
1 teaspoon grated onion
1 teaspoon sugar
1/2 teaspoon horseradish
1/2 teaspoon lemon juice
1/4 teaspoon salt
1/8 teaspoon black pepper
Dash garlic powder
6 hard-cooked eggs, peeled
   and chopped fine
8 slices rye bread
Alfalfa sprouts, optional

In medium mixing bowl, combine cream cheese and butter; stir until smooth. Stir in celery, 1 tablespoon mayonnaise, onion, sugar, horseradish, lemon juice, salt, pepper and garlic powder. Fold in eggs. Cover; chill at least 1 hour. Let stand at room temperature about 15 minutes before making sandwiches. If desired, stir in 1 to 2 tablespoons additional mayonnaise. For each sandwich, spread about 1/2 cup egg mixture on 1 slice of rye bread. Top with another bread slice. Garnish with alfalfa sprouts, if desired. **Yield:** 4 sandwiches.

BEEF AND POTATO NACHO CASSEROLE
Gloria Warczak, Cedarburg, Wisconsin

2 pounds lean ground beef
3/4 cup chopped onion, *divided*
1 package (1-1/4 ounces) taco seasoning mix
3/4 cup water
1 can (8 ounces) tomato sauce
1 can (4 ounces) chopped green chilies, drained
1 can (16 ounces) red kidney beans, rinsed and drained
1 package (24 ounces) frozen O'Brien potatoes, thawed
1 can (11 ounces) nacho cheese soup, undiluted
1/2 cup milk
1/4 cup chopped green pepper
1/4 teaspoon sugar
1 teaspoon Worcestershire sauce
Paprika

Brown ground beef and 1/2 cup onion in skillet; drain excess fat. Stir in taco seasoning, water and tomato sauce. Bring to boil and simmer 1 minute. Spread meat mixture into a greased 9-in. x 13-in. baking pan. Top with chilies, beans and potatoes. In mixing bowl, combine soup, milk, remaining onion, pepper, sugar and Worcestershire sauce; pour over potatoes. Sprinkle with paprika. Cover with foil and bake at 350° for 1 hour. Remove foil and bake another 15 minutes or until lightly browned. Allow to stand 10 minutes before cutting into squares. **Yield:** 8 servings.

TUNA-CHIP CASSEROLE
Janis Plourde, Smooth Rock Falls, Ontario

1 bag (7 ounces) plain potato chips, *divided*
1 can (7 ounces) water-pack tuna, drained
1 can (19 ounces) asparagus tips *or* 10 ounces frozen asparagus tips, precooked for 3 minutes, drained
SAUCE:
2/3 cup evaporated milk
1 tablespoon lemon juice
1/4 teaspoon dry mustard
1/8 teaspoon white pepper
TOPPING:
1/4 cup shredded cheddar cheese
1/2 cup sliced almonds

Crush chips and place half in greased 10-in. x 8-in. x 2-in. baking dish. Arrange tuna over chips; top with asparagus. Cover with the remaining chips. Combine sauce ingredients and pour over all. Sprinkle with cheese, then almonds. Bake at 325° for 20-25 minutes. Remove from oven; let stand 5 minutes before serving. **Yield:** 6 servings.

CREAMY ITALIAN POTATO SALAD
Jody Steinke, Nekoosa, Wisconsin

12 cups (about 3 pounds) peeled cubed red salad *or* new white potatoes*
2/3 cup grated Parmesan cheese
1 cup (9 ounces) ricotta cheese
4 garlic cloves, minced
1/2 medium red onion, sliced in thin rings
1/2 cup olive oil
6 tablespoons cider vinegar
Salt and pepper to taste
1/2 cup chopped fresh parsley
1/2 teaspoon leaf oregano, crushed

*Potatoes may be scrubbed and left unpeeled, if preferred. Cook potatoes in boiling salted water until just tender. While potatoes cook, combine remaining ingredients except last two. Drain potatoes. While potatoes are still hot, stir in cheese mixture. Cover; chill. Just before serving, stir in parsley and oregano. **Yield:** 10-12 servings.

ZUCCHINI LASAGNA
Charlotte McDaniel, Williamsville, Illinois

1 pound lean ground beef
1/4 cup chopped onion
1 can (15 ounces) tomato sauce
1/2 teaspoon salt
1/2 teaspoon dried oregano
1/2 teaspoon dried basil
1/4 teaspoon ground pepper
4 medium zucchini (1-1/4 pounds)
1 cup creamed cottage cheese
1 egg, beaten
3 tablespoons all-purpose flour
1 cup (4 ounces) shredded mozzarella cheese

In large skillet, brown beef and onion over medium heat; drain fat. Add tomato sauce and seasonings. Bring to boil; simmer 5 minutes. Meanwhile, slice zucchini crosswise into 1/4-in. slices. In small bowl, combine cottage cheese and egg. In a greased 12-in. x 8-in. x 2-in. baking pan, place half the zucchini and sprinkle with half the flour. Top with cottage cheese mixture and half the meat mixture. Repeat layer of zucchini and flour. Sprinkle with mozzarella cheese and remaining meat mixture. Bake at 375° for about 40 minutes or until heated through. Remove from oven and sprinkle with additional cheese, if desired. To cut more easily, let stand 10 minutes before serving. **Yield:** 6-8 servings.

CORN/OKRA CREOLE
Ruth Aubey, San Antonio, Texas

1 cup chopped green pepper
1/2 cup chopped onion
3 tablespoons vegetable oil
2 cups fresh *or* frozen corn *or* 1 can (17 ounces) whole-kernel corn
1-1/2 cups sliced fresh okra *or* 1 package (16 ounces) frozen okra
3 tomatoes, peeled and chopped (1-1/2 cups)
1 tablespoon tomato paste
1/4 teaspoon thyme
Salt to taste
1/4 teaspoon coarsely ground black pepper
1/2 teaspoon hot pepper sauce, optional

Saute pepper and onion in oil for 5 minutes. Add corn and okra; cook over medium heat for 10 minutes, stirring occasionally. Add tomatoes, tomato paste, thyme, salt, pepper and hot pepper sauce, if desired; mix thoroughly. Cover and simmer for 3-5 minutes, stirring occasionally. **Yield:** 4-6 servings.

CREAM CHEESE/ CHUTNEY APPETIZER
Alice Sunseri, St. Louis Park, Missouri

1 package (8 ounces) cream cheese, softened
1 jar (8 ounces) chutney *or* spiced peach jam
1/4 cup finely sliced green onions
Snack crackers

Press softened cream cheese into oiled mold of desired shape. (For easy removal, spray mold with no-stick cooking spray and line with plastic wrap, if desired.) Unmold on chilled plate. Pour chutney over mold; sprinkle with onions. Ring plate with crackers (buttery crackers are especially good with this). Serve immediately. **Yield:** 24 appetizer servings.

COUNTRY INNS

The Churchill House Inn

Route 73 East
Brandon, Vermont 05733

Phone: 1-802/247-3078

Directions: From Burlington, take Rt. 7 south to Brandon, then left (east) on Rt. 73, 3.7 miles to the inn.

Innkeepers: Roy and Lois Jackson

Schedule: Open December 26 through mid-March; mid-May through October.

Accommodations and Rates: Eight rooms with private baths, $70-$80 per person; includes full breakfast and four-course dinner. Llama treks, bike rentals, guided hikes and bird-watching available, as well as inn-to-inn bike, hike or ski packages. Wheelchair access: difficult.

A day at The Churchill House Inn may begin with a stack of orange whole wheat pancakes featuring Vermont maple syrup, bacon, fresh melon and blueberries. Lunch may be a tasty picnic (prepared by innkeeper Lois Jackson) consisting of fried chicken, pasta salad, cantaloupe, gingersnaps and some refreshing lemonade.

In the evening, guests gather around an old oak table for a four-course dinner of homemade soups, breads, creatively prepared entrees and desserts. For the main course, you might choose delicious baked salmon in a crunchy crust, fresh green beans, sweet corn and warm homemade bread. Top it all off with a dessert of fresh peach slices and blueberries in cream or a slice of their tempting chocolate tart.

If you can't get away to The Churchill House Inn for a pleasant dose of their country cooking, try these recipes, compliments of the Jacksons:

ORANGE WHOLE WHEAT PANCAKES

2 eggs, room temperature
1 teaspoon vanilla extract
1/2 teaspoon almond extract
1-1/2 cups orange juice
1/4 cup vegetable oil
2 cups whole wheat flour
1/2 teaspoon baking soda
1/2 teaspoon salt

Beat eggs with extracts. Mix in orange juice and oil; set aside. In a separate bowl, mix flour, baking soda and salt. Add liquid mixture to dry ingredients, stirring just enough to mix. Cook on grill or griddle over medium heat. **Yield:** 6 servings.

BARBECUED BUTTERFLIED LAMB

2 garlic cloves
1/4 cup soy sauce
3/4 cup (6 ounces) pineapple juice
1/4 cup sherry, optional
1 tablespoon brown sugar
1 butterflied leg of lamb
(6 pounds)
Orange twists and fresh mint leaves for garnish
Mint sauce and chutney, optional

Combine first five ingredients and marinate lamb for up to 24 hours. Grill meat about 20 minutes per side for medium doneness. Garnish with orange twists and mint leaves. Serve with mint sauce and/or chutney, if desired. **Yield:** 12 servings.

CHOCOLATE TART

SHELL:
3/4 cup butter
1/3 cup confectioners' sugar
1-1/2 cups all-purpose flour
FILLING:
1-1/4 cups sugar
1/4 teaspoon salt
4 tablespoons cornstarch
2 cups milk
2 egg yolks, beaten
2 squares unsweetened chocolate
1 teaspoon vanilla extract

Preheat oven to 350°. For shell, cream butter and sugar until light and fluffy. Gradually add flour at low speed until completely blended into soft dough. Press dough evenly into 12-in. false-bottomed tart pan. Prick bottom and sides of dough with fork. Bake for 22-27

minutes or until golden brown. Cool. For filling, mix sugar, salt, cornstarch and milk in double boiler. Cook, stirring constantly, until thickened. Add a little hot mixture to egg yolks, then return to double boiler. Melt chocolate completely and add to mixture. Cook 5 minutes, stirring constantly. Beat in vanilla and pour into shell. Chill. **Yield:** 10-12 servings.

MARINATED BAKED SALMON

1/2 cup olive oil
2 tablespoons lemon juice
2 garlic cloves
4 salmon fillets (6 to 8 ounces each)
1 cup seasoned stuffing crumbs
1/2 cup grated Parmesan cheese
1/4 cup chopped fresh parsley
Lemon wedges and parsley for garnish

Combine the oil, lemon juice and garlic. Marinate salmon for 30 minutes. Combine crumbs, cheese and parsley. Dredge salmon in crumb mixture and place in an ovenproof dish. Sprinkle with some of the marinade. Bake at 450° for 15 minutes. Garnish with lemon wedges and parsley. **Yield:** 4 servings.

SEVEN-LAYER SALAD

3 cups torn spinach
3 cups lettuce leaves
3 bacon slices, cooked and crumbled
2 hard-cooked eggs, sliced
1 can (6 ounces) sliced water chestnuts, drained
1 package (12 ounces) frozen peas
1 red onion, sliced in rings
1 cup mayonnaise
1 teaspoon sugar
1/2 teaspoon salt
1/2 teaspoon pepper
2 cups (8 ounces) shredded cheddar cheese

Wash spinach and lettuce and let drain. Place spinach in bottom of a 9-in. x 13-in. pan or a large round bowl. Sprinkle with bacon and eggs. Completely cover bacon and egg layer with lettuce. Mix peas and water chestnuts and sprinkle over lettuce. Cover with red onion rings. Mix together mayonnaise, sugar, salt and pepper and spread over salad, sealing at edges. Sprinkle with cheese. Refrigerate for up to 24 hours before serving. **Yield:** 12 servings.

Best Cook

**Dolores Deegan
Pottstown, Pennsylvania**

Special occasions are great reasons for special meals. But this "Best Cook" turns holiday meals into thematic banquets!

Her personal approach to cooking makes Dolores Deegan of Pottstown, Pennsylvania a "Best Cook in the Country" winner, thanks to an enthusiastic nomination from her daughter Diane.

"*Every* holiday is an event at our house," Diane told us. "Bread is Mom's specialty, and on holidays she makes 'theme' loaves—heart-shaped bread for Valentine's Day, shamrock-shaped biscuits for St. Patrick's Day and bunny-shaped rolls at Easter."

We phoned Dolores—known as "Mom" to family *and* friends—to learn more about her personalized cooking.

"Birthdays are my favorite," Dolores chuckled. "On their birthday, each of our five children selects their favorite dinner menu and cake ingredients. Whatever their choice, I aim to please!"

And please she does! For her husband, who loves *The Wizard of Oz*, Dolores topped a green tablecloth with a yellow strip of fabric to depict the Yellow Brick Road...then topped his birthday cake with tiny "ruby slippers"!

"I like things to *look* pretty as well

as taste good," Dolores told us. "And I think a good cook can make a tasty meal without it costing a lot of money."

CHOLESTEROL-FREE OMELET

4 egg whites
1 tablespoon skim milk
3 drops yellow food coloring
1 tablespoon diced onion
Salt and pepper to taste
1/2 cup cooked rice *or* leftover mashed potatoes
3 slices cholesterol-free cheese, cubed
1 green pepper and 1 sweet red pepper, chopped, optional
1 tomato, chopped, optional

In a mixing bowl, combine egg whites, milk, food coloring, onion, salt and pepper with a fork. Coat a 9-in. baking dish with no-stick cooking spray. In center of dish, place rice or potatoes in a mound and flatten. Pour egg mixture over all and top with cheese. Add chopped green and red pepper and tomato, if desired. Bake at 350° for about 15 minutes. **Yield:** 1-2 servings.

CHOCOLATE-TOPPED PEANUT BUTTER SPRITZ

1 cup margarine
1 cup peanut butter
1 cup sugar
1 cup packed brown sugar
2 eggs
2 cups all-purpose flour
1 teaspoon baking soda
1/2 teaspoon salt
CHOCOLATE TOPPING:
1-1/2 cups semisweet chocolate chips
1 tablespoon shortening
Chopped peanuts

In a mixer bowl, cream together margarine, peanut butter and sugars. Beat in eggs until fluffy. Stir together flour, soda and salt; add to creamed mixture; blend well. Chill 15 minutes. Use a cookie press with a zigzag end plate to make strips. Bake at 350° on ungreased sheet for 8-10 minutes. (Watch carefully—cookies brown quickly.) For topping, melt chips with shortening. Using a cake-decorating bag or a heavy plastic bag with corner tip removed, run a strip of chocolate down center of each cookie and top with chopped peanuts. **Yield:** 16 dozen cookies.

FRIED TOMATOES

4 to 5 medium tomatoes
1/2 cup evaporated milk
1-1/8 cups all-purpose flour, *divided*
1 cup bread crumbs
1/2 pound bacon
2 cups milk
Salt to taste

Slice each tomato in 3 thick slices. Pour evaporated milk in small bowl and place 1 cup flour and the bread crumbs in separate piles on waxed paper. Dip tomatoes in flour, then milk, then crumbs, coating well. Place in refrigerator to dry, about 1 hour. Fry bacon in large skillet until crisp; remove and set aside. In bacon drippings, saute tomato slices until brown. Remove to a large platter. Pour off all but about 2 tablespoons of drippings. Add remaining flour; cook and stir until bubbly. Add milk and bring to a boil, stirring constantly. Cook and stir for 2 minutes more. Season to taste. To serve, place tomato slice on plate, pour sauce over and top with a bacon slice. **Yield:** 8 servings.

GRINDER REMINDER: To quickly clean a food grinder after chopping nuts, raisins, etc., run half a peeled apple or half a cup of dry cereal through the grinder to pick up the remaining bits of goodies. Then add this to your batter.
● After grinding meats, run a few crackers through the grinder. This, too, can be added to other dishes, such as meat loaf or meatballs.

EGGS-CELLENT IDEA: To easily peel hard-cooked eggs, pour off all of the water from the container in which the eggs were cooked. Cover the container and knock the eggs around in it to loosen the shells. Add cold water, and the shells will fall off!

CASSEROLE HINTS: Cooking for only a couple? Divide casserole ingredients into two smaller dishes and freeze one for later. Casseroles that don't freeze well can be shared immediately with a friend or a neighbor.
● For fast, budget-stretching casseroles, keep canned cream-style soups on hand to mix with leftover meats, seafoods, frozen vegetables, rice, macaroni or potatoes.
● To avoid oven spills, place aluminum pizza pans sprayed with cooking oil under casseroles when baking.

Casseroles and *country cooking* are almost interchangeable—what could be heartier fare than a fresh-from-the-oven dish deliciously deep in meat or poultry, cheese, vegetables and sauce?

The dishes featured here provide a full-flavored response to that question! Any of these "classic casseroles" would make a lasting impression at an Easter brunch, as a "dish to pass" at a potluck, or around your table all year!

FOR EASTER...OR ANYTIME: Clockwise from lower left—**Shrimp and Asparagus Casserole**, Joan Vallem, Arroyo Grande, California (Pg. 27); **Western Beef and Corn Casserole**, Deb Poitz, Fort Morgan, Colorado (Pg. 27); **Egg Foo Yung Casserole**, Barb Fore, Mason, Michigan (Pg. 27); **Chicken Crescent Almondine**, Nancy Reichert, Thomasville, Georgia (Pg. 28); **Sausage and Rice Casserole**, Joyce Green, Bettendorf, Iowa (Pg. 28); **Zippy Baked Carrots**, Jean Muldoon, Cincinnati, Ohio (Pg. 27); **Scalloped Potatoes Etc.**, Arlene Oliver, Waterloo, Iowa (Pg. 28); **Squash Casserole**, Angie Monk, Quitman, Texas (Pg. 27).

Need hearty food in a hurry? Nothing's quicker or easier to prepare than a casserole. These main dishes make marvelous meals for family gatherings, picnics, potlucks or any occasion that calls for flavorful "fast food".

Ham and Asparagus Casserole is a guaranteed crowd-pleaser, and pizza-loving kids go crazy over zesty Zucchini Pizza Casserole. For an international flair, put Chicken Normandy or Italian Heritage Casserole on the table. Prepare any one of these the night before—or freeze it for future use. Either way, you'll be pleased with the results.

DIG IN! Clockwise from top—**Italian Heritage Casserole**, Anne Frederick, New Hartford, New York (Pg. 28); **Zucchini Pizza Casserole**, Lynn Bernstetter, White Bear Lake, Minnesota (Pg. 28); **Chicken Normandy**, Mary Jane Cantrell, Turlock, California (Pg. 29); **Ham and Asparagus Casserole**, Donetta Brunner, Savanna, Illinois (Pg. 29).

Meals in Minutes

IF Barianne Wilson of Falfurrias, Texas had a "theme song", it would likely be *On the Road Again*! Three days a week, this busy young wife of a ranch manager and mother of a 2-year-old drives 120 miles round-trip to teach at her church's preschool.

Sandwiched in between are 40-mile trips to the nearest market. "By the time I get home most days, it's late afternoon," Barianne says. "And that leaves me only about 30 minutes to get a meal on the table."

Making good use of those minutes means using quick-cooking standbys like ground beef and chicken...and reliable recipes like the ones featured here! Barianne shares one of her family's favorite fast menus—Saucy Chicken Strips with Rice Pilaf—along with some time-cutting tips.

"I begin with the flavored rice, since that takes the longest to cook. Then, while the Saucy Chicken Strips simmer, I get the apple topping for the dessert ready to cook."

Next comes a nice green vegetable —often steamed fresh broccoli or zucchini, or canned or frozen whole green beans.

Just before mealtime, Barianne microwaves the dessert topping so that it can cool slightly during the meal. "You can substitute plain yogurt for half the sour cream," she notes. "Either way, it's a tasty finale for a fast meal."

❈ SAUCY CHICKEN STRIPS

- 4 skinless chicken breast halves
- 2 tablespoons butter *or* margarine
- 1/2 cup chopped onion
- 1/2 cup chopped green pepper
- 1 can (4 ounces) sliced mushrooms, drained
- 1 package (1-1/4 ounces) onion soup mix
- 1-1/4 cups water
- 1 tablespoon Worcestershire sauce
- 1 tablespoon cornstarch
- 3 tablespoons water

Cut chicken breasts in 2-in. x 1/2-in. diagonal strips. Melt butter in a large skillet; add chicken and brown on all sides. Remove chicken from skillet, reserving drippings. Add onion, green pepper and mushrooms; saute until crisp-tender. Return chicken to skillet. In a small bowl, combine soup mix, water and Worcestershire sauce; mix well and pour over chicken. Cover. Reduce heat; simmer for 10 minutes. Remove chicken to a warm platter. Combine cornstarch and water; add to sauce. Boil 1 minute or until thick. Pour sauce over chicken. **Yield:** 4 servings.

❈ RICE PILAF

- 2-1/2 cups chicken broth
- 1 teaspoon dried parsley flakes *or* fresh minced parsley
- 2 tablespoons butter *or* margarine
- 1 cup uncooked long-grain rice

Combine broth, parsley and butter in a saucepan; bring to boil. Stir in rice; cover. Reduce heat; simmer 20 minutes. **Yield:** 4 servings.

❈ APPLE CREAM CUPS

Vanilla ice cream
Chopped peanuts, optional

TOPPING:
- 3/4 cup chopped peeled apple
- 1 tablespoon water
- 1 cup packed brown sugar
- 1 cup (8 ounces) sour cream *or* 1/2 cup sour cream plus 1/2 cup plain yogurt
- 1/4 teaspoon ground cinnamon

Combine apple and water in a small saucepan or glass bowl. Cover; cook on stove-top or microwave until water boils. Stir in remaining topping ingredients; cook until sugar melts, stirring once. Let cool slightly; serve warm over ice cream. Top with peanuts, if desired. **Yield:** 4 servings.

REAL "SOFTIES": Soften brown sugar by placing a piece of bread or an apple slice in the bag and closing it tightly. The sugar will draw moisture from the bread or fruit and become soft again.

● To soften cookies that have gotten too crisp for your liking, put them in a plastic bag with a piece of bread. The next morning you'll have soft cookies again!

Bring on spring! Tickle your taste buds with the unique flavors and textures of the fresh foods of the budding season—spinach, asparagus, rhubarb, radishes and early peas.

Capture the tart taste of rhubarb in a molded salad, a creamy layered dessert for a special occasion or a fresh-baked pudding cake served with vanilla sauce.

Savor spring vegetables in an asparagus quiche, zippy spinach appetizer or dressed-up side dish of garden peas and scallions accompanied by dill-flavored bread.

Then, complete this taste-bud sensation with chicken stir-fried in a quick-and-easy main dish.

SPRING SENSATIONS: Clockwise from lower left—**Wild Asparagus Quiche**, Mary Weaver, Glenwood Springs, Colorado (Pg. 29); **Stir-Fried Chicken Fajitas**, Arlyn Kramer, El Campo, Texas (Pg. 29); **Spring Rhubarb Salad**, Joy Hansmeier, Waukon, Iowa (Pg. 29); **Dilly Casserole Bread**, Mrs. Delbert Hull, Spokane, Washington (Pg. 30); **Rhubarb Pudding Cake**, Sharon Merchant, Ithaca, Michigan (Pg. 30); **Party Spinach Spread**, Marie Macy, Fort Collins, Colorado (Pg. 30); **Rhubarb Cream Delight Dessert**, Eleanor Timmerman, River Falls, Wisconsin (Pg. 30); **French Peas**, Ann Nace, Perkasie, Pennsylvania (Pg. 30).

Spring has sprung—and here's a four-star feast to prove it! Each delectable dish features healthy, garden-fresh fruits and vegetables.

Ladle out cups of Cream of Asparagus Soup, a delicate bisque of asparagus and green onion...serve a lovely Layered Spinach Salad...taste a hint of mint in Lamb Chops with Mint Stuffing...and sample Rhubarb/Strawberry Pie for a sweet-tart finish to a fabulous feast.

GLORIOUS GREENS: Clockwise from top—**Layered Spinach Salad**, Connie Blommers, Pella, Iowa (Pg. 31); **Cream of Asparagus Soup**, Westelle Griswa, Monroe, Connecticut (Pg. 31); **Lamb Chops with Mint Stuffing**, Ione Banks, Jefferson, Oregon (Pg. 31); **Rhubarb/Strawberry Pie**, Sandy Brown, Lake Worth, Florida (Pg. 31).

SQUASH CASSEROLE
Angie Monk, Quitman, Texas

(PICTURED ON PAGE 20)

4 eggs, beaten
1/2 cup vegetable oil
1 cup biscuit mix
1 can (4 ounces) chopped green chilies with juice
1 medium onion, chopped
1 garlic clove, minced
2 cups (8 ounces) shredded cheddar cheese, *divided*
4 cups coarsely chopped summer squash *or* zucchini *or* yellow summer squash

Combine eggs, oil and biscuit mix. Stir in chilies, onion, garlic and half of the cheese. Stir in squash. Pour into a greased 13-in. x 9-in. x 2-in. baking dish. Bake at 350° for 40 minutes; sprinkle with remaining cheese and bake 5 minutes more. **Yield:** 8-10 servings.

WESTERN BEEF AND CORN CASSEROLE
Deb Poitz, Fort Morgan, Colorado

(PICTURED ON PAGE 20)

FILLING:
1 pound ground beef
1/2 teaspoon salt
1/2 teaspoon chili powder
1 cup (4 ounces) shredded cheddar *or* American cheese
1/2 cup hickory-flavored *or* regular barbecue sauce
1-1/2 cups (12 ounces) canned Mexicorn whole kernel corn, drained
1 can (8 ounces) tomato sauce

CRUST:
1 cup all-purpose flour
1/2 cup yellow cornmeal
2 tablespoons sugar
1 teaspoon salt
1 teaspoon baking powder
1/4 cup butter *or* margarine
1 cup (4 ounces) shredded cheddar *or* American cheese, *divided*
1/2 cup milk
1 egg, beaten

Brown ground beef; drain. Stir in the remaining filling ingredients and set aside. To make the crust, stir together flour, cornmeal, sugar, salt and baking powder; cut in butter. Blend in remaining crust ingredients except 1/2 cup of cheese. Spread crust mixture over the bottom and sides of a greased (not oiled) 9-in.-square baking pan. Pour filling into crust. Bake at 400° for 25-30 minutes; sprinkle with reserved cheese during last few minutes of baking. **Yield:** 6-8 servings.

EGG FOO YUNG CASSEROLE
Barb Fore, Mason, Michigan

(PICTURED ON PAGE 20)

CASSEROLE:
8 eggs, beaten
1-1/2 cups thinly sliced celery
1 can (16 ounces) bean sprouts, drained
1/2 cup nonfat dry milk powder
2 tablespoons chopped onion
1 tablespoon chopped parsley
1/2 teaspoon salt
1/8 teaspoon ground pepper

MUSHROOM SAUCE:
2-1/2 tablespoons cornstarch
1-1/2 cups chicken broth, *divided*
1 tablespoon soy sauce
1 can (4 ounces) sliced mushrooms, drained
2 tablespoons sliced green onions

Stir together all casserole ingredients; pour into a greased 12-in. x 8-in. x 2-in. baking dish. Bake at 350° for 30-35 minutes or until knife inserted in center comes out clean. To make the sauce, combine cornstarch with 1/4 cup broth. Heat remaining broth to boiling in a saucepan; gradually whisk in cornstarch-broth mixture and soy sauce. Cook, stirring, until thickened and smooth; add mushrooms and green onions. To serve, cut casserole into squares and top with mushroom sauce. **Yield:** 6 servings.

SHRIMP AND ASPARAGUS CASSEROLE
Joan Vallem, Arroyo Grande, California

(PICTURED ON PAGE 20)

2 packages (10 ounces *each*) frozen asparagus cuts, *divided*
1/4 cup butter *or* margarine
1/4 cup all-purpose flour
1 cup milk
3/4 cup light cream
1/4 cup dry white wine *or* 1/4 cup more cream *or* 1/4 cup chicken broth
1/2 teaspoon salt
1/8 teaspoon pepper
1 egg yolk, slightly beaten
1/2 cup grated Parmesan cheese
1 pound cooked small shrimp
1/2 cup buttered soft bread crumbs

On stovetop or in a microwave oven, blanch all of the asparagus for 3 minutes. Drain well; set aside. In a small saucepan, melt butter. Stir in the flour; cook, stirring constantly, for 1 minute. Gradually whisk in milk and cream; cook until thickened. Stir in wine or substitute. Season with salt and pepper. Stir in egg yolk, cheese and shrimp. In a buttered 2-1/2-qt. casserole, arrange half the asparagus; pour on half the sauce. Repeat layers. Top with crumbs. Bake at 350° for 30 minutes. **Yield:** 6 servings.

ZIPPY BAKED CARROTS
Jean Muldoon, Cincinnati, Ohio

(PICTURED ON PAGE 21)

5 to 6 cups sliced carrots (about 2 pounds), cut 1/4 inch thick, *divided*
6 slices Swiss cheese, *divided*

SAUCE:
1 small onion, minced
4 tablespoons butter *or* margarine
3 tablespoons all-purpose flour
1 teaspoon salt
1 teaspoon chili powder
2 cups milk

TOPPING:
1 cup soft bread crumbs
2 tablespoons butter *or* margarine, melted
5 slices bacon, cooked and crumbled

On stovetop or in a microwave oven, blanch the carrots in a covered dish until crisp-tender. Layer half of the carrots in shallow 2-qt. baking pan; cover with half of the cheese. Repeat layers. To make sauce, saute onion in butter for 2 minutes; blend in flour and seasonings. Cook, stirring, for 1 minute. Add milk all at once; stir until thickened. Pour sauce over carrot-cheese layers. Combine bread crumbs and butter; sprinkle over all. Top with bacon. Bake at 350° for 25 minutes. **Yield:** 8 servings.

SCALLOPED POTATOES ETC.

Arlene Oliver, Waterloo, Iowa

(PICTURED ON PAGE 21)

 This tasty dish uses less sugar, salt and fat. Recipe includes *Diabetic Exchanges*.

SAUCE:
  2 tablespoons butter
  2 tablespoons all-purpose flour
  3/4 teaspoon salt
  1/4 teaspoon black pepper
  2 cups milk
CASSEROLE:
  4 cups peeled 1/8-inch thick potato slices, *divided*
  1 cup 1/8-inch thick carrot chunks, *divided*
  1/4 cup chopped onion, *divided*
  1/4 cup chopped green pepper, *divided*
  1 cup cooked cubed ham, *divided*
  1 cup (4 ounces) shredded sharp cheddar cheese

For sauce, melt butter in small saucepan; stir in the flour, salt and pepper. Cook, stirring constantly, for 1 minute. Gradually whisk in the milk; cook until thickened. Set aside. In a buttered 2-qt. casserole, layer half of all vegetables and ham; cover with half of sauce. Repeat layers. Sprinkle cheese over all. Bake, covered, at 350° for 1 hour. Uncover; bake 10 minutes more. **Yield:** 4-6 servings. **Diabetic Exchanges:** One serving equals 1 protein, 1 bread, 1 vegetable, 2 fat; also, 233 calories, 387 mg sodium, 43 mg cholesterol, 20 gm carbohydrate, 13 gm protein, 12 gm fat.

SAUSAGE AND RICE CASSEROLE

Joyce Green, Bettendorf, Iowa

(PICTURED ON PAGE 21)

  1 pound sage-flavored pork sausage
  1 cup sliced celery
  1/2 cup chopped onion
  1/4 cup chopped sweet red pepper
  1/4 cup chopped green pepper
  1/2 cup sliced fresh mushrooms
  1 can (8 ounces) sliced water chestnuts, drained
  1 cup uncooked converted rice
  2 cups chicken broth
  1/2 teaspoon salt
  1/8 teaspoon ground pepper

Brown sausage in a heavy skillet over medium heat; transfer to a 2-1/2-qt. greased casserole dish. In the drippings, saute celery, onion, peppers and mushrooms until lightly browned; transfer to the casserole. To casserole add water chestnuts, rice, broth and seasonings; mix well. Cover tightly and bake at 350° for 1 to 1-1/2 hours or until rice is fluffy and tender. **Yield:** 6 servings.

CHICKEN CRESCENT ALMONDINE

Nancy Reichert, Thomasville, Georgia

(PICTURED ON PAGE 21)

  1 can (10-3/4 ounces) cream of chicken soup, undiluted
  2/3 cup mayonnaise *or* salad dressing
  1/2 cup sour cream
  2 tablespoons instant minced onion
  3 cups cooked cubed chicken
  1 can (8 ounces) sliced water chestnuts, drained
  1 can (4 ounces) mushroom stems and pieces, drained
  1/2 cup chopped celery
  1 tube (8 ounces) crescent dinner rolls
  2/3 cup shredded Swiss *or* American cheese
  1/2 cup slivered almonds
  2 tablespoons butter *or* margarine, melted

In a large saucepan, combine soup, mayonnaise, sour cream and onion. Stir in chicken, water chestnuts, mushrooms and celery; cook over medium heat until mixture is hot and bubbly. Pour into ungreased 13-in. x 9-in. x 2-in. baking dish. Unroll the crescent roll dough and separate into two rectangles, trimming to fit dish. Place dough rectangles over hot chicken mixture. Combine cheese and almonds; sprinkle over the dough. Drizzle with butter. Bake at 375° for 20-25 minutes or until crust is a deep golden brown. Serve immediately. **Yield:** 8 servings.

ITALIAN HERITAGE CASSEROLE

Anne Frederick, New Hartford, New York

(PICTURED ON PAGE 22)

  6 potatoes, peeled and quartered
  1 sweet red pepper, cut in

lengthwise strips
  1 green pepper, cut in lengthwise strips
  1 teaspoon oregano
  1 teaspoon paprika
  1/2 teaspoon garlic powder
  1/2 teaspoon salt
  1/2 teaspoon black pepper
  1 frying chicken (3 pounds), skinned and cut in pieces *or* 6 chicken breast halves, cut in chunks
  1 pound sweet *or* mild Italian sausage, cut in 1-inch to 2-inch chunks

Spray a 13-in. x 9-in. x 2-in. baking dish with no-stick cooking oil; arrange potatoes and peppers in bottom of the dish. Combine the seasonings; sprinkle a third of the seasoning mixture over vegetables. Layer chicken pieces and sausage over vegetables; sprinkle remaining seasoning mixture on top. Cover tightly with foil; bake at 425° for 30 minutes. Reduce oven temperature to 375°; bake 30 to 40 minutes more. **Yield:** 6 servings.

ZUCCHINI PIZZA CASSEROLE

Lynn Bernstetter, White Bear Lake, Minnesota

(PICTURED ON PAGE 22)

  4 cups unpeeled shredded zucchini
  1/2 teaspoon salt
  2 eggs
  1/2 cup grated Parmesan cheese
  1 cup (4 ounces) shredded cheddar cheese, *divided*
  2 cups (8 ounces) shredded mozzarella cheese, *divided*
  1 pound ground beef
  1/2 cup chopped onion
  1 can (15 ounces) Italian-flavored tomato sauce *or* 15 ounces tomato sauce with 1/4 teaspoon *each* oregano and basil
  1 medium green pepper, chopped

Place zucchini in strainer; sprinkle with salt. Let drain for 10 minutes. Squeeze out moisture. Combine zucchini with eggs, Parmesan cheese and half of the cheddar and mozzarella cheeses. Press into greased 13-in. x 9-in. x 2-in. baking pan; bake at 400° for 20 minutes. Meanwhile, brown ground beef with onions. Drain and add the tomato sauce; spoon over baked zucchini mixture. Top with remaining cheeses and sprinkle with green pepper. Bake for 20 minutes more. **Yield:** 6-8 servings.

HAM AND ASPARAGUS CASSEROLE

Donetta Brunner, Savanna, Illinois

(PICTURED ON PAGE 22)

1 package (10 ounces) frozen cut asparagus *or* 1 pound fresh asparagus, 1/2-inch cuts
4 hard-cooked eggs, peeled and chopped
1 cup cooked cubed ham
2 tablespoons tapioca
1/4 cup shredded American cheese
2 tablespoons chopped green pepper
2 tablespoons chopped onion
1 tablespoon chopped fresh parsley
1 tablespoon lemon juice
1/2 cup light cream *or* evaporated milk
1 cup undiluted cream of mushroom soup

TOPPING:
1 cup soft bread crumbs
2 tablespoons butter *or* margarine, melted

On stovetop or in a microwave oven, blanch asparagus cuts in covered dish for 3 minutes; drain thoroughly. In a 2-1/2-qt. baking dish, combine asparagus, eggs and ham; sprinkle tapioca evenly over all. Add the cheese, green pepper, onion and parsley; mix gently. In a small bowl, blend the lemon juice, cream and soup; add to casserole and mix thoroughly. Mix topping ingredients; sprinkle over top of casserole. Bake at 375° for 25-30 minutes. Let stand a few minutes before serving. **Yield:** 6 servings.

CHICKEN NORMANDY

Mary Jane Cantrell, Turlock, California

(PICTURED ON PAGE 22)

CRUST:
1 package (8 ounces) seasoned bread stuffing mix
1/2 cup butter *or* margarine, melted
1 cup water

FILLING:
2-1/2 cups cooked diced chicken
1/2 cup chopped onion
1/2 cup chopped celery
1/2 cup mayonnaise *or* salad dressing
1 teaspoon salt
2 eggs
1-1/2 cups milk

TOPPING:
1 can (10-3/4 ounces) cream of mushroom soup, undiluted
1 cup (4 ounces) shredded cheddar cheese

The day before serving, combine crust ingredients; mix lightly. Spread half of crust mixture in buttered 13-in. x 9-in. x 2-in. baking pan. In a bowl, combine chicken, onion, celery, mayonnaise and salt. Spread chicken mixture over bottom crust; top with reserved crust mixture. Beat together eggs and milk; pour over all. Cover with foil and refrigerate overnight (or freeze for future use). An hour before cooking, remove casserole from refrigerator (or let thaw, if frozen); spread mushroom soup over top. Bake at 325° for 40 minutes. Sprinkle with cheese; bake 10 minutes more. **Yield:** 12 servings.

SPRING RHUBARB SALAD

Joy Hansmeier, Waukon, Iowa

(PICTURED ON PAGE 24)

4 cups diced fresh rhubarb
1-1/2 cups water
1/2 cup sugar
1 package (6 ounces) strawberry-flavored gelatin
1 cup orange juice
1 teaspoon grated orange rind
1 cup sliced fresh strawberries

Combine rhubarb, water and sugar in saucepan. Cook and stir over medium heat until rhubarb is tender. Remove from heat; add gelatin and stir until dissolved. Add orange juice and rind. Chill until syrupy. Add strawberries. Pour into 6-cup mold; chill until set. **Yield:** 8-10 servings.

WILD ASPARAGUS QUICHE

Mary Weaver, Glenwood Springs, Colorado

(PICTURED ON PAGE 24)

CRUST:
1 cup all-purpose flour
1/2 cup vegetable shortening
1 teaspoon salt
1/4 cup ice water

FILLING:
1-1/2 cups low-fat small curd cottage cheese
2 tablespoons all-purpose flour
4 eggs
2 cups low-fat milk
1 teaspoon Dijon mustard
Dash hot pepper sauce

2 cups sliced fresh wild asparagus (cut in 1/2-inch pieces)
2/3 cup shredded Swiss cheese
Paprika

For crust, combine flour, shortening and salt; mix to a "crumb" consistency. Add ice water; mix well and form dough into ball. On floured board, roll out dough to fit 10-in. quiche pan. Place dough in pan; prick bottom with fork. Bake at 350° for 15 minutes. Cool. For filling, combine in blender cottage cheese, flour, eggs, milk, mustard and hot pepper sauce; blend until smooth. Pour into crust. Arrange asparagus evenly over filling. Sprinkle with Swiss cheese and paprika. Bake at 375° for 25 minutes or until knife comes out clean when inserted near center. **Yield:** 6 servings.

STIR-FRIED CHICKEN FAJITAS

Arlyn Kramer, El Campo, Texas

(PICTURED ON PAGE 24)

 This tasty dish uses less sugar, salt and fat. Recipe includes *Diabetic Exchanges*.

4 boneless skinless chicken breast halves, cut in thin strips
3/4 cup bottled Italian dressing
1 small mild onion, sliced and separated into rings
1 small green pepper, sliced in strips
1 small sweet red pepper, sliced in strips
1 small yellow pepper, sliced in strips
1 cup sliced fresh mushrooms
1/2 teaspoon garlic salt
2 tablespoons fresh lemon *or* lime juice
Salt and pepper to taste
Flour tortillas
Picante sauce
Sour cream

In a heavy plastic bag, combine chicken strips and dressing; refrigerate for several hours or overnight, turning bag occasionally. Drain juice. Heat a 12-in. non-stick skillet over medium-high; stir-fry chicken strips and onion for 2 minutes. Add pepper strips and mushrooms; stir-fry until chicken is done and peppers are crisp-tender. Season with garlic salt, lemon juice and salt and pepper. Serve in warm tortillas. Top with picante sauce and sour cream. **Yield:** 4 servings. **Diabetic Exchanges:** One serving equals 3 protein, 1 vegetable, 1 bread; also, 326 calories, 694 mg sodium, 78 mg cholesterol, 21 gm carbohydrate, 29 gm protein, 14 gm fat.

29

FRENCH PEAS
Ann Nace, Perkasie, Pennsylvania

(PICTURED ON PAGE 24)

✓ This tasty dish uses less sugar, salt and fat. Recipe includes *Diabetic Exchanges.*

- **2 green onions, diced**
- **1 cup finely shredded lettuce**
- **1 tablespoon vegetable oil**
- **1 teaspoon all-purpose flour**
- **1/4 cup water**
- **1 package (10 ounces) frozen or fresh peas, cooked**
- **1 can (8 ounces) sliced water chestnuts, drained**
- **Dash black pepper**

In a saucepan, cook onions and lettuce in oil over low heat for 5 minutes. Set aside. Combine flour with water; add to onion mixture and cook, stirring, until thickened. Add peas, water chestnuts and pepper. Heat through and serve. **Yield:** 8 servings. **Diabetic Exchanges:** One serving equals 1 vegetable, 1/2 fat; also, 54 calories, 48 mg sodium, 0 cholesterol, 8 gm carbohydrate, 2 gm protein, 2 gm fat.

RHUBARB CREAM DELIGHT DESSERT
Eleanor Timmerman, River Falls, Wisconsin

(PICTURED ON PAGE 25)

CRUST:
- **1 cup all-purpose flour**
- **1/4 cup sugar**
- **1/2 cup butter *or* margarine**

RHUBARB LAYER:
- **3 cups sliced fresh rhubarb (cut in 1/2-inch pieces)**
- **1/2 cup sugar**
- **1 tablespoon all-purpose flour**

CREAM LAYER:
- **12 ounces cream cheese, softened**
- **1/2 cup sugar**
- **2 eggs**

TOPPING:
- **1 cup (8 ounces) sour cream**
- **2 tablespoons sugar**
- **1 teaspoon vanilla extract**

For crust, mix flour, sugar and butter; pat into 10-in. pie plate. Set aside. For rhubarb layer, combine rhubarb, sugar and flour; toss lightly and pour into crust. Bake at 375° for about 15 minutes. Meanwhile, prepare cream layer by beating together cream cheese and sugar until fluffy. Beat in eggs one at a time, then pour over hot rhubarb layer. Bake

at 350° for about 30 minutes or until almost set. Combine topping ingredients; spread over hot layers. Chill. **Yield:** 12-16 servings.

PARTY SPINACH SPREAD
Marie Macy, Fort Collins, Colorado

(PICTURED ON PAGE 25)

- **1 package (10 ounces) frozen chopped spinach**
- **1/3 cup fresh parsley, stems trimmed and discarded**
- **2 tablespoons chopped onion**
- **1 teaspoon salt**
- **1 teaspoon ground black pepper**
- **1/2 cup mayonnaise**

Thaw spinach and drain thoroughly, squeezing out extra liquid. Wash parsley; pat dry on paper towel. In a food processor, chop the parsley using steel blade. Add spinach and remaining ingredients; pulse until combined. Store in airtight container in refrigerator. Serve with thin wheat crackers, buttery crackers or celery and cheese sticks. **Yield:** 1-1/2 cups.

RHUBARB PUDDING CAKE
Sharon Merchant, Ithaca, Michigan

(PICTURED ON PAGE 25)

CAKE:
- **1 cup sugar**
- **1 egg**
- **2 tablespoons butter *or* margarine, melted**
- **1 cup buttermilk *or* sour milk**
- **1/2 teaspoon salt**
- **1/2 teaspoon baking soda**
- **1 teaspoon baking powder**
- **2 cups all-purpose flour**
- **1 cup diced fresh rhubarb**

TOPPING:
- **2 tablespoons margarine, melted**
- **1/2 cup sugar**

VANILLA SAUCE:
- **1/2 to 1 cup sugar**
- **1/2 cup margarine**
- **1/2 cup evaporated milk**
- **1 teaspoon vanilla extract**

Blend together sugar, egg and butter. Beat in buttermilk until smooth. Stir together salt, baking soda, baking powder and flour. Stir dry ingredients into buttermilk mixture; mix well. Stir in rhubarb. Pour into a greased 9-in. square baking pan. Combine topping ingredi-

ents; sprinkle on top of batter. Bake at 350° for 45 minutes or until cake tests done. For sauce, mix sugar, margarine and milk; bring to boil and cook 1 minute, stirring constantly. Remove from heat; stir in vanilla. Serve sauce over cake. **Yield:** 12 servings.

DILLY CASSEROLE BREAD
Mrs. Delbert Hull, Spokane, Washington

(PICTURED ON PAGE 25)

✓ This tasty dish uses less sugar, salt and fat. Recipe includes *Diabetic Exchanges.*

- **1 packet active dry yeast**
- **1/4 cup warm water (110°-115°)**
- **1 cup cottage cheese, lukewarm**
- **2 tablespoons sugar**
- **1 tablespoon instant minced onion**
- **1 tablespoon butter**
- **2 tablespoons dill seed**
- **1 teaspoon salt**
- **1/4 teaspoon baking soda**
- **1 unbeaten egg**
- **2-1/4 to 2-1/2 cups all-purpose flour**

Soften yeast in water; set aside. In mixing bowl combine cottage cheese, sugar, onion, butter, dill seed, salt, soda and egg. Mix until blended. Stir in softened yeast. Gradually add flour to form stiff dough. Cover; let rise in warm place for about 1 hour. Stir down dough. Turn into well-greased 8-in. round casserole, about 1- to 1-1/2-qt. size. Let rise 30-40 minutes. Bake at 350° for 35-45 minutes. Brush with additional butter. Cut in wedges to serve. **Yield:** 10 servings. **Diabetic Exchanges:** One serving equals 2 bread, 1/2 fat; also, 181 calories, 319 mg sodium, 34 mg cholesterol, 30 gm carbohydrate, 7 gm protein, 3 gm fat.

BAKING WITH BISCUITS: Inexpensive canned biscuits can be used in a variety of ways:
- Cut a hole in the middle and deep-fry them in fat for doughnuts.
- Flatten them for mini pizza crusts.
- Stretch and wrap them around wieners and bake.
- Make cheesy snack crackers by adding 1/2 cup shredded sharp cheese to one can of biscuits, rolling the dough thin, cutting it into small squares, and baking them until crisp.
- For delicious tea biscuits, flatten them, spread with butter, then sprinkle with sugar and cinnamon and bake.

LAYERED SPINACH SALAD
Connie Blommers, Pella, Iowa

(PICTURED ON PAGE 26)

1/2 to 3/4 pound fresh spinach
1/2 medium cucumber, thinly
   sliced
1/2 cup thinly sliced radishes
1/4 cup thinly sliced green onions
2 hard-cooked eggs, sliced
3/4 cup ranch-style salad
   dressing
5 slices bacon, crisply fried and
   crumbled
1/2 cup Spanish peanuts

Remove and discard spinach stems. Rinse leaves well; drain and pat dry. Tear into bite-size pieces and arrange in a salad bowl. Evenly layer cucumber slices, radishes, green onions and eggs on top of spinach. Spread dressing over top; do not mix. Cover; chill up to 24 hours. Just before serving, sprinkle with bacon and peanuts. **Yield:** 6 servings.

RHUBARB/ STRAWBERRY PIE
Sandy Brown, Lake Worth, Florida

(PICTURED ON PAGE 26)

1 unbaked deep-dish pie shell
Enough pie dough for a lattice crust
FILLING:
3 cups sliced fresh rhubarb (cut
   in 1/4-inch pieces)
3 cups sliced fresh strawberries
1/2 to 3/4 cup sugar
1-1/2 tablespoons instant tapioca
1/3 cup fresh orange juice
1-1/2 tablespoons orange
   marmalade, optional
1/4 teaspoon orange peel

Combine filling ingredients in large mixing bowl; let stand for 15 minutes while tapioca softens. Pour filling into pie shell. Prepare lattice strips for top crust. Bake at 400° for 20 minutes; reduce heat to 375° and bake 30 minutes more or until rhubarb is tender. **Yield:** 6-8 servings.

RHUBARB BREAD
Grace Capen, Sacramento, California

1-1/3 cups packed brown sugar
2/3 cup vegetable oil
1 egg, beaten
1 teaspoon vanilla extract

1 cup buttermilk *or*
   soured milk
2-1/2 cups all-purpose flour
3/4 teaspoon salt
1/2 teaspoon cinnamon
1 teaspoon baking soda
1-1/2 to 2 cups finely diced rhubarb
   (1/4-inch cuts)
1/2 cup nuts, chopped

Mix together sugar and oil; blend in egg, vanilla and milk. In separate bowl, combine flour, salt, cinnamon and baking soda; add to moist ingredients. Stir in rhubarb and nuts. Divide batter between two well-greased 8-in. x 4-in. loaf pans. Bake at 350° for about 45 minutes or until bread tests done with wooden pick. Turn out onto rack to cool. **Yield:** 2 loaves.

LAMB CHOPS WITH MINT STUFFING
Ione Banks, Jefferson, Oregon

(PICTURED ON PAGE 26)

1/4 cup chopped onion
1/4 cup chopped celery
1/2 cup butter *or* margarine
2/3 cup chopped and packed
   fresh mint leaves
4 cups torn white *or* brown
   bread (3/4-inch pieces)
Salt and pepper to taste
1 egg, beaten
8 shoulder lamb chops
4 teaspoons creme de menthe,
   optional

Saute onion and celery in butter. Stir together with mint and bread pieces. Season with salt and pepper. Add egg; mix lightly. Place lamb in a shallow baking dish; brush with creme de menthe, if desired. Pile stuffing on top of chops. Bake at 350° for 1 hour. **Yield:** 8 servings.

CREAM OF ASPARAGUS SOUP
Westelle Griswa, Monroe, Connecticut

(PICTURED ON PAGE 26)

4 cups sliced fresh asparagus
   (cut in 1/2-inch pieces)
2 cups water, *divided*
5 tablespoons butter
1/4 cup very finely diced green
   onion *or* 1 teaspoon onion
   powder
5 tablespoons all-purpose flour
1/2 to 1 teaspoon salt
1/4 teaspoon white pepper
4 cups milk

1 tablespoon chicken bouillon
   granules

Cook asparagus in 1 cup water until crisp-tender. Drain, reserving liquid. Saute onion in butter until transparent. Stir in flour, salt and pepper; cook over medium heat, stirring constantly, for 1 minute. Gradually stir in milk, 1 cup water, reserved liquid and bouillon granules. Cook, stirring with wire whisk, until mixture is thickened and hot. Stir in asparagus. Heat through and serve. **Yield:** 6 servings.

BLENDER RASPBERRY SHERBET
Mary McCrackin, Hollywood, Alabama

2 cups fresh raspberries,
   pureed and frozen *or* 2 cups
   frozen whole unsweetened
   raspberries
2 tablespoons orange juice
   concentrate
1/8 to 1/4 teaspoon vanilla extract
4 tablespoons sugar *or* more
   to taste
1/2 cup plain nonfat yogurt

Puree frozen raspberries in food processor or blender; add remaining ingredients. Blend until creamy. Serve immediately or store in freezer until serving time. **Yield:** 4 3/4-cup servings.

LUSCIOUS RASPBERRY GELATIN SALAD
Bonnie Barclay, Custer, Michigan

2 packages (3 ounces *each*)
   raspberry-flavored gelatin
1 envelope unflavored gelatin
1 cup boiling water
2 cups cold water
1 can (20 ounces) crushed
   pineapple with juice
2 large ripe bananas, mashed
1 pint fresh *or* frozen whole
   unsweetened raspberries
1 cup (8 ounces) sour cream

In a large mixing bowl, combine gelatins. Add boiling water; stir until dissolved. Add the cold water, then pineapple, bananas and raspberries. Stir. Pour half of gelatin mixture into glass serving bowl or 13-in. x 9-in. x 2-in. baking dish; chill until firm. Let remaining half sit at room temperature. When gelatin is firm, spread sour cream evenly on top, then carefully pour remaining gelatin mixture over the sour cream. Chill until firm. **Yield:** 16 servings.

CHEDDAR SPOON BREAD
Barbara Clouse, Blacksburg, Virginia

2 cups milk, *divided*
1/2 cup yellow cornmeal
**1 cup (4 ounces) shredded
sharp cheddar cheese**
1/3 cup butter
1 tablespoon sugar
1 teaspoon salt
2 eggs, well beaten

Scald 1-1/2 cups milk (heat to 180°). Mix cornmeal with remaining cold milk and add to hot milk. Cook, stirring constantly, over low heat until thickened, approximately 5 minutes. Add cheese, butter, sugar and salt; stir until melted. Remove from heat; stir in eggs. Pour into 1-qt. greased baking dish; bake at 350° for about 35 minutes, or until lightly browned and set. Serve immediately. **Yield:** 6 servings.

RASPBERRY CAKE ROLL
Virginia Quelch, Las Cruces, New Mexico

6 egg whites, room temperature
1 teaspoon fresh lemon juice
1/4 teaspoon salt
1/4 cup sugar
1 tablespoon grated lemon peel
**1/2 cup plus 1 tablespoon sifted
cake flour**
**1 package (8 ounces) cream
cheese**
1/2 teaspoon vanilla extract
**1 cup frozen nondairy whipped
topping, thawed,** *divided*
1 pint fresh raspberries, *divided*

Spray a 15-in. x 10-in. x 1-in. jelly-roll pan with nonstick cooking spray; line with waxed paper and spray again. Set aside. In large bowl, beat egg whites, lemon juice and salt with electric mixer at low speed until foamy. Gradually add sugar, beating at medium-high speed until soft peaks form. With whisk or rubber scraper, fold lemon peel and flour, 1/4 cup at a time, into egg white mixture. Spread batter evenly into prepared pan. Bake at 350° for 12-15 minutes or until cake springs back when touched in center. Cool cake in pan on rack for 5 minutes. Cover with waxed paper, then a kitchen towel and baking sheet or bread board. Invert pan so cake lies flat on towel. Gently peel away waxed paper from top of cake. Beginning with narrow end, roll cake with towel, keeping towel and bottom waxed paper pressed to underside of cake. Place rolled cake on rack to cool. Prepare fill-ing by combining cream cheese, vanilla and 2 tablespoons of whipped topping. Gently fold in remaining whipped topping. Cover; refrigerate until ready to use. To fill cake, carefully unroll on flat surface. With spatula, spread filling evenly over cake to within 1/2 in. of edges. Sprinkle with 1-1/2 cups raspberries. Using towel to lift edge of cake, gently roll as before, this time pulling away towel and waxed paper. Place roll, seam side down, on serving platter. Chill. Garnish with remaining raspberries and lemon peel. Serve chilled. **Yield:** 12 servings.

MINIATURE PEANUT BUTTER TREATS
Jodie McCoy, Tulsa, Oklahoma

1/2 cup butter, softened
1/2 cup packed brown sugar
1/2 cup granulated sugar
1 egg
1/2 cup creamy-style peanut butter
1/2 teaspoon vanilla extract
1-1/4 cups all-purpose flour
3/4 teaspoon baking soda
1/2 teaspoon salt
**About 42 miniature peanut butter-
chocolate cups**

Combine butter, sugars, egg, peanut butter and vanilla in mixing bowl; beat until smooth. In separate bowl, combine flour, baking soda and salt; add to creamed mixture. Cover dough and chill. When cold enough to handle easily, roll in small (walnut-sized) balls; place each ball in greased miniature muffin tin. Bake at 375° for 8-9 minutes. Remove from oven; gently press 1 peanut butter cup into each cookie to make depression. Cool in pan 10 minutes; remove from pan and cool on rack. Store in cool place until serving time. **Yield:** about 3-1/2 dozen cookies.

BLUEBERRY/ORANGE MUFFINS
Irene Parry, Kenosha, Wisconsin

1 cup quick-cooking rolled oats
1 cup orange juice
1 teaspoon grated orange zest
1 cup vegetable oil
3 eggs, beaten
3 cups all-purpose flour
1 cup sugar
4 teaspoons baking powder
1 teaspoon salt
1/2 teaspoon baking soda
3 to 4 cups fresh blueberries

TOPPING:
1/2 cup finely chopped nuts
3 tablespoons sugar
1/2 teaspoon cinnamon

Mix oats, orange juice and zest; blend in oil and eggs; set aside. Stir together flour, sugar, baking powder, salt and baking soda. Add oat mixture; mix lightly. Fold in blueberries. Spoon batter into paper-lined muffin tins, filling two-thirds full. Combine topping ingredients; sprinkle over batter. Bake at 400° for about 15-18 minutes or until lightly browned. **Yield:** 24 large muffins.

BROADWAY BROWNIE BARS
Anne Frederick, New Hartford, New York

**1 package (8 ounces) cream
cheese,** *divided*
1-1/2 cups sugar, *divided*
**1 cup plus 2 tablespoons
all-purpose flour,** *divided*
1 cup butter *or* **margarine,
softened,** *divided*
3 eggs, *divided*
2-1/2 teaspoons vanilla extract,
divided
2 squares (1 ounce *each***)
unsweetened chocolate,**
divided
1-1/4 cups chopped walnuts,
divided
1 teaspoon baking powder
1 cup semisweet chocolate chips
2 cups miniature marshmallows
1/4 cup milk
3 cups confectioners' sugar

In a small mixing bowl, blend 6 ounces cream cheese, 1/2 cup sugar, 2 tablespoons flour, 1/4 cup butter, 1 egg and 1/2 teaspoon vanilla; set aside. In medium saucepan, over medium heat, melt 1 square chocolate and 1/2 cup butter. Remove from heat; add 1 cup sugar, 1 cup flour, 1 cup nuts, baking powder, 1 teaspoon vanilla and 2 eggs; blend well. Spray 13-in. x 9-in. x 2-in. pan with no-stick cooking spray; spread batter in pan. Spread cheese mixture over batter. In small bowl, combine 1/4 cup nuts and the chocolate chips; sprinkle over cheese layer. Bake at 350° for about 28 minutes or until almost done. Sprinkle marshmallows over all; return to oven for 2 minutes. In medium saucepan, melt 1/4 cup butter, 1 square chocolate, 2 ounces cream cheese and milk. Remove from heat; stir in confectioners' sugar and 1 teaspoon vanilla. Immediately drizzle over marshmallows. Chill well; cut into bars. **Yield:** 30 bars.

DIRT CAKE

Flo Burtnett, Gage, Oklahoma

1 package (16 ounces) Oreo
   cookies
1 package (8 ounces) cream
   cheese
1/2 cup margarine
1 cup confectioners' sugar
1 teaspoon vanilla extract
2 packages (3-1/2 ounces *each*)
   instant vanilla pudding
3 cups milk
1 container (12 ounces)
   nondairy whipped topping
2 new clay flowerpots, about
   6 inches in diameter
Heavy-duty aluminum foil
Silk flowers
Plastic garden utensils, optional

Line flower pots completely with foil; set aside. Crush cookies until they resemble potting soil. Place 1 cup crumbs (or more) in each flowerpot; set aside. Cream the cheese, margarine, sugar and vanilla together until blended; set aside. Combine pudding mix and milk; fold in whipped topping. Gently fold cheese and pudding mixtures together. Pour half the mixture into each flowerpot. Top with remaining cookie crumbs. Cover with foil; refrigerate. When ready to serve, remove foil; top with silk or plastic flowers whose stems have been wrapped in foil. Display with plastic gardening tools, if desired. **Yield:** 12 servings.

LEMON RICOTTA CHEESECAKE SQUARES

Mrs. Glenn Holcomb, Tarrington, Connecticut

2 pounds ricotta cheese
3/4 cup sugar
3 eggs, slightly beaten
Grated rind of 1 to 2 lemons
1 package (18-1/4 ounces) lemon
   cake mix with pudding
1/4 cup fresh lemon juice
Confectioners' sugar

Combine ricotta, sugar, eggs and lemon rind; set aside. In another bowl, mix cake mix according to package directions, *substituting lemon juice* for 1/4 cup of the water called for. Pour batter into greased and floured 13-in. x 9-in. x 2-in. baking pan; spoon ricotta mixture carefully on top. Bake at 350° for 60-65 minutes or until lightly browned. Cool cake. Store in refrigerator 4 hours before serving. Sift confectioners' sugar over top before cutting into squares. Serve chilled; refrigerate leftovers. **Yield:** 16-20 servings.

MORNING GLORY MUFFINS

Paddy Webber, Exeter, Ontario

2 cups all-purpose flour
1-1/4 cups sugar
2 teaspoons baking soda
2 teaspoons cinnamon
1/2 teaspoon salt
2 cups grated carrot
1/2 cup raisins
1/2 cup shredded coconut
1/2 cup chopped pecans
3 eggs
1 cup vegetable oil
1 apple, cored and shredded
2 teaspoons vanilla extract

In a large mixing bowl, combine flour, sugar, baking soda, cinnamon and salt. Stir in carrot, raisins, coconut and pecans. In a separate bowl, combine eggs, oil, apple and vanilla. Add to flour mixture. Stir only until combined. Spoon into greased or lined muffin tins. Bake at 350° for 15-18 minutes. **Yield:** about 18 muffins.

APPLE CAKE WITH LEMON SAUCE

Jean Camp, North Olmsted, Ohio

CAKE:
3 eggs
1-3/4 cups sugar
1 cup vegetable oil
1 teaspoon vanilla extract
2 cups all-purpose flour
1 teaspoon baking soda
1 teaspoon cinnamon
1 teaspoon salt
2 cups sliced peeled apples
   (cut in 1/2-inch pieces)
1 cup pecans, chopped
1 cup seedless raisins

LEMON SAUCE:
1 large lemon
2 egg yolks
1 cup sugar
2-1/2 tablespoons cornstarch
1/2 teaspoon salt
1-1/2 cups water
4 teaspoons butter *or* margarine

For cake, beat eggs; add sugar, oil and vanilla. In separate bowl, mix flour, soda, cinnamon and salt. Add flour mixture to egg mixture all at once; blend and stir. Add apples, nuts and raisins to mixture; blend well. Pour batter into a well-greased 11-in. x 7-in. x 2-in. pan (13-in. x 9-in. x 2-in. pan may be used; decrease baking time by 15-20 minutes). Bake at 375° for 55 minutes, or

until cake tests done when wooden pick is inserted in center. For sauce, grate peel from lemon; measure out 1-1/2 teaspoons rind. Squeeze lemon; measure 3 tablespoons juice. Set aside. Beat egg yolks lightly; set aside. In a separate bowl, blend sugar, cornstarch and salt. Measure water into saucepan; gradually stir in sugar mixture. Cook, stirring, until mixture boils clear and thickens. Remove from heat. Beat small amount of hot mixture into egg yolks. Return yolk mixture to saucepan; cook and stir about 2 minutes. Remove from heat; add lemon rind, juice and butter. Pour sauce over cake. **Yield:** 20-24 servings.

ORANGE DATE NUT BREAD

Joan Higgins, Waynesboro, Mississippi

BREAD:
2 eggs
2 tablespoons butter *or*
   margarine
3/4 cup sugar
1 small *unpeeled* orange, cut
   into pieces and seeded
1 cup pitted chopped dates
1-3/4 cups all-purpose flour
1 teaspoon baking soda
1 teaspoon salt
1 cup chopped pecans

SAUCE:
1/2 cup orange juice
1/2 cup sugar

For bread, place eggs, butter, sugar, orange pieces and dates in blender or food processor. Cover and process with on/off motions until finely chopped. Remove to a large mixing bowl. In separate bowl, sift together flour, baking soda and salt; add to orange mixture and mix until well-combined. Stir in pecans. Pour batter into greased 9-in. x 5-in. x 3-in. baking pan. Bake at 325° for 1 hour or until bread tests done. If bread begins to darken, cover with foil during last few minutes of baking. Meanwhile, for sauce, heat orange juice and sugar until sugar melts. When bread comes out of the oven, prick with a wooden pick and pour hot sauce over top. Let bread stand 15 minutes before removing from pan. Cool on wire rack. **Yield:** 1 loaf.

OUT OF WHIPPING CREAM? Add sliced bananas to the white of an egg. Then beat until stiff. This makes an excellent topping for puddings and pies.

NEW YEAR'S OYSTER STEW

Christa Scott, Santa Fe, New Mexico

1/4 cup butter *or* margarine
3 leeks (white part only), chopped
2 potatoes, peeled and diced
2 cups water
3 chicken bouillon cubes
2 cups milk
2 cups half-and-half cream
1/4 teaspoon cayenne pepper
4 cans (16 ounces *each*) oysters, drained
Salt and pepper to taste
Fresh chopped parsley

In large soup kettle or Dutch oven, melt butter and saute leeks until tender, about 10 minutes. Add potatoes, water and bouillon cubes; cover and simmer 20 minutes or until potatoes are tender. Allow mixture to cool, then puree in blender or food mill. Return puree to kettle; add all remaining ingredients. Heat slowly to serving temperature. Do not boil. **Yield:** 12 servings.

SOUTHWEST STEW

Lois C. McAtee, Oceanside, California

2 pounds ground beef
1-1/2 cups diced onion
1 can (28 ounces) tomatoes with juice, chopped
1 can (15 ounces) pinto beans, rinsed and drained
1 can (17 ounces) whole-kernel corn, drained
1 cup mild, medium *or* hot picante sauce
3/4 cup water
1 teaspoon ground cumin
1/2 teaspoon garlic powder
1/2 teaspoon pepper
Salt to taste
Shredded cheddar cheese, optional

In skillet, brown beef and onion. Drain any excess fat. Add remaining ingredients and bring to a boil. Simmer, covered, for 15-20 minutes. Garnish with shredded cheddar cheese, if desired. **Yield:** 8 servings.

MAPLE ALMOND BEEF

Valerie Witt, Centralia, Washington

2 tablespoons cooking oil
3 garlic cloves, minced
2 pounds round *or* sirloin steak, cut into thin strips
1/2 medium onion, thinly sliced
1 sweet red pepper, seeded and cut into strips
1/2 cup maple syrup
1/3 cup red wine vinegar
2 tablespoons soy sauce
2 tablespoons cornstarch
3/4 cup frozen tiny peas, defrosted
1/2 cup slivered almonds
Hot cooked rice

In large skillet or wok, heat oil on high. Saute garlic 1 minute. Add meat; cook until browned. Stir in onion and red pepper. Cover and steam until vegetables are crisp-tender, about 7 minutes. While vegetables cook, combine in bowl the syrup, vinegar, soy sauce and cornstarch; stir mixture into beef. Heat, stirring until thickened. Add peas and almonds; heat through. Serve on rice. **Yield:** 6-8 servings.

LASAGNA TOSS

Sharon Martin, Denver, Pennsylvania

1 pound ground beef
1/2 cup chopped onion
Dash minced garlic
1/2 teaspoon salt
1-3/4 cups spaghetti sauce
6 ounces spiral noodles, cooked and drained
1 cup cottage cheese
2 cups (8 ounces) shredded mozzarella cheese, *divided*
Grated Parmesan cheese

In a large skillet, brown beef with onion, garlic and salt. Stir in spaghetti sauce; simmer until heated. Remove 1 cup of meat sauce; set aside. Stir noodles into the remaining sauce. Place half of noodle-sauce mixture in a greased 2-qt. casserole. Cover with cottage cheese and 1 cup mozzarella cheese. Add remaining noodle-sauce mixture; top with reserved meat sauce and remaining mozzarella cheese. Sprinkle with Parmesan cheese. Cover; bake at 350° for 20-25 minutes. Let stand 5 minutes before serving. **Yield:** 6-8 servings.

MICROWAVE PIZZA CASSEROLE

Susan Slagel, Ashkum, Illinois

1 pound ground beef
1/2 cup chopped onion
1/2 cup chopped green pepper
1 can (16 ounces) pizza sauce
1 can (4 ounces) sliced mushrooms
4 ounces sliced pepperoni
1/2 teaspoon salt, optional
2 cups uncooked noodles
1-1/2 cups water
1/2 teaspoon oregano
1/2 teaspoon garlic powder
1/2 teaspoon basil leaves, crushed
3/4 cup shredded mozzarella cheese

In a 2-qt. casserole dish, microwave the ground beef for 3-1/2 minutes; stir and microwave another 2-1/2 minutes or until done. Drain thoroughly. Add remaining ingredients except cheese; mix well. Cook for 17 minutes on high, stirring twice during cooking. Sprinkle cheese on top; cook 1 minute on high until cheese is melted. **Yield:** 6-8 servings.

MOZZARELLA MEAT LOAF

Myra Innes, Auburn, Kansas

1-1/2 pounds lean ground beef
1/2 cup dry bread crumbs
1 egg, beaten
1 teaspoon instant minced onion
3/4 teaspoon salt
1/2 teaspoon leaf oregano
1 can (8 ounces) tomato sauce, *divided*
1-1/2 cups (6 ounces) shredded mozzarella cheese
1 can (6 ounces) sliced mushrooms, drained

In a large bowl, combine beef, crumbs, egg, onion, salt and oregano. Stir in 3/4 cup tomato sauce; set aside. Cut 2 pieces of waxed paper 15 in. long. Place meat mixture in center of one rectangle; cover with second rectangle. With a rolling pin, press meat into a 13-in. x 9-in. rectangle. Remove top sheet of waxed paper. Sprinkle meat with cheese and mushrooms; top with remaining tomato sauce. Roll up meat, jelly-roll fashion, starting at narrow end (use waxed paper to help). Place meat seam side down; seal ends securely. Place in nonstick 9-1/4-in. x 5-1/2-in. x 2-3/4-in. bread pan. Bake at 375° for 30 minutes. Drain off any fat that accumulates; return to oven for 30 minutes. **Yield:** 10 servings.

TASTY TOPPERS: Crumble leftover biscuits or cornmeal muffins over casserole ingredients. Dot with butter and bake as usual.

● For a crunchy casserole topping, mix 2 cups crushed corn or wheat cereal with 1 tablespoon grated Parmesan cheese and a dash of paprika.

COUNTRY INNS

Bonnymill Inn

710 Broad Street
Chesaning, Michigan 48616

Phone: 1-517/845-7780

Directions: From 1-75 Exit 131 (Clio-Montrose), take Rt. M-57 west 19 miles to Chesaning. Inn is on north side of M-57 (Broad Street) on the west edge of town.

Owners: Bonnie and Howard Ebenhoeh
Innkeepers: Carol and Greg Wirgau

Schedule: Open year-round except December 24 and 25.

Accommodations and Rates: Nineteen rooms with private baths, five suites, $65-$125 double occupancy; includes full breakfast and afternoon tea with beverages and snacks. Lunch and dinner available at family's restaurant, Chesaning Heritage House. Well-behaved children welcome. Two rooms totally accessible for handicapped guests. Bikes available for guests' use.

When dinnertime rolls around at the Bonnymill Inn, innkeepers Carol and Greg Wirgau usher guests *out* to eat—at Carol's parents' restaurant, the Chesaning Heritage House, right across the street! There, Bonnie and Howard Ebenhoeh offer a menu with eight full dinners plus lighter fare to choose from.

You might start with a bowl of cheese chowder, then taste the en croute (pastry-wrapped) tenderloin. For dessert, the Fudge Pecan Ice Cream Sundae Pie remains the number-one favorite.

Buffet breakfasts are served in the Bonnymill Inn's atrium, tempting guests with tasty baked eggs, sticky-sweet cinnamon rolls, sour cream bundt coffee cake, fresh fruit and juices.

So rise and shine, and try some of these recipes in your own kitchen!

BONNYMILL BAKED EGGS

16 eggs
3/4 cup sour cream
1 cup half-and-half cream
1-1/2 cups (6 ounces) shredded cheddar cheese
2 cups diced cooked ham *or* crumbled cooked sausage
1 tablespoon chopped chives
2 tablespoons butter *or* margarine, melted
Salt and pepper to taste

Beat eggs in large bowl; add remaining ingredients. Beat well; pour into a greased 13-in. x 9-in. pan. Bake at 350° until mixture is set and top is golden, about 45 minutes. **Yield:** 10-12 servings.

BONNIE'S POTATO SALAD

8 large potatoes, scrubbed
2/3 cup bottled Italian salad dressing
8 hard-cooked eggs, chopped
4 celery stalks, coarsely chopped
3 tablespoons finely chopped onion
1-1/4 cups salad dressing *or* mayonnaise
1 tablespoon prepared mustard
2 tablespoons sugar
Salt and pepper to taste

Cook potatoes until tender. While hot, skin and cut into pieces. Immediately pour the Italian dressing over hot potatoes (potatoes will absorb all of the dressing). Add eggs, celery and onion. Mix salad dressing, mustard and sugar; stir into potato mixture. Add salt and pepper. Cool. **Yield:** 10 servings.

BAKED BEANS

1 pound dried white beans
1/4 pound bacon, cut into small pieces
1/4 cup chopped onion
1 tablespoon salt
1 teaspoon pepper
1 tablespoon prepared mustard
2 tablespoons vinegar
2 tablespoons molasses
1/2 cup sugar
1/2 cup packed brown sugar

Soak the beans overnight. Wash and drain. Cover with water and boil until *very tender*. Drain and reserve the liquid. Add remaining ingredients to the liquid; bring to boil and cook 3 to 5 minutes. Put beans in casserole dish and pour hot liquid over beans until covered. Bake at 350° for 5 hours or until the liquid has baked down into the beans. **Yield:** 6 servings.

CORN CUSTARD CASSEROLE

1 small onion, chopped
1/2 green pepper, chopped
1/4 teaspoon salt
1/4 pound butter *or* margarine
1 can (16 ounces) whole-kernel corn
1 can (16 ounces) cream-style corn
3 eggs
1 box (8-1/2 ounces) corn muffin mix
1-1/2 cups (6 ounces) shredded cheddar cheese, *divided*

Saute onion, green pepper and salt in the butter. Combine both cans of corn, eggs, muffin mix and 1 cup of cheese. Mix with onion mixture and place in a 1-1/2-qt. casserole. Top with remaining cheese and bake at 350° for 40 minutes. **Yield:** 6 servings.

FUDGE PECAN ICE CREAM SUNDAE PIE

20 cream-filled chocolate sandwich cookies
1/2 cup butter *or* margarine, melted
2-1/2 cups French vanilla ice cream, *divided*
1-1/2 cups fudge sauce, *divided*
2 cups pecans, *divided*

Crush cookies and add butter. Press mixture into 9-in. pie tin. Press in half of the ice cream, and over it spread half of the sauce and top with 1 cup pecans. Layer remaining ice cream, sauce and pecans. Cover tightly. Freeze for 12 hours. **Yield:** 6-8 servings.

FRESH FRUIT DIP

1 cup whipped topping
1 cup (8 ounces) sour cream
1/2 cup confectioners' sugar
1/2 cup orange, pineapple *or* lemon juice

Combine all ingredients; mix well. Cover and refrigerate. It will keep well for 3-4 days. Serve with fresh fruit. **Yield:** about 3 cups.

I s there a more versatile, family favorite than *cheese*? Not if the plethora of palate-pleasing dishes on these pages is any indication!

Celebrate June Dairy Month in flavorful fashion—all year long—with cheese-based main dishes…rich cheesy desserts…refreshing salads…deliciously crusty breads…even a satisfying cheese chowder.

PLEASING CHEESE: Clockwise from lower left—**Black Bottom Cupcakes**, Julie Briceland, Windsor, Pennsylvania (Pg. 43); **Savory Cheddar Bread**, Carol Funk, Richard, Saskatchewan (Pg. 43); **Fresh Fruit/Cheese Pie**, Jody Steinke, Nekoosa, Wisconsin (Pg. 43); **Lemon Streusel Cake**, Karla Hecht, Brooklyn Park, Minnesota (Pg. 44); **Cheese/Pepper Soup**, Gay Nicholas, Henderson, Texas (Pg. 44); **Mozzarella Pasta Salad**, Violet Kycek, Austin, Minnesota (Pg. 44); **Raspberry Cream Cheese Coffee Cake**, Brenda Knautz, West Chicago, Illinois (Pg. 44); **Cheesy Fish Fillets with Spinach**, Marla Brenneman, Goshen, Indiana (Pg. 43).

You can count on the goodness of melt-in-your-mouth cheese to add zest to recipes and make meals marvelous. When you serve picture-perfect dishes like these, your whole family will "say cheese"!

Cut into the combination of peppers, tomatoes, cheeses and olives atop Three Cheese Enchiladas...munch on cheese chunks in Chopped Salad with Parmesan Dressing...dip a chip into a bowl of Hot Cheese Dip...and savor a slice of Chocolate Malt Cheesecake.

Why not give these dishes a try today and enjoy a "dairy" good meal?

MORE CHEESE, PLEASE! Clockwise from top left—**Three Cheese Enchiladas**, Gretchen Mellberg, Hawarden, Iowa (Pg. 44); **Chopped Salad with Parmesan Dressing**, Marilyn Norrie, King City, Ontario (Pg. 45); **Hot Cheese Dip**, Ardyce Piehl, Wisconsin Dells, Wisconsin (Pg. 43); **Chocolate Malt Cheesecake**, Anita Moffett, Rewey, Wisconsin (Pg. 45).

Meals in Minutes

SHE IS a teacher, farm wife and mother—so Marjorie Carey of Belfry, Montana knows the importance of making minutes count.

Marjorie's busy weekday schedule begins early in the morning with home classes for her own children. "We stick to a routine, just like any other school," she says.

Her day doesn't end when school's out, though—afternoon hours are filled with trips to the library, helping with homework…and, of course, pitching in with farm chores.

"Before I know it, dinnertime is only 30 minutes away," Marjorie reports.

Marjorie's found an added advantage to the quick, easy-to-prepare meal menu featured here—her children often can help with the preparation. "That's a good way for them to practice some of the things they learn in school, like counting and measuring," she notes.

One of Marjorie's favorite fast meals features a flavorful grilled hamburger with a zesty cheese-and-mushroom sauce, accompanied by a garden-fresh cucumber salad and strawberries for dessert.

Your children can help to mix the hamburger seasoning, make the sauce and—if they're old enough—peel and slice the cucumbers and strawberries. But even without young assistants, this appealing meal can be table-ready in just half an hour.

Try it next time you have to pick up the kitchen pace…or anytime you feel like fixing a simply good supper!

❈ PHILLY BURGER

1 pound ground beef
2 tablespoons Worcestershire sauce, *divided*
4 teaspoons Dijon mustard, *divided*
1 can (2.8 ounces) french-fried onions, *divided*
1 package (3 ounces) cream cheese, softened
1 jar (2.5 ounces) sliced mushrooms, drained
1 teaspoon parsley flakes
4 Kaiser rolls

Combine ground beef with 1 tablespoon of Worcestershire sauce, 3 teaspoons mustard and half the onions. Form into four patties and broil or grill to desired doneness. Meanwhile, in a small bowl, blend cream cheese, remaining Worcestershire sauce and mustard, mushrooms and parsley. Spread the cheese mixture on cooked patties; top with reserved onions. Broil or grill 30 seconds more or until the onions are golden. Serve on Kaiser rolls. **Yield:** 4 burgers.

❈ CUCUMBER SALAD

2 medium cucumbers, peeled and sliced 1/4 inch thick
SOUR CREAM DRESSING:
1/2 cup sour cream
1 tablespoon vinegar
1 tablespoon grated onion
Salt to taste
Freshly ground black pepper
1 to 2 tablespoons diced pimiento

Prepare cucumbers; set aside. Combine dressing ingredients in a bowl; stir in cucumbers. **Yield:** 4 servings.

❈ STRAWBERRY SPARKLER

1 quart fresh strawberries
1/2 cup strawberry-flavored yogurt*
2 tablespoons sugar

Rinse, hull and slice berries. Spoon into sherbet dishes. Combine yogurt* (to substitute plain yogurt, swirl in a few teaspoons of your favorite strawberry jam or topping) and sugar. Drizzle over berries. **Yield:** 4 servings.

STRAWBERRY STORAGE: Strawberries will stay fresh for several days if you put fresh, unwashed berries in a container and top with a folded napkin. Cover the container, turn it upside down and store in the refrigerator.

Celebrate summer country-style —with a sizzling grill, your favorite tablecloth and a sumptuous spread of seasonal foods! Tall glasses of sun-brewed iced tea go great with fun-at-the-fair foods like crispy corn dogs or fancier fare like grilled marinated lamb.

Plain or fancy, summer's a fine time to set up your picnic table and invite the neighbors to join you as you sample some of these warmweather favorites from all over the country. After all, no matter what part of the country you live in, good food tastes better when it's shared with good friends!

SUMMER SUPPER: Clockwise from lower left—**Indiana-Style Corn Dogs**, Sally Denney, Warsaw, Indiana (Pg. 46); **Huckleberry Cheese Pie**, Pat Kuper, McCall, Idaho (Pg. 45); **Rave Review Coconut Cake**, Rena Nabours, Olaton, Kentucky (Pg. 46); **Marinated Shrimp in Avocado Halves**, Ruth Larson, Ames, Iowa (Pg. 46); **Chinese Coleslaw**, Marion Stanley, Gilroy, California (Pg. 46); **West Coast Chicken**, Denise Hopper, Logan, Ohio (Pg. 45); **Sesame Cucumber Salad**, Craig Towne, Derry, New Hampshire (Pg. 45); **Barbecued Lamb Kabobs**, Gloria Jarrett, Loveland, Ohio (Pg. 46).

Don't let summer slip by without trying some of these mouth-watering dishes. Start with a succulent slab of Barbecued Salmon—a mild marinade makes this tender meat delicious. Pass a dish of easy-to-prepare Green Beans with Mushrooms. For dessert, how about a "berry" delightful slice of Southern-Style Soft Custard or a scrumptious scoopful of Heavenly Cherry Angel Food Trifle? *Umm!*

EASY EATING: Clockwise from top—**Heavenly Cherry Angel Food Trifle**, Hyacinth Rizzo, Buffalo, New York (Pg. 47); **Green Beans with Mushrooms**, Judy Miller Hasselkus, Indianapolis, Indiana. (Pg. 47); **Southern-Style Soft Custard**, Margaret Wagner Allen, Abingdon, Virginia (Pg. 47); **Barbecued Salmon**, Lynda Bridwell, Issaquah, Washington (Pg. 47).

SAVORY CHEDDAR BREAD
Carol Funk, Richard, Saskatchewan

(PICTURED ON PAGE 36)

2 cups all-purpose flour
4 teaspoons baking powder
1 tablespoon sugar
1/2 teaspoon onion salt
1/2 teaspoon leaf oregano
1/4 teaspoon dry mustard
1-1/4 cups (5 ounces) shredded sharp cheddar cheese
1 egg, well beaten
1 cup milk
1 tablespoon butter *or* margarine, melted

Combine flour, baking powder, sugar, onion salt, oregano, mustard and cheese; set aside. Combine egg, milk and butter; add all at once to dry ingredients, stirring just until moistened. Spread batter in a greased 8-1/2-in. x 4-1/2-in. loaf pan. Bake at 350° for 45 minutes. **Yield:** 1 loaf.

CHEESY FISH FILLETS WITH SPINACH
Marla Brenneman, Goshen, Indiana

(PICTURED ON PAGE 36)

✓ This tasty dish uses less sugar, salt and fat. Recipe includes *Diabetic Exchanges*.

2 tablespoons butter
2 tablespoons all-purpose flour
1 teaspoon instant chicken bouillon
Dash nutmeg
Dash cayenne pepper
Dash white pepper
1 cup milk
2/3 cup shredded Swiss *or* cheddar cheese
1 package (10 ounces) frozen chopped spinach, thawed and well drained
1 tablespoon lemon juice
1 pound fish fillets, cut in serving pieces
1/2 teaspoon salt
2 tablespoons grated Parmesan cheese
Paprika

Heat butter over low heat until melted. Stir in flour, bouillon, nutmeg, cayenne pepper and white pepper; cook over low heat, stirring constantly, until mixture is smooth and bubbly. Stir in milk; heat to boiling and cook, stirring constantly, for 1 minute. Add cheese and cook, stirring constantly, just until cheese melts. Set aside. Place spinach in ungreased 12-in. x 7-1/2-in. baking dish or 8-in.-square baking dish. Sprinkle with the lemon juice. Arrange fish on spinach; sprinkle with salt. Spread sauce over fish and spinach. Bake, uncovered, at 350° until fish flakes easily with a fork, about 20 minutes. Sprinkle with the Parmesan cheese and paprika; return to oven for 5 minutes. **Yield:** 4 servings. **Diabetic Exchanges:** One serving equals 4 protein, 2 vegetable, 1 fat; also, 307 calories, 860 mg sodium, 108 mg cholesterol, 10 gm carbohydrate, 31 gm protein, 16 gm fat.

HOT CHEESE DIP
Ardyce Piehl, Wisconsin Dells, Wisconsin

(PICTURED ON PAGE 38)

8 ounces (2 cups) shredded mozzarella cheese
8 ounces (2 cups) shredded sharp cheddar cheese
2 cups mayonnaise
1 medium onion, minced
1 can (4 ounces) chopped green chilies, drained
1-1/2 ounces sliced pepperoni
1/2 cup sliced ripe olives

In a shallow baking dish or pie plate, combine all ingredients *except* pepperoni and olives. Top mixture with pepperoni and olives. Bake at 325° about 25 minutes or until bubbly. Serve with rye chips, crackers of choice or assorted fresh vegetables. **Yield:** 36 appetizer servings.

BLACK BOTTOM CUPCAKES
Julie Briceland, Windsor, Pennsylvania

(PICTURED ON PAGE 36)

FILLING:
1 package (8 ounces) cream cheese, softened
1/3 cup sugar
1 egg
1/8 teaspoon salt
1 cup semisweet chocolate chips

CUPCAKES:
1-1/2 cups all-purpose flour
1/4 cup unsweetened cocoa
1/2 teaspoon salt
1 cup sugar
1 teaspoon baking soda
1 egg
1 cup water
1 tablespoon white vinegar
1/3 cup vegetable oil
1 teaspoon vanilla extract
TOPPING:
Sugar
Chopped almonds, if desired

Combine cream cheese, sugar, egg and salt in a small mixing bowl; blend until smooth. Stir in chips. Set aside. Sift together flour, cocoa, salt, sugar and soda. Add egg, water, vinegar, oil and vanilla; beat until well combined. Fill paper-lined muffin tins half full with chocolate batter. Drop a heaping teaspoon of filling in center of batter of each cupcake. Sprinkle with sugar and chopped almonds, if desired. Bake at 350° for 25 minutes. Cool. Refrigerate any leftovers. **Yield:** 20-24 cupcakes.

FRESH FRUIT/CHEESE PIE
Jody Steinke, Nekoosa, Wisconsin

(PICTURED ON PAGE 36)

CRUST:
1 cup walnuts, chopped
1/2 cup butter *or* margarine, softened
3/4 cup all-purpose flour
1/2 cup packed light brown sugar
1/2 teaspoon vanilla extract
FILLING:
4 cups fresh fruit (peaches, nectarines, strawberries, raspberries, banana, kiwifruit, blueberries or pineapple)
1 cup plain yogurt
1 cup small-curd cottage cheese
1/2 cup (8-ounce can) unsweetened crushed pineapple, drained
1/4 cup unsweetened shredded coconut

In a medium bowl, blend nuts, butter, flour, brown sugar and vanilla with a fork. Press evenly into a buttered 9-in. pie plate; bake at 350° for 10-15 minutes or until lightly browned. Cool on wire rack. Cut fruit(s) of choice into bite-size pieces; layer on crust. In blender, mix yogurt and cottage cheese until smooth; add pineapple and blend to desired consistency. Pour mixture over fruit. Sprinkle with coconut. Chill several hours before serving. Decorate with any combination of fruit slices. **Yield:** 12 servings.

"SOUPER" IDEA: If you're making a cream-style soup, add a cubed potato to the mixture as it cooks. When you puree the mixture, you'll love the extra body it gives the soup.

LEMON STREUSEL CAKE
Karla Hecht, Brooklyn Park, Minnesota

(PICTURED ON PAGE 37)

1 package lemon cake mix with
  pudding
1/2 cup butter
3/4 cup milk
2 eggs

FILLING:
1/4 cup sugar
1 package (8 ounces) cream
  cheese, softened
1 tablespoon lemon juice
1 teaspoon grated lemon rind

TOPPING:
1/2 cup chopped walnuts

Cut butter into cake mix until crumbly; remove 1 cup mixture for topping. To remaining mixture, add milk and eggs; beat on high with mixer for 2 minutes. Pour into greased and floured 13-in. x 9-in. x 2-in. pan. Set aside. Cream together sugar, cream cheese, lemon juice and rind; blend well. Drop by teaspoonfuls onto the batter and spread across batter to edges of pan. Add nuts to reserved crumb mixture; sprinkle over batter. Bake at 350° for 30-35 minutes or until cake is light golden brown. Store in refrigerator. **Yield:** 12 servings.

MOZZARELLA PASTA SALAD
Violet Kycek, Austin, Minnesota

(PICTURED ON PAGE 37)

2 cups corkscrew (twist) pasta,
  cooked and drained
10 ounces fresh spinach,
  washed, drained and torn in
  bite-size pieces
2 cups chopped cooked ham
  or bacon
1 can (4 ounces) diced green
  chilies, drained
2 cups cubed
  mozzarella cheese
3/4 cup shredded
  cheddar cheese
1 can (5-3/4 ounces) black
  olives, sliced or whole

PARMESAN DRESSING:
1 cup vegetable oil
1/2 cup grated Parmesan cheese
1/4 cup white wine vinegar or
  white vinegar
1/2 teaspoon black pepper
1/4 teaspoon ground cloves
1 to 2 garlic cloves, minced

Toss together pasta with remaining salad ingredients; cover and chill. To make dressing, place ingredients in blender; blend until smooth. Pour dressing over salad; toss to coat. Serve immediately. Chill leftovers. (If dressing is made in advance, keep chilled until used.) **Yield:** 12 servings.

CHEESE/PEPPER SOUP
Gay Nicholas, Henderson, Texas

(PICTURED ON PAGE 37)

1/3 cup finely chopped carrots
1/3 cup finely chopped celery
1 cup thinly sliced green
  onions
2 cups water
1 medium onion, chopped
3/4 cup butter or margarine
1 cup plus 2 tablespoons
  all-purpose flour
4 cups milk
4 cups chicken broth
1 jar (16 ounces) process
  cheese spread
1/8 teaspoon cayenne pepper
  or to taste
Salt and pepper to taste
1 tablespoon prepared mustard

Combine carrots, celery and green onion in water; cook until tender. Set aside. Saute onion in butter until limp; stir in the flour and blend well. *Do not brown.* Combine milk and broth; bring to boil. Whisk in onion/flour mixture. Add cheese spread, cayenne, salt and pepper, if desired, and mustard. Slowly stir in vegetables and water they were cooked in. Bring just to a boil; serve immediately. **Yield:** 12 servings.

RASPBERRY CREAM CHEESE COFFEE CAKE
Brenda Knautz, West Chicago, Illinois

(PICTURED ON PAGE 37)

COFFEE CAKE:
2-1/2 cups all-purpose flour
3/4 cup sugar
3/4 cup butter
1/2 teaspoon baking powder
1/2 teaspoon baking soda
1/4 teaspoon salt
3/4 cup sour cream
1 egg
1 teaspoon almond extract

FILLING:
1 package (8 ounces) cream
  cheese, softened

1/4 cup sugar
1 egg
1/2 cup raspberry jam

TOPPING:
1/2 cup sliced almonds

In a large bowl, combine flour and sugar; cut in the butter using a pastry blender until mixture resembles coarse crumbs. Remove 1 cup crumbs for topping. To remaining crumb mixture, add baking powder, soda, salt, sour cream, egg and almond extract; blend well. Spread batter over bottom and 2 in. up side of greased and floured 9-in. springform pan. (Batter should be 1/4 in. thick on sides.) For filling, in a small bowl, combine cream cheese, sugar and egg; blend well. Pour over batter in the pan. Carefully spoon jam evenly over filling. In a small bowl, combine reserved crumb mixture with almonds; sprinkle over top. Bake at 350° for about 55-60 minutes, or until cream cheese filling is set and crust is a deep golden brown. Cool 15 minutes. Remove sides of pan. Serve warm or cool. Cover and refrigerate leftovers. **Yield:** 16 servings.

THREE CHEESE ENCHILADAS
Gretchen Mellberg, Hawarden, Iowa

(PICTURED ON PAGE 38)

1-1/2 cups (6 ounces) shredded
  Monterey Jack cheese,
  divided
1-1/2 cups (6 ounces) shredded
  cheddar cheese, *divided*
1 package (3 ounces) cream
  cheese, softened
1 cup picante sauce, *divided*
1 medium red or green bell
  pepper, diced
1/2 cup sliced green onions
1 teaspoon crushed cumin
8 flour tortillas (each 7-8 inches)
Shredded lettuce
Chopped tomato
Sliced black olives

Combine 1 cup Monterey Jack cheese, 1 cup cheddar cheese, cream cheese, 1/4 cup picante sauce, red or green pepper, onions and cumin; mix well. Spoon 1/4 cup cheese mixture down the center of each tortilla. Roll and place seam side down in a 13-in. x 9-in. x 2-in. baking dish. Spoon remaining picante sauce evenly over enchiladas; cover with remaining cheeses. Bake at 350° for 20 minutes or until hot. Top with lettuce, tomato and olives; serve with additional picante sauce, if desired. **Yield:** 4 servings.

CHOCOLATE MALT CHEESECAKE

Anita Moffett, Rewey, Wisconsin

(PICTURED ON PAGE 38)

CRUST:
- 1/3 cup unsalted butter, melted
- 1 cup graham cracker crumbs
- 1/4 cup sugar

FILLING:
- 3 packages (8 ounces *each*) cream cheese, softened
- 1 can (14 ounces) sweetened condensed milk
- 1 cup semisweet chocolate chips, melted
- 3/4 cup chocolate malt powder
- 4 eggs
- 1 teaspoon vanilla extract
- Confectioners' sugar and chocolate curls, optional

Combine crust ingredients. Pat firmly in bottom and 1/2 in. up the side of a 9-in. springform pan; chill. For filling, beat cream cheese until fluffy; add remaining ingredients and blend thoroughly. Pour into prepared crust. Bake at 300° for about 65 minutes or until filling shakes only slightly near center when moved. Cool; chill thoroughly. Garnish with confectioners' sugar and chocolate curls, if desired. **Yield:** 16-20 servings.

CHOPPED SALAD WITH PARMESAN DRESSING

Marilyn Norrie, King City, Ontario

(PICTURED ON PAGE 38)

- 1/2 head iceberg lettuce, chopped in bite-size pieces
- 1 small head romaine lettuce, chopped in bite-size pieces
- 1/4 pound Italian salami, finely diced
- 1/4 pound mozzarella cheese, finely chopped
- 1 cup canned garbanzo beans (chick-peas), drained, rinsed

DRESSING:
- 5 tablespoons vegetable oil
- 2 tablespoons white wine vinegar *or* white vinegar
- 1 teaspoon dry mustard
- 1 teaspoon salt, optional
- 1/2 teaspoon black pepper
- 1/2 cup grated Parmesan cheese

Combine salad ingredients in a glass bowl; chill while mixing dressing. Combine dressing ingredients in a jar with a tight-fitting lid; shake well. Pour dress-

ing over salad just before serving and toss lightly. Serve immediately. **Yield:** 6-8 servings.

SESAME CUCUMBER SALAD

Craig Towne, Derry, New Hampshire

(PICTURED ON PAGE 40)

✓ This tasty dish uses less sugar, salt and fat. Recipe includes *Diabetic Exchanges*.

- 1 tablespoon sugar
- 1 tablespoon cornstarch
- 1/2 teaspoon salt
- 1 cup rice vinegar
- 2 tablespoons water
- 2 large unpeeled cucumbers (with small seeds), very thinly sliced
- 1 cup diagonally sliced celery
- 1/4 pound cooked small shrimp
- 1/4 pound cooked small scallops
- 1 tablespoon toasted sesame seeds

Combine sugar, cornstarch and salt in small saucepan; stir in vinegar and water. Cook over medium heat, stirring constantly, until mixture comes to a boil and thickens. Cool completely. In large bowl, combine dressing with cucumbers, celery, shrimp, scallops and sesame seeds. Refrigerate 2 hours or overnight. Stir before serving. **Yield:** 6 servings. **Diabetic Exchanges:** One serving equals 1/2 protein, 2 vegetable; also, 73 calories, 268 mg sodium, 35 mg cholesterol, 10 gm carbohydrate, 8 gm protein, 1 gm fat.

WEST COAST CHICKEN

Denise Hopper, Logan, Ohio

(PICTURED ON PAGE 41)

✓ This tasty dish uses less sugar, salt and fat. Recipe includes *Diabetic Exchanges*.

Vegetable oil
- 5 pounds chicken thighs, skinned

SAUCE:
- 2 teaspoons salt
- 1/4 teaspoon black pepper
- 1 cup frozen orange juice concentrate, thawed
- 1/3 cup butter, melted
- 2 teaspoons ground ginger
- 4 teaspoons soy sauce

Grease two 11-in. x 7-in. baking pans well with vegetable oil. Place chicken in single layer in the pans. Combine

sauce ingredients and baste chicken well. Cover; refrigerate overnight. Bake, uncovered, at 350° for about 60 minutes, basting with sauce once during baking. **Yield:** 8 (4-ounce) servings. **Diabetic Exchanges:** One serving equals 3 protein, 1 fruit, 1/2 fat; also, 316 calories, 747 mg sodium, 96 mg cholesterol, 20 gm carbohydrate, 22 gm protein, 17 gm fat.

HUCKLEBERRY CHEESE PIE

Pat Kuper, McCall, Idaho

(PICTURED ON PAGE 40)

BUTTER CRUNCH CRUST:
- 1/4 cup packed brown sugar
- 1/2 cup finely chopped nuts
- 1 cup all-purpose flour
- 1/2 cup butter

CHEESE FILLING:
- 1 package (8 ounces) cream cheese, softened
- 3/4 cup confectioners' sugar
- 1 teaspoon vanilla extract
- 1 cup whipped cream *or* frozen nondairy topping, thawed

FRUIT TOPPING:
- 1/2 cup sugar
- 1-1/2 tablespoons cornstarch
- Dash salt
- 1/2 cup water
- 2 cups fresh huckleberries*, *divided*
- 1/2 tablespoon butter

Combine crust ingredients as for pie crust, cutting butter into mixture; mixture will be crumbly. Spread mixture on cookie sheet; bake at 400° for about 20 minutes, stirring occasionally. Remove from oven. While mixture is still hot, press into a 9-in. pie pan, using a smaller-diameter aluminum pie pan to help press crumbs into form. Cool completely. For cheese filling, blend cheese, sugar and vanilla until smooth; gently stir in whipped cream or topping. Pour or spoon filling into cooled crust; refrigerate. For topping, combine sugar, cornstarch and salt in saucepan. Add water, mixing to blend, and 1 cup berries. Cook, stirring, until thickened. Add butter and remaining berries. Cool topping; pour over filling. Top with additional whipped cream, if desired. *Blueberries may be substituted for huckleberries. **Yield:** 8-10 servings.

SIMPLER "SPUD" SALAD: Potato salad is easier to prepare if you peel and dice the potatoes *before* cooking. No more waiting for the potatoes to cool or burning your fingers on hot potatoes!

INDIANA-STYLE CORN DOGS

Sally Denney, Warsaw, Indiana

(PICTURED ON PAGE 40)

1/2 cup yellow cornmeal
1 cup all-purpose flour
1 tablespoon baking powder
1 teaspoon salt
1 tablespoon sugar
1 cup evaporated milk
1 egg, beaten
1/4 teaspoon paprika
1/2 teaspoon dry mustard
Dash pepper
10 to 16 hot dogs
Wooden skewers
Vegetable oil for deep-frying

In a bowl, mix first 10 ingredients. Pour mixture into a tall glass. Skewer hot dogs with wooden skewers; dip in mixture. Deep-fry at 375° until golden brown (about 2 minutes). Drain on paper towels. **Yield:** 10-16 corn dogs.

BARBECUED LAMB KABOBS

Gloria Jarrett, Loveland, Ohio

(PICTURED ON PAGE 40)

2-1/2 pounds boneless lamb, cut into 1-inch cubes
Skewers

MARINADE:
2 tablespoons parsley flakes
2 tablespoons onion flakes
1 teaspoon salt
1/2 teaspoon black pepper
1/2 cup lemon juice
1/2 cup white wine *or* broth of choice
2 tablespoons soy sauce

DIPPING SAUCE:
1 large onion, chopped
2 garlic cloves, minced
Salt and pepper to taste
1/2 cup vegetable oil
1/2 cup lemon juice
Chopped hot peppers to taste

Combine marinade ingredients in heavy plastic bag; add lamb and marinate overnight or at least 5 hours, turning bag occasionally. Put marinated lamb on skewers; broil or grill, turning at intervals until lamb is brown and cooked (about 15 minutes on medium-hot grill). Combine first five dipping sauce ingredients in blender; add peppers last. Serve hot with warm Syrian or French bread. **Yield:** 8-10 servings.

MARINATED SHRIMP IN AVOCADO HALVES

Ruth Larson, Ames, Iowa

(PICTURED ON PAGE 41)

12 ounces fresh *or* frozen shelled medium shrimp
2 tablespoons vinegar
1-1/2 teaspoons lemon juice
1/4 teaspoon salt
1/8 teaspoon dry mustard
Dash freshly ground pepper
1 small onion, thinly sliced, *divided*
1 garlic clove, halved
3 tablespoons cooking oil, *divided*
1 small pickled jalapeno pepper, rinsed, seeded and cut in strips
2 avocados, peeled, halved, seeded and rubbed with lemon juice
Lemon
1 medium tomato, chopped

Thaw shrimp, if frozen; set aside. In bowl, combine vinegar, lemon juice, salt, mustard and pepper; set aside. In medium skillet, cook shrimp, half the onion slices and garlic in 2 tablespoons hot oil over medium-high heat for 4-5 minutes or until shrimp are cooked. Stir occasionally. Remove onion and garlic with slotted spoon; discard. Add shrimp and remaining oil to vinegar mixture, along with jalapeno pepper and remaining onion. Cover; stir occasionally. Chill overnight. To serve, lift shrimp, onion slices and pepper strips from marinade; spoon into avocado halves. Top with tomato; drizzle some of marinade over all. **Yield:** 4 servings.

CHINESE COLESLAW

Marion Stanley, Gilroy, California

(PICTURED ON PAGE 41)

5 cups coarsely chopped Chinese cabbage*
1 cup shredded raw carrots
1/2 cup sliced green onions and tops (cut several times lengthwise, then in 1-inch pieces)
1 can (8 ounces) sliced water chestnuts, drained
2 tablespoons toasted sesame seeds

DRESSING:
1/4 cup vegetable oil
1 teaspoon dark sesame oil
2 tablespoons sugar
1 tablespoon fresh cilantro *or* parsley, minced

1/2 teaspoon salt
1/4 teaspoon black pepper
1/2 teaspoon ground ginger
2 tablespoons wine vinegar
1 tablespoon soy sauce

Toss together vegetables and sesame seeds. Combine dressing ingredients in small bowl; whisk until well blended. Pour dressing over cabbage mixture; toss and cover. Refrigerate 2 hours before serving; toss again before serving. *Chinese cabbage is also sold as Napa cabbage—it is *not* the same as Bok Choy. **Yield:** 12 servings.

RAVE REVIEW COCONUT CAKE

Rena Nabours, Olaton, Kentucky

(PICTURED ON PAGE 41)

CAKE:
1 package (18-1/4 ounces) yellow cake mix
1 package (3-1/2 ounces) instant vanilla pudding mix
1-1/3 cups water
4 eggs, room temperature
1/4 cup vegetable oil
2 cups coconut
1 cup chopped pecans

FROSTING:
4 tablespoons butter, *divided*
2 cups coconut
1 package (8 ounces) cream cheese
2 teaspoons milk
1/2 teaspoon vanilla extract
3-1/2 cups confectioners' sugar

In large bowl, blend cake mix with pudding mix, water, eggs and oil. Beat at medium speed for 3 minutes. Stir in coconut and nuts. Pour into three greased and floured 8-in. cake pans. Bake at 350° for 25-30 minutes or until cake springs back when touched in center. Cool in pans for 10 minutes. Remove to rack to complete cooling. For frosting, melt 2 tablespoons butter in skillet; add coconut and stir constantly over low heat until golden brown. Spread coconut on paper towel to cool. Cream remaining butter with cream cheese, milk and vanilla. Add sugar, beating well to blend; stir in 1-1/2 cups of the toasted coconut. Frost top and sides of cake. Sprinkle remaining coconut over cake. **Yield:** 16-20 servings.

SMOKE SIGNAL: When a film of smoke begins to rise from the hot fat, it's the right temperature for frying doughnuts.

BARBECUED SALMON
Lynda Bridwell, Issaquah, Washington

(PICTURED ON PAGE 42)

1/2 cup fresh lemon juice
1/2 cup vegetable oil
1 teaspoon Worcestershire sauce
2 pounds 1-inch-thick fresh salmon steaks *or* fillets*
1/2 cup wood chips (mesquite, hickory *or* alder)
1/2 teaspoon seasoned salt
1/2 teaspoon leaf thyme, crumbled
Cooking oil for grill

In a flat container, mix the lemon juice, vegetable oil and Worcestershire sauce. Place salmon in mixture; marinate 30 minutes. Meanwhile, soak wood chips in enough water to moisten for 15 to 30 minutes. Season salmon with salt and thyme; let stand a few minutes. Preheat charcoal or gas grill to medium-high. Just before cooking, coat grill's grate with cooking oil. Sprinkle wood chips over coals. Cook fish until it loses its translucent appearance and is uniformly colored throughout (about 6 minutes per side for 1-in. cut). *Fillets should be placed skin side down and cooked without turning for total cooking time. Charred skin will peel off easily. **Yield:** 6-8 servings.

GREEN BEANS WITH MUSHROOMS
Judy Miller Hasselkus, Indianapolis, Indiana

(PICTURED ON PAGE 42)

 This tasty dish uses less sugar, salt and fat. Recipe includes *Diabetic Exchanges.*

2 garlic cloves, minced
1/4 pound small fresh mushrooms, trimmed and sliced
1 tablespoon butter
1 medium red onion, cut in thin strips
1 pound fresh green beans, trimmed
Fresh ground pepper
1 teaspoon dill weed
2 tablespoons toasted almonds *or* pine nuts

Saute garlic and mushrooms in butter until tender. Stir in onion; set aside. Steam or cook beans in small amount of water until crisp-tender; drain. Combine beans with mushroom mixture; add pepper and dill weed. Garnish with nuts. Serve immediately. **Yield:** 6 servings. **Diabetic Exchanges:** One serving equals

1 vegetable, 1 fat; also, 75 calories, 35 mg sodium, 6 mg cholesterol, 10 gm carbohydrate, 3 gm protein, 4 gm fat.

HEAVENLY CHERRY ANGEL FOOD TRIFLE
Hyacinth Rizzo, Buffalo, New York

(PICTURED ON PAGE 42)

5 cups angel food cake cubes
1/4 cup cherry liqueur, optional
1 cup confectioners' sugar
1 package (3 ounces) cream cheese, softened
8 ounces frozen nondairy whipped topping, thawed, *divided*
1/2 cup toasted chopped pecans
1 can (21 ounces) cherry filling *or* topping

Place cake cubes in large bowl. Sprinkle with liqueur, if desired; let stand 30 minutes. In medium bowl, combine confectioners' sugar and cream cheese; beat until blended. Reserve 2 tablespoons whipped topping; fold remaining topping into cheese mixture, then stir with pecans into cake cubes and mix well. Spoon cake mixture into a pretty glass or crystal bowl. Spread cherry filling evenly over top. (Or, if desired, layer half the cake mixture and cherry filling; repeat layers.) Cover; refrigerate at least 3 hours. Garnish with reserved whipped topping. **Yield:** 8-10 servings.

BAKED POTATO SKINS
Terry Hill, Hairy Hill, Alberta

8 baking potatoes
1/2 cup butter, melted
1/2 teaspoon salt
1/2 teaspoon paprika
1/2 cup finely chopped green onions
1/2 cup finely chopped cooked bacon
1/2 cup cooked shrimp *or* chopped ham, optional
1/2 cup chopped green pepper
1 cup (4 ounces) shredded cheddar cheese
1 cup (8 ounces) sour cream

Scrub and pierce potatoes; bake at 400° for 1 hour or until tender. Cool slightly; cut in half lengthwise and scoop out pulp, leaving 1/4 in. of pulp attached to skin. (The pulp you remove can be refrigerated for use later.) Cut skins into strips or halves; brush skin sides with melted butter and place on a baking sheet. Sprinkle pulp sides with salt and

paprika; cover with green onions, bacon, shrimp or ham, if desired, and green pepper. Top with cheese. Bake at 450° until cheese is melted and skins are crisp, about 10-15 minutes. Garnish each with a dollop of sour cream. Serve immediately. **Yield:** 6-10 servings.

SOUTHERN-STYLE SOFT CUSTARD
Margaret Wagner Allen, Abingdon, Virginia

(PICTURED ON PAGE 42)

3 egg yolks
4 tablespoons sugar
1/8 teaspoon salt
1 pint milk
1/2 teaspoon vanilla extract
Sliced pound cake
Fresh berries of choice

Beat together egg yolks, sugar and salt. Scald milk (heat to 180°) and pour slowly over egg mixture. Place mixture in top of double boiler and cook over simmering (not boiling) water; stir constantly until mixture coats back of spoon, about 7-10 minutes. (You should be able to run your finger down the center of the spoon and have the pattern stay intact.) Mixture will *not* have the consistency of a firm baked custard. Cool over ice water, stirring occasionally. Add vanilla. If mixture separates, beat with egg beater until smooth. Serve chilled over pound cake and top with berries. **Yield:** 8 servings.

FESTIVE HAM GLAZE
Katie Dreibelbis, Santa Clara, California

1 precooked ham (4 pounds)
GLAZE:
2 tablespoons butter
1/4 cup apricot preserves
1/4 cup prepared mustard
2 tablespoons brown sugar

Bake ham at 350° for 1 hour. Melt butter; stir in preserves, mustard and brown sugar. Brush ham generously with glaze. Bake 30 minutes longer, basting occasionally with glaze. **Yield:** 12 servings.

RASPBERRY COOLER: For a refreshing, nutritious raspberry drink, crush ripe berries in a blender on low speed, strain puree through a medium sieve, pour into ice cube trays and freeze solid. To serve, combine cubes, sugar and cold milk to taste and blend at high speed.

EVELYN'S ORIGINAL ROQUEFORT DRESSING

Evelyn Skaggs, Nixa, Missouri

1 cup (8 ounces) sour cream
1/2 cup salad dressing *or* mayonnnaise
1 teaspoon tarragon vinegar
1 teaspoon Worcestershire sauce
1 teaspoon lemon juice
1/2 teaspoon garlic salt
1/2 teaspoon garlic powder
1/2 teaspoon onion salt
Few drops hot pepper sauce
1 package (4 ounces) crumbled Roquefort cheese

Mix together ingredients in the order given. Store, covered, in the refrigerator. **Yield:** about 1 pint.

SPINACH SALAD WITH CREAMY PARMESAN DRESSING

Ruth Seitz, Conesville, Iowa

4 cups fresh spinach leaves (washed, drained and torn in bite-size pieces)

DRESSING:
1/2 cup mayonnaise
1/2 cup grated Parmesan cheese
2 tablespoons evaporated milk
1-1/2 teaspoons dill weed
1-1/2 teaspoons onion flakes
1-1/2 teaspoons lemon pepper

Combine dressing ingredients (thinning with additional milk, if necessary) and serve over spinach. Cover and refrigerate any leftovers.

CAULIFLOWER AND HAM CHOWDER

Patty Woytassek, Havana, North Dakota

1 cup thinly sliced celery
2 cups sliced fresh *or* frozen cauliflower
1 can (13 ounces) chicken broth
1 cup half-and-half *or* evaporated milk
1 can (10-3/4 ounces) cream of potato soup, undiluted
1/4 cup water

2 tablespoons cornstarch
1/8 teaspoon white pepper
2 cups diced cooked ham
1/2 cup shredded cheddar cheese
Chopped fresh parsley

In large, covered saucepan, cook celery and cauliflower in chicken broth until almost tender, about 10 minutes. *Do not drain.* Set aside. In mixing bowl, gradually stir half-and-half or milk into potato soup. Blend water, cornstarch and pepper. Stir into soup mixture; pour over cauliflower and celery. Stir in ham. Simmer over low heat for 10 minutes. Just before serving, stir in cheese. Garnish with parsley. **Yield:** 6-8 servings.

MIDWEST CHOWDER

Denae Blair, Shawnee Mission, Kansas

2 cups diced potatoes
1/2 cup sliced carrots
1/2 cup sliced celery
1/4 cup diced onion
2 cups boiling water
1 teaspoon salt, optional
1/4 cup butter
1/4 cup all-purpose flour
Pepper to taste
2 cups milk
2-1/2 cups (10 ounces) shredded sharp cheddar cheese
2 cups cream-style corn

Cook potatoes, carrots, celery and onion in boiling water (salted, if desired) for 10 minutes. While vegetables cook, melt butter, stir in flour and pepper and cook for 1 minute. Gradually stir in the milk; cook, stirring constantly, until thickened. Add cheese, stirring until melted. Stir in corn; heat through but *do not boil.* Add cooked vegetables with liquid. **Yield:** 8 servings.

WILD RICE SALAD

Elaine Sabacky, Litchfield, Minnesota

✓ This tasty dish uses less sugar, salt and fat. Recipe includes *Diabetic Exchanges.*

2/3 cup uncooked wild rice
2 cups water
2 tart unpeeled apples, chopped (mix red and green apples)
2 stalks celery, sliced
2 tablespoons brown sugar
1 tablespoon lemon juice

DRESSING:
1/2 cup low-fat yogurt
1/2 cup light mayonnaise

Wash rice thoroughly by running cold water over it in a strainer. Place rice in a saucepan with 2 cups water; bring to boil. Reduce heat to simmer; cook, covered, for 35 minutes or until kernels are tender. Uncover; fluff with fork. Drain any excess liquid. Toss cooked rice with apples, celery, sugar and lemon juice. Combine dressing ingredients; toss with rice mixture. Refrigerate at least 2 hours before serving. **Yield:** 6-8 servings. **Diabetic Exchanges:** One serving equals 1 bread, 1 fruit, 1 fat; also, 198 calories, 140 mg sodium, 7 mg cholesterol, 32 gm carbohydrate, 3 gm protein, 7 gm fat.

TWICE BAKED SWEET POTATOES

Aney Chatterton, Soda Springs, Idaho

4 medium sweet potatoes
2 tablespoons butter
1/2 teaspoon salt
1/3 cup orange juice
1 small ripe banana, mashed
1/4 cup chopped pecans
Coconut, optional

Scrub and pierce the potatoes; bake at 375° for 45-60 minutes or until tender. Cut a slice off top of each potato and scoop out the pulp, leaving skins intact. Mash potatoes with butter, salt, orange juice and banana. Spoon mixture into shells and top with the chopped pecans. Sprinkle lightly with coconut, if desired. Return to oven and bake 12-15 minutes or until heated through. **Yield:** 4 servings.

PARMESAN POTATO STICKS

Lee Herrman, Bismarck, North Dakota

2 pounds russet potatoes
1/2 cup butter, melted
1/2 cup fine dry bread crumbs
1/2 cup grated Parmesan cheese
1/2 teaspoon salt
1/8 teaspoon garlic powder
1/8 teaspoon black pepper

Scrub and peel potatoes; cut lengthwise into quarters. Cut each quarter into 3 strips. Roll in melted butter, then roll in combined remaining ingredients. Place potato sticks in a single layer on a cookie sheet. Drizzle melted butter over potatoes. Bake at 400° for 30-35 minutes or until potatoes are tender. **Yield:** 6 servings.

SURPRISE POTATOES
Ruth Montgomery, Tullahoma, Tennessee

6 medium white potatoes,
peeled
1 cup whipping cream
Salt and pepper to taste

Shred the potatoes and rinse in cold water. Drain thoroughly. Place in a greased 9-in. x 9-in. baking pan; pour cream over all and sprinkle with salt and pepper. Cover with foil and bake at 325° for 1-1/2 hours. Uncover and bake 30 minutes longer or until lightly browned on top. **Yield:** 6 servings.

POTATO NACHOS
Deb Helmer, Winfield, Kansas

1 large baking potato
1/8 teaspoon salt
1 jar (8 ounces) taco sauce
1/2 cup sliced green onions
1/2 cup chopped green chilies
1/2 cup shredded cheddar *or*
Monterey Jack cheese
1/2 cup sliced ripe olives

Scrub the potato and cut it into 1/4-in. slices. Arrange the slices in a single layer on a greased broiler pan; sprinkle lightly with salt. Broil 4 in. from heat until golden brown. Turn and broil other side until brown and tender when tested with a fork. Top with taco sauce, green onions, chilies, cheese and olives. Broil until the cheese melts. **Yield:** 2 snack servings. **Microwave Method:** Arrange the slices in a single layer on a microwave-safe pie plate or baking dish; sprinkle lightly with salt. Drizzle with taco sauce. Cover pie plate with plastic wrap. Cook on high for 4-5 minutes or until tender, rotating dish once. Add more taco sauce, top with green onions, chilies, cheese and olives. Cover again and cook 30-60 seconds or until the cheese melts.

CASHEW PORK STIR-FRY
Betty Ruenholl, Syracuse, Nebraska

1 pound pork tenderloin
2 tablespoons vegetable oil,
divided
2 large carrots, peeled and
cut diagonally
2 celery stalks, sliced
diagonally
1/2 cup cashews
Cooked rice, optional

SAUCE:
1 tablespoon grated orange
rind
3/4 cup orange juice
1 tablespoon cornstarch
3 tablespoons soy sauce
1/3 cup corn syrup
1/4 teaspoon ground ginger

Cut tenderloin into thin strips and set aside. Combine sauce ingredients, stirring well. Heat 1 tablespoon oil in large skillet over medium. Add carrots and celery; stir-fry for about 3 minutes. Remove vegetables; set aside. Heat remaining oil in skillet. Add pork; stir-fry for about 3 minutes. Return vegetables to pan; add sauce and cashews. Cook, stirring constantly, over medium-high heat, until thickened. Serve over rice, if desired. **Yield:** 4 servings.

SQUASH-APPLE BAKE
Judith Hawes, Chelmsford, Massachusetts

1 medium (about 1-1/4 pounds)
buttercup *or* butternut squash,
peeled, cut into 3/4-inch slices
2 apples, peeled, cored and cut
in wedges
1/2 cup packed brown sugar
1 tablespoon all-purpose flour
1/4 cup butter, melted
1/2 teaspoon salt
1/2 teaspoon mace

Arrange squash in a 12-in. x 8-in. baking pan. Top with apple wedges. Combine remaining ingredients; spoon over apples. Bake at 350° for 50-60 minutes or until tender. **Yield:** 4-6 servings.

BAKED STUFFED TOMATOES
Edna Jackson, Kokomo, Indiana

6 medium tomatoes
STUFFING:
1 cup garlic/cheese croutons,
crushed
2 tablespoons grated Parmesan
cheese
2 tablespoons shredded
American *or* cheddar cheese
4 tablespoons butter, melted
1/2 teaspoon salt *or* to taste
1/4 teaspoon freshly ground
pepper
Chopped fresh parsley

Hollow out a funnel-shaped hole in each tomato to make room for stuffing. Mix stuffing ingredients except parsley, which is sprinkled on top. Spoon into to-

matoes. Place tomatoes in baking dish; cover with aluminum foil to prevent over-browning of stuffing. Bake at 350° for 30 minutes, or cook on grill until done. **Yield:** 6 servings.

BARBECUED RASPBERRY CHICKEN
Lorraine Cloutier, Legal, Alberta

1/4 cup raspberry vinegar
2 tablespoons vegetable oil
1 to 2 teaspoons dried
tarragon *or* 1 tablespoon
fresh tarragon
4 chicken breast halves,
skinned and boned
Salt to taste
Fresh ground pepper to taste
Fresh raspberries and fresh
tarragon for garnish
SAUCE:
1 cup undiluted frozen
raspberry juice
1 tablespoon cornstarch

In medium-size bowl or sealable plastic bag, combine vinegar, oil and tarragon. Whisk or shake until blended. Marinate chicken in mixture for 30 minutes, then season with salt and pepper. Grease grill lightly with oil; place chicken on grill about 4 in. from hot coals. Turn and baste frequently with marinade until chicken feels springy to touch, about 15-18 minutes. While chicken cooks, whisk together sauce ingredients in a saucepan. Cook over medium-low heat, stirring constantly, until thickened and smooth, for about 5-7 minutes. When chicken is done, place sauce in a pool on warm platter; place chicken on top of sauce. Garnish with fresh berries and a sprig of fresh tarragon. **Yield:** 4 servings.

RASPBERRY VINEGAR
Francy Nightingale, Issaquah, Washington

3 cups fresh raspberries
4 cups white wine vinegar
1/2 cup sugar

Rinse the berries and air-dry on paper towels. Place berries in a 6-cup jar; set aside. In a medium saucepan, combine vinegar and sugar; bring *almost* to a boil over low heat, stirring constantly, until sugar melts. *Do not boil.* Pour hot vinegar mixture over berries; cover jar *tightly* and let stand at room temperature 48 hours. Strain through several layers of cheesecloth into a clean bottle or jar. Seal tightly with cork or lid. Store in a cool, dark place. **Yield:** 4 cups.

COUNTRY INNS

Liechty's Homestead Inn

7830 Pine Forest Road
Pensacola, Florida 32526

Phone: 1-904/944-4816

Directions: From I-10 Exit 2, take Pine Forest Road south 1/2 mile to the inn.

Innkeepers: Neil and Jeanne Liechty

Schedule: Open year-round.

Accommodations and Rates: Four rooms with private baths, $49 to $69 double occupancy; includes full breakfast and evening dessert. Second-floor guest rooms make handicapped access difficult.

Breakfast is the Homestead Inn's specialty, luring guests out of bed with the smell of thick Amish waffles with raspberry and blueberry topping and homemade vanilla ice cream! Or might it be the aroma of Neil Liechty's homemade cinnamon rolls that gets stomachs growling?

Neil and Jeanne also open guests' eyes with their cheesy spinach quiche, broccoli and ham quiche (both made with fresh-laid eggs), sausage, fresh fruit and tangerine juice.

The Liechtys' evening desserts are also hard to turn down, especially fresh strawberry pie and Homestead Lazy Woman Chocolate Cake.

Try these recipes, garnered from the Liechtys' own cookbook, *Secrets of the Mennonite Kitchen.* (If you like Mennonite cooking and would like to order a copy of their cookbook, send $10.55 to Homestead Inn, 7830 Pine Forest Rd., Pensacola FL 32526.)

AMISH WAFFLES

BATTER:
- 1 cup all-purpose flour
- 1 cup sifted cake flour
- 1-1/2 cups milk
- 2-1/2 teaspoons baking powder
- 2 eggs, well beaten
- 5 tablespoons butter *or* margarine
- 1 teaspoon vanilla extract

TOPPING:
- 1-2/3 cups water
- 2/3 cup sugar
- 2 tablespoons white corn syrup
- 2 drops red food coloring
- 2 tablespoons cornstarch
- 1 package (3 ounces) raspberry-flavored gelatin
- 8 ounces frozen blueberries, defrosted
- 8 ounces frozen raspberries, defrosted
- Vanilla ice cream, optional

Mix batter ingredients together in order just until smooth. Bake in waffle iron according to manufacturer's directions. For topping, combine water, sugar, corn syrup, food coloring and cornstarch in saucepan; cook over medium heat until thickened. Remove from heat; add gelatin, stirring until dissolved. Cool; add berries. Serve warm over waffles with a scoop of vanilla ice cream, if desired. **Yield:** 4 waffles.

ASPARAGUS CASSEROLE

- 3 cups sliced asparagus (trimmed and cut into 1-inch pieces)
- 3 tablespoons butter *or* margarine
- 3 tablespoons all-purpose flour
- 1 cup milk *or* liquid from cooking asparagus
- 1/2 teaspoon salt
- 1/2 cup grated American cheese
- 2 cups fresh bread crumbs
- Melted butter *or* margarine

Cook asparagus with salt and a small amount of water until tender. Drain well. Place in a greased 1-1/2-qt. casserole. In a saucepan, melt butter, add flour, then gradually mix in milk or liquid, stirring constantly. Cook until thick. Add salt and cheese; cook until cheese is melted. If sauce is too thick, add a little more liquid. Pour sauce over asparagus. Cover with bread crumbs and drizzle with butter. Bake at 350° for 30 minutes. **Yield:** 4-6 servings.

MEAT LOAF

- 2 pounds ground beef
- 1/2 pound bulk sausage
- 3 eggs, beaten
- 2 cups oatmeal *or* crushed soda crackers
- 2 cups crushed tomatoes
- 1 medium onion, chopped
- 1/2 cup chopped green pepper
- 1 teaspoon garlic salt
- 1 teaspoon pepper
- Salt to taste
- 1 can (10-3/4 ounces) cream of mushroom soup, undiluted

Mix together all ingredients except the soup. Put in a 9-in. x 5-in. x 3-in. pan. Pour soup over top. Bake at 350° for 1 hour. **Yield:** 8-10 servings.

HOMESTEAD LAZY WOMAN CHOCOLATE CAKE

- 2 cups sugar
- 3 cups all-purpose flour
- 1 teaspoon salt
- 5 tablespoons cocoa
- 2 heaping teaspoons baking soda
- 3/4 cup vegetable oil
- 1 tablespoon vanilla extract
- 2 tablespoons vinegar
- 2 cups cold water

Sift dry ingredients into a 13-in. x 9-in. x 2-in. ungreased baking pan. Make three holes in dry ingredients, put oil in one, vanilla in one and vinegar in one, then pour water over it all. Stir with fork until well mixed. Bake at 350° for 30 minutes or until done. **Yield:** 12 servings.

PECAN CHEESE BALL

- 1 package (8 ounces) cream cheese, softened
- 1-1/4 cups (5 ounces) shredded cheddar cheese
- 2 teaspoons chopped pimiento
- 2 teaspoons chopped green pepper
- 2 teaspoons minced onion
- 1 teaspoon lemon juice
- Dash salt and pepper
- Dash garlic salt
- 1/2 cup finely chopped pecans

In a mixer bowl, combine all ingredients except pecans. Mix thoroughly. Shape into a ball and roll in nuts. Wrap in foil or plastic wrap and refrigerate at least 4 hours. **Yield:** 4-6 appetizer servings.

Packing a basket for an impromptu picnic in the country? Need a "dish to pass" at a church potluck? Friends and family will rave over this royal-red glazed strawberry pie; and they'll request second helpings of fresh-from-the-garden vegetable salad. Bring along hard rolls with your favorite sandwich makings and you've got a meal!

BLANKET BRUNCH: Remembrance Strawberry Pie (bottom), Anna Bargfrede, Sweet Springs, Missouri (Pg. 60); Marinated Vegetable Salad (top), Sharon Mensing, Greenfield, Iowa (Pg. 60).

Best Cook

Pat Knapp
Mansfield, Ohio

I f variety is the spice of life, this "Best Cook" need never look beyond her own country kitchen!

Pat Knapp's culinary skills are well-known in Mansfield, Ohio, where she's been dazzling folks for years, both in her own home and at the weddings and parties she caters.

Her repertoire includes treasured family favorites, creative new recipes and even some authentic dishes from France, Italy, Brazil and Mexico. Her baking is tops, too—she's won over 100 first- and second-place ribbons at county fairs!

Pat was nominated for the "Best Cook" honor by JoAnn Fisher, who has obviously enjoyed many a feast at her cousin's home.

"A meal at Pat's is one you'll never forget," JoAnn told us. "It might include Cajun blackened steak, sweet potato pone, spinach salad with buttermilk dressing, and fresh rolls hot from the oven (with homemade jam or jelly, of course). Then she'll serve you lemon slice pie or homemade cherry cobbler ice cream.

"As you can tell, Pat loves to cook!"
Pat won't argue with that!

"I come from a long line of cooks," she told us. "My mother and her four sisters were all wonderful cooks, and I learned early from Mom and my aunts that hospitality starts with tasty food."

PAT'S BLACKENED FLANK STEAK

1 or 2 flank steaks
(1 to 1-1/4 pounds *each*)
1-1/2 teaspoons salt
1-1/2 tablespoons white pepper
1-1/2 tablespoons whole black
  peppercorns
1-1/2 tablespoons fennel seeds
2-1/2 teaspoons cayenne pepper
2-1/2 teaspoons dry mustard
2 tablespoons garlic powder
Olive oil

Grind all ingredients except steak and oil in a food processor or blender. Coat both sides of flank steak with the mixture. (If cooking only one steak, use half the mixture and save the rest for future use.) Coat a seasoned cast-iron skillet with olive oil; heat until smoking. (You may want to do this outside on a propane grill, as the smoke could set off a smoke alarm.) Sear steak on both sides; meat will be black. For rare meat, cook 5 more minutes on each side. For medium doneness, cook 7 minutes on each side. Slice diagonally in thin strips. **Yield:** 1 steak serves 3-4 people.

MOO GOO GAI PAN

3 whole medium chicken
  breasts, skinned and boned
2 tablespoons cornstarch,
  divided
1/2 teaspoon salt
1/3 cup chicken broth
1 tablespoon soy sauce
1 tablespoon dry sherry,
  optional
3 tablespoons peanut oil,
  divided
1 garlic clove, minced, optional
1/4 teaspoon ground ginger
3 green onions, bias-sliced into
  1-inch pieces
1/2 pound fresh mushrooms,
  sliced
1 package (16 ounces) frozen
  pea pods, partially thawed
Hot cooked rice

Coat chicken breasts with mixture of 1 tablespoon cornstarch and salt. In a small mixing bowl, combine broth, remaining cornstarch, soy sauce and sherry; set aside. In a wok, heat 1 tablespoon oil; add garlic and ginger. Stir-fry for 15 seconds. Add onions and mushrooms; stir-fry about 2 minutes or until onions are crisp-tender. Remove onion mixture from wok. Add remaining oil to hot wok. Add chicken; stir-fry 3 to 5 minutes or until done. Push from center of wok. Stir broth mixture; pour into center of wok. Cook and stir until thickened and bubbly. Return onion mixture to wok; add pea pods. Stir all ingredients together to coat with sauce. Cook and stir 1 minute more. Serve immediately on rice. **Yield:** 6 servings.

SWEET POTATO PONE

4 large fresh sweet potatoes
1/2 cup butter
2 eggs, beaten
1 cup whipping cream
1/2 cup all-purpose flour
2 tablespoons brown sugar
1 tablespoon baking powder
1 teaspoon vanilla extract
1 teaspoon grated orange rind
1 teaspoon grated lemon rind
1/2 teaspoon ground cinnamon
1/2 teaspoon ground allspice
1/2 teaspoon ground cloves

TOPPING:
1/4 cup butter, melted
1/2 cup packed brown sugar
1/2 cup chopped pecans

Cook sweet potatoes in boiling salted water until tender. Drain; peel and mash. Melt butter and brown slightly over low heat. Stir browned butter into the mashed potatoes. Put into a buttered 13-in. x 9-in. x 2-in. baking dish. Combine remaining ingredients and stir into potatoes. For topping, combine ingredients and sprinkle on top of potatoes. Bake at 350° for 30 minutes. **Yield:** 14-16 servings.

AUNT CATFISH'S BOATSINKER PIE

2/3 cup butter
1/3 cup light corn syrup
2-1/2 ounces unsweetened
  chocolate
1 cup sugar
3 eggs
1 teaspoon vanilla extract
Pinch salt
1 unbaked pie shell (9 inches)
Ice cream *or* whipped cream
Grated semisweet chocolate,
  optional

Combine butter, corn syrup and chocolate; melt together. Cool. In a mixer bowl, beat together sugar, eggs, vanilla and salt; mix well. Blend in chocolate mixture. Pour into pie shell. Bake at 325° for 15 minutes. Reduce heat to 275° and bake 40-45 minutes longer until set. Cool. Serve with ice cream or whipped cream, and, if desired, sprinkle top with grated chocolate. **Yield:** 8 servings.

ake advantage of sunny days outdoors and fill your grill—and your family's stomachs—with satisfying summer foods, such as vegetable beef kabobs. Skewers hold sizzling sirloin chunks alternated with bite-size pieces of zucchini, red peppers and onions for a flavor-filled taste that's unforgettable.

GREAT ON A GRILL: Vegetable Beef Kabobs, Mynie Lou Griffith, Hutchinson, Kansas (Pg. 60).

Raspberries! Those warm-weather treats will burst with fruity flavor in our brimming-with-red recipes.

This regal soft summer fruit is delightful in desserts, of course. So you will find a seasonful of them here. But raspberries are equally delicious *during* a meal. Try the imaginative main courses and savory salads…then dig into desserts that will make summer even sweeter!

RED RIGHT: Clockwise from bottom left—**Raspberry Ice**, Wilma Scott, Tulsa, Oklahoma (Pg. 61); **Raspberry Crumble Coffee Cake**, Shirley Boyken, Mesa, Arizona (Pg. 60); **Chocolate Dessert with Raspberry Sauce**, Marilyn Dick, Centralia, Missouri (Pg. 61); **Raspberry Custard Meringue**, Bette Berry, Alamogordo, New Mexico (Pg. 60); **Raspberry Spinach Salad**, Rita Underdahl, Fremont, California (Pg. 62); **Raspberry Cheesecake**, Lori Manthorpe, Ile Bizard, Quebec (Pg. 61); **Raspberry Chicken**, Verna Schrock, Salem, Oregon (Pg. 62); **Red, White and Blue Berry Pie**, Cindy Zarnstorff, Anchorage, Alaska (Pg. 61).

Ripe red raspberries can turn ordinary foods into delectable dishes.

Toss a few raspberries in a bowl of leaf lettuce with raspberry dressing for a tangy change of pace, or bake the little gems into Royal Raspberry Cake for a sweet-tart treat. Raspberry vinegar adds zest to fried pork chops, and Freezer Raspberry Sauce makes a great topping for ice cream or waffles and is wonderful combined with plain yogurt. Enjoy!

BERRY BEST! Clockwise from top—**Raspberry Vinegar Pork Chops**, Maurita Merrill, Lac la Hache, British Columbia (Pg. 62); **Royal Raspberry Cake**, Genevieve Priewe, Whitewater, Wisconsin (Pg. 63); **Lettuce with Raspberry Dressing**, Harriet Stichter, Milford, Indiana (Pg. 62); **Freezer Raspberry Sauce**, Katie Koziolek, Hartland, Minnesota (Pg. 62).

Meals in Minutes

SOME DAYS, chores on her family's cattle ranch near Huson, Montana can keep Helen Meadows out of the kitchen right up until almost mealtime.

What does this busy mom and 4-H foods leader do when half an hour or less is left to fix supper for her hungry clan? "Because we raise cattle, I serve beef often—even when I'm in a hurry," she writes.

Bringing beef to the table needn't take time, she adds. "I like this menu because it's quick and nutritious."

Helen's main course is a hearty beef stir-fry salad that's easily prepared. Corn on the cob takes on a lively new flavor with lime juice added to the butter. The corn is cut in 1-inch chunks for easy eating from a fork.

French bread is fast when it's split lengthwise and topped with a cheese-and-seasoned butter that's broiled to a golden brown.

Helen likes to round out her meal with a pretty platter of fresh fruit. If time permits, she mashes 2 cups of fresh raspberries with 1/2 cup sugar and serves the sauce over bananas and grapes. "If you're really rushed, simply sprinkle the fresh berries on top of the other fruit," she suggests.

Either way, your family's sure to enjoy this quick, beefy meal!

BEEF STIR-FRY SALAD

    4 romaine lettuce leaves,
      washed and crisped
    1 beef flank steak (1 to 1-1/4
      pounds) or tender beef
      steak of choice
    1 tablespoon vegetable oil
    1 teaspoon leaf basil,
      crumbled
  1/2 teaspoon minced garlic
  1/2 teaspoon black pepper
    3 medium tomatoes, cut in
      small wedges
  1/4 cup chopped green pepper
    6 green onions, sliced thin
  1/2 cup sour cream or plain
      yogurt

  1/4 cup chopped parsley
    1 avocado, peeled and sliced

Arrange a lettuce leaf on each dinner plate. Cut steak in half lengthwise, then cut across the grain into 1/8-in. slices. In a heavy skillet, heat oil over medium-high. Add beef, basil, garlic and pepper. Stir-fry just until meat loses pink color, about 2 minutes. Remove from heat. Add tomatoes, green pepper and onions; toss lightly. Transfer beef and vegetables to dinner plates; top with sour cream and parsley. Garnish with avocado slices. **Yield:** 4 servings.

CORN WHEELS WITH LIME BUTTER

    4 medium ears of corn
    2 tablespoons butter or
      margarine
    2 tablespoons fresh lime juice
  1/2 teaspoon pepper, optional

Using a cleaver or large knife, cut corn into 1-in. lengths. In a large pot, bring water to boil over high heat. Add corn wheels; cover and boil 2 minutes. Melt butter; mix with the lime juice. Transfer corn to serving platter and drizzle with lime-butter. Sprinkle with pepper, if desired. **Yield:** 4 servings.

CHEESE/GARLIC BREAD

    4 tablespoons butter or
      margarine
    1 teaspoon minced garlic or
      1/4 teaspoon garlic powder
    1 to 2 teaspoons leaf oregano,
      crumbled
    1 loaf French bread
  1/2 cup shredded sharp cheddar
      cheese
    1 teaspoon paprika

Melt butter in saucepan; add garlic and oregano. Cut bread in half lengthwise; drizzle butter evenly over cut surfaces. Sprinkle with cheese and paprika. Broil 1-2 minutes until cheese is melted and bread is golden brown. Cut into slices and serve.

FIESTA FRUIT PLATTER

Green grape clusters, washed and
    drained
Bananas, cut in 1/2-inch chunks
Fresh raspberries, rinsed gently
    and drained

Arrange clusters of grapes on platter with banana chunks. Garnish with a sprinkling of fresh raspberries.

Autumn arrives, bearing baskets of apples, pears, fresh tomatoes, ripe avocados and other produce. Your table can be a mouth-watering testament to this bountiful harvest season if you spread it with a meal as memorable as this one.

Start out with crisp, fresh garden Gazpacho, then sample the succulent Marinated Iowa Beef. Satisfy your sweet tooth with light-as-a-feather Black Raspberry Dumplings or sweet, fruit-laden Carrot Cake with Buttermilk Glaze. Country cooking never tasted so good!

FALL FEAST: Clockwise from top— **Black Raspberry Dumplings**, Jeanette Redman, Newark, Ohio (Pg. 63); **Marinated Iowa Beef**, Shary Geidner, Clear Lake, Iowa (Pg. 63); **Gazpacho**, Agnes Gates, Lubbock, Texas (Pg. 63); **Carrot Cake with Buttermilk Glaze**, Gayle Lewis, Yucaipa, California (Pg. 63).

COUNTRY INNS

Dairy Hollow House

515 Spring Street
Eureka Springs, Arkansas 72632

Phone: 1-501/253-7444

Directions: From Rt. 23N, take Rt. 62B/Spring Street through the commercial and Victorian residential area. Curve left past residential area, curve left past the Crescent Hotel, then through wooded area to the inn.

Innkeepers: Crescent Dragonwagon and Ned Shank

Schedule: Open year-round. Open to the public for dinner Monday through Saturday (Sunday brunch on holidays only), April 1 through December 31.

Accommodations and Rates: Three guest bedrooms and three suites, $95 to $145; includes breakfast in a basket delivered daily to room. Handicapped access possible.

The innkeepers at the Dairy Hollow House pride themselves on giving guests a real dining experience, from the iced Herbal Coolers stocked in the guest quarters to the six-course dinners featuring country cuisine.

Imagine flavorful garlic- and herb-roasted shiitake mushrooms, followed by vegetable soup and sizzling-from-the-skillet buttermilk corn bread.

For the main course, why not try rainbow trout Dijon with garlic and herbs? Or perhaps you'd prefer roasted Cornish game hens with lemon and herbs, or a giant three-cheese broccoli turnover with dill?

Leave room for dessert! How about a helping of homemade chocolate bread pudding with raspberry sauce, strawberries and real whipped cream?

Until you can experience your own dining pleasure at the Dairy Hollow House, give these recipes a try:

DAIRY HOLLOW HOUSE HERBAL COOLER

    8 bags Red Zinger tea
    1 quart boiling water
    1 can (12 ounces) frozen apple
        juice concentrate
    3 juice cans water
    1 orange and 1/2 lemon, sliced
Mint sprigs for garnish

Steep tea in boiling water in glass container; cool until lukewarm. Remove bags. Add apple juice concentrate, water, orange and lemon slices. Chill thoroughly. Serve coolers over ice with a sprig of mint. **Yield:** 8-10 servings.

SKILLET-SIZZLED BUTTERMILK CORN BREAD

    1 egg
Sugar to taste (2 to 4 tablespoons)
    1/4 cup corn oil *or* peanut oil
1-1/4 cup cultured buttermilk
    1 cup stone-ground yellow
        cornmeal
    1 cup unbleached white flour
    1/4 teaspoon salt
    1/4 teaspoon baking soda
    1 tablespoon baking powder
    1/4 cup butter *or* margarine

Preheat oven to 375°. Combine in one bowl with a whisk the first four ingredients. Combine in a second bowl the dry ingredients (sift in soda and baking powder if they seem lumpy). Grease an 8-in. iron skillet. Melt the butter in it. Quickly stir together wet and dry ingredients, using only as many strokes as necessary to combine. Scrape batter into hot skillet—it should sizzle when you pour it in—and immediately pop into the oven. Bake for about 25 minutes or until golden brown. Cut in wedges and serve warm. **Yield:** 8 servings.

FEATHERBED EGGS

Leftover corn bread (3 to 6 pieces),
    coarsely crumbled
    6 eggs
1-3/4 cups milk *or* cream
Salt, pepper, cayenne pepper and
    Worcestershire sauce to taste
1-1/2 cups (6 ounces) shredded
    sharp cheese, such as cheddar

Toast the corn bread lightly in a 350° oven. Place corn bread into an 8-in. square baking dish, or divide it among 4 or 5 1-cup ramekins. Beat together eggs and milk or cream; add seasonings. Sprinkle cheese over crumbs (diced ham or bacon, sauteed mushrooms or onions can also be added at this time). Pour egg mixture over all. Bake at 350° for about 20 minutes in ramekins or 30 minutes in a baking dish, or until slightly puffed and golden brown. **Yield:** 4 servings.

CRESCENT'S MOTHER'S FABULOUS MEATBALLS

    3 pounds lean ground beef
    1 cup applesauce
1-1/2 cups soft bread crumbs
    2 eggs, beaten
    2 onions, finely chopped
Salt and pepper to taste
All-purpose flour
Cooking oil
1-1/3 cups catsup
    2/3 cup chicken stock

Combine first six ingredients and form into balls. Roll meatballs in flour and brown in oil in large skillet. Transfer to a baking dish. Combine catsup and stock. Pour over meatballs. Cover tightly and bake at 350° for 40 minutes, stirring once or twice. **Yield:** 10-12 servings.

CUBAN BLACK BEAN SOUP

    2 cups black beans
2-1/2 quarts water *or* vegetable
        stock
    2 bay leaves
    1/4 to 3/4 cup olive oil
    3 large onions, chopped
    2 green peppers, chopped
    1 fresh jalapeno pepper, chopped
    4 to 6 garlic cloves, pressed
Salt to taste
Cooked white rice, optional
Sour cream, chopped onion and
    shredded cheese, optional

Cook the beans in water or stock. (If you presoak the beans, which makes them cook more quickly, count soaking water as part of the 2-1/2 qts. given in the recipe.) Add bay leaves to the simmering beans; cook, partially covered, until the beans are tender. Saute onions in oil until softened, then add peppers and saute another couple of minutes. Add garlic and saute a few seconds more. Stir onion mixture and salt into the simmering beans. Serve immediately. If desired, pour soup over rice, and top with sour cream, onion and cheese. Reheats well. **Yield:** about 2 quarts.

MARINATED VEGETABLE SALAD

Sharon Mensing, Greenfield, Iowa

(PICTURED ON PAGE 51)

1 head fresh broccoli, separated into florets
4 ounces fresh mushrooms, sliced
1 can (5 ounces) sliced water chestnuts, rinsed and drained
1 red onion, sliced and separated into rings
1 bottle (8 ounces) Italian salad dressing
1 to 2 cups cherry tomatoes, halved

Combine broccoli florets, mushrooms, water chestnuts, onion and dressing in a large bowl. Cover; marinate several hours, stirring occasionally. Just before serving, add cherry tomatoes, stirring gently to combine. **Yield:** 6 servings.

REMEMBRANCE STRAWBERRY PIE

Anna Bargfrede, Sweet Springs, Missouri

(PICTURED ON PAGE 51)

1 cup sugar
3 tablespoons cornstarch
1 cup water
3 tablespoons strawberry-flavored gelatin powder
2 pints strawberries, stemmed and halved
1 pie shell (9 inches), baked
Whipped cream or nondairy whipped topping

Mix the sugar, cornstarch and water in saucepan; stir constantly, cooking until thickened. Remove from heat; stir in gelatin until dissolved. Pour over strawberry halves; mix well. Pour into pie shell; refrigerate until set. Top with whipped cream or topping. **Yield:** 6-8 servings.

VEGETABLE BEEF KABOBS

Mynie Lou Griffith, Hutchinson, Kansas

(PICTURED ON PAGE 53)

1-1/2 pounds boneless beef sirloin
2/3 cup dry white wine or beef broth
1/3 cup soy sauce
1 teaspoon grated gingerroot or 1/4 teaspoon ground ginger

2 tablespoons vegetable oil
1 garlic clove, minced
1/2 teaspoon dried tarragon
18 small whole onions
3 to 4 small zucchini, bias-cut in 1-inch pieces
2 large sweet red peppers, cut in 1-inch pieces

Cut beef in 1-1/4-in. cubes; place in self-sealing plastic bag. In a small bowl, combine wine or broth, soy sauce, oil, ginger, garlic and tarragon; pour over meat in bag. Seal bag; let stand at room temperature for 45 minutes. Drain meat, reserving marinade. Thread meat, onions, zucchini and peppers alternately on six skewers. Grill over medium-hot coals, turning occasionally and basting with marinade. Cook about 12 minutes or to desired doneness. **Yield:** 6 servings.

RASPBERRY CRUMBLE COFFEE CAKE

Shirley Boyken, Mesa, Arizona

(PICTURED ON PAGE 54)

FILLING:
2/3 cup sugar
1/4 cup cornstarch
3/4 cup water or raspberry juice
2 cups fresh or frozen whole unsweetened raspberries
1 tablespoon lemon juice

CAKE:
3 cups all-purpose flour
1 cup sugar
1 tablespoon baking powder
1 teaspoon salt
1 teaspoon cinnamon
1/4 teaspoon mace
1 cup butter or margarine, softened
2 eggs, slightly beaten
1 cup milk
1 teaspoon vanilla extract

TOPPING:
1/4 cup butter or margarine
1/2 cup all-purpose flour
1/2 cup sugar
1/4 cup sliced almonds

For filling, combine sugar, cornstarch, water or juice and berries; cook over medium heat until thickened and clear. Add lemon juice. Set aside to cool. In a bowl, combine flour, sugar, baking powder, salt, cinnamon and mace. Cut in butter to form fine crumbs. Add eggs, milk and vanilla; stir until blended. Divide in half. Spread half of the batter into two buttered 8-in.-round baking pans. Divide filling and spread evenly over batter in each pan. Drop remain-

ing batter by small spoonfuls over filling; spread. For topping, cut butter into flour and sugar; stir in nuts. Spread topping on cakes. Bake at 350° for 40-45 minutes. (If desired, one coffee cake can be baked in 13-in. x 9-in. x 2-in. baking pan for 45-50 minutes.) **Yield:** 16-20 servings.

RASPBERRY CUSTARD MERINGUE

Bette Berry, Alamogordo, New Mexico

(PICTURED ON PAGE 54)

MERINGUE:
4 egg whites
1/2 teaspoon salt
1/4 teaspoon cream of tartar
1 cup sugar
1 teaspoon vanilla extract
1 cup finely chopped walnuts

CUSTARD:
1/4 cup butter or margarine
1/4 cup all-purpose flour
3 to 4 egg yolks
2 cups milk
1-1/2 teaspoons vanilla extract
1/8 teaspoon salt
3/4 cup sugar

TOPPING:
8 ounces whipping cream
1/3 cup semisweet chocolate chips
3 tablespoons butter or margarine
1 quart fresh raspberries

For the meringue, beat the egg whites, salt and cream of tartar till soft peaks form. Add sugar, 1 tablespoon at a time, beating until whites are thick and glossy. Add vanilla. Fold in the nuts by hand. To form crust, place meringue mixture on parchment paper; spread in a 14-in.-diameter circle (or in several smaller circles for individual servings). Bake at 275° for 1 hour; turn off heat and leave meringue in oven for at least 1 hour longer. Cool slowly. For custard, melt butter and add flour to make a paste. In a separate bowl, stir eggs with fork; add milk. Whisk milk mixture into flour mixture slowly; add vanilla, salt and sugar. Cook over low heat until thickened and bubbly. Pour into bowl; cover with plastic wrap and cool completely. (Can be made the day before using.) Just before serving, whip cream and sweeten to taste. Melt the chocolate chips with butter in a small saucepan. Spoon custard mixture on meringue; top with whipped cream and fresh berries. Drizzle with chocolate mixture. **Yield:** 12-14 servings.

RASPBERRY ICE
Wilma Scott, Tulsa, Oklahoma

(PICTURED ON PAGE 54)

 This tasty dish uses less sugar, salt and fat. Recipe includes *Diabetic Exchanges*.

2 cups fresh raspberries
1/4 cup sugar
1/2 cup water
2 tablespoons orange juice
2 egg whites
1/4 teaspoon cream of tartar
Pinch of salt
Fresh mint leaves, optional

In blender container, combine raspberries, sugar, water and juice. Process until smooth. Pour mixture into a saucepan; cook on low heat for 5 minutes, stirring occasionally. Let cool. Pour into mixing bowl; freeze 45 minutes. Meanwhile, combine egg whites, cream of tartar and salt. Beat until stiff peaks form; set aside. Beat partially frozen raspberry mixture until fluffy; fold in egg whites. Freeze until firm. Garnish with mint leaves, if desired. **Yield:** 6 servings. **Diabetic Exchanges:** One serving equals 1 fruit; also, 61 calories, 26 mg sodium, 0 cholesterol, 14 gm carbohydrate, 2 gm protein, .2 gm fat.

RED, WHITE AND BLUE BERRY PIE
Cindy Zarnstorff, Anchorage, Alaska

(PICTURED ON PAGE 54)

1 pie crust (9 inches), baked

BERRY LAYERS:
1-1/2 cups sugar
4-1/2 tablespoons cornstarch
1-1/2 cups water
4-1/2 tablespoons raspberry-flavored gelatin powder
1 pint fresh *or* frozen whole unsweetened blueberries
1 teaspoon fresh lemon juice
1 pint fresh *or* frozen whole unsweetened raspberries

CREAM LAYER:
4 ounces cream cheese, room temperature
1/3 cup confectioners' sugar
4 ounces nondairy frozen topping, thawed

For berry layers, combine sugar, cornstarch and water in medium saucepan, stirring to dissolve. Cook until thick and clear. Add gelatin; stir until dissolved. Divide mixture in half. Stir blueberries and lemon juice into half of the mixture;

spread over bottom of pie shell. Refrigerate. Fold raspberries gently into remaining half of mixture; set aside. For cream layer, beat together cheese and sugar until smooth. Mix in the topping; spread over blueberry layer. Refrigerate until set. Carefully spread raspberry layer over cream layer. Chill at least 4 hours before serving. **Yield:** 8 servings.

RASPBERRY CHEESECAKE
Lori Manthorpe, Ile Bizard, Quebec

(PICTURED ON PAGE 55)

CRUST:
3/4 cup all-purpose flour
3 tablespoons sugar
1 teaspoon finely shredded lemon peel, *divided*
6 tablespoons butter *or* margarine
1 egg yolk, slightly beaten
1/2 teaspoon vanilla extract, *divided*

FILLING:
3 packages (8 ounces *each*) cream cheese, softened
1 cup sugar
2 tablespoons all-purpose flour
1/4 teaspoon salt
2 eggs
1 egg yolk
1/4 cup milk

RASPBERRY SAUCE:
1 package (10 ounces) frozen raspberries, thawed and crushed
1 tablespoon cornstarch
1/2 cup black *or* red currant jelly

TOPPING:
3 cups fresh *or* frozen whole raspberries

For the crust, combine flour, sugar and half of lemon peel. Cut in butter until crumbly. Stir in egg yolk and half of vanilla. Pat 1/3 of dough on bottom of 9-in. springform pan with the side removed. Bake at 400° for 7 minutes or until golden; cool. Attach side of pan to bottom; pat remaining dough onto side of pan to height of 1-3/4 in. Set aside. For filling, beat cheese, remaining lemon peel and vanilla until fluffy. Combine the sugar, flour and salt; beat into the cream cheese mixture, mixing well. Add eggs and yolk, beating at a low speed just until combined. Stir in milk. Pour into crust-lined pan. Place on a shallow baking pan in oven. Bake at 375° for 35-40 minutes or until center appears to be set. Cool for 15 minutes. Loosen sides of cheesecake from pan

with spatula. Cool 30 minutes; remove side of pan. Cool for 1-2 hours longer. Chill well. To make sauce, combine ingredients in saucepan; cook and stir over medium heat until thickened and bubbly. Cook and stir 1 minute more. Remove from heat; strain to remove seeds. Cool. Just before serving, top cheesecake with raspberries and sauce. **Yield:** 12 servings.

CHOCOLATE DESSERT WITH RASPBERRY SAUCE
Marilyn Dick, Centralia, Missouri

(PICTURED ON PAGE 54)

16 squares (1 ounce *each*) semisweet chocolate
2/3 cup butter
5 eggs
2 tablespoons sugar
2 tablespoons all-purpose flour (amount *is* correct)

SAUCE:
2 cups fresh *or* frozen whole unsweetened raspberries
1-3/4 cups water
1/4 cup sugar
4 teaspoons cornstarch
1 tablespoon water
Whipped cream
Fresh whole raspberries to garnish

Line bottom of a 9-in. springform pan with parchment paper; set aside. Place chocolate and butter in top of double boiler. Bring water to boil; reduce heat and stir chocolate until melted. In a large mixing bowl, beat eggs for 2 minutes. Slowly add chocolate mixture to eggs, beating at medium speed about 10 minutes. Blend in sugar and flour just until mixed. Pour into prepared pan. Bake at 400° for 15 minutes (cake will *not* be set in the middle). Chill. For the sauce, combine raspberries, 1-3/4 cups water and sugar in a saucepan. Bring to boil. Reduce heat; simmer, uncovered, for 30 minutes. Put through sieve; discard the seeds. Add water if needed to make 2 cups juice. Combine cornstarch and 1 tablespoon water in small bowl; stir until smooth. Add cornstarch mixture to raspberry mixture. Cook over medium heat, stirring constantly, until mixture comes to a boil; cook and stir 1 minute more. Remove from heat; cool. To serve, spoon about 2 tablespoons sauce on each dessert plate; place a thin wedge of chocolate dessert on sauce. Garnish with whipped cream and raspberries. **Yield:** 16-20 servings (2 cups sauce).

RASPBERRY CHICKEN
Verna Schrock, Salem, Oregon

(PICTURED ON PAGE 55)

4 medium chicken breasts, split, skinned and boned*
2 tablespoons all-purpose flour
1-1/2 tablespoons butter *or* margarine
1 tablespoon vegetable oil
6 tablespoons raspberry vinegar
1/2 to 3/4 cup chicken broth
1/2 cup heavy cream
Fresh raspberries to garnish

Coat chicken with flour. Melt butter in large skillet; add oil. Brown chicken, turning once. Add vinegar and broth to skillet; stir over low heat until combined. Simmer, uncovered, until the chicken is done, about 12-15 minutes. Remove chicken to serving platter and keep warm. Add cream to skillet; boil sauce until slightly thickened, about 10 minutes, stirring occasionally. Pour sauce over chicken; garnish with raspberries (and watercress, if desired). Serve at once. *Pork chops may be substituted for chicken. **Yield:** 8 servings.

RASPBERRY VINEGAR PORK CHOPS
Maurita Merrill, Lac la Hache, British Columbia

(PICTURED ON PAGE 56)

 This tasty dish uses less sugar, salt and fat. Recipe includes *Diabetic Exchanges*.

1 tablespoon butter *or* margarine
1 tablespoon olive oil *or* vegetable oil
3 pounds pork chops *or* pork tenderloin, cut 1 inch thick*
1/2 cup raspberry vinegar, *divided*
3 garlic cloves, sliced thin
2 tomatoes, seeded and chopped
1 teaspoon dried sage *or* thyme, tarragon *or* basil
1 tablespoon fresh *or* dried parsley
1/2 cup chicken stock
Salt and pepper to taste
Fresh raspberries and sage to garnish

Melt butter in a large skillet; add oil. Brown the pork on each side over high heat. Pour off oil; reduce heat to medium-low. Add 2 tablespoons vinegar and garlic. Cover; simmer for 10 minutes. Remove pork to heated contain-

er; cover to keep warm. Add remaining vinegar; stir up browned bits from bottom of skillet. Raise heat and boil until the vinegar is reduced to a thick glaze. Add the tomatoes, sage, parsley and chicken stock. Boil until liquid is reduced to half of the original volume. Strain sauce; season with salt and pepper. Spoon over chops. Garnish with fresh raspberries and sage. *Chicken breasts may be substituted for pork. **Yield:** 8 servings. **Diabetic Exchanges:** One serving equals 2 meat, 1 vegetable, 1 fat; also, 216 calories, 115 mg sodium, 60 mg cholesterol, 4 gm carbohydrate, 20 gm protein, 13 gm fat.

RASPBERRY SPINACH SALAD
Rita Underdahl, Fremont, California

(PICTURED ON PAGE 55)

2 tablespoons raspberry vinegar
2 tablespoons raspberry jam
1/3 cup vegetable oil
3/4 pound fresh spinach, rinsed well and drained
3/4 cup whole pecans, toasted, *divided*
1 cup fresh raspberries, *divided*
2 large kiwifruit, peeled and sliced 1/4 inch thick

With a whisk or blender, blend vinegar and jam. Add oil in thin stream while whisking. Set aside. Mix spinach, half of nuts, half of raspberries and all of dressing. Top salad with remaining nuts, berries and kiwifruit. Mix again before serving. **Yield:** 4-6 servings.

LETTUCE WITH RASPBERRY DRESSING
Harriet Stichter, Milford, Indiana

(PICTURED ON PAGE 56)

 This tasty dish uses less sugar, salt and fat. Recipe includes *Diabetic Exchanges*.

6 cups leaf lettuce, washed, drained and chilled
1/2 cup coarsely chopped walnuts, toasted
DRESSING:
1/3 cup vegetable oil
3 tablespoons sugar
2 tablespoons raspberry vinegar
1 tablespoon sour cream
1-1/2 teaspoons Dijon mustard
1/2 cup fresh raspberries

Whisk together all dressing ingredients except raspberries. Fold in raspberries; refrigerate, covered, for at least 1 hour. Place lettuce in glass bowl; add walnuts. Toss with dressing. Serve immediately. **Yield:** 6 servings (3/4 cup dressing). **Diabetic Exchanges:** One serving equals 1/2 fruit, 1 vegetable, 2 fat; also, 157 calories, 22 mg sodium, .8 mg cholesterol, 11 gm carbohydrate, 2 gm protein, 13 gm fat.

FREEZER RASPBERRY SAUCE
Katie Koziolek, Hartland, Minnesota

(PICTURED ON PAGE 56)

3 cups mashed fresh raspberries (mash in layers as for jam)
3 cups sugar
1 cup light corn syrup
1 package (3 ounces) liquid fruit pectin
2 tablespoons lemon juice
4 cups whole fresh raspberries

Combine the 3 cups berries, sugar and corn syrup; stir until well mixed. Let stand 10 minutes. In small bowl, combine pectin and lemon juice. Stir into fruit mixture; mix for 3 minutes to distribute pectin evenly. Add remaining whole berries, stirring carefully to distribute fruit but leave berries whole. Ladle into 1-pint freezer containers; seal and let stand at room temperature for 24 hours or until partially set. Store in the refrigerator up to 3 weeks or in the freezer for up to 1 year. Thaw and stir before using. Serve over ice cream, sponge cake, shortcake or waffles, or combined with plain yogurt. **Yield:** 4 pints.

BERRY BASICS: Store berries in small, shallow containers so that the weight of the top berries doesn't crush those underneath.
• To wash raspberries, place them in a colander and submerge twice in a sinkful of cold water. Drain well.
• To freeze, coat a cookie sheet with a fine layer of nonstick spray; spread berries in a single layer on the sheet and freeze solid. Transfer frozen berries to plastic bags.
• For fresh-tasting frozen raspberries, thaw 1 pint of frozen berries in a syrupy solution of 2 cups water to 1/2 cup sugar. Drain and use immediately.
• Freeze smashed or crumbly berries in heavy plastic bags for winter jam-making.

ROYAL RASPBERRY CAKE

Genevieve Priewe, Whitewater, Wisconsin

(PICTURED ON PAGE 56)

CAKE:
2 cups all-purpose flour
1/2 teaspoon salt
1 tablespoon baking powder
1/3 cup butter *or* margarine, room temperature
1 cup sugar
1 egg, room temperature
1 cup milk, room temperature
1 teaspoon vanilla extract
3-1/2 cups fresh *or* frozen whole unsweetened raspberries

GLAZE:
1-1/2 cups confectioners' sugar
2 tablespoons cream *or* milk with melted butter
1 teaspoon vanilla extract

Stir together first three ingredients in a bowl with wire whisk; set aside. Cream softened butter with mixer; add sugar gradually, beating well after each addition, until mixture is fluffy and light. Stir in egg; beat 1 minute. Combine milk and vanilla. Add dry ingredients alternately with milk/vanilla mixture, beating well after each addition. Spread cake batter in greased, floured 13-in. x 9-in. x 2-in. baking pan. Spread the berries evenly over top of batter. Bake at 350° for 30-35 minutes or until center of cake springs back when lightly touched. Cool 5 minutes. Combine glaze ingredients; spread over cake, leaving berries exposed. Serve warm, with vanilla ice cream if desired. **Yield:** 16-20 servings.

BLACK RASPBERRY DUMPLINGS

Jeanette Redman, Newark, Ohio

(PICTURED ON PAGE 58)

1 quart fresh *or* frozen black raspberries
1-1/4 cups sugar, *divided*
1 cup water
3 tablespoons cornstarch
3 cups prepared baking mix
1 cup milk
Dash nutmeg

In a 6-qt. pan, combine raspberries, 1 cup sugar, water and cornstarch; stir to blend. Bring to a boil, stirring often. Turn heat to low. Meanwhile, combine baking mix, milk and remaining sugar, mixing until soft dough forms. Drop by spoonfuls onto boiling berries. Cook over low heat, uncovered, 10 minutes; cover. Cook 10-15 minutes more, or until dumplings are cooked through. For glazed effect, sprinkle dumplings with additional sugar and a dash of nutmeg before serving. **Yield:** 10 servings.

CARROT CAKE WITH BUTTERMILK GLAZE

Gayle Lewis, Yucaipa, California

(PICTURED ON PAGE 58)

CAKE:
2 cups all-purpose flour
2 teaspoons baking soda
2 teaspoons cinnamon
1/2 teaspoon salt
3 eggs
2 cups sugar
3/4 cup vegetable oil
3/4 cup buttermilk
2 teaspoons vanilla extract
1 can (8-1/4 ounces) crushed pineapple, well drained
2 cups very finely grated carrots
1 cup chopped walnuts
1 cup flaked coconut

BUTTERMILK GLAZE:
1 cup sugar
1/2 cup buttermilk
1/2 cup butter
1 tablespoon white corn syrup
1/2 teaspoon baking soda
1 teaspoon vanilla extract

Sift together flour, soda, cinnamon and salt; set aside. Beat eggs in bowl until lemon-colored; beat in sugar, oil, buttermilk and vanilla. Stir in flour mixture, then the pineapple, carrots, nuts and coconut. Pour batter into lightly greased and floured 13-in. x 9-in. x 2-in. baking pan. Bake at 350° for 55-60 minutes or until cake tests done when wooden pick is inserted in center. For glaze, combine all ingredients except vanilla in saucepan; bring to boil. Boil 5-6 minutes, until thick and syrupy; add vanilla. Poke holes in top of cake a fork or wooden pick; pour glaze over top while cake is still hot. Serve warm or store in refrigerator. **Yield:** 16-20 servings.

GAZPACHO

Agnes Gates, Lubbock, Texas

(PICTURED ON PAGE 58)

SOUP BASE:
2-1/2 cups tomato juice
3 tablespoons wine vinegar
1/2 teaspoon Worcestershire sauce
2 tablespoons vegetable *or* olive oil
1 teaspoon minced garlic
2 teaspoons snipped parsley
1/8 teaspoon hot pepper sauce *or* to taste
1/2 teaspoon salt
1/8 teaspoon pepper
1 tablespoon lemon juice

VEGETABLE GARNISHES:
1 cup finely chopped tomatoes
1/2 cup finely chopped celery
1/2 cup finely chopped green pepper
1/2 cup finely chopped onion
1 small cucumber, peeled, seeded and finely chopped

TOPPING:
Peeled chopped avocado
Croutons

Combine soup base ingredients; mix well. Stir in vegetable garnishes and refrigerate at least 4 hours or overnight. Top with avocado and croutons; serve cold. **Yield:** 5 cups.

MARINATED IOWA BEEF

Shary Geidner, Clear Lake, Iowa

(PICTURED ON PAGE 58)

 This tasty dish uses less sugar, salt and fat. Recipe includes *Diabetic Exchanges*.

1 beef chuck roast *or* thick sirloin (3 to 4 pounds)
Sliced tomatoes
Sliced sweet onion

MARINADE:
1 package (.6 ounces) Good Seasons Zesty Italian Dressing mix
1/4 cup extra-virgin olive oil
1/3 cup tarragon wine vinegar
1/2 teaspoon meat tenderizer, optional

Combine marinade ingredients. Pour small amount (enough to cover bottom) in a 13-in. x 9-in. x 2-in. baking pan. Place beef in pan; top with remaining marinade. Pierce meat generously with sharp fork; turn meat and pierce again. Cover; refrigerate for at least 8 hours or overnight, piercing and turning meat often. Before cooking, let beef come to room temperature. Grill over medium coals about 6 minutes per side for medium rare cuts 1 in. thick; 8 to 9 minutes per side for thicker cuts. Serve with tomato and onion slices. **Yield:** 6-8 servings. **Diabetic Exchanges:** One serving equals 5 lean meat; also, 303 calories, 505 mg sodium, 36 mg cholesterol, 3 gm carbohydrate, 37 gm protein, 15 gm fat.

ORANGE SHERBET PARTY PUNCH

Lannis Blunk, Mascoutah, Illinois

4 cups water, *divided*
2 packages (3 ounces *each*) strawberry-flavored gelatin
1-1/2 cups sugar
1 can (46 ounces) pineapple juice
1 can (46 ounces) orange juice
1 cup lemon juice
1/2 gallon orange sherbet, softened
1 bottle (33.8 ounces) ginger ale, chilled

Heat 2 cups water to boiling; add gelatin and sugar, stirring until dissolved. Add 2 cups cold water and fruit juices. Chill until ready to serve. Just before serving, spoon in sherbet and pour in ginger ale. **Yield:** 6-1/2 quarts.

EAST COAST CRAB APPETIZERS

Mrs. William Hitchens, Georgetown, Delaware

1/2 pound process cheese spread
3/4 cup butter *or* margarine
1 pound crab meat, shredded
1 can (4 ounces) mushrooms, chopped
2 packages English muffins, toasted lightly and quartered

Melt cheese and butter; add crab meat and mushrooms. Spoon onto muffins. Place under broiler until lightly browned. Serve hot. **Yield:** 12-14 servings.

MEXICAN APPETIZER

Jean Jenner, Isanti, Minnesota

2 cups (8 ounces) shredded cheddar cheese
2 cups (8 ounces) shredded Co-Jack cheese
5 eggs
1 cup salsa
Tortilla chips

Combine cheeses and spread half of mixture in well-greased 13-in. x 9-in. x 2-in. baking pan. Beat eggs well, mix in salsa and pour on cheese. Sprinkle remaining cheese on top. Bake at 350° for 30 minutes. Cool for 10-15 minutes or until set. Cut into 1-in. squares and serve on tortilla chips. **Yield:** about 100 appetizers.

CHEESE/GRAPE APPETIZERS

Eleanor Grofvert, Kalamazoo, Michigan

2 packages (2 ounces *each*) ground almonds
1 package (8 ounces) cream cheese, room temperature
2 ounces crumbled blue cheese, room temperature
2 tablespoons cream, room temperature
2 tablespoons chopped fresh parsley
1 to 1-1/4 pounds red and green seedless grapes, washed and thoroughly dried
Chilled greens

Spread almonds on baking pan; bake at 275°, stirring twice, until they are golden brown. Combine cheeses, cream and parsley; beat with electric mixer until smooth. Place cheese mixture in shallow dish. Roll grapes in mixture to thoroughly coat. Roll coated grapes in toasted almonds. Place on waxed paper-lined tray; refrigerate until ready to serve. Serve chilled; refrigerate leftovers. **Yield:** 10-12 appetizer servings.

HAM AND CHEESE SPREAD

Lorna Graham, Carberry, Manitoba

1 package (8 ounces) cream cheese
1/4 cup mayonnaise
1/2 pound boiled *or* baked ham, cut in small pieces
4 tablespoons chopped fresh parsley, *divided*
1/4 teaspoon dry mustard
1/4 teaspoon hot pepper sauce
1 tablespoon chopped green onion

Combine all ingredients except 2 tablespoons of parsley in food processor or blender and pulse until ham is minced. *Do not overprocess.* Roll into a ball; chill until firm. Cover outside of ball with remaining parsley. Serve with a variety of crackers. **Yield:** 24 appetizer servings.

TEX-MEX BEAN DIP

Helen Suter, Rosenberg, Texas

1 can (16 ounces) refried beans
1 cup (8 ounces) sour cream
1 package (8 ounces) cream cheese
1 can (4 ounces) chopped green chilies
1 package taco seasoning
1 cup (4 ounces) shredded cheddar cheese
1 cup (4 ounces) shredded Monterey Jack cheese
6 green onions, chopped, *divided*
Tortilla chips

Mix all ingredients except 1 tablespoon onions and the chips in fondue pot or chafing dish. Heat and stir until cheese melts. Top with reserved onions. Serve warm with tortilla chips. **Yield:** 30 appetizer servings.

FRESH SALSA DIP

Pam Friesen, Merced, California

2 cans (4 ounces *each*) chopped ripe olives
2 cans (4 ounces *each*) minced green chilies
3 finely chopped green onions (tops included)
3 to 4 firm red tomatoes, finely cubed
2 to 3 tablespoons vinegar and oil dressing *or* bottled Italian dressing
About 2 tablespoons finely chopped fresh cilantro
Corn chips

Combine olives, chilies, onions, tomatoes and dressing. Chill overnight. Top with cilantro; mix gently. Serve with corn chips. **Yield:** about 6 cups.

EXTRA-QUICK YEAST ROLLS

Eleanor Paine, Junction City, Oregon

1 package (1/4 ounce) quick-rise yeast
1 tablespoon sugar
3/4 cup warm water (110°-115°)
2-1/2 cups buttermilk biscuit mix

Dissolve yeast and sugar in warm water. Stir in biscuit mix and turn out onto a lightly floured surface. Knead until smooth and elastic, about 5 minutes. Shape into dinner-size rolls or cut with 2-1/2-in. round biscuit cutter. Place on greased baking sheet. Cover and let rise in a warm place until doubled, about 30 minutes. Bake at 400° for 10-15 minutes or until golden brown. **Yield:** 24 rolls.

CRABMEAT-CHEESE APPETIZERS
Marion Bedient, Cameron, Wisconsin

1 jar (5 ounces) Old English
  cheese spread
1 tablespoon mayonnaise *or*
  salad dressing
1 teaspoon lemon juice
2 tablespoons finely minced
  green onion (white portion)
1 can (6 ounces) crabmeat,
  well drained
1 tube (8 ounces) refrigerated
  crescent rolls
1 tablespoon thinly sliced
  green onion tops
Paprika

Combine cheese spread, mayonnaise, lemon juice, white part of onion and crabmeat. Remove crescent rolls from tube; do not unroll. Cut each section into 12 slices. Place slices on ungreased baking sheet. Divide crab mixture over 24 crescent roll slices. Sprinkle with green onion tops and paprika. Bake at 375° for 10-12 minutes or until puffed and lightly browned on bottom. Serve immediately. **Yield:** 24 appetizers.

RASPBERRY HOT FUDGE SUNDAE
Cindy Lou Hickey, Kingston, Massachusetts

1-1/2 cups frozen raspberries
  (without syrup)
1 quart vanilla ice cream,
  softened
RASPBERRY SAUCE:
1 cup sugar
1/4 cup water
3 cups raspberries (without
  syrup)
HOT FUDGE SAUCE:
2/3 cup milk
1/4 cup butter
1/4 teaspoon salt
1 package (12 ounces)
  semisweet chocolate chips
1 teaspoon vanilla extract
**WHIPPED ALMOND
  CREAM TOPPING:**
1 cup whipping cream
1 teaspoon almond extract

Gently fold raspberries into vanilla ice cream; place in covered freezer container and freeze until firm. For raspberry sauce, place sugar and water in 2-qt. saucepan; boil over medium heat for 1 minute. Remove from heat; cool for 15 minutes. Gently stir in raspberries and refrigerate. For fudge sauce, combine milk, butter and salt in top of double boiler over hot (not boiling) water. Heat until butter melts; add chocolate, stirring until chips melt and mixture is smooth. Remove from heat and stir in vanilla. Just before serving, whip cream until soft peaks form; fold in almond extract. In large dessert bowl or sundae dish, top ice cream with 2-3 tablespoons of each sauce. Garnish with a dollop of whipped topping. **Yield:** 6-8 servings.

SEAFOOD GUMBO
Ruth Aubey, San Antonio, Texas

1 cup all-purpose flour
1 cup vegetable oil
4 cups chopped onion
2 cups chopped celery
2 cups chopped green pepper
1 cup sliced green onions
  (including tops)
4 cups chicken broth
8 cups water
4 cups sliced okra
2 tablespoons paprika
2 tablespoons salt
2 teaspoons oregano
1 teaspoon ground black pepper
6 cups seafood (such as
  shrimp and scallops)
1 cup snipped parsley
2 tablespoons gumbo file

In a heavy Dutch oven, combine flour and oil until smooth. Cook over medium-high heat for 5 minutes, stirring constantly. Reduce heat to medium. Cook and stir about 10 minutes more, or until mixture is reddish-brown (the color of a penny). Add onion, celery, green pepper and onions; cook and stir for 5 minutes. Add broth, water, okra, paprika, salt, oregano and pepper. Bring to boil; reduce heat and simmer, covered, for 10 minutes. Add seafood and parsley. Simmer, uncovered, about 5 minutes or until seafood is done. Remove from heat; stir in file. **Yield:** about 6 quarts.

CLEVER CASSEROLE TIP: Store unbaked frozen casseroles in foil for quick, easy meals—and to keep your casserole dishes available for other uses. First, line casserole dish with foil, fill and freeze. Once ingredients are frozen solid, lift (foil and all) from dish; wrap well and return to freezer. To heat, simply pop the frozen block of ingredients back into casserole dish and bake. The foil lining also makes for easy cleanup!

BEST-EVER BREADSTICKS
Carol Wolfer, Lebanon, Oregon

3/4 cup milk
1 tablespoon sugar
1 teaspoon salt
1 tablespoon butter *or*
  margarine
1 package (1/4 ounce)
  quick-rise yeast
1/4 cup warm water (110°-115°)
3 to 3-1/4 cups all-purpose
  flour, *divided*
1 egg white, beaten
1 tablespoon water
Coarse salt

In a saucepan, heat milk, sugar, salt and butter. Cool to lukewarm. Dissolve yeast in warm water. Combine milk mixture, yeast mixture and 1-1/2 cups flour; beat until smooth. Add enough remaining flour to form a stiff dough. Turn out onto a lightly floured surface and knead until smooth and elastic, about 6-8 minutes. Place in a greased bowl, turning once to grease top. Cover and let rise in a warm place until doubled, about 30 minutes. Punch dough down. Pinch off golf ball-size pieces; roll into pencil-size strips. Place on greased baking sheets 1 in. apart. Cover and let rise 15 minutes. Combine egg white and water; brush over sticks. Sprinkle with coarse salt. Bake at 400° for 10 minutes or until golden. **Yield:** about 18 breadsticks.

SWISS CHEESE BREAD
Karla Boice, Mahtomedi, Minnesota

1 loaf (18-20 inches) French
  bread
1 cup (2 sticks) butter *or*
  margarine, softened
2 cups (8 ounces) shredded
  Swiss cheese
3/4 teaspoon celery seed
3/4 teaspoon garlic powder
3 tablespoons dehydrated
  parsley flakes

Trim top and side crusts from bread, leaving bottom crust intact. Make diagonal cuts, 1 in. thick, through the bread but not through the bottom. Combine all remaining ingredients. Spread half the butter mixture between bread slices. Use remaining mixture to frost top and sides of bread. Place bread in foil boat; cover loosely with another sheet of foil. Bake at 425° for 20-30 minutes. For last 5 minutes, remove foil to allow bread to brown. **Yield:** 18-24 servings.

FAVORITE PIZZA CRUST

Kathleen Miller, Battle Ground, Indiana

> 1 package (1/4 ounce)
>   quick-rise yeast
> 2 cups warm water
>   (110°-115°), *divided*
> 2 teaspoons salt
> 2 tablespoons sugar
> 1/4 cup vegetable oil
> 1 cup cornmeal
> 5 cups all-purpose flour,
>   *divided*
> **Pizza toppings of choice (sauce,
> meat, vegetables, cheese)**

Dissolve the yeast in 1/4 cup of warm water. In a large mixing bowl, combine yeast mixture with remaining water, salt, sugar, oil, cornmeal and 2 cups flour; mix well. Add enough remaining flour to form a soft dough. Turn out onto a floured surface and knead until smooth and elastic, about 5-6 minutes. Place dough in a greased bowl, turning once to grease top. Cover and let rise in a warm place until doubled, about 30 minutes. Punch the dough down and divide in half. Roll dough into two 16-in. circles; place on greased pizza pans. Top with desired pizza ingredients. Bake at 400° until crust is lightly golden brown, about 15-20 minutes. **Yield:** 2 16-inch pizzas.

BUTTERHORNS

Debbie Bertsch, Salisbury, Missouri

> 1 cup butter, softened
> 1-1/2 cups (12 ounces) cottage
>   cheese
> **Dash of salt**
> 2 cups all-purpose flour
> **FROSTING:**
> 2 tablespoons butter, melted
> 2 teaspoons milk
> 1/2 teaspoon vanilla extract
> 2 cups confectioners' sugar

Cream butter and cheese together with mixer until blended; beat in salt and flour until smooth. Cover; refrigerate 4 hours or overnight. Divide into 3 parts; form into balls. On lightly floured surface, roll out flat into circles 12 in. in diameter. Cut into 12 pie-shaped wedges. Roll each wedge from wide to small end. Place on greased cookie sheet with tips turned under. Bake at 350° for 30 minutes or until light golden brown. While butterhorns bake, mix frosting ingredients. Spread over tops of slightly warm rolls. Cool completely; store in covered container. **Yield:** 36 butterhorns.

PIE POINTER: When freezing fruit for pies, mix in all the ingredients called for in the recipe. Then line a pie pan with plastic wrap and pour in the filling. Cover this and freeze the filling in the pie pan. When the filling is completely frozen, remove it to a plastic bag. That way, the filling is ready to drop into a pie shell and bake at a moment's notice.

EASY PEACH CREAM PIE

Opal Back, Elko, Nevada

> 1-1/2 pounds fresh peaches,
>   peeled and sliced (3 cups)
> 1 unbaked pie shell (9 inches)
> 2 eggs
> 1 cup sugar
> 1/4 cup all-purpose flour
> **Dash salt**
> 1 cup heavy cream
> 1 teaspoon vanilla extract

Place peaches in pie shell. In a bowl, beat eggs slightly; blend in sugar, flour and salt. Stir in cream and vanilla; blend well. Pour over peaches. Bake at 375° for 40-50 minutes or until center shakes slightly when moved. (To prevent crust edges from becoming too brown, cover edges with foil, if desired.) Serve warm; or, for firmer pie, chill before serving. Refrigerate leftovers. **Yield:** 8 servings.

JIFFY CINNAMON ROLLS

Eula Colle, Marion, Kansas

> 4 to 5 cups all-purpose flour,
>   *divided*
> 1 box (9 ounces) one-layer
>   white cake mix
> 2 packages (1/4 ounce *each*)
>   quick-rise yeast
> 1 teaspoon salt
> 2 cups warm water (120°-130°)
> 2 tablespoons butter *or*
>   margarine
> 1/2 cup sugar
> 1 tablespoon cinnamon

In a large mixing bowl, combine 3 cups flour, cake mix, yeast, salt and warm water; mix until smooth. Add enough remaining flour to form a soft dough. Turn out onto a lightly floured surface; knead until smooth, about 6-8 minutes. Roll dough into a 9-in. x 18-in. rectangle. Spread with butter and sprinkle with sugar and cinnamon. Roll dough jelly-roll style, starting with the long end. Slice the roll into 1-in. circles; place on greased cookie sheets. Cover and let rise in a warm place until doubled, about

---

15 minutes. Bake at 350° for 15-18 minutes. Frost, if desired. **Yield:** 18 rolls.

PILLOW POTATO BISCUITS

Jacqueline Thuma, Orange Park, Florida

> 1/2 cup instant mashed potato
>   flakes
> 1 teaspoon sugar
> 2 tablespoons butter *or*
>   margarine, softened
> 1/2 cup hot water
> 1/3 cup cold water
> 3 cups prepared biscuit mix
> **Milk, optional**

Combine potato flakes, sugar, butter and hot water; mix well. Add cold water and biscuit mix, stirring until well blended. Add a little more cold water if necessary to make a soft dough. Turn out on a lightly floured surface; knead about 10 times. Roll dough to 1/2- to 3/4-in. thickness; cut with 2-in. biscuit cutter or jar lid. Place on ungreased baking sheet; brush with milk, if desired. Bake at 450° for about 13 minutes or until lightly browned. **Yield:** 12-18 biscuits, depending on thickness and size.

NO-KNEAD WHOLE WHEAT BREAD

Barbara Ann Gross, APO, New York

> 1 package (1/4 ounce)
>   quick-rise yeast
> 1-1/4 cups warm water (110°-115°)
> 2 tablespoons honey
> 2 tablespoons butter *or*
>   margarine
> 1 teaspoon salt
> 1-1/2 cups whole wheat flour
> 1-1/2 cups all-purpose flour

In a large mixing bowl, dissolve yeast in warm water. Stir in honey; add butter, salt and whole wheat flour. Beat on low speed until well blended. Stir in all-purpose flour. Cover and let rise in a warm place until doubled, about 30 minutes. Stir 30 strokes with a spoon; pour batter into a greased 8-1/2-in. x 4-1/2-in. bread pan. Cover and let rise in a warm place until batter reaches edge of pan, about 30 minutes. Bake at 375° for 30-40 minutes. Cool on wire rack. **Yield:** 1 loaf.

YEAST TIP: Use a candy thermometer to get correct water temperature for recipes that use yeast. No more failures!

Best Cook

Debra Dennis
Convent, Louisiana

Food means more than just nourishment for Debra Dennis of Convent, Louisiana—it's part of what keeps her big family so close!

Debra learned to cook as a teenager when her mother became ill. She first cooked for their family of nine, but soon was making meals for workers on the family sugarcane farm, too.

These days, Debra's still a double-duty chef. She cooks every day at her father's house, whips up Cajun feasts for her own family of five...and cooks for big family gatherings each Sunday!

"When Mama died, I wanted to make sure everybody kept coming to Daddy's place on Sundays. So I always made sure they had something to eat," Debra explained.

Her sister, Lisa Rouillier, says Debra's recipes—particularly her original seafood dishes—are always a big hit.

"She has Cajun cooking down pat," Lisa says. "She's a natural cook—she never measures or writes down anything.

"And even though she's cooking and cleaning for two households, this fantastic woman always can whip up a feast for anyone who drops by."

Since Debra's *also* attending school 4 hours a day to become a medical assistant, we wondered whether she ever tires of cooking for a crowd.

"Never," she answered. "This is my hobby—it's what I do for relaxation."

❖✳❖

CAJUN CORN SOUP
WITH SHRIMP

1/2 cup vegetable oil
1/2 cup all-purpose flour
1 small onion, chopped
1/3 cup chopped green onions
2 quarts hot water *or* heated chicken broth
2 cans (14-1/2 ounces *each*) stewed tomatoes, cut up
8 cups cut corn *or* 4 cans (16 ounces *each*) whole-kernel corn, drained
2 pounds shrimp, peeled and deveined
Salt and pepper to taste

In a heavy 8-qt. pot, combine oil and flour until smooth. Cook over medium-high heat for 5 minutes, stirring constantly. Reduce heat to medium. Cook and stir about 5 minutes more or until mixture is reddish-brown (the color of a penny). Add onions; cook for 5 minutes, stirring often. Turn heat to high. Add hot water or broth, tomatoes and corn. Bring to boil; reduce heat. Cover and simmer 15 minutes. Add shrimp; simmer about 5 minutes more, until shrimp are done. Season to taste. **Yield:** 12 servings.

❖✳❖

NEW ORLEANS
BREAD PUDDING

5 slices stale white bread
1 can (12 ounces) evaporated milk
1/2 cup margarine, softened
1-1/4 cups sugar, *divided*
3 eggs, *separated*
1 can (8 ounces) crushed pineapple in juice
3/4 cup dark raisins
3/4 cup golden raisins
1 tablespoon vanilla extract

Tear bread into small pieces; soak in milk for 2 minutes. In a medium mixing bowl, combine margarine, 1 cup sugar and egg yolks. Add bread and milk mixture; stir well. Drain pineapple; reserve juice and set aside 2 tablespoons for the meringue. Add remaining pineapple juice, pineapple, raisins and vanilla to bread mixture; mix gently. Place in 2-qt. casserole dish; bake at 400° for about 40 minutes or until light brown. Meanwhile,

prepare meringue by whipping egg whites until soft peaks form; gradually blend in remaining sugar, then reserved pineapple juice. After pudding is baked; spread meringue on top. Return to oven until topping is lightly browned, about 5-7 minutes. **Yield:** 8-10 servings.

❖✳❖

EGGPLANT AND SHRIMP
CASSEROLE

3 medium eggplants (about 2 pounds)
Salt water, optional
2 tablespoons vegetable oil
1 large onion, chopped
1/2 cup chicken broth, optional
1 pound shrimp, peeled and deveined
Salt and pepper to taste
Cayenne pepper to taste
1/2 cup seasoned bread crumbs *or* 1 cup seasoned croutons

Peel eggplants; cut into small cubes. If desired, soak cubes in salt water for 15 minutes; turn under several times. Drain and discard water. In large saucepan or a medium Dutch oven, heat oil over medium-high; add onion. Cook and stir until onion is tender. Add eggplant and chicken broth, if desired; bring to a boil. Reduce heat; cover and simmer for 20 minutes, stirring occasionally. Add shrimp; cook and stir about 10 minutes or until shrimp turns pink. Season to taste. Place in a 2-qt. casserole dish; sprinkle with bread crumbs or croutons. Bake at 350° for 20 minutes. **Yield:** 8 side-dish servings.

❖✳❖

PORK CHOPS
AND GRAVY

8 pork chops (1 inch thick)
Salt and pepper to taste
1/3 cup vegetable oil, *divided*
1/2 cup all-purpose flour
1/2 cup water
1 large onion, chopped
1 cup chopped green onions

Trim excess fat from chops; season with salt and pepper. In a large heavy skillet, brown chops in 2 tablespoons oil over medium heat, about 4 minutes per side. Remove. To drippings, add remaining oil and flour; mix until smooth. Cook over medium-high heat 5 minutes, stirring constantly. Reduce heat to medium; cook and stir 5 minutes. Return chops to skillet; add water and onions. Reduce heat to low; simmer 20 minutes or until meat is tender. **Yield:** 8 servings.

On a blustery day, chase away the chill with a bowl of steaming Potato Corn Chowder or a pan of hot-from-the-oven Honey-Mustard Baked Chicken. Pizza Joes are a great after-school snack and a crowd-pleaser, and the recipe doubles easily. Cap off a hot meal in cold weather with moist and tangy citrus-glazed Golden Lemon Cake.

AUTUMN EATING: Clockwise from left—**Potato Corn Chowder**, Michelle Howell, Greentown, Indiana (Pg. 76); **Honey-Mustard Baked Chicken**, Kate Peterson, Cincinnati, Ohio (Pg. 76); **Golden Lemon Cake**, Mary E. Riggin, Martinez, Georgia (Pg. 76); **Pizza Joes**, Barbara Gorden, Hanover, Pennsylvania (Pg. 76).

Meals in Minutes

SOME working mothers resort to frozen dinners or fast-food restaurants for weekday meals. Anita Foster of Fairmount, Georgia counts on another kind of convenience instead.

"On the weekends," says this busy mother of two young sons, "my life's at a slower pace. During the week, though, there's often little time for anything else *but* 'Meals in Minutes'!"

Anita developed her own 30-minute meal after enjoying a beef and peppers dish at a local restaurant. Back at home, she perfected the recipe. Adding glazed carrots and a tasty fruit salad dessert produced a fast, hearty feast.

"The boys especially love the fruit salad dessert," she notes. "I start out by tossing the fruit with the whipped topping and mayonnaise in a big bowl. Then I chill it until just before serving." At mealtime, she adds, the dessert can be turned out onto a platter like a molded salad.

Next comes the main course. "If, like mine, your husband is a hunter, you can substitute venison for the beef," Anita points out. "Do cook the venison a little longer than beef, though."

Lastly, while the beef and peppers simmer, Anita prepares the glazed carrots, using some fresh or canned carrots from her own garden.

"The garden is a family affair," she smiles. "The boys like shelling peas and shucking corn, and I enjoy 'putting up' the fruits of our labor."

We know you'll enjoy the convenience of Anita's quick, delicious dinner menu at busy times or anytime!

BEEF AND PEPPERS

    2 tablespoons cooking oil
1-1/4 pounds beef round *or* sirloin
      steak, cut into 1-inch cubes
    1 garlic clove, minced
    1 medium onion, cut into
      wedges
    1 medium sweet red pepper,
      seeded and cut into strips
    1 medium green pepper,
      seeded and cut into strips
    1 can (10-1/2 ounces) beef
      broth
  1/4 cup water
    3 tablespoons cornstarch
Salt and pepper to taste
Hot cooked rice

Heat oil in a skillet; brown beef cubes on all sides. Add the garlic and continue to cook for 2 minutes. Add onion, peppers and broth; cover and simmer 20 minutes. Combine the water and cornstarch; stir into broth. Cook and stir until gravy is thick and shiny. Add salt and pepper. Serve on rice. **Yield:** 4 servings.

GLAZED BABY CARROTS

    1 pound fresh, frozen *or*
      canned whole baby carrots
    2 tablespoons butter *or*
      margarine
  1/4 cup packed brown sugar

Cook carrots in a small amount of water until tender. Drain. In a saucepan, combine butter and brown sugar; heat until sugar dissolves. Add carrots and toss to coat. Heat through. **Yield:** 4 servings.

AUTUMN FRUIT SALAD

    2 bananas, sliced
    1 apple, cored and cut into
      chunks
    2 tablespoons orange juice
    1 can (11 ounces) mandarin
      oranges, drained
  1/2 cup raisins
  1/4 cup chopped walnuts
    4 tablespoons frozen whipped
      topping
    2 tablespoons mayonnaise

Toss banana and apple pieces with the orange juice to prevent discoloration. Drain any excess juice. Toss with all remaining ingredients. Chill. **Yield:** 6 servings.

GOOD GRAVY! Gravies and soups too thin? Dry mashed potato flakes are a good thickener.

PERFECT PANCAKES: Pancakes will brown beautifully if you add 1 tablespoon of molasses to your batter.

Best Cook

Elsie Pritschau
Ravenna, Nebraska

Elsie Pritschau of Ravenna, Nebraska does everything the old-fashioned way—right down to cooking with a vintage Home Comfort stove!

Elsie also grinds her own flour—wheat for bread, milo for pancakes and cornmeal for corn bread—and grows her own produce for her delicious pies and vegetable dishes. "I love sharing food with others and seeing that my guests eat a hearty meal," Elsie told us.

Elsie learned to cook by helping her mother bake bread, kolaches, crescent rolls, pies and cakes. Her mom also taught her three daughters how to make such delights as homemade noodles, sauerkraut and dumplings.

"All of us loved cooking, and we especially enjoyed having Sunday dinner guests. We even liked cooking for a hungry threshing crew!" Elsie said.

"I still like inviting guests over for dinner, and I always try to have something special on hand for my husband, Bud, when he comes in from his woodworking shop for a coffee break."

Lawrence Burman, a friend of the Pritschaus', is a fan of Elsie's baked goods, too. "There's nothing like sitting in the warmth of Elsie's Home Comfort stove and sharing a cup of coffee and one of her rolls, or a slice of her fresh bread with homemade jelly," he wrote us. "It makes our friendship that much more rewarding."

SAUSAGE AND WILD RICE CASSEROLE

 1 package (6 ounces) long-grain and wild rice mix
 1 pound bulk pork sausage
 1 can (10-3/4 ounces) cream of mushroom soup, undiluted
 1 cup sliced fresh mushrooms
 1/2 cup chopped onion
 1/2 cup chopped green pepper
 1/2 cup shredded sharp cheddar cheese
 1/2 cup chicken broth
 1/4 cup minced celery
 1 teaspoon parsley flakes
 1/2 teaspoon pepper

Cook rice according to package directions. Meanwhile, brown sausage in a skillet; drain excess fat. Combine rice, sausage and remaining ingredients in a greased 2-qt. casserole. Bake at 350° for 1 hour. **Yield:** 6-8 servings.

CZECH KOLACHES

 2 packages (1/4 ounce *each*) active dry yeast
 1/2 cup sugar, *divided*
 1/2 cup warm water (110°-115°)
 1/2 cup butter *or* shortening
 2 eggs, beaten
 2 cups warm milk (110°-115°)
 2 teaspoons salt
 5 to 6 cups all-purpose flour

TOPPING:
Fruit, poppy seed *or* cheese filling
 1/2 cup butter *or* margarine, softened
 1/2 cup sugar
 1/2 cup all-purpose flour
Confectioners' sugar icing, optional

Dissolve yeast and 1 teaspoon sugar in water. Meanwhile, mix butter, remaining sugar and eggs until smooth. Add the milk, salt, yeast mixture and enough flour to form a soft dough. Place dough in a greased bowl, cover and allow to rise in a warm place until doubled, about 1-1/2 hours. Punch dough down and allow to rise again. Punch dough down and divide in half. On a lightly floured board, roll half of the dough to 1/2 in. thick. Using a 3-in. cookie cutter or glass, cut dough and place on a cookie sheet. Repeat with remaining dough. Cover cookie sheets and allow to rise 1 hour. For topping, make a depression in the center of each dough circle with a glass; fill with a heaping tablespoon of filling. Combine butter, sugar and flour to make a coarse meal. Sprinkle over filling. Let rise 10 minutes. Bake at 375° for 10-12 minutes or until lightly browned. Drizzle with a confectioners' sugar icing, if desired. **Yield:** 4-5 dozen.

MY FAVORITE CHOCOLATE CAKE

 1/2 cup baking cocoa
 1 cup boiling water
 1/2 cup butter *or* margarine
 1-1/2 cups sugar
 3 eggs, *separated*
 2-1/2 cups all-purpose flour
 1 teaspoon baking soda
 3/4 teaspoon salt
 1 cup buttermilk

In a large mixing bowl, dissolve cocoa in water. Cool. Mix in butter, sugar, egg yolks, flour, soda, salt and buttermilk until smooth. In a separate bowl, beat egg whites until stiff peaks form. Carefully fold into batter. Spread into two greased 9-in. round cake pans or a greased 13-in. x 9-in. x 2-in. baking pan. Bake at 350° for 25-35 minutes or until a toothpick inserted in center of cake comes out clean. **Yield:** 12 servings.

ANGEL BISCUITS

 1 package active dry yeast
 1/4 cup warm water (110°-115°)
 3-1/2 to 3-3/4 cups all-purpose flour, *divided*
 1/2 teaspoon baking soda
 2 teaspoons baking powder
 1/2 teaspoon salt
 1/4 cup sugar
 1/2 cup shortening
 1 cup buttermilk
 1 egg, beaten

Dissolve the yeast in warm water; set aside. In a medium mixing bowl, mix 3-1/2 cups flour with other dry ingredients; cut in shortening. Stir in buttermilk, yeast mixture and egg; blend thoroughly. Turn out onto a lightly floured surface; knead slightly, adding remaining flour if needed. Roll out dough to 1/2-in. thickness. Cut with a 2-in. biscuit cutter, dipping cutter into flour as needed. Place on a lightly greased baking sheet; let dough rise slightly. Bake at 400° for 12-15 minutes or until lightly browned. **Yield:** about 24 biscuits.

Maybe somebody should switch that old "meat and potatoes" expression around! When it comes to tasty ways to feed a hungry family anytime of day, there are *plenty* of reasons to put potatoes first.

You'll agree when you see the hearty and filling dishes we've cooked up for you here. So take your pick of potatoes—there's more than enough here for everyone!

PERFECT POTATOES! Clockwise from top—**Berry Mallow Yam Bake**, Connie Bolton, San Antonio, Texas (Pg. 76); **Dublin Potato Salad**, Kathy Scott, Hemingford, Nebraska (Pg. 76); **Tex-Mex Stuffed Potatoes**, Karen Johnston, Stouffville, Ontario (Pg. 77); **Porky-Pine Waffles**, Ferne Lanou Moe, Northbrook, Illinois (Pg. 77).

Pass the potatoes, please! That's what you'll hear when you serve your family one or more of these nutritious and delicious potato dishes. Packed with vitamins and minerals, the potato is the world's most widely grown—and perhaps most versatile—vegetable.

Potatoes are tops whether they're baked, boiled, fried or mashed! So try these lip-smacking dishes, and settle once and for all that spuds need not be duds!

TOP TATERS: Clockwise from lower left—**Fat Rascals**, Naomi Giddis, Grawn, Michigan (Pg. 77); **Perfect Potato Pancakes**, Mary Peters, Swift Current, Saskatchewan (Pg. 77); **Sweet Potato Salad**, Ellen Moore, Springfield, New Hampshire (Pg. 77); **Potato Crust Quiche**, Nancy Smith, Scottsdale, Arizona (Pg. 77); **Crunchy Swiss and Ham Appetizers**, Wendy Mitchell, Weyburn, Saskatchewan (Pg. 78); **Ranch Potato Casserole**, Lydia Schnitzler, Kingsburg, California (Pg. 78); **Potato Cheese Soup with Salmon**, Nancy Horsburgh, Everett, Ontario (Pg. 78); **Potato Onion Supreme**, Claire Stryker, Bloomington, Illinois (Pg. 78).

For hearty home cooking at its finest—and a tableful of country compliments—try the recipes pictured here. Each one is sure to become a family favorite. Kick off the feast with cups of savory Cherry Soup, then help yourself to Pork Loin Roast with Yam-Stuffed Apples. Pass the Arkansas-inspired Razorback Corn Bread, and top off your dinner with moist, marshmallowy Cranberry Crunch Cake. Now that's country cooking!

FANTASTIC FOOD! Clockwise from top—**Pork Loin Roast with Yam-Stuffed Apples**, J. Wrigley, Lynden, Washington, (Pg. 79); **Cherry Soup**, Sue Gronholz, Columbus, Wisconsin (Pg. 79); **Razorback Corn Bread**, Louise Ford, Junction City, Arkansas (Pg. 78); **Cranberry Crunch Cake**, Adelaide Krumm, Manasquan, New Jersey (Pg. 79).

COUNTRY INNS

Capt. Samuel Eddy House

609 Oxford Street South
Auburn, Massachusetts 01501

Phone: 1-508/832-5282
or 832-3149

Directions: From I-90, take Exit No. 10 and follow Rt. 12 to Faith Avenue. Turn left on Faith Avenue, which becomes Oxford Street South after it crosses Highway 20. Continue 1/8 of a mile to the inn.

Innkeepers: Carilyn and Jack O'Toole

Schedule: Open year-round. Open to inn guests and the public for dinner; reservations must be made in advance.

Accommodations and Rates: Five bedchambers with private baths, $60 to $85; includes full breakfast and afternoon tea. Dinners, $14.95 to $19.95. Limited smoking. Outdoor swimming pool. Handicapped access only for dinner.

For heavenly, herb-flavored eating, the Capt. Samuel Eddy House is tops. Guests agree when they taste the crab appetizer flavored with curry, fresh dill and chives, or the green salad's vinegar-and-oil dressing sparked with mustard and maple syrup.

Carolyn O'Toole previously operated a small herb farm, so she extended her love for growing and cooking with herbs to the colonial inn she and her husband, Jack, now run.

Palate-pleasing main dishes may include poached salmon with orange-blueberry sauce, roast duck and fresh baked haddock. Enticing entrees are usually served with roasted potatoes, cauliflower, and squash with herb butter.

If you can't visit the historic house yourself, you still can try their favorite, flavorful recipes.

CHICKEN FRICASSEE

2 tablespoons olive oil
1 chicken (3 to 4 pounds), quartered
1/2 teaspoon salt
1/2 teaspoon cracked black pepper
2 medium onions, cut in eighths
2 garlic cloves, finely minced
2 tablespoons all-purpose flour
1 can (14-1/2 ounces) chicken broth
1/2 teaspoon dried marjoram leaves
1/4 cup dry white wine, optional
6 plum tomatoes, quartered
1 can (14 ounces) artichoke hearts, drained and halved

In 5-qt. ovenproof Dutch oven, heat oil. Season chicken pieces with salt and pepper. Cook the chicken in oil until all sides are well browned; remove. Add onions and garlic; saute until onions are lightly browned. Add the flour and cook, stirring constantly, for 1 minute. Stir in broth, marjoram and wine, if desired. Bring to a boil. Return chicken to Dutch oven; cover and bake at 350° for 45 minutes. Add tomatoes and artichoke hearts. Bake 15 minutes more or until chicken is tender. Serve immediately. **Yield:** 4 servings.

LEMON BREAD

2 cups all-purpose flour
1 tablespoon baking powder
1/4 teaspoon salt
1/2 cup unsalted butter, softened
1 cup sugar
2 eggs
Grated zest of 1 lemon
1 teaspoon lemon extract
3/4 cup lemonade

Preheat oven to 350°. Grease and flour a 9-in. x 5-in. x 3-in. loaf pan. Line bottom with waxed paper. Butter and flour waxed paper. In a medium bowl, thoroughly stir together flour, baking powder and salt. Set aside. In a mixer bowl, beat butter and sugar at medium speed until light and fluffy. Add eggs, one at a time, beating well after each addition. Beat in lemon zest and extract. At low speed, beat in dry ingredients alternately with lemonade, just until blended. Spread evenly in pan. Bake at 350° for 60-65 minutes or until pick inserted in center comes out clean. Cool in pan on rack for 10 minutes. Remove bread from pan, peel off waxed paper, cool on rack. **Yield:** 1 loaf.

CAROLYN'S BREAKFAST SOUFFLE

4 slices white *or* wheat bread, crusts removed, torn into pieces
3 slices ham, bacon *or* sausage
2 slices sharp process cheese
9 eggs
3/4 to 1 cup milk
Pinch salt and pepper
1/2 tablespoon *each* minced chives and herb of choice
Pinch cinnamon

Grease a 6-1/2-in. souffle dish and cover bottom with bread pieces, then layer meat and cheese. Mix eggs, milk and seasonings together; pour over all. Cover and refrigerate overnight. Bake at 350° for 10-12 minutes. Serve hot. **Yield:** 4-5 servings.

PUMPKIN CHEESECAKE PIE

1 deep-dish pie crust (9 inches)
1 package (8 ounces) cream cheese
1/4 cup sugar
1/2 teaspoon vanilla extract
3 eggs, *divided*
1 cup canned solid pack pumpkin
1/3 cup sugar
1/4 teaspoon ginger
1/4 teaspoon nutmeg
3/4 teaspoon cinnamon
1/4 teaspoon salt
1 can (5 ounces) evaporated milk

Preheat oven and baking sheet to 350°. In a small bowl, combine cream cheese, 1/4 cup sugar, vanilla and 1 egg. Beat until smooth and creamy. Spread over the bottom of crust. In a medium bowl, combine pumpkin, 1/3 cup sugar and spices. Slightly beat remaining eggs and add to mixture with milk; mix well. Pour over cream cheese mixture. Bake on preheated baking sheet for 50-55 minutes or until puffy and set. Cool on a wire rack. **Yield:** 8 servings.

HOMEMADE HERB VINEGAR: In a clear jar, put one cup of fresh, coarsely chopped herbs (thyme, basil, marjoram, tarragon, rosemary, fennel, dill or mint) and 2 or 3 cups of white or cider vinegar. Cap jar. Set on a sunny windowsill for about 2 weeks to let the flavors mellow. Then strain into a clean jar. Identify it by inserting a fresh herb stalk.

POTATO CORN CHOWDER

Michelle Howell, Greentown, Indiana

(PICTURED ON PAGE 68)

2 ounces thick-sliced bacon, diced
1 pound white potatoes, peeled and cubed
1/2 cup chopped onion
2 garlic cloves, minced
1 cup chicken broth
1/2 teaspoon dried red pepper, optional
4 cups milk, room temperature, *divided*
1 tablespoon cornstarch
1 tablespoon salt
3 cups fresh *or* canned corn
1/3 cup diced green pepper
1/3 cup diced sweet red pepper
2 tablespoons diced green onion
2 tablespoons chopped fresh parsley

MICROWAVE DIRECTIONS: In a 4-qt. microwave-safe bowl, cook bacon at full power until crisp, about 2-3 minutes. Add potatoes, onion and garlic; stir to coat with bacon drippings. Cover bowl; microwave at full power 5 minutes. Add broth and dried red pepper, if desired. Cover; return to microwave and cook until potatoes are tender, about 8-10 minutes. In separate bowl, stir 2 tablespoons milk into cornstarch; add to potatoes with remaining milk, salt, corn and peppers. Stir well. Cover and cook, stirring twice, until vegetables are just tender, about 6-8 minutes. Just before serving, stir in green onion and parsley. **Yield:** 8 servings.

PIZZA JOES

Barbara Gorden, Hanover, Pennsylvania

(PICTURED ON PAGE 68)

1 pound Italian sausage, casings removed
1 medium green pepper, chopped
1 small onion, chopped
1/2 cup fresh chopped mushrooms
2 teaspoons Italian seasoning
1 garlic clove, minced
1 can (8 ounces) tomato sauce
6 English muffins, split and toasted
2 cups (8 ounces) shredded mozzarella cheese

Brown sausage in skillet; drain any excess fat. Add pepper, onion, mush-

rooms, seasoning and garlic; cook 2 minutes. Stir in tomato sauce and simmer, uncovered, for 10 minutes. Top each muffin half with 2 tablespoons meat sauce; sprinkle with cheese. Broil until cheese melts and filling is hot. Serve immediately. **Yield:** 12 servings.

HONEY-MUSTARD BAKED CHICKEN

Kate Peterson, Cincinnati, Ohio

(PICTURED ON PAGE 68)

2 whole chickens, cut up
1/2 cup butter *or* margarine
1/2 cup honey
1/4 cup Dijon mustard
1 teaspoon curry powder
1/2 teaspoon salt

Place chicken parts in a large shallow baking pan. In saucepan, melt butter; stir in remaining ingredients and heat through. Brush glaze over chicken. Bake at 350° for 1-1/4 hours or until chicken is golden brown. Baste chicken frequently with sauce while baking. **Yield:** 6-8 servings.

GOLDEN LEMON CAKE

Mary E. Riggin, Martinez, Georgia

(PICTURED ON PAGE 68)

1 package (18-1/4 ounces) white cake mix
3/4 cup vegetable oil
3/4 cup warm tap water
4 eggs
1 package (3 ounces) lemon-flavored gelatin
1 teaspoon lemon extract
TANGY CITRUS GLAZE:
2/3 cup orange juice
3 tablespoons sugar
2 tablespoons lemon juice
3/4 cup confectioners' sugar

For cake, combine all ingredients in large mixing bowl. Beat at low speed until moistened, then at medium speed for 2 minutes. Pour batter into greased and floured 12-cup tube pan. Bake at 350° for 40-50 minutes or until toothpick inserted in center comes out clean. Let cool 10 minutes, then remove cake and place on wire rack. For glaze, combine ingredients in saucepan; bring to a boil and simmer 5 minutes. Let cool at least 10 minutes. Place platter under wire rack. Using toothpick, poke holes in top of cake; pour glaze over top and sides. Allow cake to cool completely before cutting. **Yield:** 8-10 servings.

BERRY MALLOW YAM BAKE

Connie Bolton, San Antonio, Texas

(PICTURED ON PAGE 71)

1/2 cup all-purpose flour
1/2 cup packed brown sugar
1/2 cup dry oatmeal
1/2 teaspoon cinnamon
1/3 cup butter *or* margarine
2 cups fresh *or* frozen cranberries
2 tablespoons sugar
1 can (17 ounces) cut-up yams, liquid drained and reserved
Miniature marshmallows, optional

In a small bowl, combine flour, brown sugar, oatmeal and cinnamon. Cut in butter as for pastry; blend until crumbly. Set aside. Sprinkle cranberries with sugar. In a 2-qt. casserole, layer half the yams, half the cranberry mixture and half the crumb mixture. Repeat layers, ending with crumbs. Pour reserved yam liquid over all. Bake at 350° for 35 minutes or until heated through. If desired, place several rings of marshmallows around the outer edge of casserole and return to oven just until marshmallows are puffed and lightly browned. **Yield:** 8 servings.

DUBLIN POTATO SALAD

Kathy Scott, Hemingford, Nebraska

(PICTURED ON PAGE 71)

3 large white potatoes (about 1-1/2 pounds)
2 tablespoons white vinegar
2 teaspoons sugar
1 teaspoon celery seed
1 teaspoon mustard seed
3/4 teaspoon salt, *divided*
2 cups finely shredded cabbage
12 ounces cooked *or* canned corned beef, cubed
1/4 cup chopped dill pickle
1/4 cup sliced green onion
1 cup mayonnaise
1/4 cup milk

Cover potatoes in lightly salted water and boil until tender. Drain, peel and cube. Combine vinegar, sugar, celery seed, mustard seed and 1/2 teaspoon salt; drizzle over still-warm potatoes. Cover and chill. Just before serving, gently fold in cabbage, corned beef, pickle and onion. Combine mayonnaise, milk and remaining salt; pour over salad. Gently toss. Serve in cabbage-lined bowl. **Yield:** 8 servings.

76

PORKY-PINE WAFFLES
Ferne Lanou Moe, Northbrook, Illinois

(PICTURED ON PAGE 71)

2 cups leftover mashed
    potatoes
1/2 cup shredded cheddar cheese
3 eggs
1/2 cup milk
1 can (8 ounces) pineapple
    tidbits, juice drained and
    reserved
2 tablespoons butter *or*
    margarine, melted
1 cup all-purpose flour
2 teaspoons baking powder
1/2 pound fresh pork sausage
    links
1 cup maple syrup

Combine the potatoes and cheese in a mixing bowl. Beat eggs with milk, reserved pineapple juice and butter; stir into potato mixture and mix well. Combine flour and baking powder; stir into potato mixture and mix well. Set aside. Brown pork sausage. Drain and cut into bite-size pieces. In a saucepan, combine sausages, pineapple and maple syrup; heat through. Bake the waffles. Serve waffles topped with sausage-pineapple mixture. **Yield:** 4 servings.

TEX-MEX STUFFED POTATOES
Karen Johnston, Stouffville, Ontario

(PICTURED ON PAGE 71)

6 large baking potatoes
1/2 pound lean ground beef
1 medium onion, finely
    chopped
1 garlic clove, minced
1 can (16 ounces) refried beans
1 jar (8 ounces) spicy Mexican
    salsa
Dash pepper
1 cup (8 ounces) sour cream
2 tablespoons finely chopped
    green onion
2 tablespoons finely chopped
    tomato
Corn *or* tortilla chips for garnish

Bake potatoes at 400° for 1 hour or until tender. Meanwhile, in a medium saucepan, brown beef, onion and garlic. Drain fat; add beans, salsa and pepper to taste. Simmer, stirring occasionally, 40 minutes or until thickened. To serve, cut an "x" in the top of each potato. Fluff potato pulp with a fork and spoon beef mixture over each potato. Garnish with a dollop of sour cream and sprinkle with green onion and tomato. Serve with corn chips, if desired. **Yield:** 6 servings.

POTATO CRUST QUICHE
Nancy Smith, Scottsdale, Arizona

(PICTURED ON PAGE 72)

CRUST:
4 cups coarsely shredded
    potatoes (about 4 large)
1/2 cup diced onion
1 egg, beaten
1 cup all-purpose flour
1/2 teaspoon salt
FILLING:
1-1/2 cups (6 ounces) shredded
    Colby cheese, *divided*
1/2 cup chopped onion
1-1/2 cups diced cooked ham
1-1/2 cups broccoli florets
3 eggs, beaten
1 cup light cream
1/2 teaspoon salt
Dash ground nutmeg
Paprika

Combine crust ingredients and press into a well-greased 10-in. deep dish pie plate. Bake at 400° for 20 minutes. Remove crust from oven; reduce heat to 350°. Add 1 cup cheese, onion, ham and broccoli to crust. Mix eggs, cream, salt and nutmeg; pour over all. Sprinkle with paprika and bake for 35-40 minutes or until set. Remove from the oven and top with remaining cheese. Let stand 5 minutes before serving. **Yield:** 8 servings.

FAT RASCALS
(Potato Cheese Puffs)
Naomi Giddis, Grawn, Michigan

(PICTURED ON PAGE 72)

1 cup mashed potatoes
2 eggs, beaten
1/2 cup milk
2 cups (8 ounces) shredded
    American *or* cheddar cheese
1/2 cup all-purpose flour
1/4 teaspoon baking powder
Salt and pepper to taste
Salad oil

Combine all ingredients except oil; mix well. Pour about 2 in. of salad oil into a saucepan or frying pan and heat to 375°. Drop batter by tablespoons, 4 or 5 at a time, into the hot oil. Fry 3-4 minutes or until golden brown. Serve immediately. **Yield:** about 24 puffs.

PERFECT POTATO PANCAKES
Mary Peters, Swift Current, Saskatchewan

(PICTURED ON PAGE 72)

4 large potatoes (about 3 pounds)
2 eggs
1/2 cup finely diced onion
1/2 cup all-purpose flour
1 teaspoon salt
1/8 teaspoon pepper
Salad oil
Maple syrup *or* applesauce

Peel and shred potatoes; place in a bowl of cold water. Line a colander with cheesecloth or a clean thin dish towel. Drain potatoes into cloth and squeeze out as much moisture as possible. Place potatoes in a mixing bowl. Beat eggs; add to potatoes along with onion, flour, salt and pepper. Mix well. Heat about 1/3 cup salad oil in a skillet until hot. Drop potato mixture 1/4 cup at a time into hot oil, about 3 in. apart. Flatten with pancake turner to make a 4-in. pancake. Cook pancakes until golden brown, turn and cook other side, about 4 minutes total. Remove to a cookie sheet lined with paper towel to drain. Repeat until all pancakes are cooked. Serve immediately or place in a warm oven until ready to serve. Top with maple syrup or applesauce. **Yield:** about 16 pancakes.

SWEET POTATO SALAD
Ellen Moore, Springfield, New Hampshire

(PICTURED ON PAGE 72)

4 medium sweet potatoes
1 cup pineapple chunks,
    drained
1 cup pecans, broken
1/4 cup orange juice
1 cup mayonnaise
1 teaspoon vinegar
1 teaspoon curry powder
1 teaspoon grated orange rind
1/4 to 1/2 teaspoon dried
    tarragon
2 tablespoons half-and-half
Lettuce leaves
Prepared chutney

Cook sweet potatoes until tender but firm. Peel and cut into chunks the size of the pineapple chunks. Gently toss potatoes, pineapple, nuts and orange juice. In a small bowl, combine all remaining ingredients except last two. Pour dressing over potato mixture and gently toss. Chill for several hours. Serve the salad on a bed of greens; pass the chutney. **Yield:** 6 servings.

RANCH POTATO CASSEROLE

Lydia Schnitzler, Kingsburg, California

(PICTURED ON PAGE 73)

6 to 8 medium red potatoes
(about 2 to 2-1/2 pounds)
1/2 cup sour cream
1/2 cup prepared ranch-style
dressing
1/4 cup bacon bits *or* cooked
crumbled bacon
2 tablespoons minced fresh
parsley
1 cup (4 ounces) shredded
cheddar cheese

TOPPING:
1/2 cup shredded cheddar cheese
2 cups slightly crushed corn
flakes
1/4 cup butter *or* margarine,
melted

Cook the potatoes until tender; quarter (leaving skins on, if desired) and set aside. Combine sour cream, dressing, bacon, parsley and 1 cup of cheese. Place potatoes in a greased 13-in. x 9-in. baking dish. Pour sour cream mixture over potatoes and gently toss. Top with 1/2 cup of cheese. Combine corn flakes and butter; sprinkle over casserole. Bake at 350° for 40-45 minutes. **Yield:** 8 servings.

POTATO ONION SUPREME

Claire Stryker, Bloomington, Illinois

(PICTURED ON PAGE 73)

8 medium potatoes (about 2-1/2
pounds)
2 large sweet onions, sliced
1/4 cup water
2 tablespoons chicken bouillon
granules
2 cups (8 ounces) shredded
sharp cheddar cheese
2 cups (16 ounces) sour cream
3/4 cup bread crumbs
2 tablespoons melted butter *or*
margarine
Paprika
Chopped fresh parsley, optional

Cook potatoes; peel and slice 1/4 in. thick. Set aside. Place onions, water and bouillon in a saucepan; bring to a boil, then simmer 5-7 minutes or until onions are tender. Drain and set aside. Combine cheese and sour cream. In a greased 2-1/2-qt. baking dish, layer half the potatoes, onions and cheese

mixture. Repeat layers. Combine crumbs and butter; top potato mixture. Sprinkle with paprika. Bake, uncovered, at 350° for about 20 minutes or until heated through. Garnish with parsley and several onion rings, if desired. **Yield:** 8 servings.

CRUNCHY SWISS AND HAM APPETIZERS

Wendy Mitchell, Weyburn, Saskatchewan

(PICTURED ON PAGE 73)

2 cups very stiff mashed
potatoes
2 cups finely chopped cooked
ham
1 cup (4 ounces) shredded
Swiss cheese
1/3 cup mayonnaise
1/4 cup minced onion
1 egg, well beaten
1 teaspoon prepared mustard
1/2 teaspoon salt
1/4 teaspoon pepper
3-1/2 cups corn flakes, crushed

Combine all ingredients except corn flakes; chill. Shape into 1-in. balls and roll in corn flakes. Place on greased cookie sheet and bake at 350° for 25-30 minutes. Serve while hot. **Yield:** about 8 dozen.

POTATO CHEESE SOUP WITH SALMON

Nancy Horsburgh, Everett, Ontario

(PICTURED ON PAGE 73)

1/4 cup butter *or* margarine
1 large onion, thinly sliced
1-1/4 cups diced celery
3-1/2 cups peeled and sliced
potatoes
1 cup chicken broth
3 cups milk, room temperature,
divided
1 cup half-and-half
2 cups (8 ounces) shredded
sharp cheddar cheese
1 teaspoon dried thyme
1 tablespoon Worcestershire
sauce
1 can (7-1/2 ounces) red sockeye
salmon, well drained, bones
and skin removed
Salt and pepper to taste
Chopped fresh parsley

In a 2-qt. saucepan, melt the butter and saute onion and celery until tender but not brown. Add potatoes and chicken broth; cover and cook on low heat until

potatoes are tender. Puree potato mixture in a blender with 2 cups milk. Return to saucepan; add remaining milk, cream, cheese, thyme, Worcestershire and salmon. Heat on low, stirring often, until hot. Season with salt and pepper. Garnish with parsley. **Yield:** 6 servings.

RAZORBACK CORN BREAD

Louise Ford, Junction City, Arkansas

(PICTURED ON PAGE 74)

8 ounces bulk pork sausage
2 cups cornmeal
1/2 cup all-purpose flour
3 teaspoons baking powder
1 teaspoon baking soda
1 teaspoon salt
2 eggs, beaten
3 hot canned peppers, chopped
1 large onion, chopped
1 can (11 ounces) Mexican-style
or whole-kernel corn, drained
2 cups buttermilk
1/2 cup shredded cheddar cheese

In a deep 10-in. cast-iron skillet, fry sausage until its done. Reserve 2-3 tablespoons of the drippings. Crumble sausage. Combine cornmeal, flour, baking powder, baking soda and salt. In separate bowl, combine eggs, peppers, onion, corn, buttermilk and cheese. Add egg mixture to the cornmeal mixture. Stir in sausage and reserved drippings. Pour into the greased skillet and bake at 450° for 20-25 minutes or until done. Serve warm from skillet. **Yield:** 12 servings.

GERMAN POTATOES

Janice Scherman, Sentinel Butte, North Dakota

6 slices bacon, diced
1 small green pepper, diced
3 tablespoons chopped onion
3 large potatoes, peeled,
boiled and diced
Salt and pepper to taste
1/2 cup shredded
cheddar cheese
6 eggs

In a skillet, fry bacon. Drain all but 3 tablespoons drippings; add green pepper, onion and potatoes. Season with salt and pepper. Cook and stir until golden brown, about 5 minutes. Sprinkle with cheese and stir. Break eggs over potato mixture, one at a time. Cook over low heat until eggs are set and cooked to desired doneness. Serve immediately. **Yield:** 6 servings.

PORK LOIN ROAST WITH YAM-STUFFED APPLES

J. Wrigley, Lynden, Washington

(PICTURED ON PAGE 74)

1/4 teaspoon ground sage
1/4 teaspoon pepper
1-1/2 teaspoons salt, *divided*
1 boneless pork loin roast
    (3 to 4 pounds)
8 to 10 large baking apples
1 can (24 ounces) yams, liquid
    drained and reserved
1/4 cup packed brown sugar
1/4 teaspoon cinnamon
1/2 cup slivered almonds, toasted,
    divided
1/4 cup butter
1/4 cup maple syrup

Combine sage, pepper and 1 teaspoon salt; rub over pork roast. Place roast, fat side up, on rack in open pan. Roast, uncovered, at 325° 2-1/2 to 3-1/4 hours or until meat thermometer registers 160°-170°. Meanwhile, core each apple, removing enough pulp to make 1-1/4-in. opening. Reserve pulp. Mash yams; combine with 1/4 cup reserved yam liquid, apple pulp, brown sugar, remaining salt, cinnamon and half the almonds. In saucepan, heat butter and maple syrup until butter melts. Drizzle half the butter mixture into apple cavities. Fill apples with yam mixture; garnish with remaining almonds. Place apples around roast or in separate baking dish, timing so that apples will bake 45-60 minutes and be done at the same time as the roast. Baste apples occasionally with remaining butter mixture. To serve, arrange roast and stuffed apples on heated platter. **Yield:** 8-10 servings.

CHERRY SOUP

Sue Gronholz, Columbus, Wisconsin

(PICTURED ON PAGE 74)

SOUP:
4 cups fresh, frozen *or* canned
    red tart pitted cherries
2 cups water
1/4 to 1-1/4 cups sugar
1/4 teaspoon cinnamon
DUMPLINGS:
2 cups all-purpose flour
2 teaspoons baking powder
Dash salt
1 cup milk

In 3-qt. saucepan, place cherries, water, sugar and cinnamon. Bring to a boil,

cooking cherries until tender, about 15 minutes. Adjust sugar, if necessary, depending on tartness of the cherries. For dumplings, combine flour, baking powder and salt; stir in milk. Drop dumplings by teaspoonfuls into boiling soup. Cook, covered, 10-15 minutes, or until dumplings are fluffy. Serve hot. **Yield:** 8 servings.

CRANBERRY CRUNCH CAKE

Adelaide Krumm, Manasquan, New Jersey

(PICTURED ON PAGE 74)

1/2 cup butter
1 cup sugar
2 eggs
1-1/2 cups all-purpose flour
2 teaspoons baking powder
1/2 teaspoon salt
3/4 cup milk
1 teaspoon vanilla extract
1 cup cranberries
1-1/2 cups miniature marshmallows
1/2 cup packed light brown sugar
1/2 cup chopped pecans
2 tablespoons butter, melted

In large mixing bowl, cream butter and sugar. Add eggs; beat until well combined. In separate bowl, combine flour, baking powder and salt. Add flour mixture alternately with milk and vanilla to egg mixture. Fold in cranberries. Spread batter in a greased 13-in. x 9-in. baking pan. Top with marshmallows; press into batter. Sprinkle with the brown sugar and nuts, and drizzle with melted butter. Bake at 350° for 25-30 minutes. **Yield:** 12-15 servings.

CRANBERRY-GLAZED CORNISH HENS

Betty Nichols, Eugene, Oregon

1/2 cup jellied cranberry sauce
1 tablespoon Dijon mustard
1 can (10-1/2 ounces) chicken
    gravy
1 teaspoon grated orange peel
3 Cornish hens (1-1/2 pounds
    each)
Salt and pepper to taste
Cooked wild rice
Orange slices

In 1-qt. saucepan, combine cranberry sauce, mustard, gravy and orange peel. Cook over low heat, stirring constantly, until glaze is smooth. Cut hens in half lengthwise; rinse and pat dry. Sprinkle with salt and pepper. Place on rack with drip pan, skin side down; brush hens

generously with glaze. Bake at 400° for 15 minutes. Turn hens, brush with glaze, and bake 30 minutes, or until juices run clear when hens are pricked with a fork. While roasting, brush often with glaze. Serve on bed of wild rice and garnish with twists of thinly sliced orange. **Yield:** 6 servings.

NEW ENGLAND APPLESAUCE

Marilyn Tarr, Palos Heights, Illinois

4 pounds Rome Beauty *or*
    McIntosh apples
1 cup honey
1 cup water
1/2 cup lemon juice
1 teaspoon grated lemon rind
1/4 teaspoon cinnamon
2 tablespoons grenadine, optional

Peel, core and cut apples in wedges. In a large kettle, combine all ingredients except grenadine; bring to a boil. Reduce heat and simmer 20-25 minutes or until apples are fork-tender. Mash apples to a chunky texture or process with food mill for smooth sauce. Stir in grenadine, if desired. **Yield:** 2 quarts.

SPINACH PIE PARMA

Nancy Reichert, Thomasville, Georgia

2 cups seasoned croutons,
    coarsely crushed
1/4 cup butter, melted
1/4 cup grated Parmesan
    cheese
1 package (10 ounces) frozen
    chopped spinach, thawed and
    drained
1 cup small-curd cottage
    cheese
1 cup (4 ounces) shredded
    Monterey Jack cheese
3 eggs, beaten
1/2 teaspoon instant minced
    onion
2 tablespoons sour cream
1/2 teaspoon garlic salt
Thin tomato slices, optional
2 tablespoons grated Parmesan
    cheese, optional

Combine croutons and butter; mix well. Press into bottom of an ungreased 9-in. pie pan. Mix together remaining ingredients except last two. Spoon over crust. Bake at 350° for 35 minutes. Garnish with tomato slices sprinkled with Parmesan cheese, if desired. Let stand 5 minutes before serving. **Yield:** 6-8 servings.

GRANDPA'S AUTUMN WAFFLES

June Formanek, Belle Plaine, Iowa

2 tablespoons butter *or* margarine
1/4 cup packed brown sugar
2 baking apples, cored and sliced
1/4 cup raisins
1/4 cup chopped pecans
2 cups all-purpose flour
2 teaspoons sugar
2 teaspoons baking powder
1/4 teaspoon salt
3 eggs
5 tablespoons butter *or* margarine, melted and cooled
3/4 cup milk
3/4 cup light cream
Maple syrup

In skillet, melt butter and brown sugar. Add apples, raisins and pecans. Cook until apples are tender, about 3-4 minutes; keep warm. Sift together flour, sugar, baking powder and salt; set aside. In a separate bowl, beat eggs; add butter, milk and cream. Stir in dry ingredients, mixing only until moistened. Lumps will remain. Bake in preheated waffle iron according to manufacturer's directions until golden brown. Serve with a spoonful of apple topping and heated maple syrup. **Yield:** 5 waffles (7-1/2 in. each).

MUSHROOM BRUNCH TOAST

Ann Nace, Perkasie, Pennsylvania

1/4 cup butter *or* margarine
8 ounces fresh mushrooms, sliced
2 garlic cloves, minced
1/4 cup whipping cream
1 teaspoon lemon juice
1/2 teaspoon salt
Dash pepper
Dash nutmeg
4 slices white bread, toasted
2 tablespoons chopped fresh parsley

In skillet, melt butter; saute mushrooms until lightly browned. Add garlic, cream, lemon juice, salt, pepper and nutmeg. Cook, stirring constantly, until cream thickens and its volume is reduced by half. Divide mushroom mixture and spoon over toast. Sprinkle each serving with 1/2 tablespoon parsley. Bake at 450° for 5-8 minutes or until sauce is bubbly. Serve immediately. **Yield:** 4 servings.

SOUR CREAM COFFEE CAKE

Sandra Munyon, Watertown, Wisconsin

TOPPING:
1/3 cup packed brown sugar
1/4 cup sugar
2 teaspoons cinnamon
1/2 cup chopped pecans

CAKE:
1/2 cup butter, softened
1 cup sugar
2 eggs
1 cup (8 ounces) sour cream
1 teaspoon vanilla extract
2 cups all-purpose flour
1 teaspoon baking powder
1 teaspoon baking soda
1/4 teaspoon salt

Combine all topping ingredients; set aside. For cake, cream butter and sugar in mixing bowl. Add eggs, sour cream and vanilla; mix well. Combine flour, baking powder, baking soda and salt. Add to butter and egg mixture; beat until combined. Pour half the batter into a greased 13-in. x 9-in. baking pan. Sprinkle with half the topping mixture. Add remaining batter and topping. Bake at 325° for 40 minutes or until done. **Yield:** 12-15 servings.

GERMAN CHOCOLATE RING

Anne Frederick, New Hartford, New York

1 cup semisweet chocolate chips, *divided*
1-1/4 cups flaked coconut, *divided*
3/4 cup chopped pecans
3 eggs, *divided*
4-1/2 to 5 cups all-purpose flour, *divided*
1/2 cup sugar
1 teaspoon salt
1 package (1/4 ounce) active dry yeast
1 cup milk
5 tablespoons butter *or* margarine, *divided*

In medium bowl, mix 3/4 cup chocolate chips, 1 cup coconut, pecans and 1 egg; set aside. In large mixing bowl, combine 1 cup flour, sugar, salt and yeast. In saucepan, heat milk and 4 tablespoons butter to 120°-130°; add to flour mixture, beating until smooth. Add the remaining 2 eggs with enough remaining flour to make a soft dough. Turn dough onto a lightly floured surface. Knead until smooth and elastic, about 6-8 minutes. Shape dough into a ball. Place in greased bowl,

---

turning once to grease top. Cover; let rise in warm place until doubled, about 1 hour. Punch dough down; turn onto lightly floured surface. Roll dough into 18-in. x 10-in. rectangle. Melt remaining 1 tablespoon butter and brush over dough; spread with chocolate mixture. Starting with long side, roll up dough jelly-roll style; pinch long edge to seal. Place on greased baking sheet, seam side down. Form into ring; pinch edges together. Make cuts three-fourths of the way through ring at 1-in. intervals. Twist each section to one side, filling facing up. Cover; let rise in warm place until doubled, about 1 hour. Bake at 350° for 20-25 minutes, or until golden brown. Sprinkle with remaining chips; let stand 5 minutes. Spread melted chips; sprinkle with remaining coconut. Carefully remove ring to wire rack to cool. **Yield:** 20-24 servings.

NO-COOK RED RASPBERRY FREEZER JAM

Eileen Sterk, Bellingham, Washington

2 quarts fresh red raspberries (3-1/4 cups pulp)
1/4 cup lemon juice
1 package (3 ounces) liquid pectin
1 cup light corn syrup
4-1/2 cups sugar

Wash and mash the berries. In a 4-qt. saucepan, measure 3-1/4 cups pulp; add lemon juice. Slowly stir in pectin; mix thoroughly. Set aside for 30 minutes, stirring frequently to allow the pectin to dissolve. Add syrup; mix well. Add sugar gradually, stirring well to dissolve completely. Warm mixture to 100°, using a candy thermometer to confirm temperature. Let set for 10-15 minutes; stir occasionally to keep fruit equally dispersed. Pour into jars or freezer containers and seal. Store in refrigerator for up to 1 month or in freezer for up to 1 year. **Yield:** 7 jars, 8 ounces each.

PICKING RASPBERRIES: Raspberries are ripe when they slip off the stem into your hand without resistance.

• During hot weather, pick raspberries every day or they'll become overripe.

• Wait until morning dew has disappeared before picking raspberries—dry fruit is less perishable than wet.

• When buying raspberries, avoid red-stained containers. Those indicate overripe, wet fruit.

FROZEN CRESCENT ROLLS

Linda Wilson, Anderson, Missouri

2 cups milk
2 packages (1/4 ounce *each*)
   active dry yeast
1 cup sugar
1 cup shortening
2 teaspoons salt
6 eggs, beaten
9 cups all-purpose flour, *divided*
1/2 cup butter *or* margarine,
   melted

Heat milk to 110°-115°. Add yeast; stir until dissolved. In large mixing bowl, cream sugar, shortening and salt. Add eggs; mix well. Add half the flour; then add milk mixture, mixing until flour is moistened. Add remaining flour by hand. Turn out dough onto floured board. Knead until smooth and elastic, about 6-8 minutes. Place dough in greased bowl; cover and let rise in warm place until doubled, about 1-1/2 hours. Divide dough into 4 parts. Roll each into a circle and brush with melted butter. Cut each circle into 16 pie-shaped pieces. Roll each piece into a crescent, starting at wide end. Place on baking sheet and freeze immediately. When frozen, place in plastic freezer bags and seal. Store in freezer until ready to use. To bake, place on greased baking sheet and cover; let rise until doubled, about 3-4 hours. Bake at 350° for 12-15 minutes. **Yield:** 64 rolls.

RICOTTA-STUFFED FRENCH TOAST

Christopher Sellers, Waterbury, Vermont

1 loaf (1 pound) Italian bread
1 cup ricotta cheese
4 eggs
1/2 cup light cream
1 tablespoon vanilla extract
1/2 teaspoon nutmeg
1/2 teaspoon cinnamon
1 tablespoon butter *or* margarine
Confectioners' sugar
Maple syrup, optional

Slice bread into 24 thin slices. Spread 12 slices with ricotta cheese; top with remaining bread slices. Beat eggs, cream, vanilla, nutmeg and cinnamon together. Dip each sandwich into egg mixture. In skillet, melt butter. Grill sandwiches slowly until golden brown; turn and grill other side. Dust with confectioners' sugar. Serve with maple syrup, if desired. **Yield:** 12 servings.

POPPY SEED POUND CAKE MUFFINS

Shirley McCluskey, Colorado Springs, Colorado

2 cups all-purpose flour
1 tablespoon poppy seeds
1/2 teaspoon salt
1/4 teaspoon baking soda
1 cup sugar
1/2 cup butter *or* margarine
2 eggs
1 cup plain yogurt
1 teaspoon vanilla extract

In small mixing bowl, stir together flour, poppy seeds, salt and baking soda. In a large mixing bowl, cream sugar and butter. Beat in eggs one at a time. Add yogurt and vanilla; mix well. Stir in flour mixture until dry ingredients are moistened. Spoon batter into greased muffin tins. Bake at 400° for 15-20 minutes or until a wooden pick inserted in center of muffin comes out clean. Cool muffins on wire rack 5 minutes before removing from pan. **Yield:** 12 muffins.

NEW ORLEANS PECAN PIE

Mitzi Adkinson, Albany, Georgia

2 eggs, *separated*
1 cup (8 ounces) sour cream
1 cup sugar
1/4 cup all-purpose flour
1/2 teaspoon vanilla extract
1/4 teaspoon salt
1 pie crust (9 inches), baked
1 cup packed brown sugar
1 cup chopped pecans

In saucepan, combine egg yolks, sour cream, sugar, flour, vanilla and salt. Cook and stir over medium heat until thickened, about 5 minutes. Pour into pie shell; set aside. In large mixing bowl, immediately beat egg whites until soft peaks form. Gradually add brown sugar; continue to beat until stiff. While filling is still warm, spread egg white topping over filling. Sprinkle with chopped pecans. Bake at 375° for 12-15 minutes or until golden. **Yield:** 8 servings.

FOILED AGAIN! When you're baking a double pie crust, here's a way to keep the outer crust edges from getting too brown: Cut out the center of a foil pie tin and place the outer ring over the pie. The center crust will get brown, but the outer edges won't burn. It's a lot easier than piecing tin foil around the edges!

APPLE BREAD

Phyllis Herlocker, Farlington, Kansas

3 cups all-purpose flour
2 teaspoons cinnamon
1 teaspoon baking soda
1/2 teaspoon baking powder
1/2 teaspoon salt
1/2 cup vegetable oil
2 cups sugar
2 eggs, beaten
1/2 teaspoon vanilla extract
2 cups coarsley chopped,
   peeled and cored apples
1 cup broken walnuts

In bowl, combine flour, cinnamon, baking soda, baking powder and salt; set aside. In large mixing bowl, place oil, sugar, eggs, vanilla and apples. Stir into flour mixture. Add walnuts and mix. Divide mixture between two greased 8-in. x 4-in. bread pans. Bake at 350° for 40-45 minutes or until breads test done. Cool for 10 minutes on wire rack before removing from pans. **Yield:** 2 loaves.

PORK TENDERLOIN WITH RASPBERRY SAUCE SUPREME

Bernice Janowski, Stevens Point, Wisconsin

1 pound pork tenderloin,
   trimmed and cut into 8
   crosswise pieces
1/8 teaspoon cayenne pepper
2 tablespoons butter
2 kiwifruit, peeled and thinly
   sliced crosswise
Fresh raspberries for garnish

RASPBERRY SAUCE:
6 tablespoons red raspberry
   preserves
2 tablespoons red wine vinegar
1 tablespoon catsup
1/2 teaspoon horseradish
1/2 teaspoon soy sauce
1 garlic clove, minced

Press each tenderloin slice to 1-in. thickness; lightly sprinkle both sides of each slice with cayenne pepper. Heat butter in large heavy skillet over medium-high. Add tenderloin slices; cook 3-4 minutes on each side. Meanwhile, combine all sauce ingredients in small saucepan; simmer over low heat about 3 minutes, stirring occasionally. Keep warm. Place cooked tenderloin slices on warm serving plate; spoon on sauce and top each tenderloin with a kiwi slice. Garnish each plate with remaining kiwi slices and fresh raspberries, if desired. **Yield:** 4 servings.

OLIVIA'S APPLESAUCE CAKE

Theresa Bryant, Lynchburg, Virginia

1 cup butter, room temperature
1 cup sugar
2 eggs
3-1/2 cups sifted all-purpose flour
1 teaspoon baking soda
Pinch salt
1 teaspoon cinnamon
2 teaspoons cloves
2 teaspoons nutmeg
1 cup chopped walnuts
2 cups raisins
2 cups unsweetened applesauce

Cream butter and sugar together until light and fluffy. Add eggs; beat well. Set aside. Sift together flour, baking soda, salt and spices. Remove 1/2 cup of flour mixture and stir into nuts and raisins. Set aside. Alternately stir remaining flour mixture and applesauce into creamed mixture. Mix well. Add nut and raisin mixture; stir to blend. Pour batter into greased and floured bundt cake pan. Bake at 350° for 65-75 minutes or until cake tests done when wooden pick is inserted near center. Cool in pan 10 minutes; turn out on rack to complete cooling. **Yield:** 20-24 servings.

MOLDED CRANBERRY NUT SALAD

Eleanor Arthur, Seattle, Washington

1 envelope unflavored gelatin
1-1/2 cups cold water, *divided*
4 cups (16 ounces) fresh *or* frozen cranberries
1-1/2 cups sugar
1-1/2 cups dry red wine *or* cranberry juice
1 package (6 ounces) lemon-flavored gelatin
1-1/2 cups diced celery
3/4 cup chopped walnuts
1 cup (8 ounces) sour cream
3/4 cup mayonnaise
Celery leaves

Soften unflavored gelatin in 1/2 cup water; set aside. In a 3-qt. saucepan, combine cranberries, sugar and wine or cranberry juice; heat to boiling, stirring occasionally. Reduce heat and simmer 5 minutes, stirring frequently. Remove from heat. Add lemon gelatin and softened unflavored gelatin; stir until dissolved. Stir in remaining water. Chill until mixture is partially set. Fold in celery and walnuts. Pour into greased 8-

cup mold; cover and chill until set. Meanwhile, combine sour cream and mayonnaise; refrigerate until ready to serve. To serve, unmold gelatin and top each serving with dollop of dressing. Garnish with celery leaves. **Yield:** 10-12 servings.

BOHEMIAN KOLACHES

Maxine Hron, Quincy, Illinois

2 packages (1/4 ounce *each*) active dry yeast
1/2 cup sugar, *divided*
2 cups warm milk (110°-115°)
4 cups all-purpose flour, *divided*
4 egg yolks
1 teaspoon salt
1/4 cup butter *or* margarine, softened
2 cups canned prune, poppy seed, cherry *or* lemon pie filling
1 egg white, beaten

In small bowl, dissolve yeast and 1 tablespoon sugar in warm milk; let stand 10 minutes. In large mixing bowl, combine 2 cups flour, remaining sugar, egg yolks, salt, butter and yeast/milk mixture. Mix until smooth. Add enough remaining flour to make a stiff dough. Turn out onto a floured surface and knead until smooth and elastic, about 6-8 minutes. Add additional flour, if necessary. Place dough in a greased bowl, turning once to grease top. Cover; let rise in a warm place until doubled in bulk, about 1 hour. Punch dough down and allow to rise again. Roll out on floured surface to 1/2-in. thickness. Cut with large glass or 2-1/2-in. cutter. Place on greased cookie sheets; let rise until doubled, about 45 minutes. Firmly press indentation in center and fill each roll with a heaping tablespoon of filling. Brush dough with egg white. Bake at 350° for 10-15 minutes or until rolls are light golden brown. **Yield:** about 28 rolls.

CHOCOLATE RASPBERRY CREAM

Sally James, Lockport, New York

1 package (4 ounces) sweet cooking chocolate, *divided*
2 cups whipping cream
1 tablespoon rum *or* 2 to 3 drops rum flavoring, optional
3 cups fresh whole raspberries, *divided*
1/4 cup superfine sugar*

Grate chocolate; reserve 3 tablespoons in refrigerator. Whip cream until soft peaks form. Combine remaining chocolate and whipped cream, blending gently but thoroughly. Stir in rum or flavoring, if desired. Reserve 1/4 cup raspberries in refrigerator; toss remaining berries with sugar. (*For superfine sugar, blend granulated sugar in blender until fine.) Fold sugared berries into chocolate mixture. Spoon gently into stemmed glasses; chill for 1 hour. *Do not overchill.* Before serving, sprinkle reserved chocolate on top and garnish with reserved raspberries. **Yield:** 8 servings.

RASPBERRY STREUSEL MUFFINS

Rosemary Smith, Fort Bragg, California

MUFFINS:
1-1/2 cups all-purpose flour
1/2 cup sugar
2 teaspoons baking powder
1/2 cup milk
1/2 cup butter, melted
1 egg, beaten
1 cup fresh *or* frozen whole unsweetened raspberries, *divided*
STREUSEL TOPPING:
1/4 cup chopped pecans
1/4 cup packed brown sugar
1/4 cup all-purpose flour
2 tablespoons butter, melted

In large bowl, combine flour, sugar and baking powder. In a small bowl, blend milk, butter and egg. Stir milk mixture into flour mixture just until moistened. Spoon about 1 tablespoon batter into each of 12 greased muffin cups. Divide half of the raspberries among cups; top with remaining batter, then remaining raspberries. For topping, combine ingredients until mixture resembles moist crumbs; sprinkle over muffins. Bake at 375° for 20-25 minutes or until golden. Let stand 5 minutes; carefully remove from pans. **Yield:** 12 muffins.

WHIP UP SOME BUTTER! To make your own whipped butter, soften a stick of butter and beat with electric mixer until creamy. Slowly add 1/2 cup vegetable oil or 2 tablespoons milk, beating until light and fluffy. Store the butter, covered, in refrigerator.
● To make raspberry butter that's delicious on muffins, toast or pancakes, blend 1 cup butter (room temperature), 2 cups confectioners' sugar and 1 package (10 ounces) frozen, *thawed* raspberries. Refrigerate.

Chili may *sound* like "chilly", but it's actually named after the Spanish word for red pepper, a "hot" spice. In any case, a hot bowl of chili is a really wonderful way to warm up on a winter day!

Sally's West Coast Chili is a meaty, cheese-topped soup that's guaranteed to both cut the chill *and* please the palate. Note the unusual ingredients that give it a subtly sweet flavor…perfect with a buttered hunk of Braided Almond-Herb Bread.

HOT 'N' HEARTY: Sally's West Coast Chili (right), Sally Grisham, Oxnard, California (Pg. 90); **Braided Almond-Herb Bread** (left), Ruth Peterson, Jenison, Michigan (Pg. 90).

estive desserts and sweets are a delicious way to celebrate the holiday season—especially with the tempting treats featured here.

Top off a holiday dinner with a slice of German Chocolate Cake... or a generous serving of the creamy Swedish Rice Ring with juicy strawberries. For a treat with your evening coffee, pass a plate of rich pecan Tassies or fruity Apricot Bars.

But don't reserve these recipes just for the holidays. These dressed-up desserts are perfect for special occasions year-round!

DELECTABLE DESSERTS: Clockwise from top—**German Chocolate Cake**, Joyce Platfoot, Botkins, Ohio (Pg. 90); **Swedish Rice Ring**, Lori Jeane Schlecht, Wimbledon, North Dakota (Pg. 91); **Apricot Bars**, Jill Moritz, Irvine, California (Pg. 91); **Tassies**, Joy Corie, Ruston, Louisiana (Pg. 90).

Best Cook

Shirley Pewtress
Kaysville, Utah

Christmas is always a special time at the Kaysville, Utah home of Shirley Pewtress—as you can see from the photo above!

Shirley loves cooking and teaching others how to cook—but her favorite dishes are her Christmas treats, like the Christmas Tree Bread she's holding.

"I make steamed puddings, fruitcakes and all kinds of chocolates, candies and baked goods. With six children and 12 grandchildren, our Christmas mornings are hectic, and a piece of warm bread with hot chocolate or cider stops the hunger pangs!"

Shirley's relatives aren't the only ones to benefit from her cooking. She's known for her holiday bread-making demonstrations. She also teaches cooking and nutrition classes for low-income young homemakers, and for families at nearby Hill Air Force Base.

"She's adored by the students in her classes," says friend Jo Ann Mathis, who nominated Shirley. "She believes in down-to-earth cooking, and she's a natural at teaching people how to stretch their food budgets."

Shirley says she's happy for the opportunity to share what she's learned.

"I love teaching adults new cooking tricks and new recipes," she says.

"My favorite saying is, 'When it comes to cooking, you're only limited by your imagination.' "

CHRISTMAS TREE BREAD

BASIC SWEET DOUGH:
    1 package (1/4 ounce) active dry yeast
1/2 cup warm water (110°-115°)
1/2 cup sugar
    5 tablespoons butter *or* margarine, softened
    2 cups warm milk (110°-115°)
    1 teaspoon salt
    1 teaspoon mace
    3 eggs, beaten
    8 to 8-1/2 cups all-purpose flour, *divided*
    1 teaspoon vanilla extract
1/2 teaspoon lemon juice

PECAN CREAM FILLING:
1/4 cup butter *or* margarine
1-1/4 cups confectioners' sugar
    1 tablespoon all-purpose flour
    1 egg yolk
1/4 cup finely chopped pecans

GLAZE:
    2 cups confectioners' sugar
    4 tablespoons milk
1-1/2 teaspoons butter, melted
1/4 teaspoon vanilla extract

Red and green candied cherries

Dissolve the yeast in warm water; set aside. In a large mixing bowl, combine sugar, butter, milk, salt and mace; mix well. Add eggs and yeast mixture; mix well. Add 4 cups flour; beat well. Stir in vanilla, lemon juice and enough remaining flour to form a soft dough. Turn out onto floured surface; knead until smooth and elastic. Add more flour if necessary. Shape into ball; place in a greased bowl. Cover; let rise in warm place until doubled, about 1-1/2 hours.

For filling, cream butter, sugar and flour. Beat in egg yolk. Add pecans. Cover; set aside.

When dough has risen, punch down. Roll one-third of dough into 15-in. x 13-in. rectangle. (Using sharp knife and ruler, trim to make triangle 15 in. tall and 13 in. wide at base.) From trimmings, cut two 3-in.-high tree trunks. Place large triangle on lightly greased 17-in. x 14-in. baking sheet with no sides. Dough will shrink, so form on pan with fingers back to original shape. Center one tree trunk at base of triangle; pinch together where trunk joins tree. Fold top 2 in. of triangle under. Gently spread filling on triangle and

trunk to within 1 in. of edges.

Place second trunk over filling on trunk already attached to tree; pinch outside edges to seal. Roll remaining dough into a 15-in. square. With star-shaped cookie cutter, cut one star. With doughnut cutter, cut 25 rounds. Arrange 6 dough rounds, overlapping slightly, across the tree base. Use 5 rounds to make second row. Make third row of 5 rounds, fourth of 4, fifth of 3 and top row of 2. Place star on top. Cover; let rise until doubled, about 45-60 minutes. Bake at 375° for 20-30 minutes or until golden brown. Cool on wire rack. Combine glaze ingredients; spread over tree. Top dough rounds with candied cherries. **Yield:** about 24 servings.

Note: This recipe also can be used to make wreaths or two smaller trees.

ONE-DISH MEAL

1-1/2 **pounds ground beef**
    1 **large onion, chopped**
    1 **medium green pepper, chopped**
    2 **celery stalks, sliced**
    1 **quart tomato juice**
1-1/2 **cups catsup**
1-1/4 **cups uncooked macaroni**
    1 **teaspoon chili powder *or* to taste**
1/4 **teaspoon garlic powder**
Salt and pepper to taste

In a Dutch oven, brown beef over medium-high heat. Add onion, green pepper and celery. Continue to cook until vegetables are crisp-tender. Drain excess fat. Add all remaining ingredients. Cover and simmer 2 hours or until the macaroni is tender and the liquid is absorbed. **Yield:** 8 servings.

NO MORE "DUST": When making a chocolate cake, use cocoa instead of flour to coat your cake pan. This will keep the cake from having that white-flour "dust" on it when you remove it from the pan.

PROVEN PORK HINTS: Before opening a canned ham, run hot tap water over the container for a few minutes—the ham will slip out easily.

● For a savory seasoning on pork, use thyme, sage, basil, rosemary, chives or sweet marjoram.

● When you broil pork (or any similar meat), put some water in the bottom of the pan to prevent grease from splattering or smoking.

Want to get oohs and aahs from your family during the Christmas season? Set out a cheery Christmas Braid, serve Cream Filled Coffee Cake for breakfast, pass the Pop Up Bread with dinner, or bake any of the festive breads featured here.

If you're looking for a personalized gift to give a next-door neighbor, friend or relative, consider wrapping up one of these. Whether you're baking for family or friends...nothing quite compares to a home-baked bread from a country kitchen.

BREAD WINNERS: Clockwise from lower left—**Country Swirl Bread**, Frieda Miller, Benton Harbor, Michigan (Pg. 93); **Whole Wheat Butterhorns**, Mary June Mullins, Livonia, Missouri (Pg. 92); **Cream Filled Coffee Cake**, Betty Mezera, Eau Claire, Wisconsin (Pg. 93); **Christmas Braid**, Wendy Tschetter, Swift Current, Saskatchewan (Pg. 92); **Pop Up Bread**, Bea Aubry, Dubuque, Iowa (Pg. 93); **Cheesy Onion Burger Buns**, Dolores Skrout, Summerhill, Pennsylvania (Pg. 91); **Reuben Loaf**, Elizabeth Eissler, Osage City, Kansas (Pg. 94); **Creamy Chive Rings**, Pamela Schlickbernd, West Point, Neb. (Pg. 94).

Home-baked bread and the holidays—what a warm and wonderful match they make!

The family favorites featured here include breads for almost every occasion—breakfast and brunch, lunch and dinner, snacking and supper. But don't confine these breads to Christmas. They'll bring you compliments all year long!

BEST BREADS: Clockwise from top—**Poppy Seed Roll**, Eileen Eck, Edna, Kansas (Pg. 92); **Italian Parmesan Bread**, Frances Poste, Wall, South Dakota (Pg. 92); **Candy Cane Coffee Cakes**, Kelley Winship, West Rutland, Vermont (Pg. 91); **Oatmeal Rolls**, Jeanette Fuehring, Concordia, Mo. (Pg. 91).

Meals in Minutes

MEALTIME is never monotonous for Kathie Landmann of Lexington Park, Maryland. As the wife of a Naval Flight Officer who's always "on call", she rarely knows what time her husband will arrive home.

Raising two young daughters adds to her need for fast but nutritious family fare. Inspiration for quick meals often comes from newspaper and magazine recipes that she clips. Her tasteful collection of rapid recipes now includes *over 250* of them.

Kathie's own Parmesan Chicken recipe, which she shares below, is not only a delicious dish that's speedy to prepare—it can be assembled ahead of time and refrigerated.

The accompanying side dish of rice and green peas cooks while the chicken bakes. "I keep those staples on hand so they're ready to use at a moment's notice," says Kathie.

An appealing and extra-easy caramel apple dessert rounds out her 30-minute menu. "The whole family has fun dipping apple wedges in caramel sauce and chopped nuts. Even our 3-year-old gets into the act!"

Try Kathie's time-saving treats next time you're caught with only minutes till mealtime...your whole family will be glad you did!

PARMESAN CHICKEN

1 cup grated Parmesan cheese
2 cups soft bread crumbs
1/3 cup melted butter *or* margarine
1/2 cup regular *or* country-style Dijon mustard
6 chicken breast halves, boned and skinned

Combine cheese, bread crumbs and butter. Coat chicken breasts with mustard, then dip into crumb mixture. Place breaded chicken in a 9-in. x 13-in. baking pan. Bake at 425° for 15 minutes or until chicken is done. **Yield:** 6 servings.

RICE AND GREEN PEA SIDE DISH

1 cup uncooked long-grain rice
2 cups water
1 medium onion, chopped
2 cups frozen peas, defrosted
1 carrot, peeled and shredded
1 teaspoon chicken bouillon granules
1 teaspoon salt-free herb seasoning
Salt and pepper to taste

Place all ingredients in a 3-qt. saucepan. Cover and bring to a boil. Reduce heat to simmer and continue to cook 15 minutes or until rice is tender. **Yield:** 6 servings.

CARAMEL APPLE DESSERT

4 to 6 apples, cored and cut into wedges
1 jar (12 ounces) caramel ice cream topping
1 cup roasted chopped peanuts

Just before serving, cut apples and arrange on a platter or individual plates. Heat caramel topping according to package directions. Place peanuts in a small bowl. To serve, dip apples in warm caramel sauce and then in chopped peanuts. **Yield:** 6 servings.

COOKING PORK: Today's leaner pork can be served either "medium" (cooked to 160°) or "well done" (cooked to 170°). Pork cooked to 160° will be slightly pink in color (especially near the bone) and have more juice than a cut cooked to 170°. It's perfectly safe to eat; however, some cooks may prefer to roast to 170° until the meat is no longer pink. A pork shoulder roast should be served well done only.

● When roasting large cuts of pork, remove from the oven when the temperature is 5° below desired temperature, then "tent" the meat with foil and allow it to stand for 15-20 minutes. The temperature will rise about 5°, and the pork will be perfect for carving.

SALLY'S WEST COAST CHILI

Sally Grisham, Oxnard, California

(PICTURED ON PAGE 83)

1 pound bacon, diced
3 tablespoons reserved bacon drippings
2 pounds beef stew meat, cut into 1/4-inch cubes
2 medium onions, chopped
4 garlic cloves, minced
1 cup bottled barbecue sauce
1 cup chili sauce
1/2 cup honey
3 cans (16 ounces *each*) whole tomatoes, chopped
4 beef bouillon cubes
1 bay leaf
1 tablespoon chili powder
1 tablespoon unsweetened cocoa
1 tablespoon Worcestershire sauce
1 tablespoon Dijon mustard
1-1/2 teaspoons ground cumin
1/4 teaspoon cayenne pepper, optional
3 cans (16 ounces *each*) kidney beans, rinsed and drained
Shredded cheddar cheese

In a large Dutch oven or soup kettle, cook bacon until crisp; remove to paper towel to drain. Discard all but 3 tablespoons drippings. Brown stew meat in drippings. Add onion and garlic, cooking until onions are soft. Return bacon to kettle. Add all the remaining ingredients except beans and cheese. Bring to a boil, then reduce heat to simmer. Cover and cook until beef is tender, about 3-4 hours. Add beans and heat through. Top each serving with cheddar cheese. **Yield:** 4 quarts.

BRAIDED ALMOND-HERB BREAD

Ruth Peterson, Jenison, Michigan

(PICTURED ON PAGE 83)

 This tasty dish uses less sugar, salt and fat. Recipe includes *Diabetic Exchanges.*

1 package (1/4 ounce) active dry yeast
2 tablespoons sugar
1/4 cup warm water (110°-115°)
1/4 cup butter *or* margarine
1 teaspoon salt
1 cup warm milk (110°-115°)
3-1/2 to 4 cups all-purpose flour, *divided*

1 teaspoon dried rosemary, crushed
1 teaspoon dill weed
1/2 teaspoon dried marjoram, crushed
1/2 cup finely chopped almonds, toasted, *divided*
1 egg, beaten
1 tablespoon water

Dissolve yeast and sugar in warm water; set aside. In large mixing bowl, combine butter, salt and milk. Stir in yeast mixture, 2 cups flour, herbs and 2 tablespoons almonds. Beat until well-mixed. Stir in enough remaining flour to form a soft dough. Turn out onto a floured surface and knead until smooth and elastic, about 6-8 minutes. Place dough in greased bowl, turning once to grease dough surface. Cover; let rise in warm place until doubled, about 1 hour. Punch dough down and cut off 1/3 of dough; set aside. Divide remaining dough into three equal parts, shaping each into a 14-in. rope. Braid ropes and place on greased baking sheet. Divide set-aside dough into three ropes and braid. Place smaller braid on top of larger braid. Cover; let rise until doubled, about 1 hour. Combine egg and water. Brush over entire loaf; sprinkle with remaining almonds. Bake at 375° for 30 minutes. **Yield:** 1 loaf. **Diabetic Exchanges:** One serving equals 1-1/4 starch, 1 fat; also, 130 calories, 148 mg sodium, 15 mg cholesterol, 19 gm carbohydrate, 4 gm protein, 5 gm fat.

TASSIES

Joy Corie, Ruston, Louisiana

(PICTURED ON PAGE 84)

PASTRY:
1 package (3 ounces) cream cheese, softened
1/2 cup butter *or* margarine
1 cup all-purpose flour
FILLING:
3/4 cup packed brown sugar
1 tablespoon butter *or* margarine, softened
1 egg
1 teaspoon vanilla extract
Dash salt
2/3 cup finely chopped pecans, *divided*
Maraschino cherries, optional

For pastry, blend cream cheese and butter until smooth; stir in flour. Chill about 1 hour. Shape into 24 1-in. balls. Place in ungreased miniature muffin tins or small cookie tarts; press the dough against bottom and sides to form a shell. Set aside. In bowl, beat

brown sugar, butter and egg until combined. Add vanilla, salt and half the pecans; spoon into pastry. Top with remaining pecans. Bake at 375° for 20 minutes, or until filling is set and pastry is light golden brown. Cool and remove from pans. Decorate with maraschino cherry halves, if desired. **Yield:** 24 tarts.

GERMAN CHOCOLATE CAKE

Joyce Platfoot, Botkins, Ohio

(PICTURED ON PAGE 84)

1/2 cup water
1 bar (4 ounces) sweet cooking chocolate
2 cups sugar
1 cup butter *or* margarine, softened
4 eggs, *separated*
1 teaspoon vanilla extract
2-1/2 cups cake flour
1 teaspoon baking soda
1/2 teaspoon salt
1 cup buttermilk
FROSTING:
1 cup sugar
1 cup evaporated milk
1/2 cup butter *or* margarine
3 egg yolks, beaten
1-1/3 cups flaked coconut
1 cup chopped pecans
1 teaspoon vanilla extract
ICING:
1/2 teaspoon shortening
1 square (1 ounce) semisweet chocolate

For cake, heat in saucepan the water and chocolate until melted; cool. In large mixing bowl, beat sugar and butter until light and fluffy. Beat in 4 egg yolks one at a time. Blend in melted chocolate and vanilla. Combine flour, baking soda and salt. Add alternately with buttermilk to butter mixture. Beat until batter is smooth. In separate bowl, whip 4 egg whites until stiff; fold into batter. Pour batter into three 9-in. cake pans lined with waxed paper. Bake at 350° for 30 minutes or until the cake springs back when pressed lightly in center. Cool 15 minutes. Remove cake from pans; cool on wire racks. For frosting, mix sugar, milk, butter and egg yolks in 1-qt. saucepan. Heat, stirring constantly, until thickened. Remove from heat. Stir in coconut, pecans and vanilla. Cool until thick enough to spread. Spread frosting over tops of each cake layer. For icing, melt in saucepan the shortening and chocolate. While warm, drizzle icing down sides of cake. **Yield:** 10-12 servings.

SWEDISH RICE RING

Lori Jeane Schlecht, Wimbledon, North Dakota

(PICTURED ON PAGE 84)

2 envelopes unflavored gelatin
1/4 cup cold water
1/2 cup uncooked long-grain rice
3 cups milk
1/2 cup sugar
1/2 teaspoon salt
1 cup whipping cream
Fresh *or* frozen sweetened
    strawberries

Soften gelatin in water; set aside. In heavy 2-qt. saucepan, bring rice, milk, sugar and salt to a boil, stirring occasionally. Reduce heat and cover; cook over low heat until rice is tender, about 15-20 minutes. Remove from heat; add gelatin, stirring until dissolved. Cover; chill until partially set. In chilled bowl, whip cream until stiff; fold into chilled rice mixture. Spoon into 6-cup decorative or ring mold. Cover and chill until set, about 3 hours. To unmold, loosen edges with spatula and invert on serving platter. Serve with sweetened strawberries. **Yield:** 10-12 servings.

OATMEAL ROLLS

Jeanette Fuehring, Concordia, Missouri

(PICTURED ON PAGE 88)

2-1/3 cups water, *divided*
1 cup dry oatmeal
3 tablespoons butter *or*
    margarine
2/3 cup packed brown sugar
1 tablespoon sugar
1-1/2 teaspoons salt
2 packages (1/4 ounce *each*)
    active dry yeast
5 to 5-3/4 cups all-purpose
    flour, *divided*

In a saucepan, bring 2 cups water to a boil. Add oatmeal and butter; simmer 1 minute. Remove to a large mixing bowl and let cool to 120°-130°. Heat the remaining water to 120°-130°; add yeast. To the oatmeal mixture, add brown and white sugars, salt, yeast mixture and half of the flour. Mix well. Add enough remaining flour to make a soft dough. Turn out onto a floured board; knead 6-8 minutes or until smooth and elastic. Add additional flour if necessary. Place dough in a greased bowl, turning once to grease top. Cover and let rise until doubled, about 1 hour. Punch dough down; divide in half and shape each half into 12 balls. Place 1 in. apart on two greased 13-in. x 9-in.

baking pans. Cover and let rise until doubled, about 45-60 minutes. Bake at 350° for 20-30 minutes. **Yield:** 24 rolls.

APRICOT BARS

Jill Moritz, Irvine, California

(PICTURED ON PAGE 84)

3/4 cup butter *or* margarine
1 cup sugar
1 egg
2 cups all-purpose flour
1/4 teaspoon baking powder
1-1/3 cups shredded coconut
1/2 cup chopped walnuts
1/2 teaspoon vanilla extract
1 jar (12 ounces) apricot
    preserves

In a large mixing bowl, cream butter and sugar. Add egg; mix well. In separate bowl, combine flour and baking powder. Gradually add to butter mixture. Add coconut, walnuts and vanilla; mix thoroughly. Press two-thirds of dough into a greased 13-in. x 9-in. x 2-in. baking pan. Spread with preserves; crumble remaining dough over preserves. Bake at 350° for 30-35 minutes or until golden brown. Cool in pan on wire rack. Cut into squares. **Yield:** 36 bars.

CANDY CANE COFFEE CAKES

Kelley Winship, West Rutland, Vermont

(PICTURED ON PAGE 88)

2 cups (16 ounces) sour cream
2 packages (1/4 ounce *each*)
    active dry yeast
1/2 cup warm water (110°-115°)
1/4 cup butter *or* margarine,
    softened
1/3 cup sugar
2 teaspoons salt
2 eggs, beaten
5-1/4 to 6 cups all-purpose flour,
    divided
1-1/2 cups (12 ounces) finely
    chopped dried apricots
1-1/2 cups finely chopped
    maraschino cherries
Melted butter
ICING:
2 cups confectioners' sugar
2 to 3 tablespoons water

In a saucepan, heat sour cream until lukewarm. Set aside. Dissolve yeast in warm water. In a large mixing bowl, add yeast mixture, sour cream, butter,

sugar, salt, eggs and 2 cups flour. With an electric mixer, beat until smooth. Stir in just enough of the remaining flour to form a soft dough. Turn out onto a floured surface and knead until smooth and elastic. Place in a greased bowl, turning once to grease top. Cover and let rise in a warm place until doubled, about 1 hour. Punch dough down; divide into 3 equal parts. On a lightly floured board, roll each part into a 15-in. x 6-in. rectangle. Place on greased baking sheets. With a scissors, make 2-in. cuts at 1/2-in. intervals on the long sides of rectangle. Combine apricots and cherries; spread 1/3 of the mixture down the center of each rectangle. Crisscross strips over filling. Stretch dough to 22 in. Curve to form cane. Let rise until doubled, about 45 minutes. Bake at 375° for 15-20 minutes. While warm, brush canes with butter. Combine icing ingredients and drizzle. **Yield:** 3 coffee cakes.

CHEESY ONION BURGER BUNS

Dolores Skrout, Summerhill, Pennsylvania

(PICTURED ON PAGE 87)

5-3/4 to 6-3/4 cups all-purpose
    flour, *divided*
3 tablespoons sugar
1-1/2 teaspoons salt
2 packages (1/4 ounce *each*)
    active dry yeast
2 tablespoons butter *or*
    margarine, softened
2 cups hot water (120°-130°)
1-1/2 cups (6 ounces) shredded
    cheddar cheese
1/4 cup minced onion

In a large mixing bowl, combine 2 cups flour, sugar, salt, yeast and butter. Gradually add hot water. With electric mixer, beat 2 minutes at medium speed. Add 1 cup flour and mix on high speed 2 minutes. Stir in cheese, onion and enough of the remaining flour to form a soft dough. Turn out onto a floured surface; knead until smooth and elastic, about 6-8 minutes. Place dough in a greased bowl, turning once to grease top. Cover and let rise in a warm place until doubled, about 1 hour. Punch dough down and turn out onto a lightly floured surface. Divide dough into 20 equal pieces; shape into smooth balls and place on greased baking sheets. Cover and let rise in a warm place until doubled, about 45 minutes. Bake at 400° for 15-20 minutes. Remove from the pans and cool on wire racks. **Yield:** 20 hamburger buns.

POPPY SEED ROLL

Eileen Eck, Edna, Kansas

(PICTURED ON PAGE 88)

3/4 cup milk
1/3 cup butter *or* margarine
1/2 cup sugar
3/4 teaspoon salt
3 eggs, *divided*
1/2 teaspoon vanilla extract
1 package (1/4 ounce) active
   dry yeast
1/2 cup warm water (110°-115°)
5 to 6 cups all-purpose flour,
   divided
1 can (12 ounces) poppy seed
   filling
1-1/3 cups chopped walnuts,
   divided
1 teaspoon water
Icing

In a saucepan, heat milk, butter, sugar and salt. Cool to lukewarm. Add 2 beaten eggs and the vanilla extract. Dissolve yeast in warm water. In a large mixing bowl, combine milk mixture, yeast mixture and enough flour to form a soft dough. Turn out onto a floured surface and knead until smooth and elastic, about 6-8 minutes. Place dough in a greased bowl, turning once to grease top. Cover and let rise in a warm place until doubled, about 1 hour. Punch dough down and let rest 5 minutes. Roll dough into a 12-in. x 18-in. rectangle. Spread with poppy seed filling and 1 cup nuts. Starting with the long side, roll up dough and pinch the edges to seal. Place on a large greased baking sheet, seam side down. Curve slightly to form a crescent shape. Cover and let rise in a warm place until doubled, about 30 minutes. Beat remaining egg with 1 teaspoon water; brush over top. Bake at 350° for about 30 minutes. Cool on wire rack. Glaze with confectioners' sugar icing and top with remaining nuts. **Yield:** 1 bread.

ITALIAN PARMESAN BREAD

Frances Poste, Wall, South Dakota

(PICTURED ON PAGE 88)

✓ This tasty dish uses less sugar, salt and fat. Recipe includes *Diabetic Exchanges.*

1 package (1/4 ounce) active
   dry yeast
1 cup warm water (110°-115°)
3 cups all-purpose flour,
   divided
1/4 cup butter *or* margarine,

softened
1 egg, beaten
2 tablespoons sugar
1 teaspoon salt
1-1/2 teaspoons dehydrated
   minced onion
1/2 teaspoon Italian seasoning
1/2 teaspoon garlic salt
1/2 cup grated Parmesan cheese,
   divided
Melted butter *or* margarine

In a large mixing bowl, dissolve yeast in warm water. Add 2 cups flour, 1/4 cup butter, egg, sugar, salt and seasonings. Beat at low speed until mixed, about 30 seconds; increase speed to medium and continue beating for 2 minutes. Stir in remaining flour and 1/3 cup cheese; beat until smooth. Cover bowl and let rise in a warm place until doubled, about 1 hour. Stir batter 25 strokes. Spread batter into a greased 1-1/2-qt. casserole; brush with melted butter and sprinkle with the remaining cheese. Cover and let rise until doubled, about 30 minutes. Bake at 350° about 35 minutes or until golden brown. Cool on wire rack 10 minutes before removing from the casserole. **Yield:** 1 loaf. **Diabetic Exchanges:** One serving (1 slice) equals 1 starch, 1/2 fat; also, 97 calories, 216 mg sodium, 21 mg cholesterol, 13 gm carbohydrate, 3 gm protein, 3 gm fat.

WHOLE WHEAT BUTTERHORNS

Mary June Mullins, Livonia, Missouri

(PICTURED ON PAGE 86)

2-3/4 cups all-purpose flour,
   divided
2 packages (1/4 ounce *each*)
   active dry yeast
1-3/4 cups water
1/3 cup packed brown sugar
1/2 cup butter *or* margarine,
   divided
2 tablespoons honey
2 teaspoons salt
2 cups whole wheat flour

In a large mixing bowl, combine 1-1/2 cups all-purpose flour and yeast. Heat the water, brown sugar, 3 tablespoons butter, honey and salt to 120-130°; add to flour mixture. Beat on low for 30 seconds with electric mixer; increase speed to high and continue beating 3 minutes. Stir in whole wheat flour and enough remaining all-purpose flour to form a soft dough. Turn out onto a lightly floured surface and knead until smooth and elastic, about 6-8 minutes. Place in a greased bowl, cover and

allow to rise in a warm place until doubled, about 1-1/2 hours. Punch dough down and divide into thirds. Shape each into a ball, cover and let rest 10 minutes. On a lightly floured surface, roll the balls into three 12-in. circles. Cut each circle into 6 to 8 wedges. Roll wedges into crescent shapes, starting at the wide end. Place on greased baking sheets. Cover and let rise in a warm place until doubled, about 1 hour. Melt remaining butter and brush some on each crescent. Bake at 400° for 10-15 minutes or until golden brown. Brush again with butter while hot. **Yield:** 18-24 rolls.

CHRISTMAS BRAID

Wendy Tschetter, Swift Current, Saskatchewan

(PICTURED ON PAGE 87)

5 to 5-1/2 cups all-purpose
   flour, *divided*
1 package (1/4 ounce) active
   dry yeast
2 cups milk
1/2 cup sugar
6 tablespoons butter *or*
   margarine
1 teaspoon salt
1 egg
1 cup raisins
1 cup finely chopped mixed
   candied fruit
1/2 cup chopped nuts
1 egg yolk
1 tablespoon water

In a large mixing bowl, combine 3 cups flour and yeast. In a saucepan, heat milk, sugar, butter and salt to 120°-130°; add to flour mixture. Add egg. Beat on low speed with electric mixer for 30 seconds; increase speed to medium and continue beating for 3 minutes. Stir in raisins, candied fruit, nuts and enough remaining flour to form a stiff dough. Turn out onto a floured surface and knead until smooth and elastic, about 8-10 minutes. Place in a greased bowl, turning once to grease top. Cover and let rise in a warm place until doubled, about 1-1/2 hours. Divide dough in thirds, then divide each into thirds again. Roll each piece into a 15-in. rope. Place 3 ropes 1 in. apart on greased baking sheet. Begin braiding loosely in the middle and work toward the ends. Pinch ends together and tuck under. Repeat with remaining ropes. Cover and let rise until doubled, about 30-40 minutes. Combine egg yolk and water; brush over braids. Bake at 350° for 20-25 minutes or until browned. Cool on wire racks. **Yield:** 3 breads.

CREAM FILLED COFFEE CAKE
Betty Mezera, Eau Claire, Wisconsin

(PICTURED ON PAGE 86)

1-1/4 cups milk
1/4 cup butter *or* margarine
1/3 cup sugar
1 tablespoon salt
1 package (1/4 ounce) active dry yeast
1/4 cup warm water (110°-115°)
1 teaspoon sugar
5-1/2 to 6 cups all-purpose flour, *divided*
3 eggs, well beaten

STREUSEL TOPPING:
1/4 cup sugar
1/4 cup packed brown sugar
2 tablespoons all-purpose flour
2 teaspoons cinnamon
1/4 cup butter *or* margarine

CREAM FILLING:
1/4 cup all-purpose flour
3/4 cup milk
3/4 cup butter *or* margarine
3/4 cup sugar
3/4 teaspoon vanilla extract
3 tablespoons confectioners' sugar

Heat milk, butter, 1/3 cup sugar and salt; stir until the sugar dissolves. Set aside. Mix yeast, warm water and 1 teaspoon sugar; let stand 10 minutes. In a large mixing bowl, combine 3 cups flour, milk mixture, yeast mixture and eggs; beat until smooth. Add enough of the remaining flour to form a soft dough. Turn out onto a lightly floured surface and knead until smooth, about 6-8 minutes. Place dough in a greased bowl, turning once to grease top. Cover and let rise until doubled, about 1 to 1-1/2 hours. Meanwhile, prepare topping. Combine sugars, flour and cinnamon in a bowl. Cut in butter; set aside. Punch dough down; divide in half. Pat or roll each half to fit a greased 9-in. cake pan. With a fork, pierce entire cake top. Divide topping and sprinkle over each cake. Cover and let rise in a warm place until doubled, about 1 hour. Bake at 350° for 20-25 minutes. Remove from pans and cool on wire racks. For filling, combine flour and milk in a saucepan; cook, stirring constantly, until mixture thickens. Cool. In a mixing bowl, cream remaining ingredients until well mixed. Add flour mixture and beat until fluffy. Cut each cake in half horizontally; spread the bottom halves with half the filling, then replace top halves. Refrigerate until ready to serve. **Yield:** 2 cakes.

COUNTRY SWIRL BREAD
Frieda Miller, Benton Harbor, Michigan

(PICTURED ON PAGE 86)

DARK DOUGH:
1 tablespoon sugar
1-1/2 teaspoons salt
2 packages (1/4 ounce *each*) active dry yeast
1-3/4 cups all-purpose flour, *divided*
3/4 cup water
1/4 cup dark molasses
1 tablespoon instant coffee
1 tablespoon butter *or* margarine
1-1/4 cups pumpernickel-rye flour, *divided*

LIGHT DOUGH:
1-1/2 teaspoons salt
1 package (1/4 ounce) active dry yeast
1-1/4 cups whole wheat flour, *divided*
1-3/4 cups all-purpose flour, *divided*
1 cup water
1/4 cup honey
2 tablespoons butter *or* margarine
1/2 cup uncooked oats

Dark dough: In a mixing bowl, mix the sugar, salt, yeast and 1 cup all-purpose flour. Heat water, molasses, coffee and butter to 120°-130°; add to flour mixture. Beat with an electric mixer at medium. Add 3/4 cup rye flour and beat 2 minutes. Stir in 1/2 cup all-purpose flour and remaining rye flour. Knead for 6-8 minutes, working in the remaining all-purpose flour. Place dough in a greased bowl. Cover and let rise until doubled, about 2 hours.

Light dough: In mixing bowl, combine salt, yeast, 1 cup whole wheat flour and 1/2 cup all-purpose flour. Set aside. Heat water, honey and butter to 120°-130°; add to flour mixture. Beat 2 minutes at medium, adding remaining whole wheat flour. Mix well. Stir in 1 cup all-purpose flour and oats. Knead, working in remaining flour if necessary. Place dough in a greased bowl and let rise until doubled, about 1 hour.

Punch doughs down; let rest 15 minutes. Roll Light dough into a 16-in. x 9-in. rectangle. Roll Dark dough into a 16-in. x 8-in. rectangle and place on top of Light dough. Roll jelly-roll style, beginning with long side. Pinch to seal. Place seam side down on greased baking sheet. Cover; let rise till doubled, 45-60 minutes. Bake 40 minutes at 350°. Cool on wire rack. **Yield:** 1 loaf.

POP UP BREAD
Bea Aubry, Dubuque, Iowa

(PICTURED ON PAGE 87)

✓ **This tasty dish uses less sugar, salt and fat. Recipe includes *Diabetic Exchanges*.**

3 to 3-1/2 cups all-purpose flour, *divided*
1 package (1/4 ounce) active dry yeast
1/2 cup milk
1/2 cup water
1/2 cup vegetable oil
1/4 cup sugar
1 teaspoon salt
2 eggs, beaten
1 cup (4 ounces) shredded cheddar cheese

Combine 1-1/2 cups flour with yeast. Heat milk, water, oil, sugar and salt until warm (120°-130°), stirring to blend; add to flour mixture along with eggs and cheese. Beat with an electric mixer or by hand until batter is smooth. Using a spoon, mix in the remaining flour (batter will be stiff). Divide batter and spoon into two well-greased 1-lb. coffee cans. Cover with plastic lids. Let rise in a warm place until batter is about 1/4 to 1/2 in. below plastic lids, about 45-60 minutes. Remove lids and bake at 375° for 30-35 minutes. Cool for 15 minutes in cans before removing. Cool on wire rack. **Yield:** 2 breads. **Diabetic Exchanges:** One serving (1 slice) equals 1 starch, 1 fat; also, 111 calories, 98 mg sodium, 23 mg cholesterol, 13 gm carbohydrate, 3 gm protein, 5 gm fat.

GOOD TO THE LAST DROP: To get all the shortening out of your measuring cups when making cakes or cookies, crack an egg in the cup first. Tilt the cup to coat all sides with the egg, then pour out. Now fill the cup with shortening—it will plop right out, all in one piece. Cleanup is easier, too!

PRONTO POTATOES: For quick baked potatoes, microwave for 3 minutes, then bake for 20 minutes at 375° in a conventional oven to crisp the skins. (Remember to pierce the skins first!)

ICE BREAKER: When you're making extra ice cubes for a party, put them in a heavy brown paper bag. The heavy paper is a better insulator than plastic, so cubes won't stick together when you return them to the freezer.

CREAMY CHIVE RINGS
Pamela Schlickbernd, West Point, Nebraska

(PICTURED ON PAGE 87)

1 package (1/4 ounce) active
dry yeast
1/4 cup warm water (110°-115°)
1 cup milk
1/2 cup butter *or* margarine,
divided
1/4 cup instant potato flakes
1/3 cup sugar
1-1/4 teaspoons salt
1 egg, beaten
3-3/4 to 4-1/4 cups all-purpose
flour, *divided*
Sesame *or* poppy seeds

FILLING:
1 egg, beaten
3/4 cup whipping cream
1/3 cup chopped fresh *or* dried
chives
1/2 teaspoon salt

In a small bowl, mix yeast and warm water; set aside. In a saucepan, heat milk, 1/3 cup butter, potato flakes, sugar and salt to 110°-115°. Cool. Stir in yeast mixture and egg. Gradually add enough flour to form a stiff dough. Turn out onto a floured surface. Knead until smooth and elastic, about 6-8 minutes, adding additional flour if necessary. Place dough in greased bowl, turning once to grease top. Cover and let rise in a warm place until doubled, about 1 hour. Meanwhile, place all filling ingredients in the top of a double boiler; cook and stir until thickened. Cool. Punch dough down; divide in half. On a floured surface, roll each half into a 16-in. x 12-in. rectangle. Spread half the cream mixture on the dough. Roll up, jelly-roll style, starting at the narrow end. Seal edges. Place on a greased cookie sheet, seam side down. Shape into a ring and cut 1-in. slices almost through the roll. Lay slices flat. Melt remaining butter and brush ring. Sprinkle with sesame or poppy seeds. Repeat with remaining dough and filling. Cover rings and let rise in a warm place until doubled, about 1 hour. Bake at 350° for 20-25 minutes or until lightly browned. Cool on wire rack. (Rings freeze well.) **Yield:** 2 rings.

REUBEN LOAF
Elizabeth Eissler, Osage City, Kansas

(PICTURED ON PAGE 87)

3-1/4 to 3-3/4 cups all-purpose
flour, *divided*

1 package (1/4 ounce)
quick-rise yeast
1 tablespoon sugar
1 tablespoon butter *or*
margarine, softened
1 teaspoon salt
1 cup warm water (120°-130°)
1/4 cup Thousand Island salad
dressing
6 ounces thinly sliced corned
beef
4 ounces sliced Swiss cheese
1 can (8 ounces) sauerkraut,
drained
1 egg white, beaten
Caraway seeds

In a mixing bowl, combine 2-1/4 cups flour, yeast, sugar, butter and salt. Stir in warm water; mix until a soft dough forms. Add remaining flour if necessary. Turn out onto a lightly floured surface; knead until smooth, about 4 minutes. On a lightly greased baking sheet, roll dough to a 14-in. x 10-in. rectangle. Spread dressing down center 1/3 of dough. Top with layers of beef, cheese and sauerkraut. Make cuts from filling to edges of dough 1 in. apart on both sides of the filling. Alternating sides, fold the strips at an angle across filling. Cover dough and let rise in a warm place for 15 minutes. Brush with egg white and sprinkle with caraway seeds. Bake at 400° for 25 minutes or until lightly browned. Serve immediately; refrigerate leftovers. **Yield:** 6-8 servings.

CRUNCHY-TOP HAM &
POTATO CASSEROLE
Nancy Schmidt, Delhi, California

CASSEROLE:
2 pounds Southern-style
frozen hash brown potatoes,
thawed
1 can (10-3/4 ounces) cream
of chicken soup, undiluted
1/2 cup butter, melted
2 cups (16 ounces) sour cream
2 cups cubed cooked ham
1/2 teaspoon ground pepper
1/3 cup chopped green onion
1-1/2 cups (6 ounces) shredded
cheddar cheese

TOPPING:
2 cups crushed cornflakes
1/4 cup butter, melted

Combine all casserole ingredients and mix well. Place in 13-in. x 9-in. x 2-in. baking dish. Combine topping ingredients; sprinkle on casserole. Bake at 350° for 1 hour. **Yield:** 10 servings.

CHALUPA
(Mexican Stew)
Anne Fatout, Phoenix, Arizona

 This tasty dish uses less sugar, salt and fat. Recipe includes *Diabetic Exchanges*.

1 pork roast (3 pounds), fat
trimmed
1 package (16 ounces) pinto
beans, soaked overnight
4 to 5 garlic cloves, minced
2 tablespoons chili powder
1 to 1-1/2 teaspoons ground
cumin
1 teaspoon dried oregano
2 cans (4 ounces *each*) chopped
green chilies
Pepper to taste
5 carrots, peeled and sliced
4 stalks celery, sliced
1 can (14-1/2 ounces) tomatoes,
cut up and liquid reserved
3 small zucchini, sliced
Flour tortillas, warmed

Put first eight ingredients into a large Dutch oven or kettle. Cover with water and cook, covered, over low heat 3 to 4 hours or until meat and beans are tender. Cool slightly; remove meat from bones. Cut or shred meat into bite-size pieces; return meat to kettle. Add carrots, celery, tomatoes and tomato liquid; cover and cook until vegetables are tender. In last 10 minutes of cooking, add zucchini. Serve with warmed flour tortillas. **Yield:** 4 quarts. **Diabetic Exchanges:** One serving (1 cup) equals 1-1/2 starch, 1-1/2 meat, 1 vegetable; also, 253 calories, 11 mg sodium, 41 mg cholesterol, 26 gm carbohydrate, 22 gm protein, 7 gm fat.

BEST BEETS
Lucille Terry, Frankfort, Kentucky

3/4 cup sugar
2 teaspoons cornstarch
1/3 cup vinegar
1/3 cup water *or* beet liquid
1 teaspoon dry mustard
1 teaspoon onion powder
4 cups cooked sliced beets
3 tablespoons butter *or*
margarine
1/4 teaspoon salt
Dash white pepper

In saucepan, combine the sugar and cornstarch. Add vinegar and water or beet juice; bring to a boil. Add all remaining ingredients; reduce heat to simmer. Heat through. **Yield:** 6-8 servings.

SWEET POTATO CASSEROLE

Eleanor Sherry, Highland Park, Illinois

2-1/4 to 2-1/2 pounds (about 4 cups) sweet potatoes, cooked, peeled and mashed
1/3 cup butter *or* margarine, melted
2 eggs, beaten
1/2 cup milk
1 teaspoon vanilla extract
1/2 cup sugar

TOPPING:
1/2 cup chopped nuts
1/2 cup shredded coconut
1/2 cup packed brown sugar
3 tablespoons butter *or* margarine, melted

In large mixing bowl, combine potatoes, butter, eggs, milk, vanilla and sugar. Spread into a greased 1-1/2-qt. casserole. For topping, combine all ingredients and sprinkle over potatoes. Bake at 375° for 25 minutes or until heated through. **Yield:** 6-8 servings.

COUNTRY CHICKEN AND STUFFING

Carolyn Kent, Duncanville, Texas

2 small packages Stove Top stuffing
2 cans (10-3/4 ounces *each*) cream of chicken soup, undiluted
1 cup (8 ounces) sour cream
3 whole chicken breasts, cooked and cubed

Prepare stuffing according to package directions. In greased 13-in. x 9-in. x 2-in. baking dish, combine soup, sour cream and chicken. Top with stuffing. Bake at 350° for 25 minutes. **Yield:** 8-10 servings.

CHICKEN ANGELO

Carol Oswald, Schnecksville, Pennsylvania

✓ This tasty dish uses less sugar, salt and fat. Recipe includes *Diabetic Exchanges*.

8 ounces fresh mushrooms, sliced, *divided*
4 large chicken breast halves, skinned and boned
2 eggs, beaten
1 cup bread crumbs
2 tablespoons butter

6 ounces sliced mozzarella cheese
3/4 cup chicken broth
Hot cooked rice *or* noodles
Fresh chopped parsley

Place half the mushrooms in a 13-in. x 9-in. baking pan. Dip chicken into beaten eggs; roll in bread crumbs. In skillet, melt butter over medium heat. Brown both sides of chicken in skillet; place chicken on top of mushrooms. Arrange the remaining mushrooms on chicken; top with cheese. Add chicken broth to pan. Bake at 350° for 30-35 minutes. Serve over rice or noodles and garnish with parsley. **Yield:** 4 servings.
Diabetic Exchanges: One serving equals 6 medium-fat protein, 1 bread; also, 482 calories, 695 mg sodium, 178 mg cholesterol, 25 gm carbohydrate, 45 gm protein, 26 gm fat.

CHICKEN OR TURKEY PIE

Joy Corie, Ruston, Louisiana

FILLING:
3 tablespoons butter *or* margarine
2 stalks celery, diced
2 carrots, peeled and diced
1 small onion, minced
1/4 cup all-purpose flour
1/2 teaspoon salt
1 cup milk
1 cup chicken broth
1 can (10-3/4 ounces) cream of mushroom soup, undiluted
4 cups cooked cubed chicken *or* turkey

CRUST:
1-1/2 cups all-purpose flour
3/4 teaspoon baking powder
1 teaspoon salt
3 tablespoons butter *or* margarine
1/2 cup milk
2 cups (8 ounces) shredded cheddar cheese

In skillet, melt butter; saute celery, carrots and onion until soft. Stir in flour and salt. Gradually add milk and broth, stirring constantly until sauce thickens. Fold in mushroom soup and chicken or turkey. Spoon mixture into 9-in. x 13-in. baking pan; set aside. For crust, combine flour, baking powder and salt. Cut butter into flour mixture. Add milk and mix to form soft dough. Roll out to a 12-in. x 10-in. rectangle. Sprinkle with cheese and roll up, jelly-roll style, starting from long side. Slice into 1/2-in. wheels and place on chicken mixture. Bake at 350° for 35-40 minutes or until crust is lightly browned. **Yield:** 6-8 servings.

CHICKEN AND WILD RICE CASSEROLE

Crystal Clodfelter, Calhoun, Illinois

1 package (6 ounces) long-grain and wild rice mix
3 tablespoons plus 1 teaspoon cornstarch
1 teaspoon salt
Dash black pepper
1 can (12 ounces) evaporated skim milk
12 ounces chicken broth
2 tablespoons butter
1/4 cup chopped onion
5 cups cubed cooked chicken
1/4 cup chopped pimiento
1/4 cup chopped parsley

Cook the rice according to package directions, *omitting butter*. Set aside. In a saucepan, mix the cornstarch, salt and pepper; gradually stir in milk and broth until smooth. Add butter and onion. Bring to a boil over medium heat, stirring constantly; cook 1 minute or until mixture thickens. In 2-qt. casserole, combine the sauce, chicken, pimiento, parsley and cooked rice. Bake, uncovered, at 375° for 30 minutes. **Yield:** 6-8 servings.

GOLDEN POTATO SURPRISE

Karen Sheets, Shelton, Washington

4 to 5 medium white potatoes, peeled and diced
2 tablespoons butter *or* margarine
2 medium red onions, chopped
2 tablespoons all-purpose flour
1/2 teaspoon dried thyme
1/2 teaspoon salt
1/2 teaspoon ground black pepper
1 cup half-and-half cream
1 teaspoon Dijon mustard
1/2 cup mayonnaise
4 slices bacon, cooked and crumbled

Cook potatoes in boiling salted water until tender; drain and set aside. In saucepan, melt butter. Saute onions until soft; stir in flour, thyme, salt and pepper. Gradually add cream, stirring constantly until sauce thickens. Remove from heat; let cool slightly. Add mustard and mayonnaise; stir until well mixed and smooth. Place potatoes in 1-1/2-qt. casserole; cover with sauce. Bake at 350° for 30 minutes. Before serving, sprinkle with crumbled bacon. **Yield:** 4-6 servings.

INDEX